This book was set in Times Roman by the author using the LATEX document preparation system.

Printed and bound in the United States of America.

Library of Congress Cataloging-in-Publication Data

Nolfi, Stefano.
Evolutionary robotics: the biology, intelligence, and technology of self-organizing machines / Stefano Nolfi, Dario Floreano.
    p.    cm. — (Intelligent robots and autonomous agents)
"A Bradford book."
Includes bibliographical references and index.
ISBN 0-262-14070-5 (hc: alk. paper)
1. Evolutionary Robotics. I. Floreano, Dario. II. Title. III. Series.
TJ211.37. N65   2000
698.8′92—dc21                                                        00-028172
                                                                          CIP

# Evolutionary Robotics

The Biology, Intelligence, and Technology of Self-Organizing Machines

Stefano Nolfi and Dario Floreano

A Bradford Book
The MIT Press
Cambridge, Massachusetts
London, England

# Evolutionary Robotics

to Maria and Letizia—SN
to Krisztina—DF

# Contents

# Acknowledgments

The origins of this book go back to more than ten years ago when the authors began exploring evolution of artificial organisms at the National Research Council in Rome. Domenico Parisi played a fundamental role in getting us interested in this field, sharing his ideas, and providing a remarkably stimulating and friendly environment. His open and curious mind has had a great impact on our approach to science and technology, and his contributions can be found in many places throughout this book.

Later on, DF moved to the Laboratory of Microprocessors and Interfaces (LAMI) at the Swiss Federal Institute of Technology, Lausanne (EPFL) where Francesco Mondada, Edo Franzi, André Guignard and Jean-Daniel Nicoud were developing a new miniature mobile robot for research in bio-inspired and adaptive systems. The innovative concept of the Khepera robot has been instrumental for shaping our methodology in Evolutionary Robotics and is still used by hundreds of people in our research community. Francesco Mondada has been essential to get it all started, to provide interesting ideas and feedback, and to continuously support us with all sorts of technological tools even when he is very busy with his company. Jean-Daniel Nicoud, the LAMI director and a man with a great sense for innovation, has created the right environment for carrying out this research and has always supported us with enthusiasm and generosity.

Takashi Gomi, a globe-trotter running a company with great visions in robotics, new artificial intelligence, and mankind, realized early on the importance of Evolutionary Robotics. Along these years he has provided us with opportunities to link with other colleagues around the world and meet several interesting people from research and industry.

Many people at the Research Group of Artificial Life in Rome (GRAL) have contributed in a wide range of invaluable ways. We thank Raffaele Calabretta, Angelo Cangelosi, Federico Cecconi, Daniele Denaro, Henrik Hautop Lund, Davide Marocco, Filippo Menczer, and Luigi Pagliarini among others. Orazio Miglino in particular, significantly contributed to generate the ideas found in this book. At EPFL, Joseba Urzelai has been a companion of several fruitful discussions and has carried out important experiments mentioned in this book. He has also provided much feedback on various drafts of this book.

Inman Harvey, Phil Husbands, and Adrian Thompson of the "Sussex group" have been our *alter ego* along these years, the persons with whom we would compare and discuss our results both within the scientific circuit and in various bars around the world. Their contribution to artificial evolution and to evolutionary robotics is very important and described throughout this book.

Several other people have contributed in one way or another to this book over the last years, including Tom Ziemke, Jun Tani, Jeff Elman, and Valentino Braitenberg who often offered us the possibility to discuss the offspring of his imaginary *Vehicles* (1984) in company of his fellow neurophysiologists.

At MIT Press, Henry Stanton Bradford gave the initial enthusiastic support that allowed us to start this project. Later on, Bob Prior and his staff re-organized the project and efficiently managed the realization of this book in a very friendly atmosphere.

The authors acknowledge the forward-looking support from CNR and EPFL. DF also acknowledges the Swiss National Science Foundation, grant nr. 620-58049, that allowed completion of this book and continuation of the project.

Both authors have equally contributed to the contents of this book. In addition, SN effectively kick-started the project and always made sure that continuous progress was not hampered by other incoming projects. SN also put a major effort in preparing the camera-ready version for the press. It was a pleasure to make the final adjustments together in Rome and discover one more time how well our visions of evolutionary robotics match. We think that this book has greatly benefited from this homogeneity and hope that you will profit and enjoy reading it.

Roma and Lausanne, May 2000.

# Preface

Evolutionary robotics is a new technique for automatic creation of autonomous robots. It is inspired by the darwinian principle of selective reproduction of the fittest. It is a new approach which looks at robots as autonomous artificial organisms that develop their own skills in close interaction with the environment without human intervention. Heavily drawing from natural sciences like biology and ethology, evolutionary robotics makes use of tools like neural networks, genetic algorithms, dynamic systems, and biomorphic engineering.

The term *evolutionary robotics* has been introduced only quite recently (Cliff, Harvey and Husband 1993), but the idea of representing the control system of a robot as an artificial chromosome subject to the laws of genetics and of natural selection dates back to the end of the 1980's when the first simulated artificial organisms with a sensory motor system began evolving on computer screens. At that time, however, real robots were still machines that required accurate programming efforts and careful manipulation. Toward the end of that period, a few engineers began questioning some of the basic principles of robot design and came up with a new generation of robots that shared important characteristics with simple biological systems: robustness, simplicity, small size, flexibility, modularity. Above all, these robots were designed so that they could be programmed and controlled by people with different backgrounds and levels of technical skills. In the years 1992 and 1993, the first experiments on artificial evolution of autonomous robots were reported by our team at the Swiss Federal Institute of Technology in Lausanne, by a team at the University of Sussex at Brighton, and by a team at the University of Southern California. The success and potentials of these researches triggered a whole new activity in evolutionary robotics in labs across Europe, Japan, and the United States.

In the very last few years evolutionary robotics has gathered the interest of a large community of researchers with different research interests and backgrounds (ranging from AI and robotics, to biology and cognitive science, to the study of social behavior). Continuous investment, growth, and progress in evolutionary robotics has caused a substantial maturation of the methodology and of the issues involved, and at the same time has generated a diversification of the basic methodology. This book provides a comprehensive description of what evolutionary robotics is, of what its scientific and technological milieu are, of the various methods employed, of the results achieved so far, and of the future directions. The book aims at clarity of explanation, avoiding as much as possible (or accurately explaining) scientific jargon. The reader is gently introduced to the subject following a historical and logical path. The book describes the most used techniques (genetic algorithms, neural networks, etc.), presents several experiments of increasing complexity together with related issues as they arise, and shows the most promising future directions.

# 1 The role of self-organization for the synthesis and the understanding of behavioral systems

## 1.1 Introduction

The basic idea behind evolutionary robotics goes as follows (see figure 1.1). An initial population of different artificial chromosomes, each encoding the control system (and sometimes the morphology) of a robot, are randomly created and put in the environment. Each robot (physical or simulated) is then let free to act (move, look around, manipulate) according to a genetically specified controller while its performance on various tasks is automatically evaluated. The fittest robots are allowed to reproduce (sexually or asexually) by generating copies of their genotypes with the addition of changes introduced by some genetic operators (e.g., mutations, crossover, duplication). This process is repeated for a number of generations until an individual is born which satisfies the performance criterion (*fitness function*) set by the experimenter.

Evolutionary robotics shares many of characteristics with other approaches, such as behavior-based robotics, robot learning, and artificial life.

### Behavior-Based Robotics

The *behavior-based robotics* approach is based upon the idea of providing the robot with a collection of simple basic behaviors. The global behavior of the robot emerges through the interaction between those basic behaviors and the environment in which the robot finds itself (Brooks 1986, 1999; Arkin 1998). Basic behaviors are implemented in separate sub-parts of the control system and a coordination mechanism is responsible for determining the relative strength of each behavior in a particular moment. Coordination may be accomplished by means of competitive or cooperative methods. In competitive methods only one behavior affects the motor output of the robot in a particular moment (see, for example, the subsumption based method proposed by Brooks 1986). In cooperative methods different behaviors may contribute to a single motor action although with different strength (see, for example, the method based on behavioral fusion via vector summation [Arkin 1989]).

In this approach, as in evolutionary robotics, the environment plays a central role by determining the role of each basic behavior at any given time. Moreover, these systems are usually designed through a trial and error process in which the designer modifies the current behaviors and progressively increase the number of basic behaviors while testing the resulting global behavior in the environment. However, evolutionary robotics, by relying on an automatic evaluation process, usually makes a larger use of the trial and error process described above. Moreover, while in the behavior-based approach the breakdown of the desired behavior into simpler basic behaviors is accomplished intuitively by the designer,

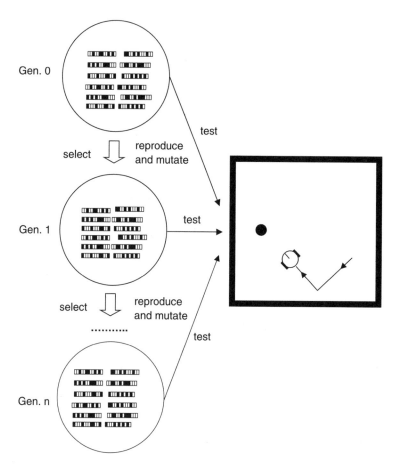

**Figure 1.1**
Basic Evolutionary Robotics methodology. A population of artificial chromosomes is decoded into
corresponding controllers which are tested one at a time in the environment. The fittest controllers are allowed to
reproduce and generate the next population of chromosomes.

in evolutionary robotics this is often the result of a self-organizing process (figure 1.2).
Indeed, the entire organization of the evolving system, including its organization into
subcomponents, is the result of an adaptation process that usually involves a large number
of evaluations of the interactions between the system and the environment (we will return
to this issue in section 3 and in chapter 5 and 6).

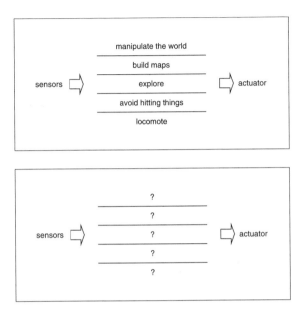

**Figure 1.2**
In the behavior-based approach the desired behavior is broken down by the designer into a set of basic behaviors which are implemented into separate sub-parts (layers) of the robot's control system (top box). In Evolutionary Robotics the designer does not need to decide how to divide the desired behavior into basic behaviors (bottom box). The way in which a desired behavior is broken down into modules is the result of a self-organization process.

## Robot learning

*Robot learning* is based on the idea that a control system (typically a neural network) can be trained using incomplete data and then allowed to rely on its ability to generalize the acquired knowledge to novel circumstances. The general motivation behind this approach is that it may produce better results than approaches based on explicit design, given the well known difficulties of engineering behavioral systems (see below). In some cases the neural control system learns to perform a mapping between sensory inputs and motor states while in other cases learning is used to develop subsystems of the controller. Different learning algorithms can be used for this purpose: back-propagation learning (Rumelhart et al. 1986); reinforcement learning (Barto et al. 1995); classifier systems (Booker et al. 1989); self-organized maps (Kohonen 1982), etc. These algorithms impose different constraints on the type of architecture that can be used and on the quantity and quality of the supervision required from the designer. For example, if used to learn a mapping from sensors to motors, back-propagation learning requires that the designer provides an explicit indication of the

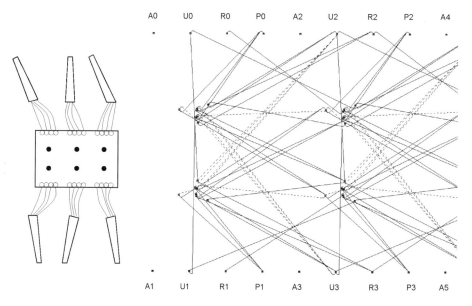

**Figure 1.3**
Example of evolved architecture for a tripod robot. **Left:** The robot body. Black circles represent original cells that develop into sub-networks connecting sensory and motor neurons (white circles) **Right:** The corresponding developed locomotion network. Labels indicate sensory and motor neurons corresponding to the white circles in the figure on the left. (From Kodjabachian and Meyer 1998a. Reprinted by permission of Taylor and Francis Ltd, http://www.tandf.co.uk/journals.)

correct values for each motor at each time step. Reinforcement learning instead only needs an evaluation of how good or bad the robot is doing at the time.[1] Evolutionary robotics shares with these approaches the emphasis on self-organization. Indeed, artificial evolution may be described as a form of learning. However, evolutionary robotics differs from robot learning in two respects. First, the amount of supervision required by evolution is generally much lower—only a general evaluation of how well an individual accomplishes the desired task is required. Second, the evolutionary method in principle does not introduce any constraint on what can be part of the self-organization process. Indeed, the characteristics of the sensors and of the actuators (Cliff and Miller 1996), the shape of the robot (Lund et al. 1997), and the architecture of the control system (Kodjabachian and Meyer 1998a, 1998b) can be included into the evolutionary process (we will return to this issue in section 1.4 and in chapter 9). Figure 1.3, for example, shows the results of an evolutionary experiment which will be further explored in chapter 9 where the architecture of the neural network controlling a tripod robot has undergone an evolutionary process.

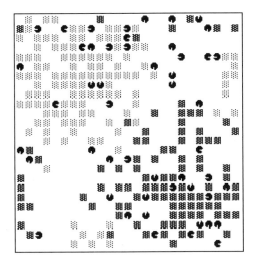

**Figure 1.4**
An example of agent for exploring Artificial Life. The environment is represented by a 2-dimensional grid of cells and the agent has sensors and actuators with infinite precision. (Reprinted with permission from Menczer and Belew 1997.)

## Artificial life

*Artificial life* represents an attempt to understand all life phenomena through their reproduction in artificial systems (typically through their simulation on a computer). More specifically, artificial life provides a unique framework for studying how entities at different levels of organization (molecules, organs, organisms, and populations) interact among themselves (Parisi 1997) although, of course, at the cost of introducing crude simplifications. To attain this ambitious goal, artificial life relies on the theory of complex dynamical systems and, from an experimental point of view, on the power of computers. A complex dynamical system is a system that can be described at different levels, in which global properties at one level emerge from the interaction of a number of simple elements at lower levels. Global properties are emergent in the sense that, even if they result from nothing else but local interactions among the elements, they cannot be predicted or inferred from a knowledge of the elements or of the rules by which the elements locally interact, given the high nonlinearity of these interactions. Evolutionary robotics shares most of these characteristics with artificial life, but it also stresses the importance of using physical devices (robots) instead of simulated agents (figure 1.4).

By using real robots, several additional factors due to the physical properties of the robot and of the environment must be taken into account (e.g., friction, inertia, ambient light, noise, etc.) (Brooks 1992). Moreover, only realistic types of sensors and actuators (instead of idealized ones that may not respect all the physical constraints or may have infinite precision) can be used. Similarly, the sensory inputs and the motor outputs should necessarily correspond to physical measures or forces; that is, they are grounded representations (Harnad 1990) and cannot include any abstract information provided by the experimenter, even unconsciously. Finally, only information truly available in the environment can be used for training.

In the following sections, we will try to show the implications of evolutionary robotics for other disciplines. Although we think that evolutionary robotics may be relevant for many different fields, we will restrict our analysis to engineering, ethology, and biology. By doing so, it will become clear that the key characteristics of this approach is the possibility to rely largely on a self-organization process (Floreano 1997).

## 1.2   An engineering perspective

It is undisputed that behavioral systems such as autonomous mobile robots are difficult to design. As one can see in everyday life, there are efficient computer programs that can play chess or solve formal problems but there are no intelligent mobile robots in our homes or towns. The main reason why mobile robots are difficult to design is that their behavior is an emergent property of their motor interaction with the environment. The robot and the environment can be described as a dynamical system because the sensory state of the robot at any given time is a function of both the environment and of the robot previous actions. The fact that behavior is an emergent property of the interaction between the robot and the environment has the nice consequence that simple robots can produce complex behavior (see Braitenberg 1984). However it also has the consequence that, as in all dynamical systems, the properties of the emergent behavior cannot easily be predicted or inferred from a knowledge of the rules governing the interactions. The reverse it also true: it is difficult to predict which rules will produce a given behavior, since behavior is the emergent result of the dynamical interaction between the robot and the environment.

The conventional strategy followed in order to overcome these difficulties has been *divide and conquer*: find a solution by dividing the problem into a list of hopefully simpler subproblems. Classical approaches to robotics have often assumed a primary breakdown into Perception, Planning, and Action. However, this way of dividing the problem has produced limited results and has been criticized by a number of researchers. Brooks (1986) proposed a radically different approach in which the division is accomplished at the level of behavior. The desired behavior is broken down into a set of simpler basic behaviors , which are modulated through a coordination mechanism. In this latter approach the control system is built up incrementally layer by layer where each layer is responsible for a single basic behavior by directly linking sensors to motors. Simple basic behaviors are implemented first, then new layers implementing other basic behaviors are added one at a time after intensive testing and debugging. This approach has proven to be more successful than the classical approach. Moreover it has been shown that both the layers (modules) responsible for simple basic behaviors and the coordination mechanism can be obtained through a self-organizing process rather than by explicit design (see Maes 1992; Mahadevan and Connell 1992; Dorigo and Schnepf 1993; Ram et al. 1994; Urzelai et al. 1998).

The approaches based on behavioral decomposition, however, still leave to the designer the decision of how to break the desired behavior down into simple basic behaviors. Unfortunately, it is not clear how a desired behavior should be decomposed and it is very difficult to perform such decomposition by hand. Even researchers who successfully adopted the behavioral decomposition and integration approach feel that this is a crucial problem. Rodney Brooks, for example, notes: "Conversely, because of the many behaviors present in a behavior-based system, and their individual dynamics of interaction with the world, it is often hard to say that a particular series of actions was produced by a particular behavior. Sometimes many behaviors are operating simultaneously, or are switching rapidly" (Brooks 1991a, pp. 584–585). Colombetti et al. (1996) note at the end of their article: "learning techniques might be extended to other aspects of robot development, like the architecture of the controller. This means that the structure of behavioral modules should emerge from the learning process, instead of being pre-designed."

To better understand why it is difficult to break down a global behavior into a set of simpler basic behaviors we have to distinguish two ways of describing behaviors: a description from the observer's point of view and a description from the robot's point of view (Sharkey and Heemskerk 1997). The *distal description of behavior* is a description from the observer's point of view in which high level terms such as approach or discriminate are used to describe the result of a sequence of sensorimotor loops. The *proximal description of behavior* is a description from the point of view of the agent's sensorimotor system that describes how the agent reacts in different sensory situations (see figure 1.5).

It should be noted that the distal description of behavior is the result not only of the proximal description of behavior (i.e., the sensory-motor mapping), but also of the environment. More precisely, the distal description of behavior is the result of a dynamical interaction between the agent and the environment. In fact, the sensory patterns that the environment provides to the agent partially determine the agent's motor reactions. These motor reactions, in turn, modify the environment or the relative position of the agent in the environment and therefore partially determine the type of sensory patterns that the agent will receive from the environment (we will come back to this point in the next section).

This dynamical interaction can explain why it is difficult to break down a global

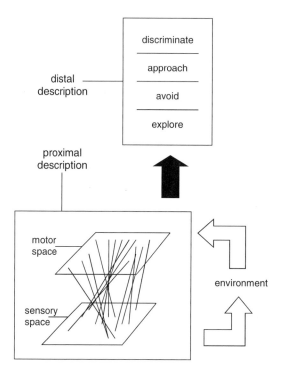

**Figure 1.5**
Proximal and distal descriptions of behavior. The distal description is from the observer's point of view and is based on words or sentences in our own language which are used to describe a sequence of sensory-motor loops. The proximal description is from the robot's point of view and is based on a description of how the robot reacts to each sensory state. The empty arrows indicate the reciprocal interactions between the sensory-motor mapping and the environment (the robot actions modify the environment and/or the relation between the robot and the environment which, in turn, modify the type of sensory pattern that the robot receives from the environment). The full arrow indicates that a distal description of behavior (top part of the figure) results from the dynamical interaction between a proximal description of behavior and the environment (bottom part of the figure).

behavior into a set of basic behaviors that are simple from the point of view of the proximal description. In general, the breakdown is accomplished intuitively by the researcher on the basis of a distal description of the global behavior. However, since the desired behavior is the emergent result of the dynamical interaction between the agent's control system and the environment, it is difficult to predict which type of behavior will be produced by a given control system. The reverse is also true—it is difficult to predict which control system will produce a desired behavior.

If there is not a one-to-one mapping between subcomponents of the agent's control system and subcomponents of the corresponding behavior from the point of view of the distal description, it is questionable whether a distal description of behavior can effectively be used to determine how the agent's control system should be structured, as hypothesized in the decomposition and integration approach. In other words, the fact that a global behavior can be divided into a set of simpler basic behaviors from the point of view of the distal description does not imply that such basic behaviors can be implemented into separate and relatively simple layers (modules) of the agent's control system.

Evolutionary robotics, by relying on an evaluation of the system as a whole and of its global behavior, releases the designer from the burden of deciding how to break the desired behavior down into simple basic behaviors.

As we will show in section 4 of chapter 5, for example, it is extremely difficult to train a controller for a Khepera robot (Mondada et al. 1993) placed in a rectangular arena surrounded by walls and containing a target object (a small cylinder) to find and stay close to the target by decomposing the desired behavior into basic behaviors. If we divide this global behavior into four basic behaviors (1. explore the environment; 2. avoid walls; 3. approach and remaining close to the target; 4. discriminate the target from the wall) and we train 4 separate neural networks to perform each basic behavior , the controller will not function properly. On the contrary, we can easily evolve a single network to produce the 4 different basic behaviors described above if we select individuals for their ability to perform the global behavior. Interestingly, in this latter case, it can be seen that a simple and homogeneous control system (a fully connected perceptron with 8 sensors and 2 outputs controlling the speed of robot's wheels) may be able to produce a global behavior which can be described (from the point of view of a distal description) as structured into the four different basic behaviors described above. For an example in which evolved controllers exhibit an emergent task decomposition in a number of different basic behaviors (from the point of view of a distal description) which are organized in a subsumption architecture like fashion, see Biro and Ziemke 1998.

In another experiment involving a Khepera robot evolved to clean an arena by carrying objects outside the walls with its gripper, simple uniform controllers have been compared with modular controllers (i.e., control systems divided into layers, or modules, used to control the robot in different environmental circumstances). As we will see in section 6.2, in this more complex case, the modular systems outperform the non modular one. However, better performance is obtained only if what each module stands for is the results of a self-organization process and not of a decision taken by the experimenter. Moreover, we will see that, after training, it is not possible to find a simple correlation between module switching and basic behaviors from the point of view of a distal description; rather, module switching is correlated with particular characteristics of sensory-motor mapping, that is with a proximal description of behavior.

## 1.3    An ethological perspective

Molecules, cells, organs, organisms, and ecosystems are all entities at different levels that are potentially relevant for the study of behavior. As a consequence the study of behavior is being conducted within different disciplines. In particular two groups of disciplines can be identified which are separated by a total heterogeneity of the concepts they use to describe, analyze, and explain their object of study: molecular biology, cellular biology, developmental biology, genetics, and neuroscience, on one side; psychology, ecology, and evolutionary biology on the other side (see Parisi 1997). On the one side neurosciences, for example, use concepts that are appropriate for describing a physical object (i.e., the nervous system). On the other side psychology uses concepts which do not normally refer to physical structures or processes. The concepts used by psychologists to talk about behavior and cognition are derived from philosophy and from the concepts that we use in everyday life to describe, predict, and explain our own behavior and the behavior of other living creatures (see figure 1.6).

Given the existence of two different vocabularies, it is only possible to look a posteriori for correlations between physical and anatomo-physiological phenomena on one side and psychological phenomena on the other. This is the task of such disciplines such as psychophysics and neuropsychology which serve as bridges. However, it is very difficult to trace back observations concerning the nervous system and observations concerning behavior to the structure of a single entity that could be described and analyzed using a single theoretical vocabulary (Parisi 1997).

In the last decade, new research fields which try to overcome this epistemological gap have been developed: connectionism (Rumelhart and McClelland 1986) and embodied cognition (Brooks 1991a; Varela et al. 1991; Pfeifer and Scheier 1999). Connectionism proposes neural networks as a unified theoretical framework for studying both behavior and cognition, on one side, and the nervous system, on the other.[2] Therefore, connectionism can be viewed as an attempt to overcome the traditional dualism embraced by psychology (Parisi 1997). Embodiment stresses the importance of the physical aspects of a system (physical shape, gravity, friction, inertia, idiosyncratic characteristics of each sensor and actuator, etc.). Moreover, it stresses the importance of the interaction with the environment (Arbib 1989; Meyer and Guillot 1991; Wilson 1991).

Perception is often viewed as a disembodied process in which the agent is passively exposed to a continuously changing stream of sensory stimulation without consideration of what the agent needs to do. In contrast, a strong coupling between action and perception is a central issue in embodied cognition which tends to view perception on a need to know basis (Arkin 1990). By exploiting their interaction with the environment (i.e., by sensory-motor coordination), agents can partially modify the stimuli they receive from the environment.

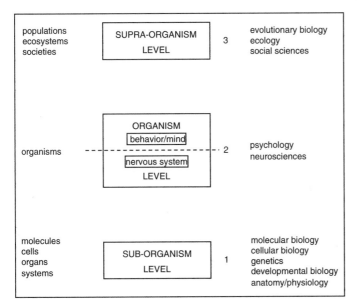

**Figure 1.6**
Three levels of entities relevant for the study of behavior and the scientific disciplines that study them. The radical separation between the concepts used by the neurosciences to describe the nervous system and the concepts used by psychologists to describe behavior and mental life creates a discontinuity within the intermediate level of the hierarchy. Courtesy of Domenico Parisi.

Therefore behavior cannot be considered a product of an agent isolated from the world, but can only emerge from a strong coupling of the agent with its own environment. In other words, a given behavior cannot be explained on the basis of internal mechanisms only. Similarly, the structure of a nervous system producing a given behavior cannot be considered in isolation from the environment. The function of an agent's nervous system, in fact, is that of coordinating perception and action in order to generate adaptive behavior (Cliff 1991; Chiel and Beer 1997).

In most robotics research, however, the power of the interaction with the environment is largely unexplored. Few notable exceptions should be mentioned. Braitenberg's vehicles are probably the first clear demonstration that a simple agent can produce complex behavior by exploiting the complexity of the environment (Braitenberg 1984). Pfeifer and Scheier showed that the problem of perception could be greatly simplified if the agent's own movement and interaction with the environment is taken into account (Scheier and Pfeifer 1995). They described a Khepera robot that can learn to discriminate between small and large cylinders by relying on three simple predesigned basic behaviors (i.e., move forward, avoid object, and turn toward object). This is possible because sensory-motor coordination makes the agent circle around objects which in turn significantly affect the type of sensory information which the robot receives from the environment.

The reason why the power of the interaction with the environment is still largely unexplored in robotics is that, as we pointed out in previous sections, adaptive behavior is difficult to obtain through design. In particular, it is hard to design systems that exploit sensory-motor coordination. For agents which interact with an external environment, in fact, each motor action has two different effects: (a) it partially determines how well the agent performs with respect to a given task; (b) it partially determines the next sensory pattern that the agent will receive from the environment, which in turn may determine if the agent will be able to solve its task or not (we will return to this issue in chapter 5). The problem is that determining which motor action the agent should perform each time by taking into account both (a) and (b) is very difficult given that: each motor action can have long term consequences; the effect of each motor action is a function also of the preceding and successive actions; the effect of each action is a function of the interaction between the agent and the environment.

Evolutionary robotics, by largely relying on self-organization, is not affected by these problems and, as a consequence, is an ideal framework for studying adaptive behavior.[3] Indeed, many of the evolved robots exploit active interaction with the environment in order to maximize the selection criterion. For example, in section 5.4 we will see that individuals evolved for their ability to discriminate between walls and cylinders solved the task by moving back and forth in front of the perceived objects. Similarly, in trying to evolve robots able to reach the upper right hand or bottom left hand corner of a rectangular box starting from eight different positions (an experimental task studied by Gallistel with rats [see Gallistel 1990]), it was found that evolved robots were able to solve the task by carefully selecting the speed of the two wheels in the absence of any sensory stimulation. Given a certain shape and dimension of the environment, this simple strategy ensured that long and short walls are encountered at significantly different angles. This in turn allows the robots to easily reach the two target corners by following or avoiding the walls depending on the angle at which they were approached (this experiment will be reported in section 5.5).

## 1.4   A biological perspective

Evolutionary robotics and biology share an interest in the following question: what are the key characteristics of natural evolution that make it so successful in producing the extraordinary variety of highly adapted life forms present on the planet? Producing better answers to this question may significantly increase both our understanding of biological systems and our ability to design artificial systems. From the point of view of evolutionary robotics this question may be restated as follows: in which conditions is an artificial evolutionary process likely to select individuals which develop complex competencies in order to adapt to their artificial environment? Possible answers to this question may be categorised into three main issues which will be described in the next three sections. As we will see, it is possible, at least in principle, to develop complex forms of behavior without increasing the amount of supervision. This may be accomplished: (a) by generating incremental evolution through competitions between or within species; (b) by leaving the system free to decide how to extract supervision from the environment; (c) by including the genotype-to-phenotype mapping within the evolutionary process.

**Incremental evolution**

From the point of view of evolutionary robotics, a key question is how artificial evolution can select individuals which have competencies that allow them to solve complex tasks (e.g. navigating in a complex environment). A related problem in biology is to understand how and in which circumstances natural evolution may discover new competencies (e.g., the ability to fly or build a nest). To avoid confusion, we should clarify here that competencies and selection criteria are different entities. In natural evolution selection is based on a simple and general criterion: the ability to reproduce. In spite of this, natural evolution has been able to produce individuals with sophisticated competencies such as the ability to swim, fly, and communicate through natural language.

If one wishes to select individuals able to solve a task that requires a specific competence through artificial evolution, the easiest thing to do is to select the individuals for their ability to solve that specific task. This amounts to design a fitness criterion that scores individuals according to their ability to solve the task. However, it is easy to show that this simple strategy can only work for simple tasks. As the complexity of the task increases, the probability that some individuals of the first generations are able to accomplish, at least in part, the task is inversely proportional to the complexity of the task itself. For complex tasks, all individuals of the first generations are scored with the same null value, and as a consequence the selection process cannot operate. We will refer to this fact as the *bootstrap problem*.

One possible solution to this problem is to increase the amount of supervision. The insights of the experimenter can be used to include in the selection criterion rewards for subparts of the desired task (an example of this technique will be described in section 6.2). Another possibility is to start the evolutionary process with a simplified version of the task and then progressively increase its complexity by modifying the selection criterion (the latter technique is usually referred to as *incremental evolution*). This idea was previously

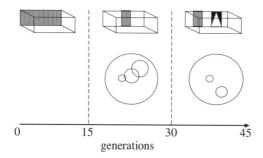

**Figure 1.7**
Incremental evolution of shape discrimination and sensory morphology (adapted from Harvey et al., 1994). The desired behavior is to approach a rectangle and avoid a triangle. The top part of the illustration shows the modification of the environment across generations. The lower part shows a schematic representation of the position and width of the receptive fields of the vision units used by the best evolved controllers (data not available for generation 15). The fitness function is significantly changed at generation 30.

proposed in the context of classifier systems by Dorigo and Colombetti (1994, 1997) who named it *shaping*, borrowing the term from experimental psychology techniques used to train animals to produce predefined responses (Skinner 1938). These techniques, by requiring more supervision, increase the risk of introducing inappropriate constraints (see section 1.2). However, from an engineering perspective, it is easier to use the insight of the experimenter for shaping the selection criterion than for designing the control system itself.

For example, Harvey et al. (1994) have incrementally evolved visually guided behaviors and sensory morphologies for a mobile robot expected to discriminate shapes and navigate towards a rectangle while avoiding a triangle (figure 1.7). The authors started with a simple version of the task that selected controllers for their ability to navigate towards a wall covered by color paper. Successively, the authors narrowed the area of the color paper on the wall and resumed evolution from the last evolved generation. Finally, the rectangular shape was displaced and a triangular shape was placed nearby. The fitness function was modified to encourage avoidance of the triangle and approach of the rectangle, and the previously evolved population was incrementally evolved in the new environment. The final evolved sensory morphology used only two pixels to detect whether the perceived shape was rectangular or triangular.

This experiment shows how manipulating the learning experiences throughout generations and introducing more constraints in the selection criterion one can solve tasks that cannot be solved otherwise, but there is a danger that additional constraints might channel the evolutionary process in wrong directions.

A more desirable solution to the bootstrap problem, however, would be a self-organized process capable of producing incremental evolution that does not require any human supervision. This ideal situation spontaneously arises in competing co-evolving populations with coupled fitness, such as predator and prey scenarios.

In chapter 8, we will investigate the conditions in which co-evolution leads to progressively more complex behavior in competing robots. We will consider the case of two competing species of predator and prey robots which are selected for their ability to catch prey and escape predators, respectively. At the beginning of the evolutionary process, predators should be able to catch prey which have a very simple behavior and are therefore easy to catch; likewise, prey should be able to escape simple predators. However, later on, both populations and their evolving challenges will become progressively more and more complex. Therefore, even if the selection criterion remains the same, the adaptation task becomes progressively more complex. A consequence discussed by Dawkins and Krebs (1979) is that competing populations might reciprocally drive one another to increasing levels of complexity by producing an evolutionary "arms race." For this reason, as we will see in section 8.7, in some cases co-evolution can solve tasks that evolution of a single population cannot.

### Extracting supervision from the environment through lifetime learning

From the point of view of a natural or artificial organism the external environment does not provide any direct cue on how the agent should act to attain a given goal. However, agents receive a large amount of information from the environment through the sensors. Such information (which is a function of both of the environmental structure and of the motor actions of the agent) may be used not only to determine how to react in different environmental circumstances but also to adapt to the current environment through lifetime learning. For example, a robot may learn the consequences of different actions in different environmental contexts.

In principle, in an evolving population, any ability which can be acquired through lifetime learning can also be genetically acquired through evolution. However these two ways of adapting to the environment differ in one important respect: ontogenetic adaptation can rely on a very rich, although less explicit, amount of supervision. From the point of view of phylogenetic adaptation, individuals are evaluated only once on the basis of a single value which codifies how well they were adapted to their environment throughout all their lifetime (i.e., the number of offspring in the case of natural evolution and the fitness value in the case of artificial evolution). Instead, from the point of view of ontogenetic adaptation, individuals receive information from the environment through their sensors throughout their whole lifetime. However, this huge amount of information encodes only very indirectly how well an individual did in different moments of its own lifetime or how it should modify behavior in order to increase its own fitness. The problem is how such information can be transformed into an indication of what the agent should do or how well it is doing.

Because of the problems discussed in sections 1.2 and 1.3, it is probably hard to design a system capable of performing a good transformation. On the other hand, we may expect that evolution solve this type of problem by producing subsystems capable of autonomously extracting supervision information that can be used for fast lifetime learning. This has been shown in two computational experiments carried out by Ackley and Littman (1991) and Nolfi and Parisi (1997) that will be described in section 7.6. In both cases the controller architecture was divided into two submodules of which the first has the function of determining how to react to the current sensory state and the latter has the function of generating a teaching signal for the former. In Ackley and Littman sensory states were transformed into reinforcement signals while in Nolfi and Parisi sensory states were transformed into self generated teaching signals. By subjecting the weights of the two sub-networks to an evolutionary process, the authors reported evolution of individuals which learn during their lifetime to adapt to the environment through self generated teaching signals by transforming sensory information into useful reinforcement signal or teaching signals. As shown by Miller and Todd (1990) and Floreano and Mondada (1996a), a similar result can be obtained by evolving neural networks with topologies that may vary evolutionarily and that learn throughout lifetime with unsupervised learning (see section 7.5). In these cases the constraints on the architecture channel the changes driven by the sensory states in the right directions.

As we said above, what can be obtained with evolution and learning can also be obtained with evolution alone. At a high level of description, for example, an individual that is born with a general strategy capable of producing a behavior which is effective in a set of different environments is equivalent to another individual capable of adapting to each environment through lifetime learning. On the other hand, at a lower level of description it is clear that these two individuals are organized in different ways. Individuals that do not start with a general strategy but adapt throughout lifetime should be able to detect the environment in which they are located, and should be able to modify their strategy accordingly (let us call these individuals *plastic general*). On the other hand, individuals that have a general strategy already suitable for different environments do not need to change (let us call these individuals *full general*). From this point of view full general individuals will be more effective than plastic general individuals because they do not have to undergo an adaptation process throughout lifetime. However, it may happen that in certain conditions full general individuals cannot be selected because a full general strategy does not exist (or because it is too complex and therefore the probability that it will be selected is very low). If this is the case, a plastic general solution is the only available option.

Evidences that this may be the case even in relatively simple environments will be described in chapter 8. As we will see, if we try to co-evolve full generals predator and prey robots by testing them against all the best competitors of previous generations we may fail. In fact, in most of the cases it is impossible to obtain predators or prey that are able to defeat a large number of competitors although it is always possible to easily find a set of different individuals with different strategies able to do so. In other words it appears that in some cases, full general strategies do not exist or are too difficult to find while a collection of simple strategies appropriate in different circumstances may be easily found. Preliminary evidence that evolving individuals that are also allowed to adapt through lifetime learning may be able to adapt their strategy to the current competitor will be described in section 8.8.

It should be made clear that, up to now, there has been only little experimental evidence within evolutionary robotics that evolution and learning can evolve more complex levels of competence than evolution alone (Floreano and Urzelai in press). However, the study of learning in an evolutionary perspective, is still in its infancy. We believe that the study of learning in interaction with evolution will produce in the next years an enormous impact on our understanding of what learning is.

### Development and evolution of evolvability

One of the aspects of natural evolution that is more crudely simplified in evolutionary robotics is development. This can explain why recently the importance of development is one of the most debated issues in evolutionary robotics. Interestingly, the importance and role of development in natural evolution is a controversial issue in evolutionary biology too.

From an evolutionary robotics perspective, this issue is usually referred to as the *genotype-to-phenotype* mapping problem. As claimed by Wagner and Altenberg, "For adaptation to occur, these systems must possess *evolvability*, i.e. the ability of random variations to sometimes produce improvement. It was found that evolvability critically depends on the way genetic variation maps onto phenotypic variation, an issue known as the *representation problem* (Wagner and Altenberg 1996).

The simplest genotype-to-phenotype transformation is a *one-to-one* mapping in which each gene codifies for a single character of the robot. However, in most of the experiments conducted in evolutionary robotics, the mapping is more complex than that. It may involve: (a) several levels of organization (e.g., genotype, nervous system, and behavior) which are hierarchically organized and involve non linear interactions between different levels (most of the experiments that will be described in this book involve different levels of organization); (b) growing instructions that are recursive in the sense that they are applied to their own results in a way that resembles the process of cell duplication and differentiation (some examples will be described in section 9.2); (c) plasticity (see chapter 7); (d) genotypes that vary in length (see chapter 9).

The opportunity to study these features of development in isolation, to manipulate the way they are modelled, to generate huge amounts of data easily, may allow evolutionary robotics to help to understand the importance and the role of development from an evolutionary perspective.

Another important difference between natural evolution and artificial evolution is that in the former case the mapping itself is subjected to the evolutionary process while in the latter the mapping is generally designed by the experimenter (although it is designed by taking inspiration from how it is accomplished in natural organisms). Unfortunately, also in this case, it is difficult to design a good genotype-to-phenotype mapping. Similarly, it is difficult to shape the mapping just by imitating nature given that not everything is known and that, for practical reasons, only some aspects of the natural process can be modeled.

All these problems and the fact that it is still not clear how the mapping itself may be subjected to the evolutionary process explain why only limited results have been obtained so far in the attempt to evolve more complex behaviors by using more biologically plausible genotypes.

## 1.5   Conclusions

In this chapter we claimed that one of the main characteristics that makes the evolutionary robotics approach suitable for the study of adaptive behavior in natural and artificial agents is the possibility to rely largely on a self-organization process. Indeed by using artificial evolution the role of the designer may be limited to the specification of a fitness function measuring the ability of a given robot to perform a desired task. From an engineering point of view the main advantage of relying on self-organization is the fact that the designer does not need to divide the desired behavior into simple basic behaviors tto be implemented into separate layers (or modules) of the robot control system. By selecting individuals for their ability to perform the desired behavior as a whole, complex behaviors can emerge from the interaction between several simple processes in the control system and from the interaction between the robot and the environment. From the point of view of the study of natural systems, the possibility of evolving robots that are free to select their way to solve a task by interacting with their environment may help us to understand how natural organisms produce adaptive behavior. Finally, the attempt to scale up to more complex tasks may help us to make hypothesis about the critical features of natural evolution that allowed the emergence of the extraordinary variety of highly adapted life forms present on the planet.

# 2 Evolutionary and neural techniques

## 2.1 Introduction

Evolutionary robotics is based on the use of evolutionary techniques for developing robotic systems. In most cases, the control systems of evolutionary robots are artificial neural networks, in other cases they are computer programs. In this chapter we provide a very concise overview of evolutionary and neural algorithms, of their combination, and of genetic programming. Readers already familiar with these techniques can skip this chapter and come back to it only if necessary. Other readers will find here a self contained introduction to adaptive algorithms sufficient for understanding and replicating all models and experiments described in this book. The algorithms described have been chosen according to the types of models presented later on, and are not intended to be a representative sample of the field of evolutionary and neural computation.

Artificial evolution of robotic control systems has been applied to three types of structures: a) neural controllers; b) parameters of a predefined control program; c) computer programs themselves. Although one finds various combinations of these three approaches, the majority of the experiments in evolutionary robotics employ some type of neural controller. This chapter is organized as follows. In the next section we shall describe the fundamentals of genetic algorithms and discuss some variations used in later chapters. We shall then provide a short description of artificial neural networks with regard to architectures, functionality, and learning. That will be followed by a section describing why neural controllers are suitable structure for evolutionary robotics and mention three ways of evolving neural networks. Finally, we shall describe genetic programming, that is evolution of computer programs.

## 2.2 Genetic algorithms

Genetic algorithms (Holland 1975) are a popular form of evolutionary computation. A genetic algorithm operates on a population of artificial chromosomes by selectively reproducing the chromosomes of individuals with higher performance and applying random changes. This procedure is repeated for several cycles (generations). An artificial chromosome (genotype) is a string that encodes the characteristics of an individual (phenotype). For example, the string may encode in binary representation the value of a variable of a function that must be optimized (figure 2.1). Alternatively, the chromosome might encode several variables, such as the connection weights of a neural network. Several types of encoding techniques (binary, grey coding, real valued, e.g.) and alphabets (binary, ternary,

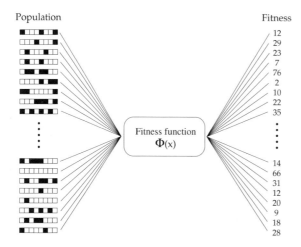

**Figure 2.1**
Assessing the fitness (performance) of the population of individuals. Each chromosome, a binary string of 0's (white) and 1's (black), is in turn decoded into the corresponding value of the variable x. The function is then evaluated for that particular value of x. In the case where we want to maximize the function, the higher the value returned by the function, the higher the fitness of the individual is. Initially, all chromosomes in the population are created in a random fashion.

etc.) have been used in the literature.

The fitness function is a performace criterion that evaluates the performance of each individual phenotype. Higher fitness values are better. For example, if one wants to optimize a mathematical function, individuals coding for values that generate higher returns will receive higher fitness. Similarly, one may attempt to minimize the difference between the value returned by the function and a target value. In this case, the fitness values will be inversely proportional to the measured error. A simple genetic algorithm (Goldberg 1989) starts with a population of randomly generated chromosomes. Each chromosome is decoded, one at a time, its fitness is evaluated, and three genetic operators—selective reproduction, crossover, and mutation—are applied to generate a new population. This generational process is repeated until a desired individual is found, or until the best fitness value in the population stops increasing.

Selective reproduction consists of making copies of the best individuals in the population. In other words, individuals that report higher fitness values tend to leave a higher number of copies of their chromosome for the next generation. Selective reproduction is often implemented with the *roulette wheel* method (figure 2.2) where each slot corresponds to an individual in the population and the size of the slot is proportional to the fitness of the individual. More precisely, given an individual phenotype $x_i$ and its fitness $f_i = \Phi(x_i)$,

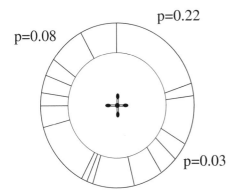

p=0.22

p=0.08

p=0.03

**Figure 2.2**
Schematic representation of roulette-wheel reproduction. Each slot in the wheel corresponds to an individuals of the population. The width of each slot is proportional to the fitness of that individual. An offspring is generated by spinning the wheel and making a copy of the chromosome of the individual where the ball stops. Individuals with higher fitness will have higher probability of generating offspring.

the size of the slot $p_i$ is proportional to the fitness value normalized by the total fitness of the population of $N$ individuals

$$p_i = \frac{f_i}{\sum_i^N f_i} \tag{2.1}$$

An offspring is generated by spinning the wheel and making a copy of the individual corresponding to the slot where the ball stops. We can consider $p_i$ as the probability of individual $i$ to generate an offspring. For a constant population, the new generation of chromosomes is obtained by spinning the wheel $N$ times. The expected number of offspring for individual $i$ is $Np_i$. This simple selection method tends to break down in two situations: when all individuals obtain similar fitness values and when one or two individuals obtain much higher fitness than the rest of the population. In the former case, all individuals will have the same probability of making offspring and evolution will amount to random search with genetic drift.[1] In the latter case, almost all offspring will be copies of the same individual who will soon dominate the population and cause premature convergence. One way to prevent these two limitations is to scale the fitness values prior to selection so that individual differences are enhanced in the former case and decreased in the latter. Another way consists of using *rank based* selection where individuals are ranked from best to worst and the probability of making offspring is proportional to their rank, not to their fitness value. A similar method, which will be often used in the experiments described in this book, is *truncation selection* which consists in ranking the individuals, selecting always the top $M$ individuals, and let them make $O$ copies of their chromosomes,

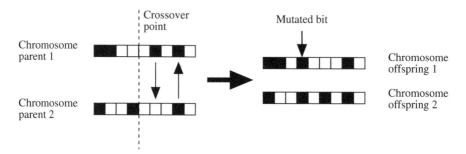

**Figure 2.3**
Crossover and mutation. Given two randomly selected offspring, genetic material is swapped between them around a randomly-selected point. After that, each location is mutated with a very small probability, for example by switching the value of the bit.

such that $M \times O = N$. For example, given a population size of 100, one may decide to reproduce always the best 20 individuals by making 5 copies of each chromosome. Yet another way of reproducing individuals is *tournament based* selection where an offspring is the result of a tournament between two randomly selected individuals. The tournament consists in generating a random number $r$ between 0 and 1; if $r$ is smaller than a predefined parameter $T$, the individual with the higher fitness makes an offspring, otherwise the other individual makes an offspring. The two individuals are then inserted back in the population. This method is more amenable to parallel implementation of genetic algorithms because it does not require global computation such as the total fitness of the population (roulette wheel) or ranking of individuals. In tournament based selection (but also in other methods) it is often useful to preserve the best individual for the next generation. This strategy, known as *elitism*, ensures that the best solution found so far is not lost and usually generates more gradual improvements of population fitness.

Once the new population has been created by selective reproduction, offspring are randomly paired, crossed over, and mutated. Crossover is applied with a given probability to a pair of chromosomes and consists of selecting a random point along the chromosome around which genetic material is swapped between the two individuals (figure 2.3). This is also called *one point crossover* to distinguish it from *multi point crossover*, and from other methods of crossing individuals and exchanging genetic material. Unless otherwise specified, in this book we shall use the term crossover to indicate one point crossover. Mutation is applied with a given probability to each location of a chromosome. For binary representations, mutation usually consists of switching the value of selected bits (figure 2.3). For real value representations, the value of a selected location is substituted with another value randomly extracted from the same range, or is incremented by a small number randomly extracted from a distribution centered around zero (*biased mutation*, Montana and Davis 1989). For other representations, mutation is implemented by substituting a selected location with a symbol randomly extracted from the same alphabet.

In distributed genetic algorithms the members of the population are thought of as distributed on a two dimensional surface (typically a toroidal grid with one individual in each cell) and selection and recombination operations are confined to local areas. This technique allows subpopulations located in different areas to explore different solutions (thus preventing a premature convergence of the population on a local minima) and at the same time, given that the local areas partially overlap, allows significant innovations to spread through the whole population (Collins and Jefferson 1991).

A generation consists of fitness evaluation of all individuals in the population, selective reproduction, crossover, and mutation. This procedure is repeated for several generations during which the average and best fitness values of the population are usually monitored. A genetic algorithm is halted when the fitness indicators stop increasing or when a satisfactory individual is found. Since almost all components of a genetic algorithms are stochastic, it is common procedure to repeat an evolutionary run several times starting from different initial conditions (e.g., with a different initialization of the random number generator) and to report collective statistics (average, standard deviations, statistical tests computed over all replications).

There are several variations on this simple genetic algorithm, as well as several other types of evolutionary algorithms. For further readings, we refer interested readers to introductory textbooks such as those by Goldberg (1989) and by Mitchell (1996).

**Building blocks and schema theory**

One way of visualizing how a genetic algorithm works is to think in terms of a fitness landscape. A fitness landscape is a multidimensional surface given by the set of fitness values for all possible combinations of genetic traits[2] (figure 2.4, left). For example, for a chromosome of length l, the fitness landscape will have l+1 dimensions (the additional dimension, or "height," of the landscape is given by the fitness value). Since a genetic algorithm selects individuals that report higher fitness, the best individual of a population moves over generations toward areas of higher fitness, as indicated by measured fitness values (figure 2.4, right).

It is a commonly held assumption that genetic algorithms efficiently explore the fitness landscapes by isolating and combining partial solutions, also known as building blocks. This notion derives from Schema Theory put forward by John Holland (1975) to describe the functioning of a genetic algorithm. A schema is a template that stands for a family of strings. A schema has an additional symbol * that can take on any value of the encoding alphabet. For example, in the case of a binary alphabet, the schema 1*1 stands

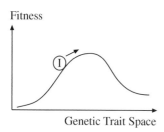

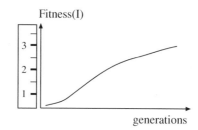

**Figure 2.4**
Schematic fitness landscape. All combinations of traits, and their corresponding fitness values, are listed along a single dimension (left). The best individual i at each population tends to move toward areas of higher fitness. This is indicated by the growth of the measured fitness values during evolution (right).

for strings 111 and 101. A population of N individuals, where each chromosome uses a binary representation and has length l, contains a number of schemata between $2^l$ and $N2^l$. Therefore schemata offer two advantages: a) they are useful for describing and isolating those components of a chromosome that provide high fitness; b) they potentially allow the exploration of a much higher number of strings than those contained in the population. Some schemata have higher fitness than other, that is strings containing those schemata will report higher fitness than other strings. John Holland showed that selective reproduction allocates a higher number of offspring to schemata with higher fitness. Furthermore, he showed that genetic algorithms process at least $N^3$ different schemata at a time, despite the fact that only N strings are evaluated (this result is known as "implicit parallelism").

Not all schemata are processed and transmitted over generations with the same efficiency. Given a set of different schemata with the same fitness, schemata whose significant components are far apart (1****1) will have a high probability of being broken down by crossover with respect to schemata whose significant component are closer (**11**). Without going into further details, a major result of the theory is that schemata with short "significant length" and high fitness will be allocated an exponential number of copies along generations. Therefore, genetic algorithms search a solution space quite efficiently. Instead of attempting to explore all possible combinations of strings, a genetic algorithm processes, selects and combines a high number of schemata with high fitness.

Within this framework schemata are the building blocks of evolution and crossover is a major genetic operator because it generates innovation by combining building blocks. Mutation, instead, would only be a local search operator. All this holds as long as one chooses a suitable genetic encoding for the problem at hand, that is an encoding whose building blocks have shorter significant length and whose combination can generate strings with higher fitness. In practice, this is very difficult and domain dependent, as we shall see in the remainder of this book.

Several practitioners reported that crossover had no influence in their experiments, or even that it lowered the performance of the genetic algorithm. In those experiments, crossover operates as a sort of macro mutation and may generate instability. Over the last years, much more attention is being paid to the mutation operator. In most of the experiments described in this book the crossover probability is zero or very small.

## Genetic algorithms and artificial evolution

Whether genetic algorithms are a plausible simulation of biological evolution is a much discussed issue that we shall not tackle here. However, for the purpose of this book it is worth asking whether artificial evolution should be implemented as a genetic algorithm. The question becomes relevant when one shifts the focus of attention from system optimization to self-organization of autonomous systems. In the former case, artificial evolution is seen as a search technique chosen for computational efficiency and genetic algorithms fit well this purpose because they are a relatively well understood and formalized technique. Instead, in the latter case what matters is spontaneous development of autonomous entities, such as artificial creatures and robots. In this context, which could be defined as a form of artificial life (Langton 1992; Steels 1994; Floreano 1998), the notions of computational efficiency, optimum, and even progress become less defined and secondary. Here, the most important aspect is emergence of complex abilities from a process of autonomous interaction between an agent and its environment.

Artificial evolution of autonomous systems differs in several subtle, but important, ways from traditional genetic algorithms. Autonomous systems are expected to survive in unknown and partially unpredictable environments by devising their own goals and finding out solutions to challenges that may arise. Therefore, it is difficult to establish a priori what abilities and achievements will be necessary to obtain higher fitness. The more detailed and constrained a fitness function is, the closer artificial evolution becomes to a supervised learning technique and less space is left to emergence and autonomy of the evolving system (aspects of fitness design will be further explored in later chapters).

As artificial evolution becomes driven more by interaction between the agent and its environment rather than by a detailed fitness function, the notion of hill climbing on a static search space becomes of less use. If the environment changes and the agent is not selected for a detailed predefined task, the course of evolution is dictated by environmental changes and local adaptations. An extreme example is the case of competitive co-evolution where competing agents are co-evolved under loose fitness constraints. In these circumstances the fitness landscape is dynamic and the notion of optimum changes over time. In chapter 8 we shall describe other aspects of traditional genetic algorithms that break down in dynamic landscapes.

## Neutral networks

The fitness landscape as a surface with peaks and valleys on which evolution performs hillclimbing driven by selective reproduction (figure 2.4) may not be a faithful representation of natural evolution. There is now biological evidence that "neutral evolution," that is random changes in the genotype that do not affect fitness values, can move the population in genotype space, possibly taking it to areas of higher fitness (Kimura 1983). A "neutral network" is a flat area (i.e., with the same fitness) of genotype space where genotypes are only one mutation away. In other words, it is possible to move along this neutral network by small mutations that do not contribute to fitness variations. A long genotype may have many neutral networks, some of which are interconnected at some point. Some networks have higher fitness than others. Small random mutations to a chromosome may move it along and across neutral networks, some of which may have higher fitness. In terms of measured fitness, one may observe long periods of fitness stagnation interrupted by sudden increments. Within this perspective, a more appropriate representation of fitness space is a complex web of genetically interconnected networks at different fitness heights.

Neutral evolution is favored by the presence of "junk DNA," that is areas of genetic code that do not correspond to phenotypic traits and whose mutation does not cause significant changes in the fitness of the individual. Moreover, neutral evolution may play an important role when there is not a direct mapping between genotype and phenotypes. For example, by evolving a population of artificial creatures whose phenotypes result from the execution of a set of "growing" instructions contained in the genotype (an encoding method which will be described in chapter 9), Miglino et al. (1996) observed long periods of stasis lasting several hundreds generations followed by rapid increases in fitness. By analyzing the effect of mutations they observed how the large majority of them were neutral. In fact while about 90% of the mutations produced changes at the level of the nervous system of the creatures, only about 20% of them affected the resulting behavior, and only 15% produced changes at the fitness level. Finally, the authors showed that, in some cases, the neutral mutations accumulated during a period of stasis provided the starting point for further changes which proved adaptive.

Inman Harvey (1995; 1997b) argues that neutral evolution is a promising approach for long term artificial evolution. Instead of using artificial evolution as an optimization tool to climb a local maximum of the fitness (from where no further movement is possible), he suggests to use fairly converged populations that move in genotype space by the effect of random mutation. Travel in neutral space may be useful for solving hard real world problems and has been detected in artificial evolution of electronic circuits (Harvey and Thompson 1996). Recent work on neutral networks in artificial evolution has addressed motion in genotype space (Barnett 1998) and their role in the interaction between evolution and learning (Mayley 1999) (see also chapter 7).

A related aspect is that of incremental and open ended evolution. As we have mentioned in the first chapter, artificial evolution of complex systems from scratch may fail because all individuals of the initial generation receive zero fitness (the bootstrap problem). Furthermore, the definition of complex and of optimum may change over time while the system evolves. These two factors require a new formulation of artificial evolution in the perspective of an incremental and open ended process. For example, Inman Harvey has proposed SAGA—Species Adaptation Genetic Algorithm—(1992a, 1992b, 1993), a form of artificial evolution characterized by variable length genotypes and a fairly genetically converged population that moves in genetic space through gradual mutations, rather than by the effect of crossover (see also box on Neutral Networks).

Additional variations to traditional genetic algorithms are introduced by inclusion of phenomena such as maturation and learning, that is changes that affect the fitness of an individual during its own life. As we shall see in chapter 7, ontogenetic changes interact with and affect the course of evolution even though induced modifications are not directly transmitted by the chromosome of an individual. Once again, under these circumstances the relevance of exponential allocation and recombination of high fitness schemata may be very minor with respect to other factors that affect selective pressure.

Some of the experiments described in this book elaborate on one or more of these aspects, whereas other experiments rely on traditional genetic algorithms. Either way, two common aspects found in artificial evolution of robots are: a) a genetic representation of the individual, and b) the fundamental importance given to autonomous interaction with a physical environment.

## 2.3   Artificial neural networks

An artificial neural network is a collection of units (neurons) connected by weighted links (synapses or connection weights) used to transmit signals (figure 2.5, left). Input and output units receive and broadcast signals to the environment, respectively. Internal units are sometimes called *hidden* because they are not in contact with the external environment. A neural network is a parallel computational system because signals travel independently on weighted channels and units can update their state in parallel. However, most neural networks can be easily simulated on serial computers.

In the simple neuron model proposed by McCulloch and Pitts (1943), the output of a unit $y_i$ is a function $\Phi()$ of the sum of all incoming signals $x_j$ weighted by connection

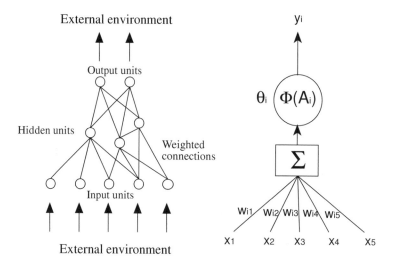

**Figure 2.5**
**Left:** An artificial feed-forward neural network. Hidden units are called so because are not in direct contact with the external environment. Signals flow from input to output. **Right:** Computing the output of a neuron. Each input signal is multiplied by the corresponding connection strength and the results added together. The net input is then passed to a function whose output may take into consideration a threshold value.

strengths $w_{ij}$ (figure 2.5, right)

$$y_i = \Phi \left( \sum_{j}^{N} w_{ij} x_j \right) \tag{2.2}$$

In some models a threshold $\theta_i$ is included in the output function. The threshold is an activity level beyond which a neuron becomes active.

Commonly used output functions include the step function, the linear function, and the sigmoid function (figure 2.6). The step function, used in the model by McCulloch and Pitts, returns 1 if the weighted sum is larger than the threshold (in figure 2.6 the threshold is always zero), otherwise it returns 0 (or $-1$)

$$\Phi(x) = \begin{cases} 1 & \text{if } x > \theta \\ 0(-1) & \text{otherwise} \end{cases} \tag{2.3}$$

The step function can transmit only one bit of information, whether the unit is on or off. Instead, the linear function can transmit more information with its graded output,

$$\Phi(x) = kx \tag{2.4}$$

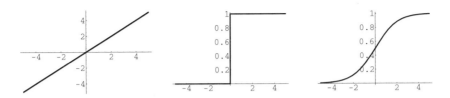

**Figure 2.6**
Three common output functions. From left to right: step, linear, sigmoid. The x axis shows the weighted sum, the y axis the value returned by the function. The threshold of the neuron is always zero. The slope constant for the latter two function is always 1.

where $k$ is a constant that controls the inclination. The sigmoid function

$$\Phi(x) = \frac{1}{1 + e^{-kx}} \qquad (2.5)$$

has a graded output, its value is automatically squashed between 0 and 1, and is nonlinear. The constant $k$ controls the slope of the response (for $k \longrightarrow \infty$, the sigmoid function approximates the step function). A function with similar properties is $\tanh(kx)$ where the asymptotes are at $-1$ and 1. In the case of continuous output function the threshold is mathematically equivalent to the weight of an additional incoming connection from a unit with constant value $-1$. This weight is sometimes called a *bias* and its input unit is called the *bias unit*. The value of the bias can be adapted with the same learning rules used for the other connections, as we shall see below.

The architecture of a neural network is defined by the number of neurons and their pattern of connectivity. Often units are organized in layers: input layer, internal or hidden layer(s), and output layer. Sometimes, the word *layer* is used for connections instead than for neurons.[3] We can distinguish two large families of architectures: feedforward and recurrent. In feedforward architectures, signals travel from input units forward to output units. If a network has an internal layer of units, the states of internal units are updated before those of output units. In recurrent architectures, instead, there may be feedback connections from neuron in upper layer or in the same layer, including connections from the same neuron. Recurrent architectures can have quite complex time dependent dynamics.

The behavior of a neural network is largely determined by the values of connection weights, also known as synaptic strengths. Except for a very few simple cases, it is difficult to determine by hand the strengths required for achieving a desired input/output mapping. Neural networks can learn a mapping by automatically finding the appropriate set of connection weights. Learning is achieved by repeatedly updating the weight values while a sample set of patterns is presented to the units of the network. Roughly speaking, we can distinguish two broad types of learning:

• In *supervised learning* synaptic strengths are modified using the discrepancy (error) between the desired output (also known as teaching signals, or teaching inputs) and the output given by the network for a given input pattern. *Reinforcement learning* (Sutton and Barto 1998) includes a class of algorithms based on a global evaluation of the network response, not on a definition of the exact output.

• In *unsupervised learning* the network updates the weights on the basis of the input patterns only. Here the learning rule and the architecture chosen determine how the network self-organizes its behavior. This type of learning is mainly used for feature extraction, categorization, and data compression.

In most cases, initial synaptic strengths are set to zero or to small random values centered around zero. Learning takes place by repeatedly presenting pairs of input/output patterns (only input patterns in the case of unsupervised learning). The modification of synaptic strength $\Delta w_{ij}$ is computed after the presentation of each pattern pair (online learning) or after the presentation of the entire training set (offline). The old weights $w_{ij}^{t-1}$ are updated by adding the newly computed modification $\Delta w_{ij}^{t}$

$$w_{ij}^{t} = w_{ij}^{t-1} + \Delta w_{ij}^{t} \tag{2.6}$$

In order to prevent wide oscillations of the weights from one change to the next, only a small rate $\eta$ (also known as learning rate) of the modification is added to the previous weights

$$w_{ij}^{t} = w_{ij}^{t-1} + \eta \Delta w_{ij}^{t} \qquad 0 < \eta \leq 1 \tag{2.7}$$

Learning algorithms therefore are concerned with the computation of $\Delta w_{ij}$. In the remainder of this section we shall present a set of learning algorithms and related architectures proceeding from simple feedforward architectures up to recurrent networks with discrete and continuous dynamics. A more detailed introduction to neural networks is given by Hertz, Krogh, and Palmer (1989), while a very comprehensive technical overview can be found in Haykin (1994). Instead, Churchland and Sejnowski (1992) describe neural networks in a wider perspective, including computer science, biology, and embodied sensory-motor computation.

**Hebbian learning**

In 1949 the Canadian psychologist Donald Hebb (1949) hypothesized that the laws of classical conditioning (a form of behavioral learning based on association between response and stimulus) reflected the functioning of the nervous system. The *hebb rule* states that when two connected neurons are simultaneously active, the synaptic weight of their connection is strengthened.

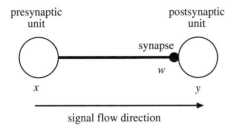

**Figure 2.7**
Presynaptic and postsynaptic neuron.

**Figure 2.8**
Learning three associations with the Hebb rule. Patterns are presented in sequence from left to right and weights are changed after each presentation. Gray connections have zero value, black connections have value 1.

If we consider the direction of signal flow, the unit before the synapse is known as *presynaptic neuron* and the unit after the synapse as *postsynaptic neuron* (figure 2.7). The hebb rule is formally described as

$$\Delta w_{ij} = y_i x_j \tag{2.8}$$

where $y_i$ and $x_j$ are the activation states of the postsynaptic neuron $i$ and of the presynaptic neuron $x_j$, respectively.

Figure 2.8 shows learning of three association with the hebb rule. After learning, the network will provide the correct output pattern also when an incomplete or corrupted version of the input pattern is presented. However, if neurons have only positive activation states, the plain hebb rule can only strengthen weights, but never decrease them. Therefore, after several presentation of different patterns, all the weights in the network will become strong and positive. As a result, the network will always activate all output units for any input pattern. In order to allow weight decrement and prevent this interference, one can use output functions where neurons can have both positive and negative values.

Other variations on the hebb rule that do not require neurons with negative activations are the postsynaptic rule and the presynaptic rule. The postsynaptic rule, or stent-singer rule (Singer 1987; Stent 1973) changes the weight only when the postsynaptic unit is active as follows: if the presynaptic unit is active too, the weight is increased, otherwise it is decreased. Conversely, the presynaptic rule (see Stanton and Sejnowski 1989 for biological evidence) changes the weight only when the presynaptic unit is active: if the postsynaptic unit is active too, the weight is increased, otherwise it is decreased. Willshaw and Dayan (1990) have studied optimal rates of increment and decrement to minimize errors due to interferences between successive presentations of different patterns.

The hebb rules are computationally appealing because they are simple and are based only on variables locally available at the synaptic site.

### Supervised error based learning

Supervised learning modifies the weights of the network in order to reduce the error between the desired output and the output provided by the network for a given input pattern. In the case of a network with one layer of connections, this learning method is known as the *delta rule*. The training set is composed of pairs of input patterns $\mathbf{x}$ and teaching patterns $\mathbf{t}$. A teaching pattern is the desired output of the network.

In the online version, the weights are updated after the presentation of each pattern pair. After obtaining the output of the network for a given input pattern $\mu$,

$$y_i^\mu = \Phi \left( \sum_j^N w_{ij} x_j^\mu \right) \tag{2.9}$$

where $\Phi()$ is a linear output function, the "delta error" $\delta^\mu$ between the teaching pattern and the output is computed as follows

$$\delta_i^\mu = \left( t_i^\mu - y_i^\mu \right) \tag{2.10}$$

The weight modification is given by the product between the delta error at the postsynaptic unit and the input at the presynaptic unit

$$\Delta w_{ij}^\mu = \delta_i^\mu x_j^\mu \tag{2.11}$$

The training patterns are presented several times in random order and the synaptic weights are updated after each presentation. It can be shown that this modification rule minimizes the objective function

$$E = \frac{1}{2} \sum_\mu^M \sum_i^N \left( t_i^\mu - y_i^\mu \right)^2 \tag{2.12}$$

also known as the *error function*, or *cost function* (so called because it must be minimized during learning), where $M$ is the total number of training patterns and $N$ the

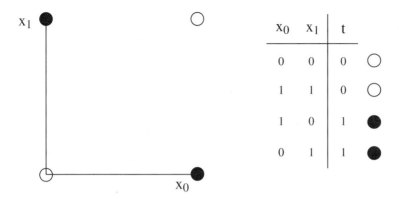

**Figure 2.9**
The XOR function has two inputs and one output. It is not linearly separable because it is impossible to separate the two groups of patterns with a line and thus it cannot be learned by a network with a single layer of connections. **Left:** Geometric visualization of the function. Each axis represents one input. The color of the dot represents the desired output. **Right:** Tabular visualization.

total number of output units. The power of two ensures that the discrepancy between target and unit activation is always positive.

The delta rule is more powerful than the hebbian rules described above, but it requires the knowledge of the correct response for each input pattern of the training set. The delta rule is applicable only to networks with one layer of connections. These networks can learn only linearly separable mappings. Two sets of vectors are said to be linearly separable if it is possible to draw a line between them. Consider a network with two input units (plus a bias unit) and a single output unit. In this simple case, the separation line is given by

$$x_2 = \frac{w_0}{w_2} - \frac{w_1}{w_2}x_1 \qquad\qquad (2.13)$$

where the index 0 refers to the bias weight, or threshold.

There are cases where the patterns are not linearly separable, such as in the XOR problem shown in figure 2.9. In order to learn nonlinearly separable mappings it is necessary to add an internal set of units (hidden units) to the network. These units recode the input vectors so that the output units can produce the desired output. The output function of the internal units must be nonlinear.[4] A typical choice is the sigmoid function described above because it is nonlinear, continuous, and differentiable.

A network with hidden units and non linear output functions requires two modifications to the delta rule: 1) addition of nonlinear behaviors introduced by the output function, and 2) a method to compute the error of the hidden units. The method of back-propagation of error (Rumelhart et al. 1986), also known as "generalized delta rule," includes both

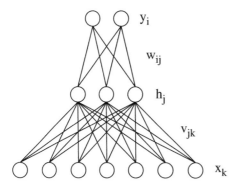

**Figure 2.10**
A feedforward neural network with hidden units.

constraints. The core of the algorithm consists of computing the error contribution of hidden units by transmitting the delta error on the output units back to the hidden units through the same weighted connections (hence the name back-propagation). Consider the multilayer network shown in figure 2.10 and the symbols associated to each entity. The values of the input units are given by the input pattern. The output of the hidden and of the output units are computed using the sigmoid function described above. The online version of the algorithms proceeds as follows:

- Initialize all weights (including biases) to small random values centered around 0.
- Set the values of the input units $x$ to the current training pattern $s$

$$x_k^\mu = s_k^\mu \tag{2.14}$$

- Compute the values of hidden units

$$h_j^\mu = \Phi\left(\sum_{k=0} v_{jk} x_k^\mu\right) \tag{2.15}$$

where $\Phi()$ is the sigmoid activation function.

- Compute the values of output units

$$y_i^\mu = \Phi\left(\sum_{j=0} w_{ij} h_j^\mu\right) \tag{2.16}$$

- Compute the delta error for each output unit. Notice that the error is multiplied by the first derivative (denoted by a dot) of the output function of that node because we are using a non-linear activation function. This was not necessary in the delta rule because the activation function was linear.

$$\delta_i^\mu = \dot{\Phi} \left( \sum_{j=0} w_{ij} h_j^\mu \right) (t_i^\mu - y_i^\mu) \tag{2.17}$$

The first derivative of the sigmoid function can be conveniently expressed in terms of the output of the unit itself. In the case of the output units, for example

$$\dot{\Phi} \left( \sum_{j=0} w_{ij} h_j^\mu \right) = y_i^\mu (1 - y_i^\mu) \tag{2.18}$$

- Compute the delta error of hidden units by propagating the delta errors at the output backward through the connection weights. Notice that the index in the sum of the weighted deltas is $i$ and refers to the output units. As before, the delta error must be multiplied by the first derivative of the output function of the unit,

$$\delta_j^\mu = \dot{\Phi} \left( \sum_{k=0} v_{jk} x_k^\mu \right) \sum_i w_{ij} \delta_i^\mu \tag{2.19}$$

- Compute the modifications to the synaptic weights of the two layers by multiplying the delta errors at the postsynaptic units by the output of the presynaptic units

$$\Delta w_{ij}^\mu = \delta_i^\mu h_j^\mu$$
$$\Delta v_{jk}^\mu = \delta_j^\mu x_k^\mu \tag{2.20}$$

- Finally, update the weights by adding a portion $\eta$ of the modifications

$$w_{ij}^t = w_{ij}^{t-1} + \eta \Delta w_{ij}^\mu$$
$$v_{jk}^t = v_{jk}^{t-1} + \eta \Delta v_{jk}^\mu \tag{2.21}$$

where $\eta$ is the learning rate and smaller than 1.

Every pair of input-output pattern in the training set is presented several times in random order until the Total Sum Squared Error computed over each output unit $i$ and each training pattern $\mu$

$$TSS = \frac{1}{M} \sum_\mu^M \left( \frac{1}{N} \sum_i^N (t_i^\mu - y_i^\mu)^2 \right) \tag{2.22}$$

until it reaches a suitable small value. Provided a suitable architecture, it can be shown that, in principle, multilayer networks trained with the method of back-propagation can learn any arbitrary mapping between input units and output units. However, adding more neurons and connections to a network in the attempt to learn complex mappings is not necessarily positive because a larger network requires a larger training set,[5] it may overfit the data (learn well the training set, but not generalize), and it may become stuck into sub optimal solutions.

**Reinforcement learning**

Despite their computational power, networks trained with the delta rule or with back-propagation can be used only in those situations where one knows the correct output for each input pattern in the training set. This is often not the case for autonomous robots where the feedback (if any) available from the environment is usually much less detailed. Reinforcement learning (Barto and Sutton 1998) includes a class of algorithms designed for situations where the feedback (reinforcement) is coarse and sparse. By "coarse" we mean that the feedback does not provide much information: for example, it could be only 0 for bad and 1 for good. By "sparse" we mean that a feedback may not always be available, but, for example, only after a long sequence of actions.

Reinforcement learning algorithms attempt to choose those actions that maximize the amount of positive reinforcement received over time. In doing so, they must solve at the same time two formidable credit assignment problems. The structural assignment problem is about which action, among all those available, should be credited for a given reinforcement value. The temporal assignment problem is about the distribution of credit among all actions involved in a sequence that ended in a single reinforcement value. In order to solve these problems, the agent (or robot) must explore several combinations of input-output patterns, also known as state-action pairs. In order to reduce the state-action space and make learning feasible in reasonable time, these algorithms are often applied to discrete simulated environments, that is grid worlds with only a few actions (move forward, turn right, stay, etc.) and highly abstract sensory information (Kaelbling et al. 1996). Much of current research is aimed at generalizing these algorithms to continuous input and output domains.

In this chapter we shall not enter in more detail about this family of algorithms because they are not used in the experiments described in this book, but we refer interested readers to the already cited book by Barto and Sutton (1998). It is worth noticing that reinforcement learning and evolutionary algorithms attempt to solve a similar class of problems, although in different ways. Despite this, to the best of our knowledge there are not yet objective comparisons between the two families of algorithms.

In an evolutionary experiment that will be described in chapter 7, Ackley and Littman have employed a method to exploit coarse feedback in multilayer networks trained with back-propagation (Ackley and Littman 1990). The algorithm, known as *complementary reinforcement back-propagation* (CRBP), consists of mapping the real valued output of the network **y** into a binary valued vector **o** with the same dimensionality. Each value $y_i$ is interpreted as the probability that the corresponding value $o_i$ is 1. The vector of binary values **o**, which is stochastically produced from the output of the network, codes for the actions of the agent. The stochastic generation of **o** provides an exploration of the state-action space. For example, Medeen (1996) employed CRBP for a car like robot equipped with two motors (the front motor for steering and the rear motor for propulsion) where the binary states of four units coded for "front motor on/off," "front motor left/right," "rear motor on/off," "rear motor backward/forward."

The core of the algorithm consists of increasing the probability of producing actions that receive positive reinforcement and decrease the probability of producing actions with negative reinforcement.[6] The learning rate $\eta$ is higher for positive feedback than for negative feedback. The error for the output units of the network is computed as follows:

- If positive feedback, then $e_i = o_i - y_i$
- If negative feedback, then $e_i = (1 - o_i) - y_i$
- If no reinforcement, then $e_i = 0$

The delta error is then computed by multiplying the error by the first derivative of the activation of the unit. CRBP is quite effective for learning simple behaviors, but it tends to get stuck into sub optimal solutions if the reinforcement program (when and what reinforcement is received) and initial synaptic weights are not well chosen, and therefore it can take advantage of evolutionary support (Medeen 1996).

## Learning in recurrent networks

The neural networks described so far have a feedforward architecture. The output of these networks depends only and entirely on the pattern currently presented as input. In some cases, such as in time series prediction, it is important to detect time dependent features in the sequence of input patterns. One way of doing so is to expand the input layer in order to present several patterns at the same time to the network. One can visualize the input layer as a window looking at several patterns and shifting across them one at a time. These so called *time delay neural networks* (TDNN) require that the user knows the appropriate size of the window, that is what is the minimum number of patterns sufficient to extract time dependent features. Furthermore, this window size is constant and the network has many more synaptic weights that must be estimated.

Another strategy consists of adding recurrent connections from neurons in the same and upper layers. These connections transmit activations with a time delay. In the simplest

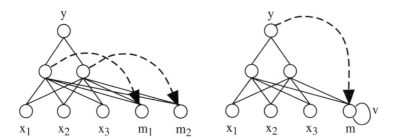

**Figure 2.11**
Two types of architectures with discrete and constant time delay. **Left:** Elman architecture. The memory units hold a copy (dashed lines) of the activations of hidden units at the previous time step. **Right:** Jordan architecture. The memory unit computes its activation by combining a copy of the output unit at the previous time step with its own previous state weighted by a self-recurrent connection.

case, where the time delay is constant and equivalent to one time step, the output of a neuron $y_i^t$ with recurrent connections is determined by its current weighted inputs plus the weighted outputs of other neurons (including itself) at the previous time step

$$y_i^t = \Phi \left( \sum_i w_{ij} x_j^t + \sum_k c_{ik} y_k^{t-1} \right) \qquad (2.23)$$

where $c_{ik}$ are the recurrent connections and $y_{ik}^{t-1}$ are the outputs at the previous time step from neurons in the same layer (including the neuron $i$ itself) or in upper layers.

Figure 2.11 shows two types of recurrent architectures that can be trained with the supervised algorithms described so far. The strategy consists of adding extra input units that hold a copy (memory) of the activations of other units at the previous time step. These extra "memory units" are connected to hidden units with feedforward connection. In Elman's (1990) architecture (figure 2.11, left) the memory units hold a copy of the values of hidden units at the previous time step. Since hidden units encode their own previous states, this network can detect and reproduce long sequences in time. In Jordan's (1989) architecture, memory units a copy of the values of output units at the previous time step is combined with the weighted activation of the memory unit itself at the previous time step (recurrent connection).

More complex time dependent dynamics can be achieved with continuous time recurrent neural networks where recurrent signals and inputs are continuously integrated over a time constant $\tau$

$$\tau_i \frac{\partial a_i}{\partial t} = -a_i + \sum_j w_{ij} \Phi \left( a_j \right) + I_i \qquad (2.24)$$

where $a_i$ is the mean activation state of the unit, $\Phi(a_i) = 1/(1 + e^{a_i})$ or another continuous function, and $I_i$ is the current sensory input to the neuron. A fully connected network of such units can be trained or evolved to generate oscillatory behaviors. Since individual units can have different time constants, the dynamics of such a network can become quite complex. For this reason, continuos time recurrent networks are used in several experiments described later on in this book.

## 2.4   Evolving neural networks

As we have mentioned in the introduction, the majority of experiments in evolutionary robotics have resorted to neural networks for the control system of the evolving robot. This choice is often justified by one or more of the following issues:

• Neural networks offer a relatively smooth search space. In other words, gradual changes to the parameters defining a neural network (weights, time constants, architecture) will often correspond to gradual changes of its behavior.

• Neural networks provide various levels of evolutionary granularity. One may decide to apply artificial evolution to the lowest level specification of a neural network, such as the connection strengths, or to higher levels, such as the coordination of predefined modules composed of predefined sub-networks.

• Neural networks allow different levels of adaptation. We can distinguish at least three types of adaptation: phylogenetic (evolution), developmental (maturation), and ontogenetic (life learning). These types can be combined in various ways. For example, the blueprint of a network architecture may be evolved, its actual structure may develop during the initial stages of the robot "life," and its connection strengths may adapt in real time while the robot interacts with the environment.

• Neural networks provide a straightforward mapping between sensors and motors. They can accommodate continuous (analog) input signals and provide either continuous or discrete motor outputs, depending on the transfer function chosen.

• Neural networks are robust to noise. Since their units are based upon a sum of several weighted signals, oscillations in the individual values of these signals do not drastically affect the behavior of the network. This is a very useful property for physical robots with noisy sensors that interact with noisy environments.

• Neural networks can be a biologically plausible metaphor of mechanisms that support adaptive behavior. They are a natural choice for those researchers interested in replicating and understanding biological phenomena from an evolutionary perspective.

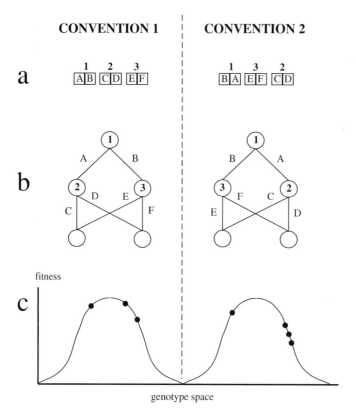

**Figure 2.12**
Competing conventions. Two different genotypes (a) may encode networks that are behaviorally equivalent but have inverted hidden units (b). The two genotypes define two separate hills on the fitness landscape (c) and thus may make evolutionary search more difficult (adapted from Schaffer, Whitley and Eshelman 1992).

Some authors (Schaffer, Whitley and Eshelman 1992; Radcliffe 1991) have suggested that evolution of neural networks is made difficult by the problem of "competing conventions" (figure 2.12). This refers to the situation when the mapping between genotype-to-phenotype is many to one. This means that very different genotypes (conventions) may correspond to neural networks with similar behavior. For example, two networks with inverted hidden nodes have very different genetic representations, but exactly the same behavior. Since the two genotypes correspond to quite different areas of the genetic space, this ambiguity generates two peaks on the fitness landscape instead of only one as it would be for back-propagation. Furthermore, crossover among competing conventions may produce offspring with very low fitness because they have duplicated structures. However, experimental studies have shown that in practice this is not a problem (Hancock 1992), but it may still be wise to use small crossover rate (much less than 100%) when evolving neural networks.

In the following subsections we shall mention three ways of evolving neural networks. More details for each method will be given later on in those chapters where these methods are employed.

## Weights and learning parameters

There are several reasons for evolving the values of synaptic weights: a) a genetic algorithm explores a population of networks, not a single network as in other learning algorithms; b) there are no constraints on the type of architecture, activation function, etc.; c) it is not necessary to have a detailed specification of the network response for each patters, as in supervised learning methods. This last point is the most important in evolutionary robotics.

The synaptic weights (including bias weights and time constants, if applicable) are directly encoded on the genotype either as a string of real values or as a string of binary values with a given precision. For the latter case, Schraudolph and Belew (1992) have suggested to encode the most significant bits early on and in later generations, when the population is almost converged, encode the less significative bits to narrow the search.

Montana and Davis (1989) have compared the performance of a genetic algorithm with that of back-propagation on a task of sonar signal classification. The results showed that genetic algorithms find much better networks and in many less computational cycles than back-propagation of error. These results have been confirmed also on a different classification task by other authors (Whitley, Starkweather and Bogart 1990).

Another strategy consists of combining evolution and supervised learning for the same task. Since back-propagation is very sensitive to initial weight values, genetic algorithms can be used to find the initial weight values of networks trained with back-propagation (Belew, McInerney and Schraudolph 1992). The fitness function is computed using the residual error of the network after having being trained with back-propagation on a given task (notice that the final weights after supervised training are not coded back into the genotype, i.e. evolution is Darwinian, not Lamarkian). Networks with evolved initial weights learn significantly faster and better (two orders of magnitude) than networks with random initial weights. The genetic string can also encode the value of the learning rate and of other learning parameters. When doing so, it was found that the best networks employed learning rates ten times higher than values suggested by common wisdom (i.e., much less than 1.0), but this result may depend on several factors, such as the order of presentation of the patterns, the number of learning cycles allowed before computing the fitness, and the initial weight values.

**Architectures**

The architecture of a network can affect quite a lot its ability of solving a problem. Genetic algorithms are an interesting way of finding suitable architectures because the space of possible architectures is infinite, not differentiable (therefore, cannot be searched by gradient descent algorithms), and noisy.

When evolving architectures, it is common practice to encode on the genotype only some characteristics of the network, such as the number of nodes, the probability of connecting them, the type of activation function, etc. This strategy is also known as "indirect encoding" to differentiate it from "direct coding" of all network parameters (Yao 1993). Fine tuning of the weights is usually obtained by applying a learning algorithm to the decoded network.

In the pioneering work by Harp, Samad and Guha (1989), the genetic string encodes a blueprint to build a network. This blueprint is composed of several segments, each corresponding to a layer of the network. Each segment has two parts: one part defines node properties, such as the number of units, their activation function, and their geometric layout, and the other part defines the properties of their outgoing connections, such as the connection density, learning rate, etc. Once decoded, the network weights are trained with back-propagation. Crossover takes place only between corresponding parts of the segments. The results showed that when the fitness function includes a penalty for the number of connections, the best networks had very few connections; instead, when the fitness function includes a penalty for the number of learning cycles needed to reach an error threshold, the best networks learned almost ten times faster, but used many more connections.

Kitano (1990) employed a developmental encoding based on a set of rewriting rules encoded on the genotype. The genotype is divided in blocks of five elements. Each block of five starts with one symbol that develops in the remaining four symbols during the construction of the network. There are two types of symbols: terminals and non terminals. A terminal symbol develops in a predetermined 2x2 matrix of 0s and 1s. A non terminal symbol develops in a 2x2 matrix of symbols. The first block of the genotype builds the initial 2x2 matrix of symbols, each of which recursively develops using the rules encoded in the genotype until a matrix of 0's and 1's is built. This matrix represents the architecture and connection pattern of the network. Synaptic weights are fine tuned by back-propagation whose residual error is used to compute the fitness function. This method can encode quite complex networks on a very compact genotype and is well suited for evolving modular networks. Gruau (1992a) has developed this method further by encoding network structures as grammatical trees and employed genetic programming (see next section). We shall describe Gruau's method it in more detail in chapter 9.

Nolfi et al. (Nolfi et. al. 1994a; Nolfi and Parisi 1995) have implemented a maturation process where the network "grows" in time while the agent moves in the environment. The neural network is conceived as a 2D tissue and the genetic string encodes the position of the neurons on this tissue, the direction of growth of axons, their length, etc. Axons that end up in areas without neurons die while others can form synaptic connections with new neurons. Since the growth process depends also on the activity of the neurons, the agent behavior affects maturation. This method will be described in more detail in chapter 9.

## Learning rules

Genetic algorithms have been employed to evolve learning rules too. A learning rule can be considered as a function of few variables, such as presynaptic activity $x_j$, postsynaptic activity $y_i$, and the current value of the synaptic connection $w_{ij}$

$$\Delta w_{ij} = \Phi \left( x_j, y_i, w_{ij} \right) \tag{2.25}$$

The genetic encoding of this function requires that the function is rewritten as a linear combination of the products between the variables weighted by constants. For example, if one takes into consideration only first and second order products, the function above becomes

$$\Delta w_{ij} = a_1 \left( x_j, x_j \right) + a_2 \left( x_j, y_i \right) + a_3 \left( x_j, w_{ij} \right) + a_4 \left( y_i, y_i \right) + a_5 \left( y_i, w_{ij} \right) + a_6 \left( w_{ij}, w_{ij} \right) \tag{2.26}$$

where the constants $a_n$ can take on discrete values $\{-1, 0, 1\}$ or continuous values in the range $[-1, 1]$. The genetic string encodes the values of the constants. A network is then trained on a set of tasks using the decoded learning rule and its performance is used to compute the fitness. The initial synaptic weights are always set to small random values centered around zero.

Chalmers (1990), who pioneered this technique, employed a fitness function based on the mean squared error (see section 3.2 above). A neural network with a single layer of connections was trained on eight linearly separable classification tasks. The genetic algorithm evolved a learning rule similar to the delta rule described above. Similar results were obtained by Fontanari and Meir (1991). Dasdan and Oflazer (1994) employed a similar encoding scheme to evolve unsupervised learning rules for classification tasks. The authors reported that evolved rules were more powerful than comparable human designed rules. Baxter (1994) encoded both the architecture and whether a synapse could be modified by a simple hebb rule (the rule was predetermined). Floreano and Mondada (1996a) evolved different learning rules for individual synapses and applied it to a mobile robot using a behavioral fitness function. This method will be described in more detail in chapter 7.

X+ (Y/(X-Z))  ———————▶   (+, X, (%, Y, (-, X, Z)))

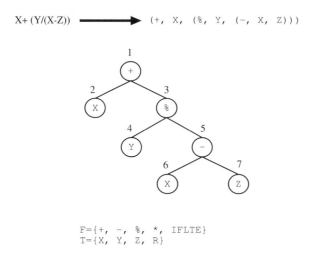

F={+, -, %, *, IFLTE}
T={X, Y, Z, R}

**Figure 2.13**
Representation of computer programs in genetic programming. **Top:** Lisp encodes programs as nested lists.
**Center:** Parse tree representation of Lisp expression. **Bottom:** Elements of a parse tree: functions and terminals.

Husbands et al. (1998) evolved a class of neural networks denoted as GasNets inspired by the modulatory effects of freely diffusing gases in real nervous systems. According to recent findings in fact, gases such as nitric oxide act as modulatory neurotransmitters. Contrary to other neurotransmitters however, these gases diffuse across the intervening cellular structures (Husbands et al. 1998). The nodes of GasNets, which are spatially distributed over a 2D surface, emit "gases" that diffuse through the network and modulate transfer function of the nodes in a concentration dependent fashion. Nodes might produce a genetically specified type of gas either when the activation of the node or the concentration of a gas at the node site exceeds a genetically specified threshold. The authors argue that the modulation caused by gas diffusion introduces a form of plasticity in the network.

## 2.5 Genetic programming

*Genetic programming* (GP) is evolution of computer programs (Koza 1992; 1994). In other words, genetic strings do not encode a solution for a specific problem, but a program to solve that problem. Although the idea of evolving programs had already being explored in earlier work (Cramer 1985, e.g.), GP employs efficient representations and simple formalisms that make it applicable to a large variety of problems.

GP is based on Lisp like expressions[7] and operates on tree representations, instead of string representations (figure 2.13). Lisp is a functional language based on nested lists. For example, a function of two variables $\Phi(a, b)$ is expressed as a list of three elements

$$(f, a, b)$$

where the first element is the function and the remaining two elements are its arguments (figure 2.13, top). Evaluating the list consists of substituting the elements with their actual values

$$(+, 2, 5)$$

which returns a value of 7. Each argument can be recursively substituted by another list,

$$(+, 2, (*, 3, 2))$$

which is a nested list equivalent to the expression $2+(3*2)$. Nested lists of various depth (levels of recursion) can be conveniently represented as trees where the branching nodes are the functions and the terminals are arguments that assume numerical values (figure 2.13, center). A program is evaluated by parsing the tree from its terminals up to the main branching node. A tree is thus composed of two elements: a function set and a terminal set (figure 2.13, bottom). The sets of functions and terminals are said to be closed if any function can accept the output produced by any other function. Some functions are protected to ensure the principle of closure. For example, protected division % returns 1 whenever division by zero is attempted.

The first step consists of choosing the initial set of functions and terminals. For example,

$$F=\{+, -, *, \%, IFLTE\}$$
$$T=\{X, Y, Z, \Re\}$$

where IFLTE is "if-less-than-or-equal" and $\Re$ is random number. Often the choice of a function set is based on the knowledge of the problem domain. It has been shown that it can be difficult or impossible to evolve programs with complex abilities using a low level function set, such as that shown above (O'Reilly and Oppacher 1992).

The second step consists of creating an initial population of random programs by randomly choosing the branching nodes from the function and terminal set within a predefined maximum depth level. Therefore, individuals can have different lengths. The fitness value is computed evaluating each program on a data set (in some cases it is necessary to set a maximum number of CPU cycles).

Crossover exchanges subtrees between parents or within the same individual by selecting two random nodes and swapping all the node dependencies (figure 2.14). It is important

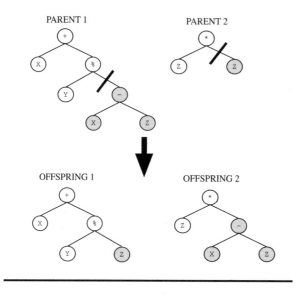

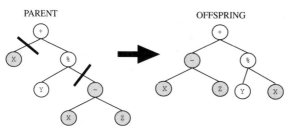

**Figure 2.14**
Two common types of crossover. **Top:** Swapping branches between parents. **Bottom:** Swapping branches within
the same individual (also known as inversion operator).

that the function set and terminal set are closed so that all possible combinations of subtrees
correspond to legal programs.

Mutation works by deleting a randomly selected node or creating a new random subtree
in its place. However, the mutation operator is not used very often in genetic programming.
Instead, it is common practice to use large populations (several hundreds or thousands)
and employ a high crossover rate to find good programs by recombining existing subtrees.
Often, a solution is found in few generations (between 5 and 50). This has led some researchers to think that GP success is largely due to the type of representation employed; in
other words, random programs expressed in a Lisp like convention have a higher probability of being "correct" than other types of conventions. Whatever the case, the combination

of genetic algorithms and tree like representations has been shown to be competitive or superior to human design for a large range of problems, from pattern classification to design of electronical circuits. Recent improvements include *Automatically Defined Functions*, a technique to define new functions that take on the role of entire subtrees. This strategy generates much more compact and efficient programs capable of exploiting regularities and reusing them.

In chapter 9 we shall describe some experiments where control systems of robots have been evolved using genetic programming.

## 2.6   Conclusions

This chapter presented a self contained introduction to adaptive algorithms sufficient for understanding and replicating all models and experiments described in this book.

Artificial evolution of robots might involve different type of structures: (a) neural networks, (b) parameters of a predefined control program, and (c) computer programs themselves. Moreover, in the case of neural networks, the evolving controllers might also adapt ontogenetically as a result of lifetime learning. For this reason, after introducing evolutionary algorithms, we described neural networks and some learning algorithms that are usually combined with artificial evolution. Finally, we described how evolutionary algorithms can be used to evolve neural networks and computer programs. In the last chapter of this book we shall address the possibility of evolving the hardware itself, that is the control circuits and the morphology of the robot.

# 3 How to evolve robots

## 3.1 Introduction

Artificial evolution of robots can take considerable time because it requires repeated fitness tests of populations of several individuals, but, as this book will show, the results obtained are worth all the time it takes. In this chapter we shall describe the methodology and technology necessary to obtain those results. In order to evolve robots, one must consider the following issues:

• Mechanical robustness. Several individuals (mainly in early generations) may produce behaviors that can be damaging for the robot hardware, such as high speed collisions against objects or sustained strong currents to motors pushing toward a wall.

• Energy supply. Evolutionary experiments last longer than the average battery duration; it is thus necessary to find a way to provide energy or bypass this problem in other ways.

• Analysis. The control system of evolved robots can be very complex, intimately related to the environment, and thus difficult to understand by simple observation. Methods inspired upon neuroethology can provide useful insights by correlating behavior and dynamics of evolved controllers.

• Time efficiency. As we shall see in the next chapters, an evolutionary run can last hours, days, or even weeks. In some circumstances this time can be considerably reduced without necessarily reducing the number of fitness tests.

• Design of fitness functions. The selection criterion can have a major influence on the results of an evolutionary run, but it can be difficult to design a priori an effective fitness function for autonomous robots expected to operate in partially unknown environments.

In the next section we shall describe the Khepera concept, an integrated methodology based on hardware and software originally developed in order to investigate adaptive and evolutionary algorithms in robotics.[1] This technology addresses the issues of mechanical robustness, energy supply, and analysis. In the section that follows, we shall discuss the use of simulations and describe some ways of simulating mobile robots. A strategic use of realistic simulations can speed up artificial evolution by several orders of magnitude without problems of energy supply and mechanical failure, but the results can easily become of little significance to real robots if certain small details are not taken into consideration. That section will show how to pay attention to some crucial details and discard others. In the section after that, we shall present a framework for describing and comparing different fitness functions, and provide some guidelines for designing fitness functions of autonomous mobile robots. Finally, the issues of time and computational

**Figure 3.1**
The miniature mobile robot Khepera by a ruler (marks in cm). See also figure 3.2.

resources will be reconsidered in the perspective of incremental open ended evolution.

## 3.2  Evolution of physical robots

Khepera (figure 3.1 and 3.2) is a miniature mobile robot with a diameter of 55 mm and a weight of 70 g used in the majority of the experiments described in this book. In order to meet the criteria detailed above, the Khepera robot has been designed on the basis of the following criteria: miniaturization, modular open architecture, expandibility, interface, and compatibility with larger robots (Mondada et al. 1993).[2]

The robot is supported by two lateral wheels that can rotate in both directions and two rigid pivots in the front and in the back. By spinning the wheels in opposite directions at the same speed, the robot can rotate without lateral displacement. The sensory system employs eight "active infrared light" sensors distributed around the body, six on one side and two on the other side. These infrared sensors can function in two modalities. In "passive mode" they measure the amount of infrared light in the environment. Unless the robot is positioned close to a heat source (that reflects infrared waves), the infrared component is roughly proportional to the amount of visible light. This is the reason why passive infrared light sensors are sometimes called *ambient light sensors*. Instead, in active mode these sensors emit a ray of infrared light and measure the amount of reflected light. The closer they are to a surface, the higher is the amount of infrared light measured. The amount of reflected light depends both on the distance and on the reflectance of the surface. The Khepera sensors can detect a white paper at a maximum distance of approximately 5 cm. Active infrared sensors are also known as "proximity or distance sensors" because their activation is roughly proportional to the proximity (or inversely proportional to the distance) of a

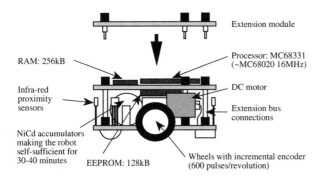

RAM: 256kB

Infra-red
proximity
sensors

NiCd accumulators
making the robot
self-sufficient for
30-40 minutes          EEPROM: 128kB

Extension module

Processor: MC68331
(~MC68020 16MHz)

DC motor

Extension bus
connections

Wheels with incremental encoder
(600 pulses/revolution)

**Figure 3.2**
The Khepera robot has a modular architecture. It can be expanded with extension modules whose input and outputs are accessible by the on-board controller (drawing courtesy of Francesco Mondada and K-Team SA).

surface. It is possible to set via software in which modality each sensor works. However, since these sensors refresh their activations every 5 microseconds, which is much faster than the time needed by a control system, one can access both passive and active readings. It is as if there were two times eight sensors. Four rechargeable NiCd batteries with a total autonomy of approximately 30–40 minutes are secured on the sensorimotor board. The CPU board encloses the robot's processor (a Motorola MC68331[3] with 128 Kbytes of EEPROM and 256 Kbytes of static RAM), an A/D converter for the acquisition of analog signals coming from the sensorimotor board, and an RS232 serial line miniature connector that can be used for data transmission and power supply from an external computer.

Robot miniaturization can bring several advantages in evolutionary experiments. For example, the experimenter can build complex environments on a limited surface. For a miniature robot like Khepera which measures 55 mm in diameter, a standard office desk of 0.9 by 1.8 m represents a working surface equivalent to that of a tennis court for a standard size robot with a diameter of 55 cm. A compact working surface also allows an easier monitoring of the robot behavior. Fundamental laws of physics give higher mechanical robustness to a miniature robot. In order to intuitively understand this physical phenomenon, compare a robot of 50 mm in diameter crashing against a wall at 50 mm/s with a robot of 1 m in diameter crashing against the same wall at 1 m/s. The miniature robot will resist the collision, the other robot will probably report serious damages.

Khepera has a modular open architecture (figure 3.2) that can be expanded with additional components allowing different configurations and experiments without changing the basic structure of the software. Modular expansion is achieved with an extension bus that makes it possible to add several turrets on the top of the basic configuration, depending on the needs of the experiments that one wishes to perform. Some of these turrets can have

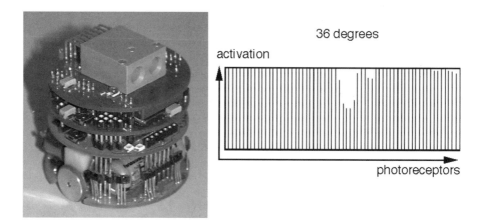

**Figure 3.3**
**Left:** The Khepera with a linear vision module (photograph courtesy of K-Team SA). One hole hosts a chip with
a line of 64 photoreceptors covering a visual field of 36 degrees; the other hole hosts an ambient light sensor to
adjust the sensitivity of the photoreceptors. **Right:** A snapshot of an image while the robot looks at a black stripe
against a white background.

their own private processors performing computation in parallel and independently of the
main onboard processor.

Some of these turrets will be used in the experiments described in this book. The
vision turret K213 (figure 3.3, left) consists of one array of 64 photoreceptors providing
a linear image composed of 64 pixels of 256 gray levels each (figure 3.3, right) and
subtending a total view angle of 36°. The optics are designed to bring into focus objects
at distances between 5 cm and 50 cm while an additional sensor of light intensity provides
information for automatic adjustement of photoreceptor sensitivity. The image is grabbed
and transformed in an array of values by a private onboard processor that communicates
with the main on board processor. The vision processor can also perform additional
feature extractions and communicate the results to the main processor. This module, as
all other modules, is automatically recognized by the main onboard processors and all its
functionalities are immediately available via software.

The gripper module (figure 3.4) has two degrees of freedom: lift/lower the arm and
open/close the segments. An optical barrier between the two segments can be used to detect
whether an object is present while a conductive sensor on the inner part of the segments can
discriminate metallic objects from non conductive objects. Another turret often used in the
experiments described in this book is a thin input/output module providing several ports
for additional sensors and motors which can be used to customize the robot for specific
experiments. For example, in the experiments described in chapter 8 the robot has been

**Figure 3.4**
The Khepera with a gripper module (photograph courtesy of K-Team SA).

fitted with conductive sensors all around the body whose signals are passed through the input/output module.

Khepera can be attached to the serial port of a computer through a thin cable and rotating contacts. The serial connection provides electrical power and supports fast data communication between the robot and the computer. The rotating contacts are very useful for performing long lasting experiments without the need to periodically straighten the cable. There are two ways of working with the Khepera. In interactive mode the user can access from the computer all sensor readings and send commands to the wheels of the robot almost in real time.[4] These operations can be performed through the keyboard or automatically executed by functions embedded in a program. In other words, the control system of the robot can run on the computer that reads in sensory data and gives motor commands in real time while the robot moves on the desk nearby. The advantage of this method is that all data from the robot are readily available on the computer for debugging, analysis, and storage. Alternatively, one can download the code of the control system on the processor of the robot and then disconnect the cable (or leave it connected for power supply and communication of other data). In the experiments described in this book we have used mostly the interactive mode.

Evolved controllers cannot be fully understood by isolating them from the environment and looking at their structure because their functioning has become intimately related to

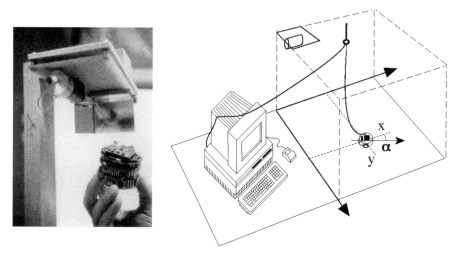

**Figure 3.5**
**Left:** A Khepera robot equipped with a positioning turret under the laser-beam emitting device. **Right:** Top view
of the experimental settings. The positioning turrets can compute every few milliseconds the robot position from
the laser beams. This information is transmitted to the computer via the serial cable for precise behavioral
analysis.

the physical interactions between the robot and the environment. Morevover, evolved neural controllers can have complex dynamical behaviors that appear only under normal autonomous behavior of the robot. This situation is similar to that faced by a neuroethologist
attempting to understand how the brain of an animal works. *In vitro* studies of brain tissue
can tell very little about the behavioral function of a neural circuit. Therefore, the common
practice is to implant electrodes in the brain and correlate neural activity with behavior
while the animal performs some tasks. From this perspective, an autonomous robot evolved
after generations of free interaction with the environment is quite similar to an animal. Extracting the evolved neural network from the robot and studying it in isolation often tells
little about the behavior of the robot. More insight can be gained by correlating the activity
of the evolved neural network with the robot behavior. In other words, the activations of the
artificial neurons are monitored while the robot autonomously moves in the environment.
This methodology holds for both simulated and physical robots, but only in former case the
robot behavior can be measured exactly at any point in time and space. In order to measure
behavior of a real Khepera robot, a device emitting laser beams at predefined angles and
frequencies is positioned on the top of the testing environment and the Khepera is equipped
with an additional turret capable of detecting laser beams and computing in real time the
robot positions and displacements (figure 3.5). This computation is carried out on a private

**Figure 3.6**
Koala shares the same sofwtare and hardware architecture of a Khepera, but is larger (32×32×20 cm), has a different shape, and a different sensorimotor system (photograph courtesy of K-Team SA).

processor placed on the turret and synchronized with the cycles of activity of the evolved neural network. While the evolved robot moves in the environment, its position and sensor readings are sent every 300 ms (or faster) via the serial cable to the computer where they are correlated with the activations of the neurons and stored away for later analysis. From its perspective, the evolved robot is not "aware" of these observations and its movements are not made difficult by the lightweight turret.

Koala (figure 3.6) is a larger robot (32 cm long, 32 cm wide, and 20 cm high; 3 kg weight) fully compatible with the Khepera robot. The six wheels of Koala are driven by two motors, as for Khepera, each controlling one side of the platform. The central wheels on the two sides are lower than the others, so that rotation of the whole platform is very similar to that of the Khepera. The infrared sensors of the Koala operate like those of the Khepera, but the measurement range is scaled up (maximum detection range is 20 cm in active mode) to the larger size of the Koala. Also, the number of sensors has been changed from 8 on the Khepera to 16 on the Koala. The Koala is a modular robot too. In addition to the serial extension bus of the Khepera, the Koala is equipped with a fast interprocessor parallel communication bus to support transfer of larger amounts of data. Finally, at the software level, the two robots are compatible, having the same low level software and the same communication facilities. In other words, one can easily switch the serial cable between the two robots without changing software and working modality. The Koala robot has been used in some experiments aimed at investigating cross platform incremental evolution. These experiments are described in chapter 4 where will be presented more details about the differences between the two robots.

In many cases, a single robot is sufficient for an evolutionary experiment (figure 3.7). In the typical situation, a Khepera robot is connected to the computer through a serial

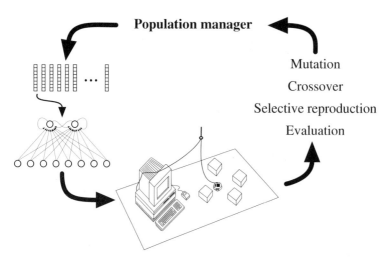

**Figure 3.7**
Artificial evolution with a single robot without human intervention. The cable between the robot and the
workstation has rotating contacts and provides energy supply and data communication between the computer
and the robot. The population of evolving individuals is stored on the computer memory, while each individual
is tested on the robot.

cable and the rotating contacts. The evolutionary algorithm and the neural controllers run
on the computer. Every 100 ms (or 300 ms, depending on the experiment), the evolving
controller on the computer reads in the sensory activations from the robot, computes the
output commands (speeds and directions of rotation), and sends them back to the robot.
The commands are executed on the robot until a new command is received. This procedure
is very convenient because it allows one to exploit the computation power of a workstation
for implementing very complex controllers and at the same time store large quantities of
data during evolution for later analysis. Since each individual in the population must be
tested for some seconds (for example, 60 seconds) on the same robot, an evolutionary
experiment may take a few hours or days but, once the Return key on the keyboard has
been hit, the robot evolves alone day and night without any further human intervention. All
the experiments described in this book, unless otherwise specified, have been carried out
with this simple method.

   The experiments on competitive co-evolution described in chapter 8 represent a notable
exception to this methodology. The dynamic situation involved in those experiments is such
that the delay necessary for transmitting visual images from the robot to the workstation
can put an handicap on the ability of the robot to cope with sudden changes in the
environment. Therefore, a hybrid solution has been adopted where the evolutionary neural

controller runs directly on the onboard processor while the genetic algorithm runs on the workstation. The serial cable is used for energy supply and to transmit the chromosomes at the beginning of a test and to receive the fitness value from the robot at the end of the test. Finally, if one is not interested in storing away chromosomes of previous generations, the whole evolutionary algorithm can run on the processor of the robot. Power supply can be provided via the cable or using other solutions, such as with power grids on the floor or on the top of the environment, or with a routine that periodically takes control of the robot and drives it to a docking station.

Before leaving this section, we wish to mention an important detail that we call *repositioning strategy* (Urzelai and Floreano 1999). Between any two individuals of the population, the robot is repositioned to a new location by executing random actions for a few seconds. This strategy is useful mainly at the beginning of an evolutionary run when almost all individuals have very poor sensorimotor abilities and tend to eventually end up against a wall or in locations of the environment that require complex sequences of actions. An individual tested on a robot abandoned by the previous individual in a difficult location is at disadvantage. Repositioning is used to give a fair starting position to each new individual tested on the robot. However, it is not necessary to reposition the robot always in the same starting location. As a matter of fact, if one does so, evolution may exploit this regularity and evolve brittle "minimalistic" solutions that rely on a fixed sequence of actions and do not generalize to different starting positions.

## 3.3   Evolving in simulation

Although evolution on real robots is feasible, serial evaluation of individuals on a single physical robot might require quite a long time. The experiment on the evolution of a homing navigation performed by Floreano and Mondada (1996b) and described in chapter 6, which is one of the most complex experiments carried out entirely on physical robots, took 10 days. In principle, having at disposal a large number of robots and testing more individuals in parallel might reduce significantly the time required. For example, by testing that entire population in parallel on 80 physical robots, the same experiment would have taken only few hours. However, one should bear in mind that different robots, even if identical from the electronic and mechanical point of view, might differ significantly between themselves. To test the population in parallel the offspring of selected individuals should be tested on different bodies. If evolved individuals are unable to adapt to new body structure during their lifetime, artificial evolution might be unable to progressively select better individuals. Watson et al. (1999), for instance, evolved individuals in parallel by using 8 identical robots. However, to avoid the problem described above they developed a

new algorithm in which successful individuals do not reproduce but transmit their genes to
the other individuals of a never dying population.

One way to avoid the problem of time is to evolve robots in simulation and then
run the most successful individuals on the physical robot. Simulated robots in fact might
run faster than their real counterpart. Moreover, the power of parallel computers can be
easily exploited for running more individuals at the same time. The advantage in term of
time, however, depends on the complexity of the simulated robot/environment interaction.
Simulated vision, for instance, is generally a time consuming process.

Simulation however present other problems. As claimed by Brooks (1992): (1) "Without regular validation on real robots there is a great danger that much effort will go into
solving problems that simply do not come up in the real world with a physical robot (or
robots)", and (2) "There is a real danger (in fact, a near certainty) that programs which
work well on simulated robots will completely fail on real robots because of the differences in real world sensing and actuation—it is very hard to simulate the actual dynamics
of the real world" (p. 4).

Several evolutionary experiments recently conducted in simulations and successfully validated on real robots demonstrated that, at least for a restricted class of robot-
environment interactions, it is possible to develop successful individual robots in simulation that generate almost identical behaviors in the real environment. Therefore, although
the evolutionary process on the physical robot, when feasible, is highly preferable (a simulation will never be an exact copy of the real robot-environment interaction) and although it
is not clear if current simulative methods can scale up to significantly more complex cases,
simulations validated on real robots may be a justifiable tool under some circumstances.
The use of simulation simplifies aspects such as energy supply and resetting the state of the
environment at the beginning of each epoch. In chapter 6, for example, we will describe
an experiment in which a Khepera robot is trained to collect cylindrical objects and release
them outside the arena where they are initially placed. The objects must be replaced inside
the arena at the beginning of each individual "lifetime." While this process is trivial in
simulation, to automate it in the real environment requires a certain effort.

Below we will describe two techniques that have been used to build simulations that
transfer relatively smoothly to real robots. The former is based on the attempt to model
as accurately as possible the real robot-environment interaction. The latter is based on the
attempt to model only those characteristics that are relevant for the emergence of a desired
behavior.

**Methods for accurately modeling robot-environment interactions**

To accurately model robot-environment interactions one must face different problems.
A first problem is due to the fact that *different physical sensors and actuators, even*

*if apparently identical, may perform differently because of slight differences in their electronics or mechanics.*

For example, an inspection of the infrared sensors of different Khepera robots shows that the responses of the sensors vary because of slight differences in the environment (e.g., ambient light settings, color, and shape of the objects). Other important sources of variation of response are the intrinsic properties of each sensor. In other words, each sensor responds in a significantly different way from other sensors when exposed to the same external stimulus. Consider for example the activation of the 8 infrared sensors of a Khepera robot placed at different angles and distances with respect to a cylindrical object (figure 3.8). Different sensors have rather different sensitivity ranges. The 8th sensor is sensitive within angle and distance ranges that are nearly twice as large those of the 4th sensor. This also implies that two different robots may perform very differently in identical conditions because of the differences in the sensory characteristics.

As suggested in Miglino et al. (1995), one way to take into account the idiosyncrasies of each sensor is to empirically sample the different classes of objects in the environment through the robot's sensors. Consider for example the case of an environment consisting of an arena surrounded by walls which contains a certain number of cylindrical objects of the same size. This simple environment contains two classes of objects: walls and cylinders. We can sample this environment by placing the robot at different angles and distances with respect to a wall and with respect to a cylinder, and recording the corresponding activation state of the infrared sensors. In the case of Miglino et al. (1995), for example, objects were sampled for 180 orientations and for 20 different distances (figure 3.8 displays the result of such a sampling procedure conducted on an individual robot in the case of a cylindrical object). The resulting matrices of activation values can then be used by the simulator to set the activation levels of the infrared sensors of the simulated robot depending on its current position in the simulated environment.

Individuals evolved in simulations based on this technique continue to perform satisfactorily well when transferred in the real environment (see for example Miglino et al. 1995; Nolfi 1996; Nolfi 1997). Unfortunately, its application to complex environments can become expensive because each class of objects must also be sampled and asymmetrical objects must be sampled from different points of view. In fact, while the perception of symmetrical objects such as cylinders is only a function of the orientation and distance of the robot with respect to the object (figure 3.9, left), for other objects, such as a rectangular box, the perceptual state is also a function of the local shape of the object (figure 3.9, center). An additional problem arises when the simulated robot is close to two different objects (for example in the case of a corner as in figure 3.9, right). One solution consists of summing up the sampled vectors that the robot would experience in the proximity of each object taken in isolation (see Miglino et al. 1995), but this may introduce significant discrepancies between the simulation and the real environment.

When the use of this sampling technique becomes too expensive one could rely on mathematical models. Also in this case, the parameters of the functions describing the robot-environment interaction can be empirically determined by using the real robot. This technique was adopted by Jacobi et. al. (1995) who developed a simulator for a Khepera robot. The authors modeled the wheel speeds, the infrared, and the ambient light sensors of the robot with a set of general equations and then set the constants of such equations by recording the activation states of the sensors and the speed of the wheels while the real robot was moving. For an attempt to use a hybrid technique based on sampling and on a geometrical model to simulate vision see Nolfi and Marocco (in press).

One second problem that should be taken into account in building a simulator is that in real robots *physical sensors deliver uncertain values and commands to actuators have uncertain effects*. Sensors do not return accurate values but just a fuzzy approximation of what they are measuring. Similarly, actuators have effects that might vary in time depending on several unpredictable causes (Brooks 1992). This problem may be alleviated by introducing noise in simulation at all levels. The addition of noise in the simulation on the values returned by the sensors and on the effects of the actuators reduces the drop in performance observed when individuals are transferred from the simulated to the real environment (Miglino et. al. 1995, Jakobi et al. 1995, Miglino et al. 1996). Noise can be introduced by adding randomly selected values within a certain range to the computed values of the sensors or to the effects of the actuators. This can be accomplished in different ways: by adding random values within a certain range at each life cycle (Miglino et al. 1995; Miglino et al. 1996; Jakobi et al. 1995); by altering the values in a random but systematic way for a certain number of life cycles (Miglino et. al. 1995, also reported in chapter 4); by randomly varying certain values in different epochs (Jakobi 1997). Adding noise in each life cycle can compensate for the stochastic properties of the robot-environment interaction, but it must be added in the appropriate amount. It has been demonstrated, in fact, that evolved neural controllers rely on the available noise. As a consequence, if the amount of noise in simulation is larger than that present in the real robot-environment interaction, evolved individuals perform poorly when transferred in the real environment because of the lack of extra noise (Jakobi et al. 1995; Miglino et al. 1996).

Finally, since evolution can exploit unforeseen characteristics of the robot-environment interaction, *the body of the robot and the characteristics of the environment should be accurately reproduced in the simulation*. This means, for instance, that grid worlds, that are often used in artificial life simulations, are meaningless for the purpose of developing robot controllers because they are inaccurate (Brooks 1992).

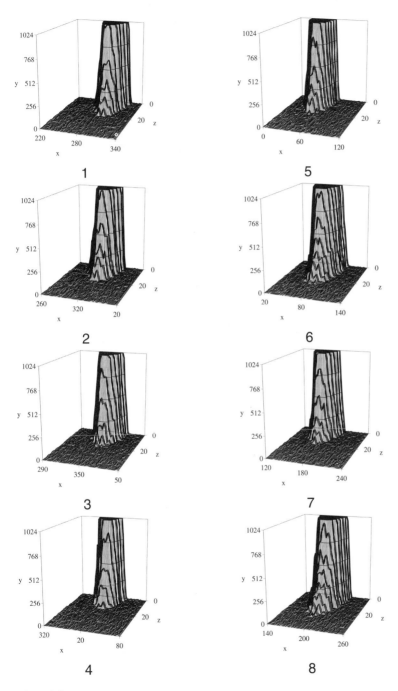

**Figure 3.8**
Sensors activation (y-axis) of an individual Khepera measured at different angles (x-axis) and distances (z-axis) with respect to a cylindrical object with a diameter of 2.3 cm covered with white paper. Labels 1–6 and 7–8 indicate the sensors located on the frontal and on the back side of the robot respectively.

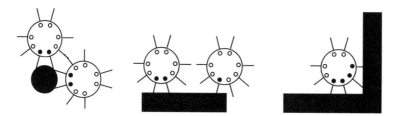

**Figure 3.9**
**Left:** In the case of a cylindrical object, the activate sensors (black dots) are a function of the angle (with respect to the robot orientation) and distance between the robot and the object. **Center:** In the case of a rectangular box, the pattern of active sensors also depends on the portion of the perceived object. **Right:** Sensors might be stimulated from more than one object. In this example, they are stimulated by two objects of the same class (i.e., two walls forming a corner).

## Minimal simulations

Recently Jakobi (1997) proposed an alternative approach based on the attempt to model only those characteristics of the robot-environment interaction that are relevant for the emergence of a desired behavior. These characteristics, that are referred to as *base set* features, should be accurately modeled in simulation. In addition to these features, simulations will include other aspects that will not have any correspondence in reality. These additional aspects, which are referred to as *implementational aspects*, should be randomly varied in different epochs in order to ensure that evolving individuals will rely on the base set aspects only. Finally, base set features should also be varied from epoch to epoch in order to allow the emergence of robust individuals able to cope with a certain amount of variation in the environment. As reported in Jakobi (1997), the overall methodology thus consists in the following steps:

*1. A base set of robot-environment interactions (that are sufficient to underlie the behavior we want to evolve) must be identified and made explicit. A simulation should then be constructed that includes a model of these interactions. This simulation will display base set aspects, which have a basis in reality, and implementation aspects, which do not.*
*2. Every implementation aspect of the simulation must be randomly varied from trial to trial so that evolving controllers that depend on them are unreliable. In particular, enough variation must be included to ensure that evolving controllers cannot, in practice, be reliably fit unless they are base set exclusive (i.e., they actively ignore each implementation aspect entirely).*
*3. Every base set aspects of the simulation must be randomly varied from trial to trial so that reliably fit controllers are forced to be base set robust. The extent and character of this random variation must be sufficient to ensure that reliably fit controllers are able to cope with the inevitable differences between the base set aspects and reality but not so large that reliably fit controllers fail to evolve at all.*

From Jakobi 1997, pp. 332–333.

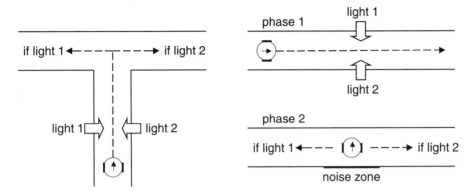

**Figure 3.10**
**Left:** The T-maze environment. Full lines represent the walls of the maze, block arrows represents the two lights on the two sides of the main corridor, the circle represent the Khepera robot, the dotted lines represent the expected trajectories of the robot depending on which light comes on. **Right:** The minimal simulation of the T-maze environment shown on the left. Phase 1 and 2 represent the two parts of the T-maze, the main corridor and the two arms, respectively. The noise zone represents the area where the activation values of the infrared sensors is randomly varied from trial to trial. Redrawn from Jakobi (1997).

As an example let us consider the case reported in Jakobi (1997) of a Khepera robot that is placed in a T-maze environment with two switchable light sources (figure 3.10, left). The robot is expected to turn left or right at the junction depending on the side where the light came on. The base set features in this experiment are the wheel motions and the activations of proximity and ambient light sensors while the robot is in the main corridor; these features have been modeled accurately in the simulation. Instead, the activation of proximity sensors during the negotiation of the junction (i.e., the part that is more difficult to simulate accurately) was considered as an implementational aspect. As a consequence, this part of the robot-environment interaction was not modeled at all in simulation.

In practice the T-maze was modeled as two segments (figure 3.10, right). The lower segment corresponds to the main corridor of the T-maze whereas the upper segment corresponds to the two arms on the top of the T. When the simulated robot reaches the end of this corridor (phase 1), it is taken out of it, rotated by 90°, and positioned into the middle of the lower segment (phase 2). At this point, a significant discrepancy between the simulated and the real environment arises (in this position the real robot has a complicated junction behind him while the simulated robot has a wall). This is due to the fact that, as we mentioned above, the negotiation of the junction is treated as an implementational aspect and is not modeled at all in the simulation. However, to prevent the possibility that evolving individuals will exploit the state of the infrared sensors oriented toward this area (i.e., the noise zone in figure 3.10, right), the values of the sensors affected by this portion of the wall were randomly varied from trial to trial. Finally, to ensure evolution of robust individuals, other aspects of the simulation such as the side with the light on, the width of the corridor, the initial orientation of the robot, the length of the corridors, and the length of the illuminated section of the corridor were randomly varied in different epochs at certain predetermined intervals.

Jakobi showed that controllers evolved in this minimal simulation continued to perform satisfactorily when transferred to the real environment. In addition to the T-maze task, the author was able to solve a visual discrimination task that will be reported in the next chapter (Jakobi 1997) and a walking task with an octopod robot (Jakobi 1998, see also chapter 10). The problem with this approach is that one must know in advance the robot-environment interactions that are crucial for producing the desired behavior (i.e., the base set features) (Watson et. al. 1999). In general, however, this is not the case. Let us consider the case of the T-maze task reported above. Jakobi (1997) hypothesized that in order to solve this task, the controllers "must involve a dependence on some internal state or (less likely in this case) external state which allows them to remember which side the lamp was on so that they can take the correct turn at the junction" (p. 339). Actually, evolved individuals appear to rely on internal states that keep a trace of the previously experienced sensory states when they decide how to turn at the junction. However, one may imagine a simpler strategy consisting in turning toward the light switched on, approaching that side of the corridor, and then perform a simple wall following behavior. This strategy can be effective in the real environment, but it cannot be exploited in a simulated environment because the modeling simplifications introduced at the T-junction prevent the possibility to perform a wall following behavior in the surrounding of this area. In other words, the robot-environment interactions that should be included in the base set of minimal simulations depend on the varieties of behavioral strategies that might be exploited during the evolutionary process which, in turn, cannot be known in advance by the designer (we will come back on this issue in chapter 5).

## 3.4   Fitness space

In artificial evolution the fitness function is used to evaluate the performance of individuals and to select the best ones. The result of an evolutionary run depends very much on the form of this function. Fitness functions for autonomous robots usually include variables and constraints that rate the performance with respect to the expected behavior, but these variables and constraints are difficult to choose because the behavior evolved by the robot is not fully known in advance. Actually, the degree of knowledge of an expected behavior is inversely proportionaly to the appeal of using artificial evolution. Even when one knows

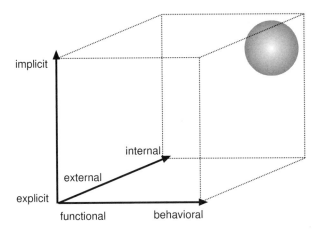

**Figure 3.11**
Fitness Space provides a framework for describing and designing fitness functions of autonomous systems (not to be confused with Fitness Landscape). The three dimensions define important criteria of fitness design along a continuum space. Fitness functions for autonomous robots are ideally located in the top right corner. See text for explanations.

in advance the most relevant variables and how to combine them in a function, it is not guaranteed that the system will be evolvable. Variables that objectively measure the fitness of a fully functional behavior may be incapable of rating the primordial appearances of that behavior in early stages of evolution. Therefore, some aspects of the robot behavior that are instrumental for the development of higher abilities may be underrated; or, even worse, all individuals of early generations may receive zero fitness.

The fitness function plays a major role in the evolvability of a system. The lack of formal principles for designing fitness functions of evolutionary autonomous systems has two major consequences: a) the results obtained with even slightly different fitness functions are hardly comparable; b) the choice of a suitable function often proceeds by trials and errors, a time consuming approach when one evolves physical robots.

We propose the *fitness space* (figure 3.11) as an objective framework for describing and comparing various fitness functions for autonomous systems. The fitness space can also help to define general guidelines for designing fitness functions and assess the implications of certain choices. The fitness space is defined by three continuous dimensions; a fitness function represents a point in this 3D space.

● The dimension *functional-behavioral* indicates whether the fitness function rates specific functioning modes of the controller or whether it rates the behavioral outcome of the controller. For example, consider evolution of walk for a legged robot equipped with a network of neural oscillators. A functional fitness would rate the oscillation frequency of the neurons in the network in order to evolve controllers whose dynamics correspond to walking patterns (Lewis et al. 1992). Instead, a behavioral function would rate the distance covered by the robot within a certain time period (Hornby et al. 1999). Fitness functions can include a combination of functional and behavioral components. The functional-behavioral dimension is applicable only where there is a distinction between the functioning of an evolving system and its behavior, which is a characteristic of autonomous embedded agents.

• The dimension *explicit-implicit* defines the amount of variables and constraints included in the function. For example, an implicit function would select only robots that do not run out of energy after a certain time. Instead, an explicit function would include variables and constraints that evaluate various components of the desired behavior, such as whether the robot approaches an energy supply area, the travel velocity, the activity of certain neurons in the controller, etc. The position of a fitness function along this dimension is given by the total number of variables, constant, and constraints (if-then, e.g.) included in the function, but not by their combination and relative weighting. For example, the function $f = 2x + y$ occupies the same position of the function $f = x - 3y$. Implicit fitness functions have no (or very few) components, such as in Latent Energy Environments (Menczer and Belew 1996b).

• The dimension *external-internal* indicates whether the variables and constraints included in the fitness function are computed using information available to the evolving agent. Notice that even if this information is available to the agent, it may not be necessarily used as an input to the controller of the agent. For example, the absolute distance between a robot and a goal is an external variable because it cannot be computed using the information coming from the sensors of the robot. Instead, the activations of ambient light sensors, or the battery charge, are internal variables because they are computable using information available to the evolving robot. If an experiment is carried out only entirely in simulation, the position of the fitness function along this dimension is not very relevant given that all types of informations are available in software. But if one plans to combine simulations and real world, or carry out an evolutionary run entirely on a physical robot, external variables may not be measurable in the real world or may require the realization of complex machineries and procedures to compute them exactly and in real time.

Deciding where to stand in the fitness space depends on the goal of an evolutionary run. If the goal is that of optimizing a set of parameters for a very complex—but well defined—control problem in a well controlled environment, then the fitness function should be located in the low left corner of fitness space. FEE (Functional, Explicit, External) functions describe how the controller should work, rate the system on the basis of several variables and constraints, and employ precise external measuring devices.

Instead, if the goal is that of evolving robots capable of autonomous operation in partially unknown and unpredictable environments without human intervention, the fitness function should tend toward the top right corner of fitness space (gray area in figure 3.11). BII (Behavioral, Implicit, Internal) functions rate only the behavioral outcome of an evolutionary controller, rely on few—if any—variables and constraints, and its components can be computed onboard. BII functions are suitable for standalone adaptive robots. They let the evolutionary system free to choose and adapt its own strategy to the characteristics of the environment, exploiting whatever the environment affords them to do. Since BII fitness functions depend less on externally imposed constraints, they are suitable for incremental open ended evolution where evolving organisms adapt to an ever changing environment with the sole purpose of survival.

The diagonal line between the FEE and the BII extremes in Fitness Space defines a continuum between traditional engineering optimization and synthesis of artificial life systems, respectively. The relative positions of the projections of fitness functions onto this diagonal give a rough comparison among the levels of autonomy of the evolving systems.[5]

*Subjective fitness* is the name used for the case where human observers rate the performance of evolving individuals by visual inspection. An early famous example of subjective fitness are the *Biomorphs* described by Dawkins (1986) where an observer can select some individuals out of a screen full of different creature like static shapes; the selected individuals, whose chromosome defines the shape of the creatures, are reproduced and mutated to create a new population of creatures. Lund et al. (1998) have applied this strategy for evolution of control systems of simulated robots whose behaviors are displayed on the screen of a computer. Human observers are asked to point at the individuals to be selected for reproduction and mutation. Subjective fitness is usually located in the bottom near corner (BEE) of the fitness space because it is based on the behavior of the robot, it relies on explicit constraints (although not objectively or verbally expressed), and the constraints are external to the evolving system. The position along the explicit-implicit dimension can vary depending on how a subject rates a robot. In some cases (as we shall see in chapter 10) the subject is asked to give a numerical value for a set of predefined abilities, in other cases subjects are free to decide on whatever criteria they wish. It may thus happen that the amount and type of constraints varies from subject to subject and even for the same subject during evolutionary time. Subjective fitness functions can be useful when it is difficult to design an objective function or in situations where it is desirable to have a machine adapt interactively with a human subject (for example in entertainment and service robotics). However, if the subject is inaccurate and inconsistent it may be difficult to obtain meaningful results (see also Floreano 1997b).

## 3.5   Conclusions

In this chapter we have described various methodologies for evolving autonomous robots and discussed advantages and limitations of different approaches. In particular we have shown that artificial evolution can be applied to a single robot with minimal or no human intervention. We have described the Khepera concept as an example of technology and methodology for conducting experiments in artificial evolution. However, this methodology can be—and has been—applied to other types of robots, as we shall see from the examples described in this book. Realistic simulations can be a useful tool to explore very quickly the space of architectures, fitness functions, and other aspects of an evolutionary system. In some circumstances, a control system evolved in simulation can be transferred to a physical robot without major performance degradation.

Simulations are often advocated as a method to accelerate evolution and spare the trouble of energy supply and mechanical failures. Although modern simulation methods, such as those described above in section 3.3, represent a powerful support tool, in the long run they cannot become a substitute of hardware evolution. This is not a problem if one conceives artificial evolution as an open ended incremental adaptation process of a mutant artificial organism in an ever changing environment. In that case, a simulated world and a simulated body would be just one of the possible worlds and bodies that the evolving organism encounters in its history of continuous adaptation. Within that context even the notion of evolutionary time length would become secondary because it would be no longer necessary to evolve control systems entirely from scratch, but simply adapt an already evolved population to the specific constraints of the problem at hand. Incremental open ended evolution of adaptive individuals is a very promising approach for the future of autonomous agents. Initial explorations in this direction have already been undertaken by Harvey (as we shall see in the next chapter), but this still remains an open field of research.

# 4 Evolution of simple navigation

## 4.1 Introduction

In this chapter we shall describe evolution of simple behaviors. In the next chapter we shall look at evolved behaviors that apparently require memory or internal states, but are instead implemented in much simpler ways by actively exploiting the interaction with the environment. Finally, in chapter 6 we shall describe complex navigation strategies where evolution exploits modular architectures and internal states.

Regardless of its complexity, any navigation ability requires the development of a suitable mapping from sensory information to motor actions. The actions performed by the robot depend upon incoming sensory information which, on its turn, depends upon the actions performed at the previous time step. This closed feedback loop makes it rather difficult to design a stable control system for realistic situations. From an engineering perspective, one might be tempted by listing all possible sensory situations and associate them to a set of predefined motor actions. In the case of autonomous robots expected to operate in partially unknown and unpredictable environments, this solution is not always viable. As we shall see later on, it is very difficult to handcraft control system even for very simple environments and navigation tasks.

In the next section we shall describe in more details some of the complexities that arise when handcrafting a simple navigation behavior and show that artificial evolution can automatically develop very efficient controllers for that purpose. It will become clear that artificial evolution builds smart controllers by exploiting interactions between the robot and the environment that might be very difficult to take into account with traditional analytical methods. We shall then describe the evolution of simple visually guided behaviors and sensory morphology in environments of increasing complexity. This will prompt us to examine in a later section two special cases of environmental change: cross platform evolution and the transfer from simulated to real environments.

## 4.2 Straight motion with obstacle avoidance

Navigation with obstacle avoidance is a classic task that most people working in mobile robotics have some experience with. A robot is put in an environment with some objects in it and is required to cover the longest possible distance without hitting the objects.

If the robot morphology (shape, motors and sensors layout) is symmetrical about at least one axis and it has two wheels, one can try to realize a Braitenberg's vehicle (Braitenberg 1984). *Braitenberg's vehicle* are conceptual robots whose wheels are directly

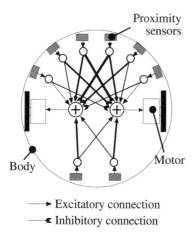

Figure 4.1
Wiring diagram of a Braitenberg-type controller (Braitenberg, 1984) for the miniature mobile robot Khepera that performs straight motion and obstacle avoidance (courtesy of Francesco Mondada). The thickness of the connection is proportional to its strength. Incoming signals are weighted (multiplied) by the values of the corresponding connections and summed up. A positive offset value on each wheel generates forward motion in absence of signals from the sensors.

linked to the sensors through weighted connections[1] very similar to the wiring of neural networks described in chapter 2. If the connection is positive (excitatory), the rotation speed of the wheel is proportional to the activation of the sensor. Instead, if the connection is negative (inhibitory), the rotation speed of the wheel is inversely proportional to the sensor activation, possibly reversing its direction of rotation. Figure 4.1 shows the wiring diagram of a Braitenberg-type controller for the miniature mobile robot Khepera that performs straight motion and obstacle avoidance (Mondada and Floreano 1995). Each wheel is linked through excitatory connections to the sensors on its own side and through inhibitory connections to the sensors on the opposite side. A positive offset value applied to each wheel generates forward motion while the weighted sum of incoming signals steers the robot away from objects.

It should be noticed that even this simple design requires careful analysis of sensor and motor profiles, and important decisions for what concerns the direction of motion (forward, backward), its straightness, and its velocity. Furthermore, the connection weights must match the sensor response properties. For example, if a sensor has a lower response profile as compared to other sensors, its outgoing connections should have stronger weights in order to obtain a good trajectory. The balance of weights is equally important. For example, if the outgoing connections from the leftmost sensor and from a front sensor

**Figure 4.2**
Bird's eye-view of the looping maze and the Khepera robot within.

have the same weights, the robot will tend to turn too much when an object is perceived on the left side or too little when an object is perceived right in front, depending on how strong the chosen values are. The strengths of the connections depend also on the offset speeds which, on their turn, depend on the refreshing rate of the sensors, on the reflection properties of the objects, and on environment clutter. In other words, different robots and different environments require different sets of carefully chosen values.

It is now worth asking whether an evolutionary approach could find a solution for straight navigation and obstacle avoidance without assuming all the prior knowledge about sensors, motors, and environment mentioned above. If such a solution is found by artificial evolution, it is also worth asking how does it work and how does it compare to a predesigned architecture such as the Braitenberg-type controller described above. We have investigated these questions with the miniature mobile robot Khepera (Floreano and Mondada 1994).

The robot was put in a looping maze whose external size was approx. $80 X 50$ cm (figure 4.2). The walls were made of lightblue polystyrene and the floor was a gray thick paper. The robot could sense the walls with the eight infrared proximity sensors. Since the corridors were rather narrow (8–12 cm), some sensors were slightly active most of the time. The environment was within a portable box positioned in a room always illuminated from above by a 60 watt bulb light. A serial cable (not pictured in the figure) for power supply and data monitoring connected the robot to a workstation in our office, a few rooms away.

The goal was to evolve a control system capable of maximizing forward motion while accurately avoiding all obstacles on its way. The definition of the fitness function $\Phi$ was based on three variables directly measurable on the robot platform,

$$\Phi = V \left(1 - \sqrt{\Delta v}\right) (1 - i)$$ (4.1)

$$0 \leq V \leq 1$$
$$0 \leq \Delta v \leq 1$$
$$0 \leq i \leq 1$$

where $V$ is the sum of rotation speeds of the two wheels, $\Delta v$ is the absolute value of the algebraic difference between the signed speed values of the wheels (positive is one direction, negative the other), and $i$ is the normalized activation value of the infrared sensor with the highest activity. This function is evaluated whenever a new sensory motor loop is executed and the resulting values are summed up and divided by the total number of sensory motor loops during which the individual is tested. The higher the value, the better is the performance of the individual. These three components encourage—respectively— motion, straight displacement, and obstacle avoidance, but do not say in what direction the robot should move (see box for further details).

The control system of the robot was a neural network with an architecture very similar to the wiring of the Braitenberg vehicle illustrated in figure 4.1. It consisted of one layer of synaptic weights from the eight infrared proximity sensors to two motors units. Each motor unit was implemented as a sigmoid neuron whose output, shifted in the range $[-0.5, 0.5]$, was used to set the rotation of the corresponding wheel (the direction of rotation was given by the sign, the speed by the absolute value). A set of recurrent connections at the output layer was implemented as in Elman networks (see chapter 2). In addition, each output unit had an additional evolvable synaptic weight from a bias unit. The bias unit is quite important in this architecture because it provides the output units with some activation even when there is no sensory input.[2]

For each generation, that took approximately 40 minutes, we recorded the average fitness of the population and the fitness of the best individual in the population (figure 4.3). Although the fitness indicators keep growing for 100 generations (after that they become stable), around the 50th generation the best individuals already exhibited a smooth navigation around the maze without bumping into walls. A fitness value of 1.0 could have been achieved only by a robot moving straight at maximum speed in an open space. In the environment shown in figure 4.2, where some of the sensors were almost always active and where several turns were necessary to navigate, 0.3 was the maximum value attained by the evolutionary controller even when continued for further 100 generations (data not shown). Figure 4.4 shows the trajectory of the best individual of the last generation.

## A fitness function for reactive navigation

The function employed for evolving straight navigation and obstacle avoidance is based only on variables directly accessible on the robot itself (in terms of fitness space, it is an *internal* function). This is useful for robots that evolve without external control. The rotation speed of each wheel on the Khepera robot is readable thanks to optical encoders. The direction of rotation is given by the sign of the read value and the speed by its absolute value. In this experiment, the rotation range is $[-0.5, 0.5]$.

The first component $V$ is computed by summing these two absolute values, thus generating a value between 0 and 1. This component is maximized by high rotation speed of the wheels, without regard to their direction of rotation, thus encouraging motion. A robot spinning on itself and a robot going straight at maximum speed would generate the same high value.

The second component $\left(1 - \sqrt{\Delta v}\right)$ instead encourages the two wheels to rotate in the same direction. $\Delta v$ is computed by adding 0.5 to each read value (thus bringing them in the range $[0,1]$), subtracting them together, and taking the absolute value of the difference. For example, if the left wheel rotates backward at speed $-0.4$ and the right wheel rotates forward at speed 0.5, Dv will be 0.9. The higher the difference in rotation, the closer $\Delta v$ will be to 1. The square root is used to give stronger weight to small differences. Since the value is subtracted from 1, this component is maximized by robots whose wheels move in the same direction, regardless of speed and overall direction. Therefore, a robot standing still and a robot going straight at maximum speed will generate the same high values for this component. The combined effect of the first and second component gives higher fitness to robots moving straight at maximum speed (forward or backward).

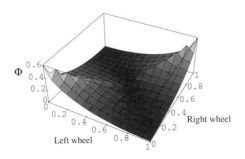

---

**A fitness function for reactive navigation** (continued)

The last component $(1-i)$ encourage obstacle avoidance. Each of the 8 proximity sensors on the Khepera emits a beam of infrared light and returns and measures the quantity of reflected infrared light up to a distance of 5 cm, depending on the reflection index of the object. The closer it is to an object, the higher the measured value in a range from 0 to 1. The value $i$ of the most active sensor provides a conservative measure of how close the robot is to an object, independently of its relative position. Since this value is subtracted from 1, this component will select robots that stay away from objects. Combined with the previous two components, it will contribute to select robots that move as straight as possible avoiding objects on their path.

Notice that this fitness function does not give a selective advantage to forward or backward motion. Since the robot has a circular shape and the wheels can rotate in both directions, in theory the direction of motion does not affect the fitness values. This is readily seen by plotting the fitness values of an imaginary robot with for all possible combination of wheel speeds (assuming that the most active proximity sensor returns 0.4). In this graph wheel speed is shown in the range 0 and 1, where 0 corresponds to maximum speed backward, 1 to maximum speed forward, and 0.5 to no motion. The two maxima correspond to the robot moving at maximum speed forward and at maximum speed backward. Notice that the function searched by artificial evolution is much more complex because it involves parameters of the control system that generate suitable speeds.

---

We can gain a better understanding of the way in which the robot evolves by analyzing the development of the three fitness components in isolation along the generations (figure 4.5).

During the initial generations the best individuals are those that move straight at very low velocities (about 2 mm/s). High oscillations of the sensory component indicates that these individuals cannot yet avoid objects and thus their performance depends very much on their starting position. Most of the remaining individuals (not plotted) in the initial generations spend their time rotating in place. In order to maximize the fitness function $\Phi$ it is necessary to find a balance among the three components because in this environment none of them can reach its maximum value without lowering at least one of the other two. A stable balance is found around the 50th generation. In the remaining 50 generations the robot increases mostly speed (continuous line).

Another way of describing the adaptation process is the *state space approach* proposed by ethologists for quantitatively measuring adaptation of biological autonomous agents

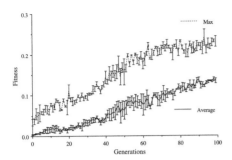

**Figure 4.3**
Average fitness of the population and fitness of the best individual in the population plotted every generation.
Error bars show standard error over three repeated runs from different initial randomization.

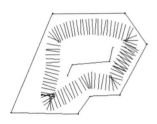

**Figure 4.4**
Trajectory of the robot controlled by the best individual of the last generation. Segments represent the line
between the two wheels of the robot. The location and orientation of the robot is recorded every 300 ms using an
external positioning device (see chapter 3).

(McFarland and Houston 1981). Within this perspective, the activity of an animal depends
on its state, which is characterized by a set of variables such as its energy level or the
perception of the environment. These state variables define an $n$-dimensional state space,
where the axes are provided by $n$ state variables considered. Adaptation is then described
as a transition from an initial oscillatory state toward a sub region of this space. This
region, which is compact and bounded, represents the equilibrium conditions of the animal
(Sibly and McFarland 1974). Within this same framework, our evolutionary robot can be
described as a point in a 3D space defined by three state variables corresponding to the
three fitness components. The graph on the left of figure 4.6 shows the position of the best
individuals at each generation within this space. After a relatively fast displacement during
the initial generations, the best individuals of the last 20 generations remain within the same
compact subregion of the space, despite the constant perturbations of the recombination

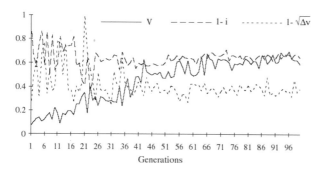

**Figure 4.5**
Values of the fitness components for the best individual of each generation (data from a single run). $V$ is maximized by wheel speed; $(1 - i)$ is maximized by low sensory activation; $\left(1 - \sqrt{\Delta v}\right)$ is maximized by straight motion (see also box on fitness design).

and mutation operators. This region represents the stability condition for the evolved controllers. Similarly, on the time scale of a single individual (graph on the right of figure 4.6), when the individual is pulled away from the equilibrium region, for example by positioning it in a corner close to two walls, it will return to the stability region that corresponds to obstacle avoidance and straight navigation (figure 4.7, right).

Let us now consider again the handcrafted solution inspired upon Braitenberg vehicles that we described earlier on (figure 4.1). When put in the looping maze, the Braitenberg-like vehicle displays a behavior very similar to the evolved individual described above, but very soon it will stop. This is due to the fact that the architecture of this controller is symmetric and feedforward. Therefore, whenever two controlateral sensors (for example the 2nd from left and the 2nd from right) receive the same input, their inhibitory and excitatory signals (summed to the offset speed) cancel out and the wheels do not move (left side of figure 4.7). These *equilibrium points* exist for many other combinations of sensors. One way of breaking symmetries is to introduce recurrent connections at the level of the output units acting as a sort of continuously decaying memory of previous states. This type of nonlinear feedback is hard to incorporate by hand design without affecting other aspects of the behavior, but has been exploited by artificial evolution. Our evolved individual has strong asymmetrical weights on the recurrent connections. These values are such that they do not interfere during navigation, but are sufficient to avoid deadlock situation (right side of figure 4.7).

Artificial evolution can thus automatically generate a control system competitive with hand designed solution without requiring as many assumptions and knowledge about the robot and the environment. Evolved solutions emerge from the interaction with the physics

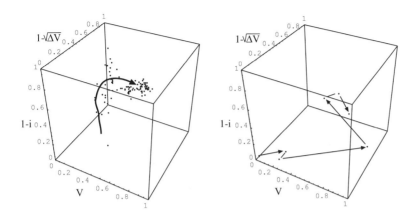

**Figure 4.6**
**Left:** State-space representation of evolutionary adaptation. Each dot is the state of the best individual of a generation. The arrow shows the direction of motion during evolution. The dots concentrate in a sub-space indicated by the arrow tip in the last 20 generations ($x = 0.6 \pm 0.07$, $y = 0.6 \pm 0.05$, $z = 0.4 \pm 0.15$). **Right:** State-space representation of the best individual of the last generation when positioned close to two walls. By moving away from the walls and starting its navigation around the maze, the controller in fact returns to the equilibrium zone ($x = 0.65$, $y = 0.6$, $z = 0.5$).

of the environment in ways that are difficult to analyze a priori, but are important for the good functioning of the robot. Two further examples of these emergent solutions[3] are the direction of motion and cruising speed.

Considering the fact that Khepera has a circular and symmetric shape, that the wheels can rotate at equal speeds in both directions, and that the fitness function does not give selective advantage to forward or backward motion, one might expect that the preferential direction adopted by evolved controllers depends solely on initial conditions (initialization of the population). Theoretically, the fitness function has indeed two maxima (see box on fitness design), one corresponding to straight forward motion and the other to straight backward motion. However, in all the experiments carried out within the looping maze shown in figure 4.2, selected individuals display a direction of motion that corresponds to the side with more sensors (figure 4.8). This direction allows the robot to approach obstacles on the side that provides better sensory resolution and larger perceptual angle. Those individuals that move backward are more likely to get stuck against an obstacle that cannot be seen and hence disappear very soon from the population. (However, rear sensors do not go out of use. The best individuals of the final generation still make use of that information to change trajectory if something is approaching the robot from the back). This preference of direction does not show up when the robot is evolved in a rectangular arena free of obstacles (an example will be shown in chapter 6).

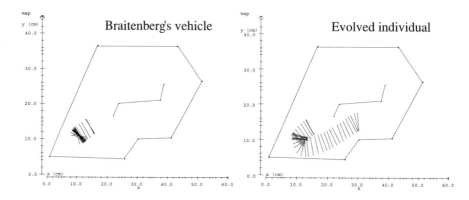

**Figure 4.7**
Feedforward architectures vs. architectures with nonlinear feedback. **Left:** A control system inspired upon Braitenberg vehicles (see also figure 4.1) with feedforward symmetric connections moves towards the bottom left corner where it stops when controlateral sensors receive the same signal intensities (small oscillations are due to sensory noise). **Right:** The evolved controller exploits nonlinear feedback coming from recurrent connections in order to avoid deadlock situations and resume smooth straight trajectory.

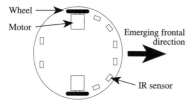

**Figure 4.8**
The direction of motion of individuals evolved in the looping maze corresponds to the side with a larger number of sensors, although the fitness function does not give explicit advantage to a direction of motion.

Finally, the overall speed of the evolved individuals never reaches the maximum value (80 mm/s), not even when the evolutionary process is continued until the 200th generation. The robot speed peaks at 48 mm/s when positioned in zones free of obstacles. This self adjustment of the maximum cruising speed has an adaptive meaning. Since sensors and motors are updated only every 300 ms and many passages in the maze are rather narrow, if Khepera moved faster it would often crash into unnoticed obstacles. Evolved individuals have adapted their behavior to the physical characteristics of their own sensory system and of the environment where they operate.

## 4.3   Visually guided navigation

On the surface of our planet vision represents a powerful sensory system. A large number of animal species have evolved receptors and nervous systems that exploit light reflected by surfaces in order to move around the environment, find food, mates, shelter, and avoid dangers.

Artificial vision is typically viewed as an expensive business in terms of hardware and computation, but the situation is rapidly changing. Visual information is traditionally gathered through a camera and a framegrabber capturing images of the scene several times a second. This equipment is expensive, fragile, and cumbersome to carry around. At the time of writing, new small CMOS[4] cameras with embedded preprocessing and very small power consumption are making their appearance on the market while miniature a VLSI (analog Very Large Scale Integration) chips resembling biological retinas are being developed and tested on mobile robots in research laboratories (Indiveri and Verschure 1997). It is very likely that by the end of the this decade almost all autonomous robots will employ vision as a primary sensory system.

Widespread availability of artificial vision for robots will open the question of how to use efficiently the large amount of information gathered in real time. It is clear that the mainstream approach to vision processing (Marr 1982), based on preprocessing, segmentation, and pattern recognition of each single image is not viable for systems that must respond very quickly in partially unpredictable environments. A drastic new approach that takes into account the ecological aspects of visual based behavior and its integration with the motor system of the robot is required. Although this approach has been claimed for long time in cognitive science (Gibson 1979; Neisser 1976), there are only few efforts in machine vision into this direction (e.g, Horswill 1993; Marjanovic et al. 1996).

Evolutionary robotics provides an ideal framework for exploring visually based strategies and mechanisms within an ecological perspective because a) it allows the development of visual processing along with motor processing in closed feedback loop with the environment; b) since it relies less on externally imposed assumptions, an evolutionary approach can exploit very simple and low resolution light sensors in non conventional ways for fast and efficient navigation; c) it allows simultaneous exploration of both controllers and sensor morphologies, such as number of receptors, position, angle, etc.

Initial explorations in this direction have been carried out by a group of researchers at the University of Sussex (Cliff et al. 1993; Harvey et al. 1994). For a more recent attempt see Nolfi and Marocco (in press). In order to circumvent the problem of tangled cables between the workstation and the mobile robot, Harvey et al. have developed a *gantry robot* (figure 4.9, left). The robot, 150 mm in diameter, is suspended from a frame with step motors that allow motion along the x and y axis relative to the gantry frame

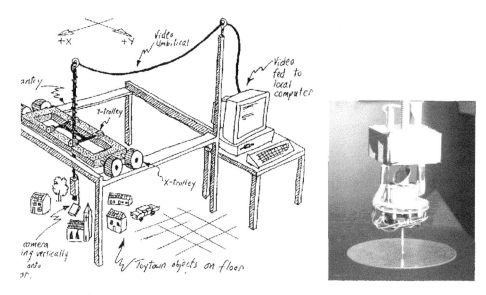

**Figure 4.9**
**Left:** Schematic drawing of the gantry-robot. A system of two rail trolleys, one moving along the x-axis and the other along the y-axis, moves a suspended camera around the environment. Input to the camera comes via a rotating mirror controlled by a step-motor positioned beneath the mirror. This system can simulate the motion of a wheeled robot like the Khepera. **Right:** Close view of the suspended robot (from Harvey et al., 1994). The CCD camera inside the black box points down at the inclined circular mirror. The mirror can be rotated by a motor underneath. The lower disk is a bump sensor suspended from a joystick that can detect collisions with obstacles from four different directions. (Reprinted with permission from Cliff et al. 1993.)

and a maximum speed of 200 mm/s along each axis. This movement, combined with a synchronized rotation of the sensory system of the suspended robot, can be considered equivalent to that of a wheeled robot with a motor system such as that of the Khepera.

The visual system of the robot consists of a CCD camera pointing down at a circular mirror inclined at 45 degrees (figure 4.9, right) through a wide angle lens providing a total visual field of 60 degrees. A 64 x 64 monochrome image is transferred by the onboard framegrabber at 50 Hz to an external workstation for filtering before passing it forward to the input units of the neural network. A bumper disk suspended from a joystick turned upside down detects collisions. The incremental approach advocated by the authors consists of progressing from simple situations and architectures to more complex settings. This methodology goes hand in hand with *species adaptation genetic algorithm* (SAGA), a form of artificial evolution characterized by variable length genotypes and a fairly genetically converged population, proposed by the authors for open ended evolution (Harvey 1992a, 1992b, 1993).

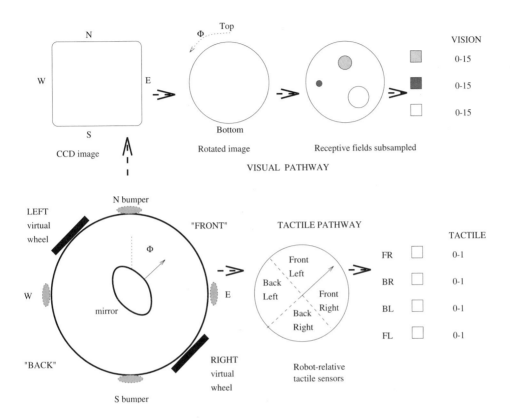

**Figure 4.10**
Schematic representation of the transformation of the sensory information (visual and tactile) being passed to the input units of the neural network. (Reprinted with permission from Harvey et al. 1994.)

According to the incremental approach suggested by the authors, the visual input is considerably reduced by sampling only a small part of the image according to genetically specified instructions. Each individual in the population is characterized by two chromosomes: a chromosome specifies the visual morphology and the other the architecture of the neural network (details of the genetic encoding can be found in Cliff et al. 1993). The visual chromosome is a fixed length bit string encoding sizes and positions of three visual receptive fields (figure 4.10, top). A receptive field is a circular patch characterized by an angle of acceptance (diameter) and position (distance of its center from the center of the visual field). For each genetically specified receptive field, 25 pixels uniformly scattered over its area are chosen and their values averaged to provide a 4 bit single value for every image provided by the camera. These three values represent the visual input to the neural network. Four additional input units receive contact information $\{0,1\}$ from the corresponding sectors of the circular bumper (figure 4.10, bottom).

The neural networks have a fixed number of input (7) and output (4) neurons and a variable number of hidden neurons and connections encoded on the network chromosome (any arbitrary recurrent path can be specified). Artificial neurons have separate excitatory and inhibitory channels and continuous activation functions that incorporate white noise (more details in Cliff et al. 1993). Four output neurons give signals to the two virtual wheels of the robot (as for a Khepera, for example). The signals to the left and right wheels in the range $[-1, 1]$ are obtained—respectively—by subtracting the activation of the first neuron from the second, and the activation of the third unit from the fourth. Artificial evolution was carried out in three stages of increasing behavioral complexity (see also section 1.4 and figure 1.7). At the end of each stage, both the environment and the fitness function were modified.[5]

In the first stage, one long wall was covered with white paper to a width of 150 cm and a height of 22 cm, effectively showing up to 2/3 in the visual field of the robot. The fitness function to be maximized encouraged the robots to move towards the white wall

$$\Phi_1 = \sum_{i=1}^{i=20} Y_i \tag{4.2}$$

where $Y_i$ is the perpendicular distance from the robot to the wall opposite to the target measured at 20 fixed time intervals $i$ throughout a trial of the robot (lasting 25 seconds). Each individual was tested for 4 trials, each starting in the same corner of the environment (opposing the white wall) at different orientations. In order to initialize the first population, the authors randomly generated several individuals and visually selected one that displayed interesting behaviors. The initial population was generated by creating clones of this individual. In about ten generations an individual was found that rotated on itself until it spotted the target wall and approached it.

In the second stage the white target surface was restricted to a 22 cm wide band positioned 2/3 of the way along the same wall. The fitness function was modified in order to encourage approaching the center of the new target

$$\Phi_2 = \sum_{i=1}^{i=20} (-d_i) \tag{4.3}$$

where $d_i$ is the distance of the robot from the center of the target measured at 20 fixed time intervals $i$. Artificial evolution was continued from the previously evolved population maintaining the same experimental conditions described above. In six generation an individual was generated that approached the narrow band and was also capable of following

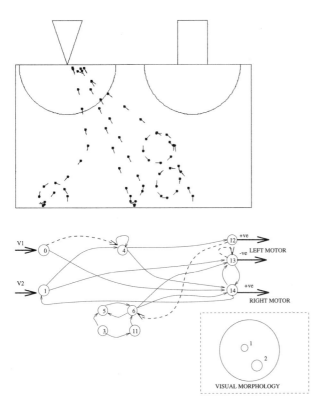

**Figure 4.11**
**Top:** Behavior of the best individual from the last generation evolved in the environment with two targets. The rectangle and triangle indicate the positions of the targets. The semicircles mark the "penalty" (near the rectangle) and "bonus score" (near triangle) zones associated with the fitness function. The oriented segments indicate positions and facing directions (point) of the robot during its trajectory from four different starting locations. **Bottom:** Active part of the neural network and visual morphology of the best individual of the last generation. (Reprinted with permission from Harvey et al. 1994.)

slowly white cylinders of the same size.

In the third stage the white paper was substituted by two white shapes, a rectangle and an isoscele triangle, both with a base of 21 cm and a height of 29.5 cm. The robot was started at four positions and orientations near the opposite wall and the fitness function was designed so that it encouraged approaching the triangle and avoiding the rectangle

$$\Phi_3 = \sum_{i=1}^{i=20} [\beta (D_{1i} - d_{1i}) - \sigma (D_{2i}, d_{2i})] \tag{4.4}$$

where $D_{1i}$ is the distance of the triangle from the gantry origin, $d_{1i}$ is the distance of the robot from the triangle, and $D_{2i}$, $d_{2i}$ are the corresponding distances for the rectangle sampled at fixed time interval $i$. The function $\beta$ is the identity function unless $d_{1i}$ is less than some threshold, in which case it becomes $\beta(D_{1i} - d_{1i})$. $\sigma$ returns 0 unless $d_{2i}$ is less than some threshold; in that case, $\sigma$ becomes $I - (D_{2i} - d_{2i})$ where $I$ is the distance between the two shapes. After 15 generations of incremental evolution from the population of the previous stage, fit individuals emerged capable of approaching the triangle while avoiding the rectangle (figure 4.11, top). The best individual of the last generation used only two receptive field positioned in such a way that they can discriminate rectangles from triangles. In fact, whereas a relatively close rectangle activates both receptors generating an avoidance behavior, a triangle activates only the lower receptor triggering an approaching behavior.

Despite the complexity of this methodology and some amount of external information (e.g., subjective choice of the individual of the initial population and fitness function using explicit distances measured on the x-y coordinates–i.e., a partially *external* function), this work indicates that an apparently complex task of visual navigation can be solved by artificial evolution of smart mechanisms tuned to the characteristics (affordances)[6] of the environment. More recent work has addressed the robustness of the evolved controllers by varying lighting conditions during evolution (Jakobi 1997a) and by using a simpler neural network and genetic encoding (Smith 1998). We think that ecological vision is going to be a very fertile area for evolutionary robotics over the next years.

## 4.4   Re-adaptation

From an engineering perspective, the price to pay for the automatic process of adaptation described above is the amount of time required by evolution carried out entirely on physical robots. As we have seen, artificial evolution often comes up with solutions that are well tailored for the conditions employed during the evolutionary process. Obviously, one can make the evolved controller less sensitive to some features by varying these features during evolution (e.g., the lighting conditions), but we think that this "trick" has some limitations. In order to do it properly, one should know in advance what are those features that require systematic variation, a problem almost as difficult as that of designing the control system of the robot. Furthermore, the relevance of a particular feature for the robustness of the evolved control system depends uniquely on the modifications that occur after artificial evolution. These modifications will affect some features (for example, a different lighting condition when the TV crew comes to shoot your amazing results), but not other (for example, the shape of the environment). Unless you can predict the future, even well planned variations may not be effective.

The question then is to what extent and at what speed an evolutionary system can generalize and/or re-adapt to modified environmental conditions without retraining it from scratch. Artificial evolution of neurocontrollers offers generalization at two levels: the individual and the population. At the individual level, generalization capitalizes on the feature invariants encoded by the neural network. At the population level, generalization is provided by diversity of the individuals. A population will sooner or later converge to a single solution, but even in the worst case the mutation operator will still maintain some variation distributed around the best individual. Artificial evolution can capitalize upon this variation very efficiently to re-adapt under a variety of new conditions. The experiments on visually guided navigation described above are indeed based upon this feature, but also employ weak human supervision in the form of changed fitness functions that reward specific behaviors for each new condition. In the following section we shall describe two further cases of re-adaptation without changing the fitness function and we will leave a further case for chapter 6.

**Cross platform adaptation**

Consider now the simple experiment described in section 4.2 where the robot learns to navigate in a looping maze (figure 4.2). The evolved neurocontroller has developed a pattern of synaptic weights that matches the morphology of the Khepera, its sensorimotor layout, and the response properties of the infrared sensors. As we have seen a miniature robot like the Khepera is very suitable for carrying out rigorous evolutionary experiments, but it might be too small for some applications or terrains. On the other hand, it might be too difficult to evolve from scratch larger robots with a more complex geometry or, if possible, these robots might be too fragile to sustain test of very bad individuals of the initial generations. Therefore, it might be desirable to continue evolution on the new robot incrementally. From the point of view of the neurocontroller, changing the sensory motor characteristics of the robot is just another way of modifying the environment.

Francesco Mondada has tested re-adaptation of evolved neurocontrollers to a larger robotic platform, the mobile robot Koala (figure 4.12). Despite its different size, the Koala robot is similar to the Khepera in some aspects. The six wheels of Koala are driven by two motors, as for Khepera, each controlling one side of the platform. The central wheels on the two sides are lower than the others, so that rotation of the whole platform is very similar to that of the Khepera. The proximity sensors of the Koala are based on the same concept used for the Khepera, but their response range is scaled up (approximately 50 cm). Both hardware and software of the Koala is perfectly compatible with modules and programs written for the Khepera.

In order to assess only re-adaptation to a new morphology and sensory motor system, the Koala robot was placed within a scaled up version of the looping maze already

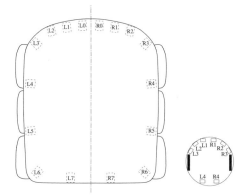

**Figure 4.12**
**Left:** Layout of infrared sensor positions of the Koala robot shown in figure 3-6. L = left; R = right (image courtesy of K-Team SA). **Right:** The khepera robot, redrawn here for comparison.

employed for the Khepera robot (figure 4.13, left). Only eight of the sixteen infrared sensors available on the Koala were selected as input to the neurocontroller (see left side of figure 4.12; from left clockwise: L4, L3, L1, R1, R3, R4, R7, L7). As for the Khepera, the response of each infrared sensor was linearly compressed within the range [0,1] before passing it to the input units of the neural network. After 106 generations of evolution on the Khepera robot in the same conditions described in section 4.2, the last population of neurocontrollers was incrementally evolved on the Koala robot until generation 150 (figure 4.13, right side) without any further change to the software parameters. After a partial drop in performance, in approximately thirty generations the best individuals report fitness values similar to those recorded during the last generations on the Khepera and are capable of performing full laps of the maze.

In this experiment, re-adaptation was mainly concerned with a new body shape and a different layout of the sensors. For example, the passage on the top right corner of the environment requires a rotation in place for the Koala whereas the Khepera—in its original maze—could go around it without stopping (Floreano and Mondada 1998). These results are quite encouraging because they hint at the fact that artificial evolution is suitable for a large variety of physical robots when approached with an incremental methodology. However, incremental evolution still requires quite a lot of research in order to accommodate more complex sensory motor systems, acquisition of new skills, modification of old ones, and preservation of evolved competencies.

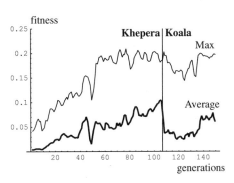

**Figure 4.13**
**Left:** The Koala robot, without the protective white shell, in a scaled-up version of the looping maze used for evolution on the Khepera (figure 4.2). **Right:** Average population fitness and fitness of the best individual across generations. Evolution begins on the Khepera and from generation 107 it continues on the Koala. Data from single run smoothed using rolling averages with window size = 3 (Floreano and Mondada 1998).

## From simulation to reality

As we have mentioned in chapter 3, simulations can provide a valuable aid to evolutionary robotics as long as they are coupled with tests on physical robots. In some cases, one might wish to explore different experimental conditions or fitness functions in simulation before moving on to experiments with the physical robot. In other cases, one might wish to carry out the initial phases of artificial evolution on a simulated robot and incrementally continue on the physical robot. Transferring an evolved controller from the simulated to the real robot is very likely to generate discrepancies in the behavior and performance of the robot caused by different properties of the sensory motor interactions between the robot and its environment. Within this perspective, the passage from simulation to real robots is equivalent to a modification of the environment and/or of the robotic platform, and it can be considered as a case for incremental evolution.

Let us go back once again to the experiment on navigation with obstacle avoidance described in section 4.2. Although good individuals already evolve in approximately one day, running all 100 generations on the physical robot took approximately 66 hours. This time could be reduced to approximately 1 hour by evolving simulated robots on a personal computer. But, how does the neurocontrollers behave once transferred onto the real robot?

Miglino et al. (1995) carried out a set of experiments investigating the transfer from simulations to real robots and evolutionary re-adaptation (see also Nolfi et al. 1994b; Miglino et al. 1994). The authors replicated the experiment on navigation with obstacle avoidance described in section 4.2 using that same fitness function (see box on fitness design) and the sampling technique described in chapter 3 for simulating the Khepera

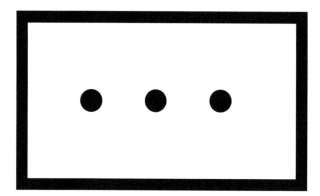

**Figure 4.14**
The environment used for navigation and obstacle avoidance in the experiments on evolutionary re-adaptation
from simulation to the physical robot.

robot. For sake of simplicity, the environment was a rectangular arena measuring 60 x 35 cm with 3 cylindrical objects placed in the center (figure 4.14). A population of 100 individuals was evolved for 200 generations in the simulated environment. At the end of this first phase, all individuals of the last generation were sequentially downloaded on the physical Khepera and evolved in the physical environment using the same procedure for additional 20 generations.[7]

Three experimental conditions were carried out. In the first condition the simulation did not include any noise (*no-noise* condition). In the second condition uniform (white) noise in the range [0.0, 0.4] was added to the values read from the simulated sensors (*noise* condition). In the third condition the sensory values were read as if the robot, after reaching its new position, had been displaced by a small random quantity in the range [−30, 30] mm along the x and y coordinates (*conservative-noise* condition). For each condition, five replications of the experiment starting from different randomly generated genotypes were carried out.

The average and best fitness values of the populations followed a trend very similar to the experiments described in section 4.2, rapidly increasing across the first 100 generations (figure 4.15, only no-noise and conservative-noise conditions shown for sake of compactness). Both in the no-noise and noise conditions the transfer from simulation to the real robot caused a small drop in performance, but no drop at all in the conservative noise condition.

From the point of view of incremental re-adaptation, the no-noise condition is the most significative because it shows the passage between two different worlds, the simulated and the real, each one characterized by its own systematic idiosyncrasies. Here artificial

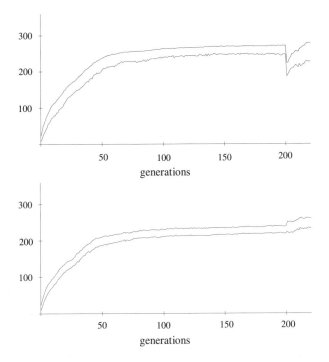

**Figure 4.15**
**Top:** Peak and average fitness for the no-noise condition. **Bottom:** Peak and average fitness for the
conservative-noise condition. Each data point is averaged over five runs with different initializations of the
population. The first 200 generations are evolved in the simulated environment, the last 20 generations in the
real environment (from Miglino et al. 1995).

evolution displays the same type of moderate performance drop and rapid re-adaptation
(figure 4.15, graph on the top) observed in the case of cross platform incremental evolution
described above (section 4.1 and figure 4.13).

The other two conditions with noise, instead, are significative within the perspective
of developing simulation tools that can effectively come closer to real world conditions.
Whereas injection of simple white noise on each sensor is similar to the no-noise condition,
the controllers of the last population (200) evolved under conservative-noise condition do
not significantly differ when tested in the simulated or real environments. Furthermore,
they can continue to improve their performance when incrementally evolved in the real
environment (figure 4.15, graph on the bottom). This result could be explained by the fact
that conservative noise is more systematic because it includes sensor variations induced
by errors in the motor system. The motor system instead is not taken into account in

the white noise condition. Furthermore, if each sensor is updated with noise extracted independently of its neighboring sensors, one assumes that reading errors are due solely to imperfections of each individual sensors. On the other hand, noise caused by external reasons (such as surfaces with different reflection indices) is more likely to be similar for neighboring sensors and is better captured by the conservative-noise condition where all sensor readings are coherently affected.

## 4.5  Conclusions

In this chapter we have presented some examples of artificial evolution applied to simple navigation tasks. In the first example, described in section 4.2, evolved robots display behavioral strategies that are competitive or better than those displayed by hand designed controllers. Evolutionary robots improve their abilities by developing strategies, such as the preferred direction of motion and the cruising speed, that capitalize upon interactions between the machine and its environment. These interactions could hardly be captured by traditional methodology using model based design of control systems. The results indicate that artificial evolution can be fruitfully applied even to tasks where a preprogrammed strategy already exists or to tasks that are apparently simple.

The methodology employed for that experiment does not need any external intervention, with the exception of power supply, because the fitness function is based only on variables accessible through the sensors of the robot. Such a self contained approach is more amenable for standalone applications of adaptive autonomous robots than one that relies on external measures of performance, on periodical manipulations of the training conditions, or on subjective selection of the individuals. However, it works as long as the choice of fitness function and of genetic encoding allows evolvability of the system. There must be a path in the genetic search space that can be discovered by the limited sample of the population considered and that takes the population to areas of increasingly higher fitness.

In the case of more complex sensory motor mappings, such as for visually guided navigation described in section 4.3, human guided incremental evolution was used to facilitate the co-development of sensory morphologies and control strategies. The incremental approach consisted in presenting the evolving robots with a set of tasks of increasing complexity. Human guidance was needed for a) subjective selection of a "good" individual to seed the initial generation; b) design of successive fitness functions; c) decision of when to stop each evolutionary phase. The fitness function relied on an external measure of behavior, the distance between the robot and the walls, that normally would not be accessible to an autonomous robot. The net result of this methodology was co-evolution of controllers and sensory systems capable of complex visual based navigation with remarkably compact resources and rich temporal dynamics. Co-evolution of sensory morphologies and control systems is a very promising approach. It can be exploited for investigating historical patterns of developments of biological organism (for example, see Enquist and Arak 1994) or for engineering machines capable of self-selecting the most suitable sensory information for a given task, environment, and hardware resources (we will come back on this issue in chapter 11).

Artificial evolution comes up with solutions that nicely match the evolutionary environment in ways that are often unpredictable from the distal perspective of an external observer. This means that even slight modifications to the environment of an evolved individual are likely to cause a drop in performance. In section 4.4 we have shown two cases where performance can be rapidly recovered and even incremented by simply exploiting the variation present in the population during a prolonged evolutionary run under changed environmental conditions: transfer to a new robot and transfer from simulations to real world. Evolutionary re-adaptation can be understood by looking at the graph on the left of figure 4.13. Even in the last generations, a population always exhibits some variation due to the mutation operator. When the selection criterion changes (either because the environment or the fitness function change), some individuals that previously were not among the best may be selected for reproduction and pull the population towards a new area of the genetic space. The concept of adaptation as displacement of a partially converged population in genetic space has been first proposed by Harvey (1992b, 1993) as a powerful strategy for incremental open ended evolution, and is behind the experiment on visually guided navigation described above.

We feel that evolutionary machines should be conceived right at the beginning as continuously adaptive systems rather than as learning systems for predefined problems. The difference is subtle, but it entails several consequences. At the implementation level, the generational process of selective reproduction and random mutation should be continuously active. At the algorithmic level, it is necessary to develop genetic encoding and operators that can support incremental open ended evolution. At the conceptual level, the notion of progress, optimum, and objective performance measure must be redefined to take into account the possibility of ever changing situations.

# 5 Power and limits of reactive intelligence

## 5.1 Introduction

Research in new wave Robotics (Sharkey 1997) often involves systems that are reactive or mostly reactive. These are systems where sensors and motors are directly linked and which always react to the same sensory state with the same motor action. In these systems internal states, if any, play a comparatively limited role in determining the motor output of the system. For this reason, researchers working with systems that are embodied and situated have often been criticized for rejecting the importance of internal representations of the external world. As claimed by Brooks this criticism does not hold. Researchers in this field in no way deny the importance of internal representations although they tend to have a different view regarding what internal representations stand for. Within the traditional Artificial Intelligence approach, in fact, there is a tendency to view internal representations as explicit representations of the external world, while those who embrace the embodied and situated approach tend to view the internal representations as partial models of the world which include only those aspects that are necessary to allow agents to achieve their goals (Brooks 1991a).

The reason why most of the systems developed within the situated and embodied approach are mainly reactive is that embodied and situated systems can solve rather complex tasks without requiring internal states or internal representations. As we will show below, this ability to solve a rather large number of tasks without the need to react differently to the same sensory states in different contexts can be explained by considering that systems that are situated and embodied (agents) can coordinate perception and action.

Agents partially determine the sensory patterns they receive from the environment by executing action that modify the position of the agent with respect to the external environment and/or modify the external environment itself. Agents can take advantage of this ability in different ways. We will refer to the process of exploiting the agent-environment interaction (i.e., the ability to select favorable sensory patterns through motor actions) as *sensory-motor coordination* (for a similar view, see Pfeifer and Scheier 1997).

That does not imply that pure reactive agents are able to solve any kind of task and that internal states or internal representations are unnecessary. As we will see, there are tasks in which sensory-motor coordination is not sufficient.

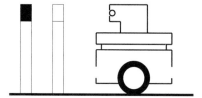

**Figure 5.1**
The robot and the environment. The robot has eight infrared proximity sensors that can detect the bottom part of
the obstacles and a linear camera that can detect the gray level of the top part of the obstacles. Objects with their
top painted in black should be avoided while objects with their top painted in white should be approached.

## 5.2   How sensory-motor coordination can cope with perceptual aliasing

The perceptual aliasing problem is a simple example where sensory-motor coordination
becomes very useful. Perceptual aliasing, a term coined by Whitehead and Ballard (1991),
refers to the situation wherein two or more objects generate the same sensory pattern,
but require different responses. A solution to this situation (i.e., when an agent receives a
sensory pattern which requires different motor responses in different circumstances) could
be that of performing actions in order to search for other sensory information that is not
affected by the aliasing problem (that is, an unambiguous sensory pattern).

Consider for example the case of a Khepera robot placed in an environment with two
types of objects: one with the top painted in black, which should be avoided, and one with
the top painted in white, which should be approached (figure 5.1). The Khepera robot is
provided with 8 infrared proximity sensors and with a linear camera providing a linear
image composed of 64 pixels of 256 gray levels each and subtending a total view angle of
36° (figure 3.3, left).

Every time such a robot approaches an object which does not happen to be in the view
angle of its camera, the robot will experience an ambiguous sensory pattern (i.e., a sensory
pattern which is affected by the aliasing problem). The same type of sensory pattern will
be experienced by the robot both in the case of objects to be approached and of objects to
be avoided. The obvious solution to this problem is to turn toward the object. By turning
until the object is within the 36° view angle of the camera, the robot will eventually receive
an unambiguous sensory pattern (i.e., frontal infrared sensors active and white image for
objects to be approached; frontal infrared sensors active and black image for objects to be
avoided). The process of selecting sensory patterns which are easy to discriminate through
motor actions is usually referred as *active perception* (Bajcsy 1988). Some examples
of processes falling within this category have been identified in natural organisms. For
example, in order to recognize certain visual patterns, the fruit fly *Drosophila* moves in

order to shift the perceived image to a certain location of the visual field (Dill et al. 1993).

One thing that should be stressed in this example is that, when the robot is experiencing a sensory pattern which is affected by the aliasing problem, different types of motor actions might have different effects. Some motor actions might lead the robot to finally experience an unambiguous sensory pattern (e.g. turning toward the object) while other actions may prevent this possibility (e.g. moving away from the object). Some actions might be more effective than others (e.g. turning always in the same direction independently from the relative position of the object is less effective than turning toward the object. The robot will finally face the object with the camera in both cases, but it will be faster in the second case). This implies that, when facing an ambiguous sensory pattern, agents should perform the actions that maximize the chance to select an unambiguous sensory pattern.

Another point that should be made here is that we could describe this process of active vision as sensory-motor coordination. More precisely, we can identify one subpart of the robot behavior (between when the robot starts to perceive an object with the infrared sensors to when the robot perceives the object also with the camera) and describe it as a sensory-motor coordination behavior. On the other hand it is clear that if we look at the way in which the robot reacts to each sensory state there is not a clear distinction between actions that have the function to select useful sensory patterns (i.e., unambiguous sensory pattern in this example) and other actions, such as move away from an object. Each action, in fact, has always two consequences: (1) it partially determines how the agent accomplishes the desired task; (2) it partially determines the sensory patterns that the agent will experience next.

A final remark concerns the limits of this strategy to solve the perceptual aliasing problem. The strategy is effective only when the robot can find at least one sensory state that is not affected by the aliasing problem.

## 5.3   How sensory-motor coordination can simplify hard problems

Another problem is the case in which groups of sensory patterns requiring different motor answers strongly overlap even if not completely. In this case, agents are facing hard perceptual problems that might be difficult or even impossible to solve with a reactive architecture. In this section we will try to show how sensory-motor coordination can turn these hard problems into simpler ones.

The distinction between simple and hard problems has been recently formalized by Clark and Thornton (1997). They introduced the term *type-2* problems to denote hard tasks in which the problem to map input patterns into appropriate output patterns is complicated by the fact that the regularities,[1] which can allow such a mapping, are marginal or hidden in

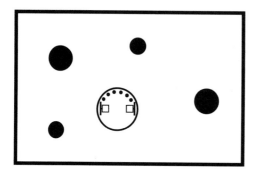

**Figure 5.2**
The robot and the environment. Small and large dark circles represent cylinders with a diameter of 1.5 and 4 cm, respectively. The lines represent the walls. The large circle represents the Khepera robot.

the sensory patterns. On the basis of this consideration they distinguished type-2 problems (i.e., hard problems) from *type-1* problems (i.e., easy problems) in which many regularities are directly available in the sensory patterns.

Type-2 problems, which require complex input-output mappings, may be reduced to type-1 (tractable) problems by recoding sensory states so to enhance useful regularities (Clark and Thornton 1997). This can be obtained in two different ways. One possibility is to internally recode sensory inputs. Elman (1993), for example, showed how complex tasks that cannot be solved by training a feedforward neural network using standard back-propagation can be solved if the network is first trained on a simpler subtask and then on the entire task. This can be explained by considering that the first learning phase affects how the sensory patterns are recoded at the level of the internal representations (Elman 1993). This recoding, by enhancing the regularities of the sensory patterns, turns the process of learning the entire task to a type-1 problem (Clark and Thornton 1997).

However, agents can also transform a type-2 into type-1 problems by actively structuring their own input through sensory-motor coordination (Scheier et al. 1998). As we will see, this strategy cannot be used by systems that are passively exposed to sensory states, that is systems which are not embodied and situated. Scheier et al. (1998) considered the case of a Khepera robot which should approach large, and avoid small, cylindrical objects located in an arena surrounded by walls (figure 5.2). The robot receives sensory input from the six frontal proximity sensors.

The task of discriminating between the two types of objects is far from trivial for an agent that is required to passively discriminate between the sensory patterns produced by the two objects (Nolfi 1996, 1997c, 1999). This was shown by training a neural network to discriminate between sensory patterns corresponding to cylindrical objects and walls, or to cylindrical objects with different diameters. Three neural architectures were used: (a) a feedforward architecture with two layers of nodes: the input layer consisted of 6 neurons coding the activation of the 6 frontal infrared sensors of the robot for different positions with respect to the objects, the output layer consisted of one neuron binarily coding for the object category; (b) an architecture with an additional internal layer of 4 units; (c) an architecture with an additional internal layer of 8 units. The networks were trained with the back-propagation algorithm (Rumelhart et al. 1986). In a set of experiments the networks were trained to discriminate between cylindrical objects with a diameter of 2.3 cm and walls while in another set of experiments they were asked to discriminate between cylindrical objects with diameters of 2.3 and 5.5 cm. A training set consisted of sensory patterns perceived by the robot at 20 different distances and at 180 different angles with respect to the two objects, for a total of 7200 different patterns.[2]

Figure 5.3 shows the percentage of positions from which the networks were success-fully capable of classifying the two types of stimuli (i.e., to produce an activation value below or above 0.5 depending on the category of the perceived object) for each of the three different architectures. When asked to discriminate between walls and small cylindrical ob-jects, networks without hidden units were capable of correctly classifying only 22% of the cases, whereas networks with 4 or 8 hidden units managed about 35% of the cases. When trained to discriminate between small and large cylindrical objects, the performance was even worse. Independently of their architecture, trained networks were able to correctly discriminate between small and large objects in less than 10% of the cases.

The fact that these networks can correctly classify the two objects only in the minority of the cases can be explained by considering that variations in distance and angle are larger than variations between the two categories of objects. As a consequence, sensory patterns belonging to different categories largely overlap. "Put differently, the distance in sensor space for data originating from one and the same object can be large, while the distance between two objects from different categories can be small" (Scheier et al. 1998, p. 1559).

If we look at figure 5.4, which represents the positions (i.e., the combination of angle and distance) from which networks were capable of correctly discriminating (black areas) between sensory patterns belonging to *walls and small cylinders*, we see that the networks produce correct answers when the objects are not more than $120^o$ to the left or the right of the robot face and no more than 32mm away. This result is not surprising if we consider that the robot relies only on 6 frontal infrared sensors, and that when the distance is high the infrared sensors are only slightly activated. However, there are two areas in which objects cannot be correctly discriminated even though they are "within sight": in the figure these are the white areas enclosed by the black outer stripes. A similar pattern emerge from figure 5.5 which represents the positions from which networks are able to correctly discriminate between sensory patterns belonging to *small and large cylinders* although the

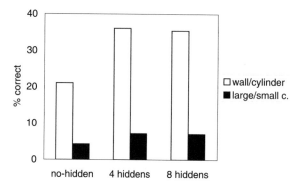

**Figure 5.3**
Percentage of positions from which sensory stimuli are successfully classified by networks with no hidden units, four hidden units, and eight hidden units. Performance of the best replication out of 10. White histograms represent the performance for the wall/cylinder discrimination task, black histograms represent the performance for the small/large cylinder discrimination task. For 20 different distances and 180 different angles (3600 different positions in all) networks were required to produce an output above or below the threshold, depending on the type of object (wall or target object). As a consequence, the total number of patterns was 7200. Responses were considered correct if, for a given position, the network was able to correctly classify both sensory patterns corresponding to the two objects. The networks were trained with back-propagation.

area corresponding to correct discriminations is significantly smaller.

It is also interesting to note that the areas in which stimuli can be correctly disambiguated are not symmetrical. This has to do with the fact that different sensors, even if identical from the electronic point of view, actually respond differently. As a consequence, it is clear that whether stimuli are ambiguous or not is a function of both the structure of the stimuli themselves and of the sensory apparatus of the robot.

From these results we can conclude that *passive networks* (i.e., networks which are passively exposed to a set of sensory patterns without being able to interact with the external environment through motor action), are mostly unable to discriminate between different objects. In other words, this is a type-2 problem. As we will show in this and in the next section however, this problem can easily be solved by agents that are left free to exploit sensory-motor coordination.

In order to develop robots capable of approaching large, and avoiding small, cylindrical objects (see figure 5.2) Scheier et al. (1998) used artificial evolution to select the weights of the robot's neural controllers.[3] As shown in figure 5.6, performances increased during the first generations and stabilized at near optimal performance (objects were almost always correctly discriminated) after about 40 generations. In other words, agents allowed to exploit sensory-motor coordination managed to solve the task. The fact that coordination between sensory and motor processes is crucial in solving this task can be clearly

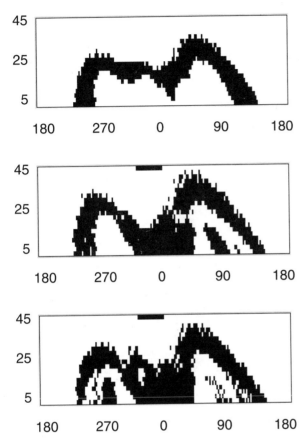

**Figure 5.4**
The areas in gray represents the relative positions from which networks are able to correctly discriminate the sensory patterns belonging to walls from those belonging to small cylindrical objects. The three pictures (from top to bottom) represent the result for the best simulation with no hidden, 4 hidden, and 8 hidden units, respectively.

demonstrated by observing the behavior of evolved individuals and by observing how the distribution of the sensory patterns changed throughout generations.

Scheier et al. (1998) report that the fittest individuals in 86% of the runs moved in the environment until they perceived an object (large or small) and then started to turn around the object eventually leaving if the object is a small cylinder (the remaining 14% of the runs they stopped in front of the objects and displayed significantly lower performance). This circling behavior is crucial in order to accomplish the discrimination between the two type of objects given that the sensory patterns that robots experience while circling the small

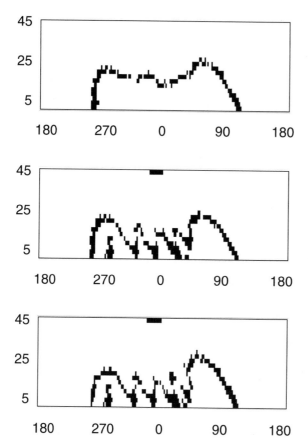

**Figure 5.5**
The areas in black represents the relative positions from which networks are able to correctly discriminate the sensory patterns belonging to large from those belonging to small cylindrical objects. The three pictures (from top to bottom) represent the result for the best simulation with no hidden, 4 hidden, and 8 hidden units, respectively.

objects is significantly different from those that robots experiences while circling large objects. In other words, the sequence of motor actions that lead to the circling behavior allows the robot to select sensory patterns that can be easily discriminated.

The role of sensory-motor coordination has been further demonstrated by analyzing the sensory-motor patterns experienced during their lifetime by individuals of successive generations. Indeed, given that the type of sensory patterns that an individual receives from the environment partially depend on how the individual reacts to each sensory state, individuals who behave differently may face harder or simpler discrimination tasks. To

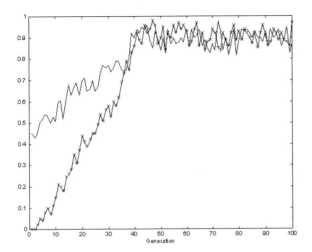

**Figure 5.6**
Performance and GSI (see the text below) throughout generations. The line with crosses shows the percentage of
trials in which evolving individuals are able to end up close to large cylindrical objects. The line without crosses
show the corresponding GSI value. Average results of 30 runs. (Reprinted with permission from Scheier et al.
1998.)

quantify the complexity of the discrimination task faced by different individuals, the
authors measured how much the two classes of sensory patterns corresponding to the two
objects (small and large cylinders) were separated in the input space. To accomplish this
measure the authors used the Geometric Separability Index (GSI) proposed by Thornton
(1997) to quantify the distinction between type-1 and type-2 problems introduced above.
In the case of this experiment, the GSI gives a measure of the separation between the
two classes and of the compactness of each class. GSI is computed by storing all sensory
patterns experienced by an individual during N lifecycles and by checking for every
sensory pattern whether the nearest pattern (euclidean distance) belongs to the same
class. The total number is then normalized by N. If the nearest pattern in sensory space
always belongs to the same class of the currently perceived object, the GSI value is 1:
this means the patterns of the two classes are well separated. Values close to 1 thus
indicate that the sensory patterns belonging to the two categories are quite separated in
the input space and easy to discriminate while values close to 0.5 indicate that the sensory
patterns corresponding to the two categories completely overlap (see figure 5.7). In the
case of patterns corresponding to only two categories (small and large objects) this can be

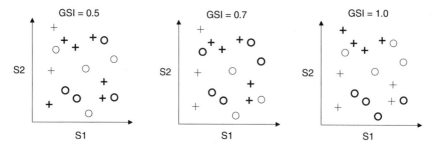

**Figure 5.7**
A schematic representation of the distribution of sensory patterns. For sake of simplicity the sensory space has
only two dimensions (S1 and S2). Crosses and circles represent the sensory patterns belonging to two classes
(e.g., small and large cylinders). Dark crosses and circles represent the sensory patterns experienced by an
individual (notice that the sensory patterns experienced by an individual depend on how it react to previous
experienced sensory states). The three figures indicate the sensory patterns experienced by three different
individuals. As shown in the figure GSI vary from 0.5 to 1.0 depending on how much the two groups of sensory
patterns overlap.

calculated in the following way:

$$GSI(f) = \frac{\sum_{i=1}^{N} \left( f(x_i) + f(x_i') + 1 \right) \bmod 2}{N} \qquad (5.1)$$

where $f$ is the category of the object ($0$ = small $1$ = large cylinder), $x_i$ are the sensory
patterns consisting of $N$ vectors, and $x_i'$ is the nearest neighbor of $x_i$ (i.e., the pattern within
the N set which has the minimum euclidean distance with respect to $x_i$).

As shown in figure 5.6 the GSI value starts at about 0.5 and monotonically increases
during the first 40 generations until it reaches a stable state around 0.9 (notice that also
performance increases during the first 40 generations). This means that individuals of
successive generations increase their ability to coordinate the sensory and motor processes
so that experienced sensory patterns corresponding to one object become more similar
between them and more different from sensory patterns corresponding to the other object.

A further indication that sensory-motor coordination is able to solve hard problems is
that the GSI for passive networks (i.e., the GSI computed by taking into account all possible
sensory states) is 0.564722 for the wall/small-cylinder discrimination and 0.500556 for
the small/large cylinder discrimination. This implies that sensory patterns belonging to
different objects overlap extensively in the first case and completely in the second case.
This is a further indication that we are dealing with type-2 problems in which regularities
are almost or entirely absent. Evolved agents use sensory-motor coordination to select a
subset of the data containing enough regularities to discriminate sensory patterns belonging

to different objects. In other words, evolved individuals are capable of transforming type-2 problems into type-1 problems through sensory-motor coordination.

## 5.4   Exploiting behavioral attractors

In this section we will describe another case of hard perceptual discrimination, similar to that described above, where sensory-motor coordination is used in a different way.

Consider the case of a Khepera robot which is asked to discriminate between walls and a cylindrical object by finding and remaining close to the cylinder (Nolfi 1996, 1997c). The environment is an arena of $60 \times 35$ cm surrounded by walls containing a cylindrical object with a diameter of about 2.3 cm located at a random position. To discriminate between walls and cylinders is difficult given that, as shown in the previous section, the sensory patterns corresponding to the two objects largely overlap.

We provide individual robots with a neural network with 6 sensory neurons encoding the states of the 6 frontal infrared sensors and 2 output neurons encoding the speed of the two wheels. If we use artificial evolution to select the weights of the controllers,[4] after few generations we obtain individuals which are capable of spending most of their lifetime close to the cylindrical object (i.e., individuals which are able to discriminate between walls and cylindrical objects avoiding the former and remaining close to the latter). In particular, as shown in figure 5.8 (thick line), after a few generations the best individuals are able to end up close to the cylindrical object within 500 cycles most of the times.

Evolved individuals do not circle around objects (as in the case of the experiment described in the previous section). On the other hand, when approaching the cylinder, evolved individuals move back and forth and/or left and right. Figure 5.9 displays the behavior of a typical evolved individual. The robot is placed in front of a wall on the bottom side of the environment. During the first 100 cycles it encounters and avoids the south, west, and north walls. Later on, it encounters the cylindrical object and remains close to it. All individuals, like the one shown in the figure, never stop in front of the target, but begin moving back and forth, and left and right by remaining at a given angle and distance with respect to the cylindrical object.

This emergent behavior could be described as a dynamical system. The positions with respect to an object at which individuals start to oscillate while remaining in about the same position is an attractor; the robot's trajectory will always converge to these positions regardless of the direction of approach to the target. Figure 5.10 shows the trajectories produced by an evolved individual while approaching walls or cylinders (top and bottom respectively). When the individual reaches a distance of about 20mm from an object, it avoids walls but approaches cylinders until it reaches the attractor area located at a distance

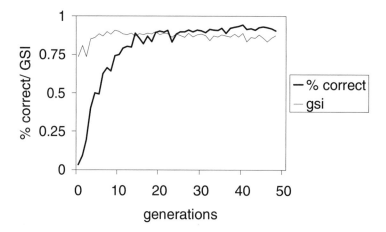

**Figure 5.8**
**Thick line:** Percentage of epochs in which the best individuals of each generation are able to end up close to the cylindrical object after 500 cycles. **Thin line:** GSI of the sensory patterns experienced by individuals of successive generations. Average results of 10 replications.

of about 15 mm and an angle of about 60 degrees. The resulting trajectories converge to the center of the area allowing the individual to keep more or less the same position relative to the cylinder.

To ascertain if these individuals, as in the case of the individuals of the experiment described in the previous section, solve the task by self-selecting sensory patterns which are easy to discriminate we calculated the GSI index for the best individuals of successive generations. As shown in figure 5.8, GSI index stabilizes at around 0.8 after the very first generation while performance keeps growing throughout 50 generations. These contrasting trends, and the fact that GSI stabilizes on a lower value with respect to the experiments described in the previous section (about 0.8 instead of 0.9), suggest that here the ability to select sensory patterns which are easy to discriminate plays a less important role. This hypothesis is also supported by the fact that the attractor area is located outside the gray area representing the relative positions from which is possible to correctly discriminate between the two type of objects without relying on sensory-motor coordination (same data shown on the top of figure 5.4).[5] These individuals can solve the problem of remaining close to the cylinder while avoiding walls by reacting to sensory states in a way that produces an attractor area close to the cylinder but not close to a wall.

To better clarify the role of sensory-motor coordination in this emergent strategy it is useful to analyze a simpler case designed so to prevent the possibility to increase the separability between groups of sensory patterns belonging to different objects through

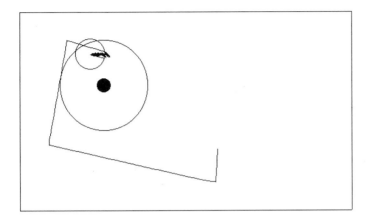

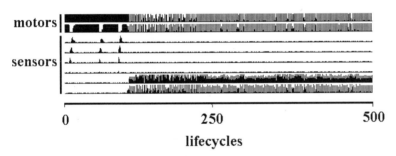

**Figure 5.9**
**Top:** Behavior of a typical evolved individual. The lines represent the walls, the full circle represents a cylindrical object, the large empty circle around it represents the area in which the robot is given fitness values, the small empty circle represents the position of the robot after 500 cycles, and the trace on the terrain represents the trajectory of the robot. **Bottom:** State of the two motor neurons and of the six infrared sensors during 500 lifecycles recorded during the trajectory displayed above.

sensory-motor coordination (see figure 5.12). As we will see, in fact, evolved individuals solve the problem by relying on a behavioral attractor also in this case.

Consider the case of a simulated agent which lives in a circular stripe divided into 40 cells (20 cells on the left and 20 on the right side). For each side of the environment, cells are labeled by numbers in the range 0–19 in *different random* orders (see figure 5.11, left). At each time step the agent occupies one single cell and perceives the number corresponding to that cell. The agent can react to the current sensory state in two different ways: move one cell clockwise or one cell counterclockwise. Starting at any position on the circular stripe, the goal of the agent is to reach and/or remain in the left part of the environment.

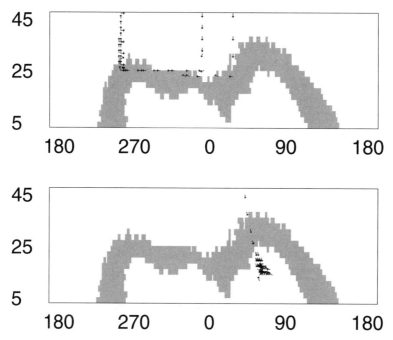

**Figure 5.10**
Angular trajectories of an evolved individual close to a wall (top graph) and to a cylinder (bottom graph). The picture was obtained by placing the individual at a random position in the environment, leaving it free to move for 500 cycles, and recording displacements at positions relative to the two types of objects for distances smaller than 45 mm. For sake of clarity, arrows are used to indicate the relative direction but not the amplitude of movements. The black area represents the positions from which the two objects can be discriminated by a passive agent (same data of figure 5.4, top).

Agents have a neural network with 20 input units locally encoding the number of the current cell, and 1 output unit binarily encoding one of the two possible actions (see figure 5.11, right). Only one sensory unit is activated each time step. Weights can assume only two values (0 or 1). Therefore, the weight from the input unit activated by the current sensory state determines the action of the agent. If the weight is 0 the output will be 0 and the agent will move clockwise; conversely, if the weight is 1 the output will be 1 and the agent will move counterclockwise. Individuals cannot keep trace of previously experienced sensory states (i.e., they react to a certain sensory state always in the same way).

What is interesting about this experimental situation is that all sensory states are affected by the aliasing problem. Whatever the sensory state is, in fact, the agent has 50% of probability to be in the left or in the right part of the environment. In other words, it is impossible to select sensory states which are not affected by the aliasing problem.

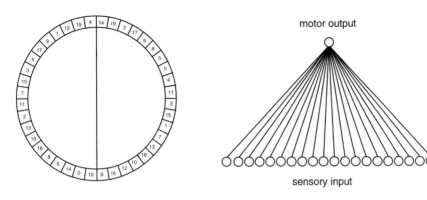

**Figure 5.11**
**Left:** The environment. **Right:** The agent's neural controller.

Moreover, being all sensory states equidistant in the input space, it is impossible to self-select the sensory states so that the two groups belonging to the two objects do not largely overlap (figure 5.12).

However, if we evolve a population of such agents by selecting those who spend a larger number of cycles in the left part of the environment, after few generations we obtain individuals which are able to move away from the right part of the environment and to remain in the left part.[6] The way in which evolved individuals solve this problem can be seen by observing the arrows in figure 5.13 which display two typical evolved strategies. In the right part of the environment individuals consistently move clockwise or counterclockwise until they abandon the right side. On the contrary, in some areas of the left side of the environment, individuals start to move back and forth while remaining in the left side for the remaining part of their lifetime.

Agents solve their task by reacting to sensory states so to produce attractors in the left part and not in the right part of the environment. Attractors consists of two adjacent cells to which the agent react clockwise and counterclockwise (following the clockwise direction, the robot should respond clockwise to the first cell and counterclockwise to the second cell, see points indicated with an "a" in figure 5.13). When the agent encounters an attractor point, it starts to move back and forth while remaining there. This strategy ensures that agents will leave the right part, but will remain in one of the attractors located in the left part.[7]

The strategy evolved by these simulated agents closely resembles the strategy evolved by the robots described above in this section. The environment has only one dimension in this experiments while it has two dimensions in the previous experiments. This explains while agents move clockwise or counterclockwise in these experiments, while robots move

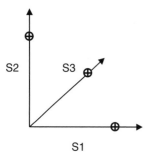

S2    S3

S1

**Figure 5.12**
A schematic representation of the distribution of the sensory patterns in the experiment of the artificial organism living in the circular environment described in figure 5.11. For sake of simplicity the figure displays a sensory space with three dimensions (S1, S2, and S3) instead of 20. As in the case of figure 5.7, crosses and circles represent the sensory patterns belonging to two classes (the left and right side of the environment in this case). In the case of this experiment however, all sensory patterns belong to both classes. Therefore crosses and circles are superimposed. In addition, all sensory patterns have the same distance between themselves. For this reasons is not possible to select a subset of the patterns so that the two groups corresponding to the two classes do not largely overlap.

back and forth and/or left and right in the previous experiments. However, the type of strategy is the same: react to sensory states in order to produce attractors (i.e., set of motor actions that, taken together, allow the individual to remain in the same position) in the left part but not in the right part of the environment in this experiments; react to sensory states to produce an attractor close to cylindrical objects, but not close to walls, in the previous experiment.

It should be noted that how an individual reacts to a particular sensory state does not have any function on its own. For example the fact that the individual shown on the left side of figure 5.13 reacts clockwise to the sensory state "3" does not have a function by itself. The way in which an evolved individual reacts to a certain sensory state makes sense only if we consider how it reacts to all other sensory states. Another interesting aspect to notice is that in these experiments we cannot distinguish between a phase in which the agent discriminates between the left and right part of the environment and a phase in which it moves to the desired part of the environment. As in the experiment with robots described above, the discrimination is an emergent result of how the robot reacts to all sensory states.

When we claim that a sensory pattern is affected by the aliasing problem or that two groups of sensory patterns which require different answers strongly overlap we implicitly assume a certain behavioral solution to a given task. In other words, we are assuming that the agent should react differently to patterns belonging to different objects or to different sides of the environment. However, tasks can usually be solved in a varieties of different ways and only some of these ways might present problems such as aliasing or

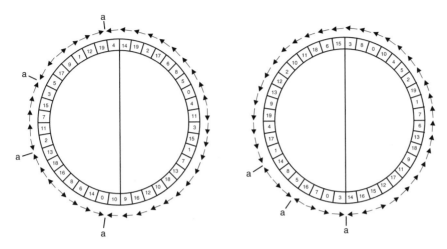

**Figure 5.13**
Two typical strategies obtained with artificial evolution. The numbers represents the sensory state experienced by the agent in each cell. Each different sensory state is present one time in the left and one time in the right part of the environment, but at different random locations. Arrows indicate the motor reaction of a typical evolved agent. Points indicated with an "a" are attractors. Notice that the two pictures represents the strategies obtained in two different replications of the experiment. In each replication the sequence of 20 cells in the two sides of the environment are randomly distributed.

lack of regularities between groups of sensory patterns that require different answers. Let us consider the last experiment of this section. When we first think of this task we assume that the only way to solve it is to react differently to sensory states present in the left and in the right part of the environment (at least to some of them). When we then realize that all sensory patterns are both present in the two sides and equally distant in the input space we feel that there is no way to solve the problem for a reactive agent (i.e., for an agent which do not have internal states which can keep a trace of previously experienced sensory states). However, when we observe the behavior of the evolved agent, we see that there is a completely different way to solve the problem that does not require to react differently to sensory states which lie in the two sides.

When we left individuals free to find their own way to solve a task by interacting with the external environments two different processes take place. On one hand, evolution, by selecting the most successful individuals, tend to select the individuals whose strategies are less affected by the aliasing problem or by the lack of regularities within groups of sensory patterns that require different answers. This is the case, for example, of the individuals who start to move back and forth in the left part of the circular stripe which do not need to react differently to the sensory patterns encountered in the two sides to leave the right side and to remain in the left part of the environment. On the other hand, given a certain selected strategy, evolution tends to select individuals that exploit sensory-motor coordination to avoid sensory pattern affected by the aliasing problems and to select the sensory patterns so to increase regularities within groups of sensory patterns which require different answers. This is the case, for example, of the experiment described in the previous section in which evolutionary improvements are highly correlated with an increasing ability to select sensory patterns easy to discriminate.

## 5.5   Exploiting constraints

From an engineering point of view the characteristics of the environment and the body structure of the robot are referred to as constraints and are generally viewed as problems to be solved in the design of control software. Typically, an engineer comes up with a solution to the problem based on a model of the environment and of the robot body, and then checks whether that solution works for the specific environment and robot (e.g. sensors with a certain level of precision, obstacles of a given shape arranged in certain configurations, etc.).

Conversely, in artificial evolution constraints may be viewed as opportunities (Ashby 1956; Scheier et al. 1998). To better illustrate this point we will consider an experiment carried out by Miglino (Miglino 1996; see also Lund and Miglino 1998) where the author used artificial evolution to train a Khepera robot to perform a navigation task that had been previously studied with rats.

Gallistel, Cheng and other researchers (Gallistel 1990; Cheng 1986; Margules and Gallistel 1988) used the experimental settings displayed in figure 5.14 to show that rats build a map[8] of the environment and use it to navigate. In one of their experiments, they let rats locate and eat a visible food patch in an open field box. They then tested the rats for their ability to locate food patches in boxes identical to the one experienced previously with the food placed in the same position, but this time buried.

When the box was covered and its orientation changed randomly to prevent the use of external cues, Margules and Gallistel (1988) observed that rats were able to correctly accomplish the task in 35% of the trials (see Table 1). Moreover, they observed that some of the errors made by the rats were systematic. In 31% of cases, rats looked for the food in an area that had the same geometric relationships as the correct location with respect to the rectangular shape of the box. For example, if the food was located in a corner, in about one third of the trials rats looked for the food in the correct location while in another third of the trials, they looked in the opposite corner with respect to the correct location of the food (figure 5.14). The authors called these *rotational errors* because rats confused the correct location of the food with a location that would be correct if the box were rotated by

target area

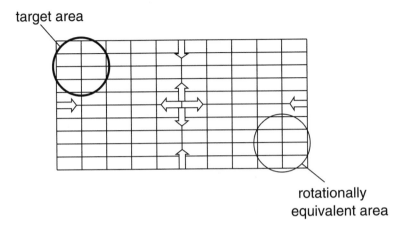

rotationally
equivalent area

**Figure 5.14**
Top view of the open field box experiment. The thick lines represent the box (120×60 cm). The thin lines show
how the box can be ideally divided into 100 12×6 cm cells. The arrows indicate the eight different starting
positions and orientations used during the test phase. The dark circle represents the area in which the food is
located (i.e., the target area) while the light circle represents the rotationally equivalent area. In the experiments
with robots the target area has a diameter of 15 cm and can be positioned at any intersection except for the
central one. A new evolutionary run is performed for each target location. Redrawn from Miglino (1996).

180 degrees. For the remaining one third of the cases, rats looked elsewhere. According to
the authors, since rotational errors can be explained only in Euclidean terms, these results
would show that rats rely on an internal representation of their environment (a map) based
on Euclidean geometry.

Miglino set up a similar experiment in which a Khepera robot was evolved to navigate
toward a target area using artificial evolution (Miglino 1996; see also Lund and Miglino
1998). The robot was placed in a rectangular 60×30 cm environment ideally divided into
100 6×3 cm cells. Each robot was allowed to move in the environment for 8 epochs, with
each epoch consisting of 80 actions. For each epoch, the robot was initially placed in one
of the 8 starting positions and orientations displayed in figure 5.14. Robots were provided
with a neural network with 8 sensory neurons encoding the state of the infrared sensors of
the robot and 2 motor neurons encoding the speeds of the two wheels (which were updated
every 100 ms). A new evolutionary run was repeated for every new position of the target
on the 80 intersections of the lines dividing the floor into 100 cells, with the exception
of the central intersection. Therefore the experiment was replicated 79 times and in each
replication the position of the food was different.[9]

Similarly to rats, evolved robots were able to locate the food area or the rotational
equivalent area in 82% of the cases and missed one of the two areas in only 18% of the

**Table 5.1**
Percent of navigation to the target area (hits), to the rotationally equivalent area (rotational errors), and to other areas (misses) for robots and for rats. Rat data from Margules and Gallistel (1988). Robot data from Miglino (1996).

|        | Hits | Rotational Errors | Misses |
|--------|------|-------------------|--------|
| Rats   | 35   | 31                | 33     |
| Robots | 41   | 41                | 18     |

cases (cf. Table 5.1). Note that, as in the case of rats, pure reactive robots navigated to the rotational equivalent area as many times as they did to the correct target area. It is important to clarify that these results do not imply that rats do not use internal representations to solve this type of task. In fact the same task could be solved in a variety of ways including those that rely on internal representations.

How can purely reactive robots solve this task? One solution could be that of discriminating between long and short walls and navigate accordingly. For example, if the food is located in the upper left corner, as in figure 5.14, an agent could follow a long wall on its own right side until a corner (or other similar strategies like following a short wall on its own left side until a corner). In the case of this food location, this strategy will produce 50% of success and 50% of rotational errors, depending on which of the two walls the agent happens to follow. However, a Khepera robot with a purely reactive control system and sensors that can detect obstacles up to a distance of about 5 cm, cannot discriminate between long and short walls. Once again evolution exploit sensory-motor coordination to find the solution to a hard perceptual problem.

Figure 5.15 shows the behavior of an evolved individual in an experiment in which the target area is located in the upper left corner. This individual follows one of the strategies described above (follow a long wall on the right until a corner), but it does not need to discriminate between short and long walls because it never encounters short walls! This favorable condition is achieved by producing a curvilinear trajectory when far from walls (i.e., when the sensors are all off). The result is that the robot always encounters long walls first.

This evolved strategy clearly exploits environmental constraints (i.e., the fact that the environment has certain dimensions, that individuals start from only 8 different positions, and that long walls are twice the length of short walls). If we test the same individual in a $1200 \times 600$ cm environment, in conditions (e) and (h) the robot actually produces two misses by performing a circular trajectory and never encountering any wall. Similarly, if we test the same individual in a $300 \times 150$ cm environment, in conditions (f) and (g) the robot produces two misses by encountering and following the short walls. In other words,

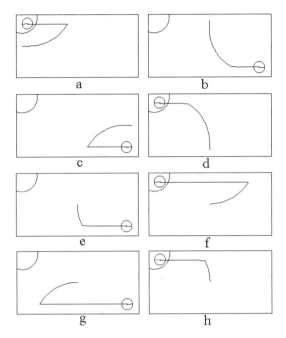

**Figure 5.15**
Behavior of a typical evolved robot. The arcs located in the upper left corner indicate the target area. In conditions (a), (b), (c), and (d) the robot is initially placed along one of the four walls delimiting the arena and is oriented toward the center of the arena itself. In conditions (e), (f), (g), and (h) the robot is initially placed in the center of the environment with four different orientations. The robot ends up four times in the target area and four times in the rotationally equivalent area. Data obtained from a replication of the experiment described in Miglino (1996).

the angular trajectory produced by the evolved robot far from walls exploits the fact that the environment has certain dimensions. This result clarifies the sense in which behavior is the result of the interaction between the robot and the environment. The ability of this robot to get to the target area, or to the rotationally equivalent area, is due both to how the robot reacts to sensory patterns and to the characteristics of the environment (its dimensions, in this case).

This issue takes us to some of the limits of purely reactive agents. These agents can solve relatively complex tasks by developing strategies that exploit environmental constraints. But what happens if some of these features are allowed to vary? In other words, what happens in less constrained environments?

Nolfi (1999) ran two new sets of experiments in which the environmental constraints

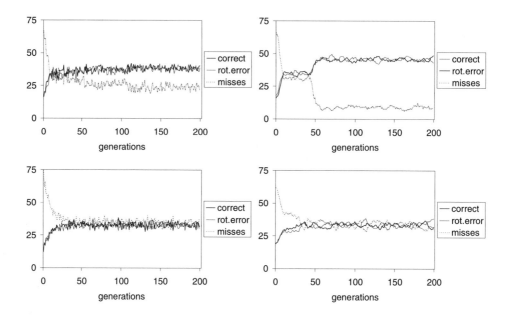

**Figure 5.16**
Performance (i.e., percentage of hits, rotational errors, and misses) throughout generations obtained by testing
the best individual of each generation for 200 different starting positions. **Top:** Results for the experiment in
which starting positions, orientations, and size of the environment varied randomly for each epoch. **Bottom:**
Results for the experiment in which also the proportion between long and short walls varied randomly. **Left:**
Average results of 10 replications. **Right:** Result of the best replication (rolling average over 7 data points).

presented in the previous experiment were progressively relaxed. The aim of these experiments was not to compare the behavior of robots and rats. Therefore, the analysis was
restricted to the case in which the food was located in the upper left corner of the environment. In this situation individuals evolved in the previous experiment reported 4 hits and 4
rotational errors out of 10 replications (see figure 5.15).

   In a first set of new experiments the environment varied in size across epochs for each
individual while maintaining the same proportion (the length of the long walls was always
twise that of the short walls, but the length of short walls was randomly selected for each
epoch and varied between 15 and 45 cm). Moreover, evolved robots were initially placed
in a randomly selected location of the environment with a randomly selected orientation
(instead of being sistematically placed in one of the eight starting positions shown in figure
5.14). In a second set of new experiments, the proportion between the length of short and
long walls varied too (the length of long walls was obtained by multiplying the length of
short walls by a number randomly selected between 1.1 and 2.0).

Evolved individuals display a rather high percentage of misses (25%) in the experiments where the size of the environment varies (figure 5.16, top left). Only in the case of the best replication does the number of misses level out at around 5% after generation 50 (figure 5.16, top right). Notice that, in the control experiment described in figure 5.15, evolved individuals displayed no misses. In the experiment where also the proportion between long and short walls was varied, the number of misses remained at 33% both in the case of average performance and in the case of the best replication (figure 5.16, bottom).

These results show that if we reduce the number of constraints available in the environment the task becomes harder and performance becomes worse (in the case of purely reactive agents). The strategy adopted by the individual displayed in figure 5.15 exploits the fact that the environment has a certain size and that the robot is initially always placed in specific starting positions. If we remove these constraints, evolved individuals will look for other constraints. Exploiting these residual constraints nevertheless appears a harder task given that in only 1 out of 10 replications are evolved individuals able to reach the food area or the rotationally equivalent area most of the times. In the experiment where one more constraint (the fixed proportion between long and short walls) has been removed, performance of evolved individuals decreases even further. The fact that also in the last experiment the number of hits is above the chance level (which is 25%, given that there are four corners) can be explained by considering that even in this experiment the environment may display some constraints. For example, since long walls are longer than short walls, a simple strategy such as "move straight until you meet a wall or your own right side and then follow it until a corner" gives success higher than chance simply because there is higher probability of encountering a long wall.

## 5.6   Discussion

Before closing this chapter we want to discuss the implications of sensory-motor coordination from an engineering point of view.

Most of the research in robotics is based on the attempt to divide the problem of developing a robot capable of performing a certain task into a list of subproblems to be implemented into separate modules of the robot (decomposition), and on the attempt to integrate these modules to solve the entire problem (integration). In the case of behavior-based approaches, for instance, the decomposition is accomplished at the level of behavior. The desired behavior is broken down into a list of simpler basic behaviors which are implemented in separate layers of the control systems and are modulated through a coordination mechanism (on this point see also below).

Within this framework, three different things have to be specified: (a) how to decom-

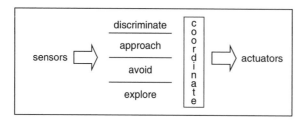

**Figure 5.17**
One possible way to proceed by following the decomposition and integration approach. The desired behavior is
broken down into four basic behaviors that are implemented in separate modules and coordinated through an
additional module or set of priority links.

pose the desired behavior into basic behaviors; (b) how to implement each basic behavior;
(c) how to coordinate the behavioral modules (layers). Several authors have shown how (b)
and (c) (i.e., the layers responsible for simple basic behaviors or the coordination mechanism) can be obtained through a self-organizing process rather than by explicit design (see
Maes 1992; Mahadevan and Connell 1992; Dorigo and Schnepf 1993; Ram et al. 1994;
Urzelai et al. 1998). In all cases, (a)—the decision of how to break the desired behavior
down into simple basic behaviors—is left to the designer. Unfortunately, it is not clear how
a desired behavior should be decomposed and it is difficult to perform an effective decomposition by hand. A distinctive characteristics of evolutionary robotics is that the designer
may be released from the burden of deciding how a desired behavior should be broken
down into basic behaviors. As we will see in the next chapter, evolved robot controllers
might be organised into separate parts or modules where the decomposition is the result of
a self-organization process and not a decision of the experimenter.

To clarify the difficulties of operating a decomposition by hand, let us consider the
problem of building a robot which should avoid walls and remain close to cylindrical
objects (the task described in section 5.4). If we decide to follow the decomposition and
integration approach we have to divide this behavior into a set of simpler basic behaviors.
A reasonable way to decompose the problem is to divide the behavior into four basic
behaviors: (1) move in order to explore the environment; (2) avoid objects; (3) approach
and remain close to an object; (4) discriminate objects. Once we have implemented these
behaviors into separate modules of the control systems we have to design a coordination
mechanism capable of selecting the right module at the right time (see figure 5.17).

Unfortunately, as we know from the results described in section 5.4, one of these basic
behaviors (the ability to discriminate between walls and cylinders) is more complex than
the whole behavior (the ability to avoid walls and to remain close to cylinders). While
the whole desired behavior can be produced by a simple perceptron (see figure 5.9), the

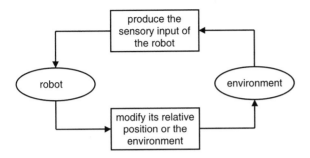

**Figure 5.18**
Behavior can be seen as an emergent result of the dynamical interaction between the robot and the environment. The dynamics arise because the robot, by acting, modifies its relative position with respect to the environment which in turn affects the sensory states experienced by the robot itself. This loop explains why reactive agents, which cannot have internal dynamics, can still produce dynamic behaviors (e.g., back and forth trajectories described in section 5.4).

discrimination behavior, which is supposed to be a subpart of the whole behavior, cannot be solved by such a network (see figure 5.3). Therefore, decomposition does not necessarily produce a simplification of the problem but, on the contrary, may transform the problem into a list of subproblems that are more complex than the original problem itself.

This does not implies that decomposition is always ineffective or counter productive, but that it is far from trivial. We know from section 5.3 that better discrimination between two types of objects can be obtained as an emergent result of the interaction between the robot and the environment, and that in order to obtain such an emergent behavior the discrimination process cannot be separated from approach and avoid behaviors. We would have not known that without running the evolutionary experiments described above.

The fact that a human designer cannot always figure out which is the best way to break a behavior down into basic behaviors is not restricted to this particular task. This difficulty can be explained by considering that the behavior of an autonomous robot is often the emergent result of a dynamical interaction between the robot and the environment (see figure 5.18). This makes it hard to predict the emergent properties of the dynamical interaction, especially when several variables are involved. Therefore, simple forms of sensory-motor coordination that rely on environmental constraints, may be overlooked by human designers concerned with a decomposition and integration approach.

These difficulties also explains why the solutions found through artificial evolution are often qualitatively different from solutions partially or totally handcrafted by human designers. To design a system producing a behavior that relies on the dynamic interaction with the environment, human designers have to predict the form of behavior that will result from the dynamical interaction between a given control system and the environment.

Being such a prediction extremely hard, human designers are generally unable to exploit emergent forms of behavior. This in turn has the consequence that we humans: (a) tend to see only a limited number of ways to solve a problem, and (b) tend to build robots that solve problems by relying mostly on internal mechanisms (robots which are rather complex in their control systems and body structure). In the case of evolution instead, different forms of emergent behavior are spontaneously produced by introducing random changes into individuals' offspring. As a consequence, artificial evolution: (a) tends to produce a variety of different solutions for a single problem, and (b) tends to select solutions that rely on emergent behavior resulting from the interaction between the robot and the environment, and less on internal mechanisms (i.e., robots that are rather simple in their control systems and, if also the body structure can be changed evolutionarily, robots that have rather simple body structures).

As we claimed in the first chapter, to better understand this point we have to distinguish between a proximal description of behavior (i.e., a description from the point of view of the agent's sensorimotor system indicating how the agent reacts to different sensory states) and a distal description of behavior (i.e., a description from the observer's point of view where high level terms such as "approach" or "discriminate" are used to describe the result of a sequence of sensorimotor loops). The behavior from a distal description point of view is the emergent result of the interaction between the behavior from a proximal description point of view and the environment (see figure 1.5). In decomposing a behavior into basic behaviors the designer operates at the level of the distal description of behavior. However, since there is not a one-to-one mapping between subcomponents of the agent's control system and subcomponents of the corresponding behavior from the point of view of the distal description, decompositions that appear to produce a simplification of the problem at the level of the distal description of behavior might result ineffective and even counter productive at the level of the proximal description of behavior.

## 5.7   Conclusions

We have presented a set of experiments showing that rather complex tasks can be solved by exploiting sensory-motor coordination. In particular, we have shown that agents can use sensory-motor coordination to: (a) select sensory patterns which are not affected by the aliasing problem and avoid those that are (section 5.2); (b) select sensory patterns for which groups of patterns requiring different answers do not overlap too much (section 5.3); (c) exploit behavioral attractors resulting from the interaction between the robot and the environment (section 5.4). More generally we have seen how agents can exploit the constraints present in the environment by using sensory-motor coordination. A consequence of this is that progressively reducing the number of constraints available in the environment makes a task harder and harder until a point is reached where a purely reactive agent is unable to solve it. In these circumstances pure sensory-motor agents show their limitations.

# 6 Beyond reactive intelligence

## 6.1 Introduction

In the previous chapter we have presented a set of experiments involving reactive robots controlled by simple neural networks (i.e., fully connected perceptrons without internal layers and without any form of internal organization). As we have seen, these robots can display not only simple behaviors, such as obstacle avoidance, but also behaviors capable of solving complex problems involving perceptual aliasing, sensory ambiguity, and sequential organization of sub-behaviors. Those examples have been included to show the power, but also the limits, of reactive sensory-motor coordination. In this chapter we will describe two experimental situations that can only be solved by robots allowed to exploit modular architectures and/or internal dynamical states.

In section 6.2 we shall describe a garbage collection task and see that in this case modular neural controllers outperform simple non modular ones. By comparing different types of architectures, we shall show that the best results can be obtained using an emergent modular architecture, that is an architecture where what a module stands for is not predetermined by the experimenter, but is the result of an evolutionary process. Moreover, by analyzing the internal organization of evolved individuals, we will see that there is not a one-to-one correspondence between architectural modules and basic behaviors (elementary components of a global behavior derived from a distal description).

In section 6.3 we shall describe evolution of homing navigation where a robot is asked to navigate in an arena with a limited, but rechargeable, energy supply. The abilities to locate a battery charger and periodically return to it are achieved without introducing explicit indications in the fitness function. Evolved homing strategies are based on autonomous development of an internal neural topographic map (that was not predesigned) allowing the robot to choose appropriate trajectories as function of location and remaining energy.

Finally, in section 6.4 we shall discuss the implications of these experiments from the point of view of the emergence of complex behaviors.

## 6.2 Investigating the role of modularity

Modularity is an integral part of the decomposition and integration approach. The desired behavior is broken down into a set of basic behaviors, or reflexes (such as "approach" or "avoid"), that are correspondingly allocated to a set of components (modules) of the controller.

Instead, in an evolutionary approach this use of modularity is not mandatory. As we

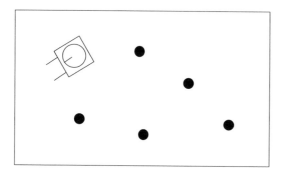

**Figure 6.1**
The robot and environment for the garbage collecting experiment. Lines represent the walls of the arena. Full circles represent the target objects. The empty circle and the rectangle represent the Khepera robot with the gripper module.

have shown in section 5.4, a monolithic control system can produce a global behavior that would normally be decomposed into a set of basic behaviors (in that case, explore the environment, avoid walls, approach and remain close to cylinders).

Should we expect that behaviors of any complexity can be produced by homogeneous non modular controllers or rather suspect that architectural modularity may be beneficial for certain tasks? And, assuming that we evolve modular controllers but let the evolutionary process free to determine the functionality of each different modules, will architectural modules correspond to basic behaviors? In the next subsections we shall present a set of experiments aimed at answering these questions.

**Evolving a garbage collection robot**

Consider the case of a Khepera robot placed in an arena surrounded by walls; the robot is expected to keep the arena clean by removing the objects contained in it (Nolfi 1997a, 1997b). The robot is provided with a gripper module with two degrees of freedom. The arm of the gripper can move through any angle from vertical to horizontal while the gripper can assume only the open or closed position (see figure 3.4).

The environment is a rectangular arena $60 \times 35$ cm surrounded by walls containing 5 target objects (garbage). The walls were 3 cm in height, made of wood, and covered with white paper. Target objects consisted of cylinders with a diameter of 2.3 cm and a height of 3 cm. They were made of cardboard and covered with white paper. Targets were positioned randomly inside the arena.

To keep the arena clean, the robot must look for garbage, grasp it, and release it outside the arena. The whole task involves a rather long sequence of subtasks: (a) explore the environment, avoiding walls; (b) recognize a target object and move to an angle and

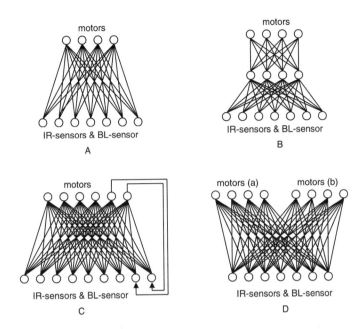

**Figure 6.2**
Four different control architectures: (A) a standard feedforward architecture; (B) an architecture with an internal layer of hidden units; (C) a recurrent architecture; (D) a modular architecture with two pre-designed modules.

distance from where the object can be grasped; (c) pick up the target object; (d) move toward the walls while avoiding other target objects; (e) recognize a wall and move at an angle and distance from where the object can be safely dropped outside the arena; (g) release the object. Each of these subtasks can be further broken down into a sequence of simpler components. For example (a) may be broken down into: ($a_1$) go forward when sensors are not activated, and ($a_2$) turn left at a given speed when right sensors are activated, etc.

To assess the role of modularity we tried several different network architectures. All architectures had 7 sensory neurons and 4 motor neurons although they differed in their internal organization. The first 6 sensory neurons were used to encode the activation level of the corresponding 6 front infrared sensors, while the seventh sensory neuron was used to encode the light barrier sensor on the gripper. This latter sensor becomes active whenever an object is detected within the two segments of the gripper. Four motor neurons respectively coded for the speeds of left and right motors and for the triggering of *object pick up* and *object release* procedures (see below).

The simplest architecture used was a 2 layers feedforward neural network (figure

6.2A). The second architecture was also a feedforward neural network, but had an internal layer of four units (figure 6.2B). We then tried a recurrent architecture (Elman style) in which the activation levels of two additional output units were copied back into two additional input units (figure 6.2C). Finally, we tried two modular architectures. These were networks in which different parts or modules could assume control in different sensory situations. The first modular architecture (figure 6.2D) had two modules for which the corresponding behavior was predetermined by the designer. The first module (the sub-network on the left) assumed control when the gripper was empty; therefore, it was responsible for the ability to avoid walls, find a target, and pick it up correctly. The second module (the sub-network on the right) assumed control when the gripper was carrying a target; therefore it was responsible for the ability to avoid other targets, find a wall, stop in front of it, and release the target. The partition of the required behavior into these two basic behaviors and into the corresponding neural modules was arbitrary. It appeared a reasonable choice given that the robot was expected to perform two very different behaviors depending on the state of the gripper. Instead, the second modular architecture (figure 6.3), called *emergent modular architecture*, did not require the designer to do such a partition in advance. The designer had to decide the number of available neural modules (in this case two for each motor output), the architecture of each module, and the arbitration mechanisms. However, the number of modules actually used by the controller, the combination of modules used each time step, and the weights of the modules themselves were evolved while the robot interacted with the environment. Consequently, the decomposition of the global behavior into basic behaviors and their allocation to different architectural modules were completely emergent.

The emergent modular architecture considered here had 2 modules for each of the four previously described effectors (left motor, right motor, pick up, release). A module was composed of two output units fully connected to the sensory units. The first output neuron determined the state of the corresponding effector when the module was in control, while the second output neuron (selector) competed with the selector neuron of the other module in charge of the same effector in order to determine which of the two modules assumes control at a given instant. A similar architecture has been proposed by Jacobs and Jordan (1991). The synaptic weights of these five different architectures were separately evolved and compared.[1]

The activation of the sensors and the state of the motors were updated every 100 milliseconds. However, when the activation level of the object pick up or of the object release neurons reached a given threshold, a sequence of actions occurred that required up to three seconds to complete (pick up procedure: move a little further back, close the gripper, move the arm up; release procedure: move the arm down, open the gripper, and move the arm up again).[2]

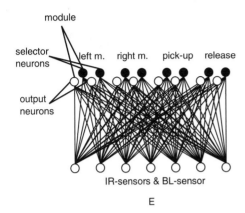

**Figure 6.3**
The emergent modular architecture (E).

The evolutionary process was carried out in simulation using the sampling technique described in chapter 3. Robots were scored by counting the number of objects correctly released outside the arena. In order to facilitate the evolutionary process, individuals were also scored—with much lower fitness values—for their ability to pick up targets. In addition, it was found important to expose the robots to useful training experiences (that is, to artificially increase the number of times the robot encountered a cylindrical object while carrying another object) in order to help the evolutionary process select individuals capable of avoiding objects when the gripper was full. This was accomplished by artificially positioning a new target object in the frontal area of the robot each time the gripper was filled (we will come back to this point in section 6.4).

This task presents several forms of complexity. In order to decide when to activate the pick up or release procedure, the robot should be capable of discriminating target objects from walls. Given that the pick up and release procedures last only a single step (i.e., no additional spreading of activation occur until the procedures ends), this decision must be taken on the basis of a single sensory state. This means that the robot cannot rely on emergent forms of behavior similar to those described in section 5.3 where discrimination is achieved through a sequence of motor actions. Neither can it rely on sensory-motor strategies that select sensory states which can be easily told apart, as in the case of the experiments described in section 5.2. In this case in fact, to correctly pick up or release objets, the robot should discriminate the two objects from its frontal side.[3] The discrimination task is further complicated by the fact that the robot should produce quite different responses for similar sensory states. Not only the robot should react differently for sensory states corresponding to walls and targets that largely overlap. The robot should also react quite differently to identical values of the infrared sensors depending on the state of the light barrier sensor: when the sensor is on, it should avoid objects, when it is off it should approach them, and the converse for walls.

Another form of complexity is due to the fact that this task requires the robot to perform a long sequence of different sub-behaviors. These are: (a) explore the environment avoiding the walls; (b) recognize a target object and move to a relative angle and distance so that it can be grasped; (c) pick up the target object; (d) move toward the walls while avoiding other target objects; (e) recognize a wall and move to a relative angle and distance so that the object can be safely dropped outside the arena; (g) release the object. We have already shown in the previous chapter that a simple perceptron, where sensors are directly linked to motors, can produce a sequence of different behaviors such as (i) explore the environment avoiding the walls, and (ii) recognize a target object and remain close to it. However, one may expect that the longer the sequence of behavior is the less the probability that a simple controller will succeed.

Therefore this task is particularly well suited to investigate: (a) the role of internal units (e.g. an internal layer of units which can be used to recode the sensory states so to enhance the differences between states requiring different answers); (b) the role of internal dynamics (internal units with recurrent connections that may allow a robot to react differently to the same sensory state depending on the previously experienced sensory states); (c) the role of modularity (the possibility to divide the sensory states in subgroups to be processed by different neural modules).

**Emergent modularity accelerates evolution and allows the development of more robust controllers**

If we measure the average number of epochs (out of 15) where individuals correctly pick up and release a target outside the arena for simulations with different architectures, we can see that the ability to accomplish the correct sequence of behaviors evolves in all conditions (see figure 6.4). Remember that an epoch is terminated after 200 actions or after an object has been correctly released. Therefore, the largest number of targets that could be released outside the arena is equal to the maximum number of epochs (15). However, individuals evolved with different architectures vary in performance at the end of evolutionary training and in the time needed to reach their maximum performance. If we look at performance of generation 999 we can see that all types of architectures have reached relatively high performances with the exception of the simple feedforward architectures (A). On the opposite end, emergent modular architectures begin to outperform all other architectures after a few generations, and maintain a large difference until generation 500. A one way ANOVA test (analysis of variance) of performance in the five different conditions was performed each 100 generations. The results show that performance in condition E

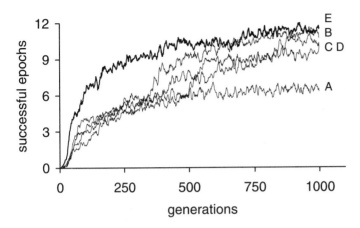

**Figure 6.4**
Number of epochs (out of 15) in which individuals with different architectures correctly picked up and released a target object throughout generations. Each curve represents the average performance of the best individuals from 10 different replications. Data smoothed by calculating rolling averages over preceding and succeeding three generations. A,B,C,D,E indicate the five different architectures described in figures 6.2 and 6.3.

(emergent modular) is significantly higher than in the other four conditions at generation 199 and performance in condition A (perceptron) is significantly lower than the other four conditions at generation 999 ($p < 0.05$).

By downloading the best controllers of generation 999 (from each of 10 replications of the simulation) into the robot and testing them in the real environment with 5 objects for 5000 sensory-motor cycles, we observe that architecture (E) outperforms all other architectures (figure 12). The best individuals of 7 (out of 10 simulations) with the emergent modular architecture were capable of cleaning the arena without displaying any incorrect behavior while only 1 or 2 individuals (out of 10) with other architectures were capable of accomplishing the task.

These results indicate that the emergent modular architecture (E) enables the evolutionary process to find a correct solution to the task earlier than other architectures and, in particular, earlier than the handcrafted modular architecture (D). Physical tests of controllers evolved in simulations indicate that emergent modular architectures allow evolution to develop more robust controllers, i.e., controllers displaying only limited performance loss when transferred into the real robot.

**There is no correspondence between evolved modules and distal behaviors**

Let us now turn to the second question mentioned at the beginning of this section: Can we find in evolved individuals a correspondence between distal behaviors (e.g. look for a

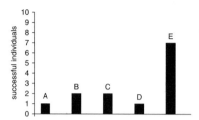

**Figure 6.5**
Number of evolved individuals for each type of control architecture capable of correctly picking up and then releasing outside the arena the five targets objects within 5000 cycles without displaying incorrect behavior (crashing into walls, trying to grasp a wall, or trying to release a target over another target). A,B,C,D,E indicate the five different architectures described in figures 6.2 and 6.3.

target while avoiding walls; look for a wall while avoiding targets; etc.) and neural modules for architecture E?

The analysis of evolved controllers gives a negative answer. Figure 6.6 displays the behavior of a typical evolved individual. Individuals with emergent modular architecture have two different modules for each of the four motor outputs and therefore can use up to $2^4 = 16$ different combinations of neural modules. However, if one of the two competing modules of a given effector never wins the competition, the number of functional neural modules and of combinations of neural modules actually used can be lower. The evolved individual described in figure 6.6 (one of the most successful) uses only one of the two neural modules for the left motor, the pick up procedure, and the release procedure (LM, PU, and RL), and it uses both modules only for the right motor (RM). In this individual therefore, only two different combinations of neural modules are in charge in different moments (which of the two neural modules is on at each time step is indicated by the "mod" graph of figure 6.6). It is interesting to note that those two modules competing for the control of the right motor are both used throughout the whole sequence of basic behaviors (see graphs a–h of figure 6.6): (a) when the gripper is carrying a target and the robot has to look for a wall (sensor LB is on); (b) when the gripper is empty and the robot has to look for a target (sensor LB is off); (c) when the robot perceives something and has to disambiguate between walls and targets (W/T graph shows upper or bottom line); (d) when the robot does not perceive anything (W/T graph does not show any line); (e) when the robot is approaching a target (when sensor LB is off and the perceived object is a target); (f) when the robot is approaching a wall (sensor LB is on and perceived object is a wall); (g) when the robot is avoiding a target (sensor LB is on and perceived object is a target); (h) when the robot is avoiding a wall (sensor LB is off and perceived object is a wall). For a systematic analysis of the relation between neural modules and distal behaviors in these experiments see Calabretta et. al. (1998).

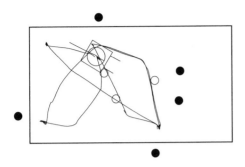

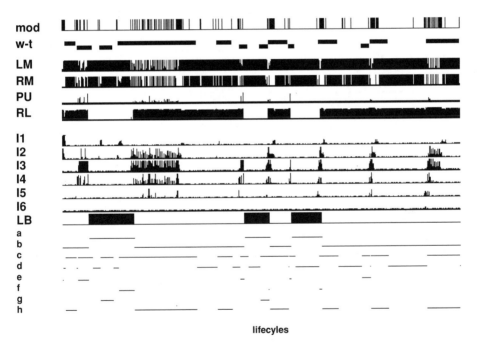

**Figure 6.6**
The top of the figure represents the behavior of a typical evolved individual in its environment. Lines represent walls, empty and full circles represent the original and final position of the target objects respectively, the trace on the terrain represents the trajectory of the robot. The bottom part of the figure represents the type of object currently perceived (w on top = wall; t on bottom = target; nothing = no object), the states of the motors, and the states of the sensors for 500 cycles. The "mod" graph indicates whether the first or the second module controlling the right motor has control (white = module 1, black = module 2). In the case of the remaining three effectors, always the same module has control. The "LM", "RM", "PU", and "RL" graphs show the state of the motors (left and right motors, pick-up and release procedures, respectively). The graphs "i1" to "i6" show the state of the six infrared sensors. The "LB" graph shows the state of the light-barrier sensor. Finally, a–h graphs display different distal behaviors (see text). The activation state of sensor and motor neurons is represented by the height with respect to the baseline (in the case of motor neurons, only the activation state of the competing winning neuron is shown).

As we pointed out in the previous chapter, the decomposition of a behavior into a list of basic behaviors from a distal description point of view can be accomplished in many different ways. Whatever is the way in which we divided a behavior into a list of distal sub-behavior, however, sensory-motor loops that are close in time tend to belong to the same sub-behavior. The fact that in evolved individuals, such as the individual shown in figure 6.6 the arbitration tends to produce a rapid switching between competing modules demonstrates that in these experiments competing modules do not tend to be responsible for different distal behaviors independently from how sub-behaviors have been identified.

Similar results can be obtained by analyzing other evolved individuals. When many competing neural modules are involved it becomes difficult to understand what is going on. However, the general picture remains the same: neural modules, or combinations of neural modules, do not correspond to sub-behaviors described from a distal perspective. On the contrary, different modules contribute to the implementation of different distal sub-behaviors.

To understand the function of neural modules in these evolved individuals we should abandon the perspective of distal behaviors and concentrate on a proximal perspective. By looking at the way in which individuals respond to different sensory patterns, it appears that one of the main functions of module arbitration is to produce different motor responses for similar sensory states when necessary. Different neural modules, in fact, tend to alternate especially when the robot has an object on its front side and must decide whether to approach, avoid, or try to pick it up. This is the case, for example, of the individual described in figure 6.6.

That modularity is used to produce sharp discontinuities in behavior can be demonstrated by comparing individuals with different architectures for their ability to discriminate between targets and walls by triggering the picking up or the releasing procedures in the right environmental circumstances. Figure 6.7 shows the result of a test in which the best individuals of the last generation are placed at 180 different angles and 20 different distances in front of target and walls with the gripper full or empty (for a total of 14.400 different robot/environmental states). As it can be seen, individuals with the simple perceptron architecture correctly pick up and release targets from a large number of positions; however, they also produce a large number of errors triggering the two procedures at incorrect positions. Instead, individuals with the other architectures are more selective, i.e. they trigger the two procedures in a smaller number cases, but they also produce significantly less errors. In particular, architecture (B) and (E) are those that produce the lower number of errors on the average.[4] In addition, in the case of architecture (B) and (E) two individuals out of 10 never produce discrimination errors while all individuals with architecture (A) and (D) always produce some errors. It is important to notice that the fact that individuals produce errors when tested in all possible positions does not implies that they produce

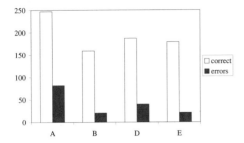

**Figure 6.7**
Number of relative positions from which evolved individuals trigger the pick-up and release procedures. White histograms represent the number of correct decisions (i.e., the number of times in which individuals trigger the pick-up procedure in front of a target and trigger the release procedure in front of a wall). Black histograms represents the number of incorrect decisions (i.e., the number of times in which individuals trigger the pick-up procedure in front of a wall and trigger the release procedure in front of a target). Average results of the best individuals of generation 999 for 10 replications. (A), (B), (D), and (E) refers to the experiments with the corresponding architectures described in figures 6.2 and 6.3.

errors when they freely interact with the environment. In that case, in fact, not all positions are experienced. As we will see below, individuals can self-select the experienced sensory patterns so to avoid positions from where they would produce discrimination errors.

Emergent modules therefore do not seem to be used to produce different sequences of sensory-motor loops (i.e., different sub-behaviors). Rather, one of the main function of neural modules is to enhance the ability to discriminate between different objects (a similar outcome, as we saw above, is obtained by providing an internal layer of neurons). This ability however, as all other distal behaviors, result from the contribution of different neural modules.

It should be noted that the results described in figure 6.7 (in particular the results obtained with architecture (B)) contrast with the results described in section 5.3 in which we showed how networks with an internal layer which was trained by back-propagation produced about 65% of errors when asked to discriminate between walls and targets. Both in the case of the experiments described in the previous chapter and in the case of the experiment described above in fact, networks are asked to produce the correct discrimination on the basis of the current sensory state only. The fact that these evolved networks are able to produce much better performance on the average and 100% correct performance in 2 replications out of 10 can be explained by considering that these networks are not required to produce a discrimination action for all sensory states. In other words, these individuals are allowed to select a subset of sensory states to be discriminated.

Figure 6.8 shows the relative positions from which one evolved individual with the emergent modular architecture responds by triggering the picking up or the releasing

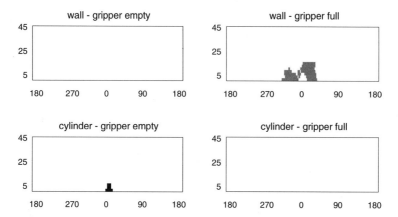

**Figure 6.8**
Relative positions from which an evolved individual responds by triggering the pick-up or the release procedures (black and gray areas, respectively). **Top:** The individual is close to a wall. **Bottom:** The individual is close to a cylinder. **Left:** The individual has the gripper empty. **Right:** The individual is carrying a cylinder with its gripper. Results for an individual with the emergent modular architecture placed at 180 different angles and 20 different distances (ranging from 5 to 45 mm) in the four different conditions described above.

procedures (black and gray areas respectively). This is one of the two individuals who never produce discrimination errors (i.e., it never triggers the picking up procedure in front of a wall or the releasing procedure in front of a target). This individual, however, picks up cylinders only when they are slightly on its right side. Moreover, it does not release the carried object if it has a wall on its frontal side, but only if the wall is slightly on the left or on the right side.

If we look at another evolved individual with the emergent modular architecture (E) we see that it produces some discrimination errors (see figure 6.9). By testing this individual in all possible positions with respect to the two objects, we can see that responds by triggering the releasing procedure not only when it is facing a wall (top right graph of figure 6.9) but also, erroneously, when it is facing a cylinder at about $45^o$ on the right side (bottom right graph of figure 6.9). Despite of that, this individual apparently displays a perfectly correct behavior in natural circumstances (i.e., when it is left free to move in the environment). The reason for that is that this individual it is very unlikely to experience those states that may trigger incorrect responses. Figure 6.10 shows the states experienced by this individual during 100 epochs in which the robot was placed in a randomly selected position of the environment and left free to collect cylinders for 500 cycles. As can be seen, these individual experienced about one half of all the possible environmental states. However, it never experienced a cylinder at about $45^o$ on its right side and at a short distance (i.e., it never experienced the sensory states from which it produces wrong responses).

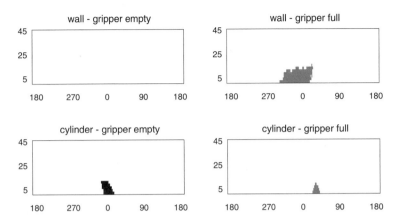

**Figure 6.9**
Relative positions from which an evolved individual responds by triggering the pick-up or the release procedures
(black and gray area respectively). This individual correctly triggers the pick-up procedure in front of a cylinder
when the gripper is empty (bottom-left graph) and the release procedure in front of a wall when the gripper is
full (top-right graph). However it also erroneously triggers the release procedure with a cylinder slightly on its
right side (bottom-right graph).

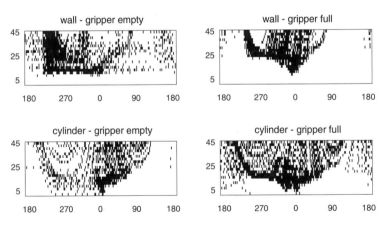

**Figure 6.10**
Environmental states experienced by the same individual described in Figure 6.9. The relative positions
displayed in black represent robot/environmental states experienced by the individual at least once. Area
displayed in white represents robot/environmental states never experienced by the individual. Data obtained by
testing the evolved individual for 100 epochs lasting 500 cycles each. At the beginning of each epoch the robot
is place in a randomly selected location of the environment which is replenished with five targets randomly
distributed. One can see that the robot never happens to go those positions from where it could make an error
(compare with figure 6.9).

As we stressed in the previous chapter, robots partially determine the sensory patterns they receive from the environment and can exploit this ability for different purposes. Here we see another potential function of sensory-motor coordination. Robots can use sensory-motor coordination to increase the frequency of environmental states that can be tackled effectively and reduce the frequency of environmental states that cause erroneous reactions (for a systematic analysis of this function of sensory-motor coordination see Nolfi and Parisi 1993b).

**Discussion**

In section 5.8 we claimed that the main problem of the decomposition and integration approach is that the decision of how to break a desired behavior down into simple component behaviors is left to the designer and that, unfortunately, it is not clear how such a decomposition should be made. We showed that such decomposition may result into component behaviors (e.g., discriminating between walls and targets) whose implementation may be more difficult than the global behavior (finding and remaining close to a cylinder while avoiding walls).

To investigate the role of modularity, we introduced an architecture denoted as *emergent modular architecture* where two or more alternative neural modules compete for control of each motor output. This architecture allows evolving individuals to use different neural modules to produce different sub-behaviors, but releases the designer from the burden to decide how the whole behavior should be broken down. Moreover, it allows artificial evolution to select both how a desired behavior should be broken down into sub-behaviors corresponding to different neural modules and how each neural module should produce the sub-behavior for which it is responsible. Artificial evolution of robots with emergent modular architectures reported better results than all other architectures, including a modular architecture where the breakdown of the required behavior into component behaviors had been handcrafted. Moreover, analysis of evolved individuals showed that there is no one-to-one correspondence between evolved modules and distal description of behaviors. In evolved individuals with emergent modular architectures the sequence of sensory-motor loops that may be described as component behaviors from a distal perspective is the result of the contribution of different neural modules. These results suggest that the engineering oriented approach based on decomposition and integration can have serious limitations in the case of behavioral systems (such as mobile robots) where the observed behavior is the result of the dynamical interaction between the robot and the environment.

The fact that the individuals described in this chapter rely on internal mechanisms (e.g. neural modules which process different sets of sensory patterns) does not implies, however, that these individuals do not exploit sensory-motor coordination. As we have shown in the previous section, in fact, these individuals act so to avoid the sensory states to which they are not able to react effectively. Sensory-motor coordination and internal mechanisms can coexist and cooperate. In other words, sensory-motor coordination can play a role even in individuals that have complex internal mechanisms.

## 6.3   Robots with an internal dynamics

Another way to enrich the computational power of a neural controller is to provide it with recurrent connections. This type of networks might take into account previously experienced sensory states and therefore might react differently to the same sensory states. Therefore, these robots might display internal dynamics.

Floreano and Mondada (1996b) run a set of experiments where a Khepera robot equipped with limited—but rechargeable—energy was asked to navigate in an arena. The environment included a battery charger illuminated by a light source where the robot could replenish its own energy supply. Although the fitness function did not specify the location of the battery station or the fact that the robot should reach it, the robot evolved the ability to find and to periodically return to the charging station while exploring the area. This emergent homing behavior, as we will see, is based on the autonomous development of an internal neural topographic map (that was not predesigned) allowing the robot to choose the appropriate trajectory as a function of its own location and of remaining energy.

The environment consisted of a $40 \times 45$ cm arena delimited by walls of lightblue polystyrene and the floor was made of thick gray paper (see figure 6.11). A 25 cm high tower equipped with 15 small DC lamps oriented toward the arena was placed in one corner. The room did not have other light sources. Under the light tower, a circular portion of the floor at the corner was painted black. The painted sector, that represented the recharging area, had a radius of approximately 8 cm and was intended to simulate the platform of a prototype of battery charger under construction at the Microcomputing Laboratory of the Swiss Federal Institute of Technology. When the robot happened to be over the black area, its simulated battery became instantaneously recharged.[5]

Khepera was equipped with its basic set of eight infrared sensors. Two among these sensors, one on the front and one on the back, were also enabled for measuring ambient light. Additionally, another infrared sensor was placed under the robot platform, pointing downward. Its signal value was thresholded so that it returned always 1, except when over the black painted area in the corner (figure 6.12). The robot was provided with a simulated battery characterized by a fast linear discharge rate and a maximum duration of 20 seconds, and with a simulated sensor providing information about the battery status. The reason why we simulated the battery and the battery charger, rather than using the hardware available, was evolutionary time. Considering that the built in battery lasts about 40 minutes and it

**Figure 6.11**
The environment of the experiment on battery recharge. The light tower is positioned in the far corner over the recharging area which is painted black. There are no other light sources in the room.

requires further 30 minutes for a full recharge, a complete evolutionary run with the same parameters used here would have taken something like 6 years, whereas our experiment lasted only 10 days.

The neural network controlling the robot was a multi layer perceptron of continuous sigmoid units (figure 6.13). The hidden layer consisted of 5 units with recurrent connections (Elman 1990). We did not attempt to optimize the number of units required and the pattern of connectivity. Each individual started with a fully charged battery which was discharged by a fixed amount at each time step: a fully charged battery allowed a robot to move for 50 time steps (20 seconds). If the robot happened to pass over the black area the battery was instantaneously recharged and consequently its life was prolonged. An upper limit of 150 steps (60 seconds) was allowed for each individual, in order to eventually terminate the life of robots that kept sitting on the recharging area or that regularly passed over it.

Each individual was evaluated according to a simplified version of the fitness function used in the experiment on navigation and obstacle avoidance described in section 4.2. Indeed one of the goal of this new experiment was to test the hypothesis that, when

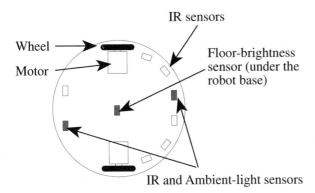

IR sensors

Wheel

Motor

Floor-brightness
sensor (under the
robot base)

IR and Ambient-light sensors

**Figure 6.12**
Sensory-motor layout of the Khepera robot used in the battery recharge experiment.

employing an evolutionary procedure, more complex behaviors do not necessarily have
to be specified in the objective fitness function, but rather emerge from a mere change of
the physical characteristics of the robot and of the environment. More precisely, we were
interested in observing whether the robot discovered the presence of a place where it could
recharge its (simulated) batteries and modify its global behavior by using an even simpler
version of the fitness function employed in the previous experiment described in chapter 4.
The fitness criterion $\Phi$ was a function of two variables directly measured on the robot at
each time step, as follows,

$$\Phi = V(1 - i) \tag{6.1}$$
$$0 \leq V \leq 1$$
$$0 \leq i \leq 1$$

where $V$ is a measure of the average rotation speed of the two wheels and $i$ is the
activation value of the proximity sensor with the highest activity. The function $\Phi$ has two
components: the first one is maximized by speed and the second by obstacle avoidance.
With respect to the experiment described in chapter 4, the component responsible for
straight motion has been removed: thus a robot could achieve a reasonable performance
even by simply spinning in a place far from the walls. The fitness value was computed
and accumulated at each step, except when the robot was on the black area (although later
observations showed that the fitness function itself yielded values extremely close to 0
when the robot was on the black area).[6] The accumulated fitness value of each individual
(which depended both on the performance of the robot and on the length of its life) was then

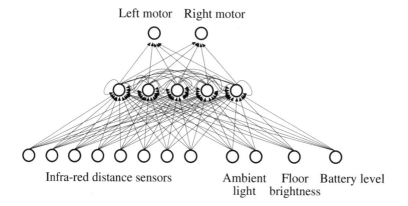

Left motor   Right motor

Infra-red distance sensors          Ambient   Floor   Battery level
                                    light   brightness

**Figure 6.13**
The neural network. The input layer consists of twelve receptors, each clamped to one sensor (8 for infrared emitted light, 2 for ambient light, 1 for floor brightness, and 1 for battery charge) and fully connected to five hidden units. A set of recurrent connections (Elman, 1990) are added to the hidden units. The hidden units are fully connected to two motor neurons, each controlling the speed of rotation of the corresponding wheel.

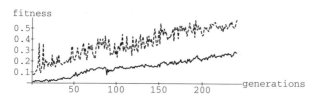

**Figure 6.14**
Average population fitness (continuous line) and fitness of the best individual (dotted line) at each generation. Theoretical values of 1 could not be practically reached; empirical calculations based upon the maximum feasible speed and the characteristics of the environment give a maximum achievable fitness of 0.7.

divided by the maximum number of steps (150) and stored away for the genetic operators.[7]

## Results

The evolutionary procedure was carried out entirely on the physical robot without human intervention. The Khepera was left in a dark room lit only by the small light tower for the next 10 days (each generation, initially lasting approx. 45 minutes, took increasingly longer time as the individuals started to locate the recharging area). From time to time somebody went into the room to replace some of the small light bulbs, but evolution was never stopped. Both the population average fitness and the fitness of the best individual steadily increased along the corresponding 240 generations (see figure 6.14).

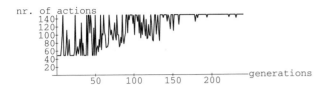

**Figure 6.15**
Number of actions during life for the best individual at each generation. 50 actions (approximately 20 seconds) represent the minimum life length because each individual starts with a full battery. If an individual performs more than 150 actions, its life is automatically truncated and the next individual is evaluated.

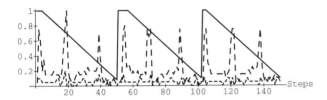

**Figure 6.16**
Battery level (continuous line) and motor activities (dotted lines) during the life of the best individual of the last generation. The robot starts on the recharging area facing the light. Motor activity 0.5 means stasis, activity 0 corresponds to backward max. speed, activity 1 to forward max. speed. Spikes in only one motor activity indicate fast turning in place. Most of the time the robot moves backward at nearly maximum speed.

The increasing number of actions performed by the best individuals at each generation (figure 6.15) suggests that the robot gradually "learned" to pass over the recharging zone. The combined data of the best fitness values and of the corresponding life durations showed that, mainly in the last 90 generations, the individuals increased their own life duration and spent shorter periods of time over the recharging area (recall that no fitness value is given while the robot is over the recharging area).

**Neuro-ethological analysis**

In order to understand the behavior and mechanisms evolved by the best individual of the last generation, the authors resorted to a method of analysis traditionally employed by ethologists and neurophysiologists. The robot was put in a number of different situations and let free to move while its internal (battery charge and neuron activations) and external (position, sensor activations, motor activations) variables were recorded and correlated. For this purpose, Khepera was fitted with an additional module for measuring its absolute position (see figure 3.5). The measuring device was synchronized with the neural network activation loops (one measure every 380 ms).

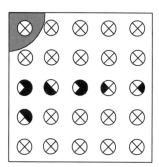

**Figure 6.17**
Map of success/failures to reach the recharging area for each starting location and direction. Each sector in the circles indicates a different initial orientation; the circles correspond to the robot circumference. Black sectors correspond to starting orientations/locations from where the robot missed the recharging area after a full path (most of the misses were within a few millimeters, the largest was 3 cm).

In the first test the robot was placed in the recharging area and left free to move. In the meantime, the battery level and motor activities of the robot were recorded (figure 6.16). The robot rapidly moved out of the recharging area where it returned only when its battery level was about 0.1 (that means about less than two seconds before a complete discharge, or approx. 5 steps). The robot was always extremely precise in timing its return to the recharging area, as it can be seen by the regularity of the peaks in the line corresponding to the battery level. The period of time spent over the recharging area was reduced to a minimum necessary to turn on itself and move out, as documented by the sharp increment of activity difference between the two motors in correspondence of the full charge level. The robot displayed a preferential direction of motion (see figure 6.16) although the sharpest turns in correspondence of the walls were performed by full acceleration of one wheel and full inversion of the other (thus turning in place). Most of the time the robot moved at nearly full speed along a slightly bended trajectory, and it always turned to the right when a wall was encountered.

Once the robot had found the recharging zone, without regard to the starting position in the arena, it always managed to return there a very large number of times, without necessarily performing always the same trajectories. However, the robot did not find the recharging zone in the first place from a few starting positions and orientations in the arena (figure 6.17). It should be noted that the robot could indeed reach the recharging area from these locations if it was already moving: in fact, due to the recurrent connections on the hidden nodes, the same sensory information may yield different actions depending upon the previous history of the individual.

In another series of tests we positioned the robot at various locations and left it free

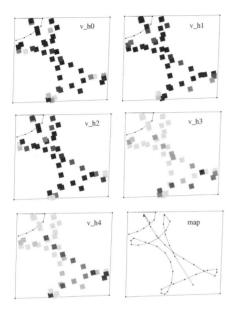

**Figure 6.18**
Visualization of the hidden node activations while the robot moves in normal conditions. Each node is plotted on a separate window. The bottom-right window plots only the trajectory. Darker squares mean higher node activation. The robot starts in the lower portion of the arena. The recharging area is visible in the top left corner of each window.

to move while we recorded its position and the corresponding activations of the hidden nodes (figure 6.18) every 380 ms. Hidden nodes were labelled as v_h0, v_h1, v_h2, v_h3, and v_h4. These measures revealed a non stereotypical behavior and very complex internal processing. Most of the time the robot performed long nearly straight trajectories across the arena until it arrived very close to a wall, where it performed a sharp turn. Although the trajectories were very different even when the robot started from the same location because of noise in the sensors, friction against the floor and sometimes against the walls, and internal recurrent states, it generally performed 3 or 4 turns before moving toward the recharging area. In order to understand the strategies employed for homing, we performed an analogous test with the light tower switched off (figure 6.19).

By comparing the behaviors in the two conditions (light on and light off), it becomes apparent that in both cases the robot relies on a set of semi-automatic procedures to perform the turns at the walls and the semi-linear trajectories (although they are more curved when the light is off). However, when the battery reaches a critical level, a somehow different behavioral strategy takes control trying to correct the trajectory in order to reach the

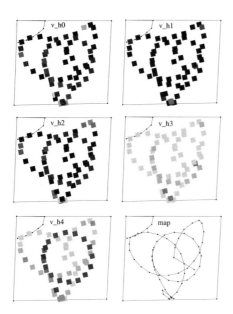

**Figure 6.19**
Visualization of the hidden node activations while the robot moves when the light tower is switched off. The robot starts approximately in the center of the arena and ends up in circular trajectory during the last 18 steps.

recharging area by using a combination of local light gradient and memory of previous trajectory (the light gradient is available through the robot sensors only in a very narrow stripe at the center of the arena). When the light is off, this behavioral switch is documented by the beginning of the circular path in the middle of the arena in the attempt to find a light source during the last 18 steps. These tests indicate that the robot starts planning the trajectory that will lead it to the recharging zone when the battery level is about one third of full charge, that is before the last turn against one of the walls in normal operating conditions.

A confirmation of this hypothesis comes from the analysis of the states of the hidden nodes. Although their functioning is distributed and highly dependent on their previous states (in tests where all the recurrent connections were cut off the robot could not even move properly), it is possible to detect a certain degree of specialization. In particular, the node labelled v_h4 seems to be responsible for battery check and path planning during the last steps. In all our "live tests" it always kept a constant low level of activation (except for the two steps after the turns), but when the battery reached the critical level it progressively raised its activation state until the robot reached the recharging area. Hidden nodes v_h0

 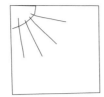

**Figure 6.20**
Trajectories with full battery (left) and low battery (right). Four different paths are shown for each condition.
Both the trajectories and the environment contours have been plotted using the laser positioning device.

and v_h2 were nearly always highly active, except when approaching a wall: therefore, they are very likely to account for the automatic behavior of straight navigation and obstacle avoidance. Finally, hidden nodes v_h1 and v_h3 may contribute to path planning: the temporary change in activity of node v_h1 after a turn suggests that it partially controls the trajectory, while the slight rise in activity of node v_h3 when the battery is low is synergic with the activity of node v_h4.

To definitely ascertain the choice of different behavioral strategies depending upon the battery charge level, the authors performed another test where they compared the trajectories of the robot with a fully charged battery (level 1.0) and a nearly exhausted battery (level 0.12, i.e., max. 6 steps left). In both conditions the robot was positioned at four different locations equidistant from the recharging area and regularly spaced. As clearly shown in figure 6.20, the robot accurately avoided the recharging area when the battery was charged and it moved straight toward it when the battery was low. This strategy minimized the amount of time spent on the recharging station where no fitness could be accumulated.

In another test, the authors clamped the signal coming from the recurrent connections to the average node activity and measured the activation levels of each hidden unit while the robot was placed at several regularly spaced positions in the arena. These "shots" of activation levels for every location were taken in four different conditions: a) low battery and facing light, b) low battery and facing direction opposite to light, c) full battery and facing light, and d) full battery and facing direction opposite to light.[8] These measures can be displayed as four maps—each for one of the measuring conditions—of the environment with the corresponding activity level of a single hidden unit. The resulting activity maps of node v_h4 (figure 6.20) display remarkable topographical representations of the environment with respect to the robot trajectory. This map is head direction specific because the major change corresponds to the change of the robot's facing direction. Similar activations map neighbouring locations in the environment. The organization of

Facing light          Facing opposite corner

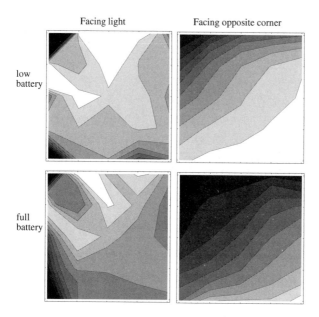

low
battery

full
battery

**Figure 6.21**
Contour map of the activation levels of node v_h4 for different conditions while the robot was positioned at various locations in the environment. The recharging area is located at the top left corner of each map. See text for explanation.

the resulting map is regularly oriented toward the recharging area when the robot faces the corner opposite to the light tower, but it displays a completely different pattern when the robot faces the light tower. Although the geometrical organization in the former situation is more regular, in the latter situation (when the robot faces the light) one can still recognize the recharging area and a sort of gate before it (the entrance of this virtual gate actually corresponds to the robot preferred approaching direction). Also the other neurons display a topological organization (but not so precise), except for node v_h0. Most of them are not head direction specific (although node v_h3 displays an activity pattern close to that of node v_h4).

**Re-adaptation to layout variations**

One way of testing the generalization properties of evolved neurocontrollers consists in manipulating the arrangement of the environment. Consider the experiment with the battery charger described above. The first frame of figure 6.22 shows a typical trajectory of the best neurocontroller after 240 generations. If the battery is not automatically recharged when the robot arrives to the charging area, the robot will keep moving over the black area

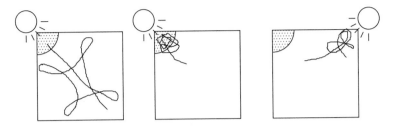

**Figure 6.22**
Trajectories of best individual of generation 240 in three environmental conditions. **Left:** Test in training conditions. The robot starts with a full battery in the bottom right corner (only the first 50 actions are displayed). **Center:** The battery is not automatically recharged when the robot arrives on the charging area. The robot starts in the centre of the environment with an almost discharged battery. **Right:** The light source is positioned on the top right corner, but the charging area remains at the original location.

until all the residual energy is exhausted (figure 6.22, center). If the light source is moved to the top right corner (but the charging area is not moved), the robot will head toward the light and move in its surroundings until all the energy is exhausted (figure 6.22, right). Therefore, the position of the light tower represents an important perceptual cue (indeed, as we said above, it was observed that if the light was switched off during the return to the charger, the robot performed wide circular trajectories looking for gradient information).

The population of neurocontrollers of generation 240 was tested and incrementally evolved in three new environmental conditions, each one identified by positioning the light tower in a different corner of the environment (top-right, bottom-right, and bottom-left). For each condition, the genetic algorithm was restarted on the population of generation 240 and continued for 80 additional generations. Data for all conditions are displayed in figure 6.23, including data from the previous ten generations for the sake of comparison. The presence of several individuals which were "suboptimal" in the original environment, but resulted fitter in the new environment prevented a dramatic drop of the both fitness indicators. Re-adaptation of the population to each new condition took place relatively quickly; approximately 20 generations (10% of the time required by evolution from scratch) were sufficient to generate an individual perfectly adapted to the new environment which reported the same performances already measured for the best individual of generation 240 in the original environment. Re-adaptation was extremely rapid when the light source was positioned in the corner opposite to charging area (figure 6.23, *b*); this indicates that the mirror symmetry of the new environment does not require a drastic change in the internal representation developed by the neurocontrollers. In other words, whereas conditions *a* and *c* require a 90-degree rotation of the mapping from sensors to actions, involving changes in several synaptic weights, condition *b* can be successfully solved by changing few synaptic weights which result in a 180-degree rotation of the sensorimotor mapping. If this is

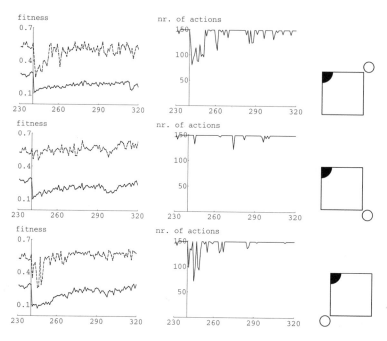

**Figure 6.23**
Re-adaptation in environments with a new light position. Each row (a, b, c) shows: (left) the average population fitness (continuous line) and the fitness of the best individual (dotted line) across generations; (center) the number of actions during life for the best individual at each generation; (right) a sketch of the light position (small circle) in the environment (the black sector represents the charging area). For sake of comparison, each plot includes data for the last ten generations of the original run (see figures 6.14 and 6.15) shown here to the left of the y axis.

the case, then one would expect that only few best individuals (i.e., those which already developed a correctly oriented map in the original environment) could benefit from mirror symmetry of the new environment; this is indeed shown by the sharp contrast between the performance of the best individual and the average performance of the population which displays the same initial drop and recovery rate as in conditions *a* and *c*.

**Discussion**

The behavior of the evolved individuals relies on a topological neural representation of the world that is gradually built through a process of interaction with the environment. The few failures in reaching the recharging area from some starting locations (figure 6.17) thus might be due to a suboptimal or not fully formed map (when artificial evolution was halted, the fitness measure was still increasing, as one can see in figure 6.14). The functioning of node v_h4 (figure 6.20) vaguely resembles the classic findings about the organization of the rat hippocampus, where most of the cells are *place cells*, i.e. they fire only when the rat is in a particular portion of its environment (O'Keefe and Nadel 1978). Given the constraints of our neural model (few nodes, continuous activation, discrete dynamics, and homogeneous properties), the similarity between the rat hyppocampus and the control system of the robot is only *functional*: whereas the rat "knows" its own location by the firing of some specific place cells, the evolved agent represents this information in terms of specific activation levels. With regard to the head direction activity of node v_h4, agreement (in functional terms) is found with recent findings about the existence of few head direction' cells (whose firing modality depends upon the direction of the rat's head) in regions neighbouring the rat hippocampus (Taube, Muller and Ranck 1990). All this amounts to saying that the behavior of the evolved robot cannot be purely explained by a stimulus-reaction paradigm because it is mediated by the autonomous development of an internal representation of the environment which reflects the goals defined by the robot itself (a similar conclusion was reached nearly 50 years ago in psychology (Tolman 1948) and formed the basis for a large conceptual revolution). One might further speculate that the reason why both rats and the evolved robots employ similar computational strategies, despite the diversity of their neural architectures, may be due to the fact that this type of internal representation is particularly efficient to optimize a navigation behavior in this environment.

A rather interesting result comes from the dual role played by node v_h4 as an orienteering device and as a controller of battery charge. The latter role is masked during the single shot measures taken for drawing the maps of figure 6.21. To make things even more complicated, under that measuring condition the activation levels of this node are very similar in the two battery conditions (low battery and full battery). Node v_h4 is nevertheless responsible for monitoring the battery level, but this feature is revealed only during the free running of the robot (figures 6.18 and 6.19).[9] On the other hand, the orienteering function is not apparently revealed when the measures are taken during a free run: in this case the underlying representation of the environment is masked by the pattern of temporal activity sustained by the continuous (approximated by discrete dynamics) flow of information from the recurrent connections that is used to monitor the battery charge. Such a dual and concurrent processing modality has been hypothesized for biological neurons (Abeles 1991) too, but it can be hardly analyzed in living organisms because of technical difficulties. However, it can be displayed and thus analyzed in artificial neural network models with recurrent (discrete or continuous) dynamics. It remains to be seen whether this feature emerges only when the neural network is embedded in a sensorimotor agent and learning is not controlled by gradient descent techniques, or whether it is a more general computational strategy of these types of networks.

## 6.4   Emergence of "complex" behaviors

All experiments reported in this chapter show that it is possible to perform behavior engineering of intelligent agents without resorting to explicit design of their cognitive abilities and artificially restricting the range of actions. Let us now discuss the role of fitness design within the perspective of fitness space introduced in chapter 3. Two different methods can be used to develop behaviors through artificial evolution. The first method consists in a detailed specification of the fitness function that is tailored for a precise task. This is the case, for example, of the experiment described in section 4.2 in which all required abilities (i.e., keep far from obstacles, move fast, move as straight as possible) are explicitly indicated in the fitness function. Although this choice may provide interesting and successful results, the behavior of the evolved agent depends upon the choice of the experimenter. In this sense, there is not much difference between the tuning of the objective function in a supervised neural algorithm and the engineering of the fitness function in the genetic algorithm. In this case, the design of the fitness function even for a simple task requires some effort and empirical trials because it is not possible to identify and specify in advance the desired actions of an autonomous agent (Beer and Gallagher 1992; Steels 1994). Additionally, the evolved agent can hardly be said to be autonomous because its behavior is largely dictated by the experimenter (Steels 1993).

An alternative method is to consider the fitness measure not as a detailed and complex function to be optimized in order to achieve a desired behavior, but rather as a general survival criterion that is automatically translated into a set of specific constraints by the characteristics of the interactions between the organism and the environment. If one follows this approach, the adaptation process yields ecologically grounded behavior (i.e., necessary for survival), rather than a mere *task*. The experiment described in section 6.3 has been conceived within this latter framework. With respect to the simple obstacle avoidance behavior described in chapter 4, no additional constraints have been introduced in the fitness function (on the contrary one constraint has been removed). Straight navigation, location of the battery charger, and timely homing therefore are subgoals created by the agent itself in order to maximize a more general and indirectly related fitness function. Similarly, in the experiment described in section 6.2, although the ability to pick up cylinders was explicitly rewarded, the exploration of the environment, the ability to discriminate between walls and cylinders, and the ability to approach/avoid walls/cylinders depending on gripper state emerged without explicit indications in the fitness function.

Obviously the latter method is preferable, because it releases the engineer from the burden of designing the controller and possibly constraining its adaptive potentials. The problem is to see how well this simple method can scale up to more complex cases. The experiment described in section 6.3 was successfully replicated by starting with different

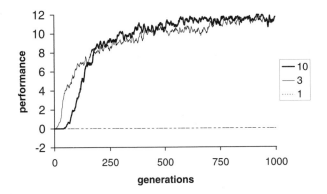

**Figure 6.24**
Number of epochs (out of 15) in which individuals pick up and then release a target object outside the arena for fitness formulae with 1, 3, and 10 components throughout generations. Each curve represents the average of the best individuals of each generation for 10 replications of the simulation. Data smoothed by calculating rolling averages over preceding and succeeding three generations.

initial synaptic weight values. In another experiment where a number of obstacles with a circular shape were introduced in the environment however, the robot did not evolve the ability to reach regularly the recharging area. Better performance could only be achieved by relying on an incremental approach, i.e. by introducing obstacles only after the robot learned to locate the recharging area. A similar situation has been observed in the case of the experiment described in section 6.2. Successful behaviors could only be achieved by introducing at least an additional constraint in the fitness function (i.e., a reward for the ability to pick up objects). By rewarding individuals only for their ability to release objects outside the arena, in fact, performance did not increase at all throughout generations (figure 6.24, see the curve labeled with "1"). This is a case of the bootstrap problem mentioned in the first chapter. The probability that a robot with random weights can manage to complete a whole desired behavior (find a cylinder while avoiding walls, grasp it, and release it out of the arena) is extremely low. Under these circumstances, all networks of the initial generations are scored with the same null values and the evolutionary algorithm does not perform better than a random search.

In order to solve the bootstrap problem, it was necessary to introduce intermediate fitness scores and additional constraints. Therefore, robots were rewarded also for their ability to pick up objects and were exposed to "good" learning experiences (the number of time the robot encountered an object while it was carrying another object was increased).

However, simply adding constraints to the fitness function does not guarantee better evolvability of the system. In one of the preliminary attempts to evolve the garbage collecting behavior described in section 6.2 above, a fitness function with 10 components was used. Later on it was realized that 7 of them not only were unnecessary but actually retarded the evolution of good behaviors (see figure 6.24, curve labeled with "10"). The 7 unnecessary components were the following: (1) a reward when the robot is close to the target object; (2) a reward if the target object is in front of the robot; (3) a reward if the robot tries to pick up the object; (4) a reward if the robot gets close to a wall when it has an object in the gripper; (5) a reward for the ability to bring objects close to walls; (6) a punishment when the robot crashes into walls while carrying an object; (7) a punishment when the robot releases an object on another object. This attempt to channel the evolutionary process toward a desired behavioral sequence may actually favor the selection of individuals that satisfy only parts of the constraints, but not the ultimate goal of releasing objects outside the arena.

We believe that the fitness function should be as simple as possible and the selection criterion should be as general as possible. The spirit of this approach consists in making artificial evolution closer to natural evolution where the selection criterion has no sense of predetermined goal directedness. In natural evolution in fact, the selection process admits a very large number of alternative ways of survival. In artificial evolution, instead, we usually select individuals on the basis of a very specific criterion and therefore set up problems that can be satisfied only in a limited number of ways. From this point of view it is not surprising that artificial evolution may get stuck in a suboptimal solution.

From the point of view of scalability we believe that, rather then trying to channel the evolutionary process by using the insight of the experimenter, we should include in these simple models other mechanisms of adaptation and self-organization exploited by natural evolution such as plasticity, co-evolution, and development. These issues will be discussed in chapters 7, 8, and 9 respectively.

## 6.5    Conclusions

In this chapter we have described two experiments where the structure of the evolving controller allows the development of complex behaviors. In section 6.2 we have investigated evolution of modular architectures and showed that the functionality and dynamics of these modules are correlated with low level sensory-motor aspects rather than with an observer's description of primitive behaviors. Evolutionary modularity is a promising approach to the development of complex abilities where traditional decomposition and integration fails to capture the most relevant aspects of the task from the perspective of the control system.

On a similar vein, in section 6.3 we have described a case where internal representations spontaneously emerge in a relatively simple architecture instead of being imposed by an external designer. Notice the difference between this approach and that typically used in the literature on adaptive map based navigation. In the latter case, the experimenter makes the assumptions that: a) internal representations are necessary to solve a certain navigation task; b) these representations take a given form, for example a graph that connects locations in the environment; c) these representations are based on certain architectural structures, such as place cells, units with lateral connections, different layers with dedicated functions, etc.; d) the agent is rewarded when it reaches the target location. In other words, the system is explicitly designed to perform navigation to a target location with internal representations. The evolutionary approach employed here is completely different in that none of these constraints have been employed. This experiment shows that artificial evolution can develop mechanisms that go beyond reactive behavior when this is necessary without being explicitly told to do so.

Finally in section 6.4 we discussed different methods for scaling up in complexity and discussed the role of fitness design. We concluded that the most promising direction is to include in the evolutionary process other mechanisms such as ontogenetic plasticity that might enhance the adaptation power of the evolutionary process without increasing the role of human designer. This hypothesis will be explored in more detail in the next chapter.

# 7 Learning and evolution

## 7.1 Introduction

Evolution and learning are two forms of biological adaptation that differ in space and time. Evolution is a process of selective reproduction and substitution based on the existence of a geographically distributed population of individuals displaying some variability. Learning, instead, is a set of modifications taking place within each single individual during its own life time. Evolution and learning operate on different time scales. Evolution is a form of adaptation capable of capturing relatively slow environmental changes that might encompass several generations, such as perceptual characteristics of food sources for a given bird species. Learning, instead, allows an individual to adapt to environmental changes that are unpredictable at the generational level. Learning might include a variety of mechanisms that produce adaptive changes in an individual during its lifetime, such as physical development, neural maturation, and synaptic plasticity. Finally, whereas evolution operates on the genotype, learning affects only the phenotype and phenotypic changes cannot directly modify the genotype.

In this chapter we will use the term *learning* to indicate modifications to the synaptic weights of a neural network that produce changes during lifetime of an individual increasing the adaptivity of the individual itself. However, adaptive changes may also be obtained by modifying other entities, such as the activation states of some neurons or the neural architecture. Changes affecting these entities tend to be identified with different processes such as memory and development. Connectionists, for example, usually refer to long lasting changes in the synaptic weights as *learning* and to the activation states of neurons with recurrent connections as *memory*. In general, researchers draw a sharp distinction between mechanisms responsible for producing a given behavior, and those responsible for learning. "However, this distinction is difficult to defend biologically, because many of the same biochemical processes are involved in both processes" (Yamauchi and Beer 1994, pp. 243). Indeed, changes in the pattern of activations of internal neurons and changes affecting the synaptic weights are both form of plasticity in that they may produce similar outcomes from a behavioral point of view. Yamauchi and Beer (1995), for example, have evolved and analyzed continuous time recurrent neural networks that give the external appearance of performing reinforcement learning while in fact they had fixed connection weights and used only the dynamics of the neuron activations. In the case of these experiments therefore learning was the results of changes affecting the activation states of the neurons, i.e. changes which tend to be identified with behavior regulation and not with learning. In other experiments, which will be described in section 7.5, synaptic weights continually change and are responsible for behavioral regulation. In the case of these experiments therefore, behavior regulation results from changes affecting the synaptic weights, that is changes that are usually identified with learning. These results suggest a much tighter integration between behavior and learning than is usually assumed.

## 7.2   The adaptive functions of learning in evolution

Within an evolutionary perspective, learning has different adaptive functions:

• *It allows individuals to adapt to changes in the environment that occur in the lifespan of an individual or across few generations.* As mentioned in the previous section, learning has the same function attributed to evolution: adaptation to the environment. Learning supplements evolution in that it enables an organism to adapt to changes in the environment that happen too quickly to be tracked by evolution (Todd and Miller 1991; Nolfi et al. 1994a; Floreano and Nolfi 1997b; Nolfi and Parisi 1997; Sasaki and Tokoro 1997).

• *It allows evolution to use information extracted from the environment thereby channelling evolutionary search.* Whereas ontogenetic adaptation can rely on a very rich, although not always explicit, amount of feedback from the environment, evolutionary adaptation relies on a single value which reflects how well an individual coped with its environment. This value is the number of offspring in the case of natural evolution and the fitness value in the case of artificial evolution. Instead, from the point of view of ontogenetic adaptation, individuals continuously receive feedback information from the environment through their sensors during the whole lifetime. This huge amount of information encodes only very indirectly how well an individual is doing in different moments of its life or how it should modify its own behavior in order to increase its fitness. However, ontogenetic and phylogenetic adaptation together might be capable of exploiting this information. Indeed evolution may be able to transform sensory information into self generated reinforcement signals or teaching patterns (Ackley and Litmann 1991; Nolfi and Parisi 1993a; Nolfi and Parisi 1994; Floreano and Mondada 1996a; Nolfi and Parisi 1997)

• *It can help and guide evolution.* Although physical changes of the phenotype, such as strengthening of synapses during learning, cannot be written back into the genotype, Baldwin (1896) and Waddington (1942) suggested that learning might indeed affect the evolutionary course in subtle but effective ways. Baldwin's argument was that learning accelerates evolution because suboptimal individuals can reproduce by acquiring during life necessary features for survival. However, since learning requires time (and might thus be a disadvantage), Baldwin suggested that evolution tends to select individuals who have already at birth those useful features which would otherwise be learned. This latter aspect of Baldwin's effect, namely indirect genetic assimilation of learned traits, has been later supported by scientific evidence and defined by Waddington (1942) as a canalization effect. Recently, Hinton and Nowlan (1987) have provided a clear computational model that demonstrates how learning may help and guide evolution. Nolfi et al. have further investigated this issue in a case where the learning task differs from the evolutionary task (Nolfi et al. 1994a; Nolfi 1999).

• Other advantages. Learning might allow the production of complex phenotypes with short genotypes by extracting some of the information necessary to build the corresponding phenotype from the environment (Todd and Miller 1991; Mayley 1997). Moreover learning can allow the maintenance of more genetic diversity. Different genes, in fact, have more chances to be preserved in the population if the individuals who incorporate those genes are able to learn the same fit behaviors (Whitley, Gordon and Mathias 1994)

However, learning has costs:

• A delay in the ability to acquire fitness. Learning individuals will necessarily have a suboptimal behavior during the learning phase. As a consequence they will collect less fitness than individuals who have the same behavior genetically specified. The longer the learning period, the more accumulated costs have to be paid (Mayley 1997).

• Increased unreliability. "Since learned behavior is determined, at least partly, by the environment, if a vital behavior defining stimulus is not encountered by a particular individual, then it will suffer as a consequence. The plasticity of learned behaviors provides the possibility that an individual may simply learn the wrong thing, causing it to incur an incorrect behavior cost. Learning thus has a stochastic element that it is not present in instinctive behaviors" (Mayley 1997, pp. 216).

• Other costs. In natural organisms or in biologically inspired artificial organisms learning might imply additional costs. If individuals are considered juvenile during the learning period, learning also implies a delayed reproduction time (Cecconi et al. 1996). Moreover, learning might imply the waste of energy resources for the accomplishment of the learning process itself (Mayley 1997) or for parental investment (Cecconi et al. 1996). Finally, while learning, individuals without a fully formed behavior may irrevocably damage themselves (Mayley 1997).

In the next sections we will present a set of models and experiments devised to study the interaction between learning and evolution and we will discuss the implications from the different perspectives described above. Some of the models which will be described in the next sections do not involve mobile robots but only simulated agents (animats). We decided to discuss them in detail because they are useful to understand relevant aspects of the interaction between learning and evolution.

### 7.3   How learning can "help and guide" evolution: Hinton and Nowlan's model

In the effort to explain evolutionary gaps in the fossil records, more than a century ago Baldwin (1896) advanced the idea that evolution could be influenced by learning during life without assuming that learned features could directly modify the genotype (as hypothesized by Lamarck 1914).[1] Baldwin's argument was that learning accelerates evolution because suboptimal individuals can reproduce by acquiring during life necessary features for survival. However, since learning requires time (and might thus be a disadvantage), Baldwin suggested that evolution tends to select individuals who have already at birth those useful features which would otherwise be learned. This latter aspect of Baldwin's effect, namely *indirect genetic assimilation of learned traits*, has been later supported by scientific evidence and defined by Waddington (1942) as a *canalization effect*.

Hinton and Nowlan (1987) have described a simple computational model that shows how learning might help and guide evolution in some circumstances. The authors considered the case in which "a neural network confers added reproductive fitness on an organism only if it is connected in exactly the right way. In this worst case, there is no reasonable path toward the good net and a pure evolutionary search can only discover which of the potential connections should be present by trying possibilities at random. The good net is like a needle in a haystack" (p. 495). In their experiment individuals have genotypes with 20 genes which encode a neural network with 20 potentials connections. Genes can have three alternative value: 0, 1, and ? that represent, respectively, the presence of the connection, the absence of the connection, and a modifiable state (presence or absence of the connection) that can change its value according to a learning mechanism. The learning mechanism is a simple random process that keeps changing modifiable connection weights until a good combination (if any) is found during the limited life time of the individual.

In the absence of learning (i.e., when genes can only have 0 and 1 values), the probability of finding a good combination of weights would be very small given that the fitness surface (see also inset on fitness landscape) would look like a flat area with a spike in correspondence of the good combinations (see figure 7.1, thick line). On such a surface genetic algorithms do not perform better than any random search algorithm. However, if learning is enabled, it will be more probable that some individuals will achieve the good combinations of connection values at some point during life and start to collect fitness points. The addition of learning, in fact, produces an enlargement and a smoothing of the fitness surface area around the good combination which can be discovered and easily climbed by the genetic algorithm. This is due to the fact that not only the right combination of alleles, but also combinations which in part have the right alleles and in part have unspecified (learnable) alleles, report an average fitness greater than 0 (fitness monotonically increases with the number of fixed right values because the time needed to find the right combination is inversely proportional, on the average, to the number of learnable alleles).

---

### Fitness landscape

The fitness landscape is a metaphor often used to visualize the search space of an evolutionary algorithm. A fitness landscape associates combinations of genetic traits to fitness values. The dimensions of the landscape are given by the number of genetic traits. For example, for an organism characterized by only two genes corresponding to length and mass, the fitness landscape will look like a surface. The height of the landscape at any given point is determined by the fitness value of the "potential" individual resulting from that specific combination of genetic traits. In practice, the fitness landscape is largely unknown because only a tiny fraction of all potential individuals is generated and tested. Even in the simplest computational models, though, the genetic traits under evolution are often much more than two. In that case, a one dimensional visualization of the fitness landscape might still be useful assuming that we unfold the multi dimensional space into a single dimension by plotting all fitness values one after the other.

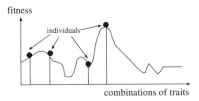

The figure shows a one dimensional representation of a fitness landscape with four individuals. This simple representation does not take into consideration changes that take place during the life of the individual, it ignores environmental modifications, and it assumes that there is a one-to-one mapping between genes and traits. These three factors, which have important consequences on the evolutionary process, are considered in this chapter, in chapter 8, and in chapter 9, respectively.

---

In other words, learning makes the fitness surface smoother, and this, in turn, simplifies the search which should be performed by evolution. As claimed by Hinton and Nowlan, with learning "it is like searching for a needle in a haystack when someone tells you when you are getting close" (1987, p. 496). This simple model also accounts for the Baldwin effect that postulates that characters that are initially acquired through learning may later be fixated in the genotype. Once individuals which have part of their genes fixed on the right values and part of their genes unspecified (learnable) are selected, individuals with less and less learnable genes tend to be selected given that fitness monotonically increases

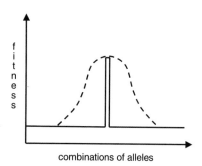

combinations of alleles

**Figure 7.1**
Fitness surface with and without learning. In absence of learning, the fitness surface is flat, with a thin spike in correspondence of the good combinations of alleles (thick line). When learning is enabled, the fitness surface has a nice hill around the spike which includes the alleles combination which have in part right fixed values and in part unspecified (learnable) values (dotted line). The thick line represents the fitness for each possible combination of two alleles ([0, 1]) while the dotted line represents the fitness for each possible combination of three alleles [0, 1, ?]). Redrawn from Hinton and Nowlan (1987).

by decreasing the number of learnable genes (an equilibrium point is eventually reached, see Hinton and Nowlan 1987). In other words, characters that were first acquired through learning tend to become genetically specified later on.[2]

In the representation adopted in figure 7.1 each individual is represented as a point on the fitness surface with a height corresponding to the average fitness of the individual during its lifetime. This is a static representation where changes in performance during lifetime cannot be visualized. Another way of representing the individuals in the search space is to imagine that each individual network corresponds to a point in the phenotype space. In this case changes of connection weights introduced by learning correspond to a movement of the learning individual in the phenotype space and on the fitness surface. As a consequence, changes in performance correspond to movements toward higher or lower areas of the fitness surface. By using this type of representation the interaction between learning and evolution in the Hinton and Nowlan's model can be explained in the following way. The fitness surface (i.e., the distribution of fitness value that are assigned to each possible combination of 0 and 1 alleles) is flat with the exception of one spike of high fitness both in the case of learning and non learning individuals. The initial population will be represented as a set of fixed points randomly distributed on the fitness surface (see cross marks in figure 7.2). Non learning individuals do not move in the phenotype space during their lifetime while learning individuals do (given that some of their connections continually change value during lifetime). Clearly, the probability that at least an individual will step on the spike will be much higher in the case of learning individuals. In other words we can say that learning allows the evolutionary process to explore the landscape

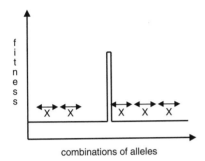

combinations of alleles

**Figure 7.2**
Representation in the phenotype space of the same fitness surface described in figure 7.1. The full line represents the fitness for each possible combination of two alleles (0, 1). The crossmarks represent the positions of the individuals at birth. The arrows represent the movements of the individual in the search space corresponding to changes of modifiable alleles. Notice however, that only learning individuals move in the search space during lifetime.

neighborhood of each candidate for reproduction (Nolfi et al. 1990).

If learning is represented as a random process (such as in the case of Hinton and Nowlan's model), the representations shown in figures 7.1 and 7.2 are functionally equivalent. However, as we will see in the next sections, the latter representation is more appropriate in cases where learning is modeled as a form of change with some directionality.

Despite its explicative power, Hinton and Nowlan's model has several limitations: (1) learning is modeled as a random process; (2) there is no distinction between the learning task and the evolutionary task; (3) the environment does not change; (4) the learning space and the evolutionary space are completely correlated. The two spaces are correlated if genotypes which are close in the evolutionary space correspond to phenotypes which are close in the phenotype space (Mayley 1997).

The results obtained by Hinton and Nowlan may not generalize completely to other circumstances in which these limitations are released. In particular, they may not generalize to cases where learning and evolutionary spaces are less correlated. In the case of the Hinton and Nowlan model, learning and evolution operate on the same entities with the same operators (i.e., both changes produced by mutations and changes produced by learning correspond to substitutions of genes with new randomly selected values). Therefore the two spaces are completely correlated. By systematically varying the cost of learning and the correlation between the learning space and the evolutionary space, Mayley (1997) showed that: (1) the adaptive advantage of learning is proportional to the correlation between the two search spaces; (2) the assimilation of characters first acquired through learning is proportional to the correlation between the two search spaces and to the cost of learning (i.e., to the fitness lost during the first part of the lifetime in which individuals have suboptimal performance); (3) in certain situations learning costs may exceed learning benefits.

In the next sections we will presents other models in which most of these limitations are released.

## 7.4   Evolving individuals which learn a task different from what they are selected for

As we claimed in the previous section, one of the limitations of Hinton and Nowlan's model is that there is no distinction between the learning task and the evolutionary task. This is possible because the experimenter provides supervision signals both for the evolutionary and the learning task. In natural evolution, instead, the environment does not usually provide cues that directly indicate to the individual how it should change in order to produce more adapted behavior. Natural selection is the only source of "supervision" for many living systems. However, natural organisms can use environmental information made available to them through their sensors in order to acquire competencies (such as the ability to predict the next sensory states; see Nolfi and Tani 1999) that may indirectly increase their ability to reproduce.

Nolfi et al. (1994a) have studied the case of artificial agents (also known as *animats*, see Wilson 1987) that evolve (to become fitter at one task) at the population level and learn (a different task) at the individual level. In particular, individuals which were selected for their ability to find food in their environment were also asked to learn to predict the sensory consequences of their motor actions during their lifetime. Notice that the supervision necessary for learning this task is directly available from the environment (i.e., the correct prediction corresponds to the state of the sensors at the next time step).

Each individual animat lives in a 2D grid world where a number of food tokens are randomly distributed (figure 7.3, left). Each food token occupies one cell; if the animat happens to step on one of these cells, the food token is automatically "eaten" and the animat's fitness is increased. Individuals are equipped with a neural network interfaced to a sensorimotor system that provides input information on the distance and angle (with respect to the facing direction of the animat) of the nearest food token, and on the planned motor action (figure 7.3, right). Two input units encode the angle and the distance of the nearest food token and two other units (thresholded to the nearest binary value) encode one of four possible actions: turn 90° right, turn 90° left, move one cell forward, and remain still. At each time step, the neural network receives as input the sensory information on the nearest food token and the current planned motor action and produces as output the next planned action and a prediction of the sensory state after the execution of the current

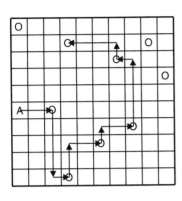 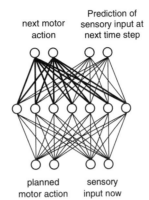

**Figure 7.3**
**Left:** The environment containing 10 food tokens "O" and the animat "A". The arrows represent the trajectory of a typical evolved individual. **Right:** Neural network architecture. All connections are inherited. Connections represented with thin lines are also modified by prediction learning during the lifetime of the individual while connections represented with thick lines are not.

planned action. At this point: (a) the planned action that was used as input is executed and the next planned action is passed as new input; (b) the freshly gathered sensory information is used both as input and as teaching signals for the output units encoding the predicted state of the sensors (the new sensory state is compared with the predicted state and the difference is used to adjust by back-propagation the connection weights between the four input, the seven hidden, and the two prediction units).[3]

The results showed that, after a few generations, individuals learning to predict also increased their ability to find food during life (figure 7.4).

Moreover, by comparing the results of the experiments described above with another set of experiments in which individuals were not allowed to learn to predict during their lifetime, it was shown that learning populations displayed faster and higher fitness values across generations than populations without learning (figure 7.5). The same type of results were obtained in other cases and in particular in cases in which the learning task and the evolutionary task were clearly "uncorrelated" (see Parisi et al. 1992; Harvey 1997).

Since here the learning criterion is different from the evolutionary goal and learning has a directionality (i.e., the weights are not changed in a random fashion), the explanation by Hinton and Nowlan depicted in figures 7.1 and 7.2 is not sufficient for explaining these results. A new explanation of the interaction between learning and evolution has been proposed (Nolfi et al. 1994a; Parisi and Nolfi 1996). Imagine two different search surfaces, an evolutionary surfaces and a learning surface (figure 7.6). Changes due to learning produce a movement of the individual phenotype both on the learning and on

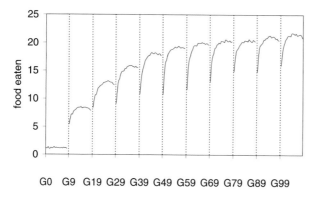

GO   G9   G19  G29  G39  G49  G59  G69  G79  G89  G99

**Figure 7.4**
Average number of food elements eaten by populations of successive generations that learn to predict. Each
curve represents performance prior to learning and then for each of the 20 epochs of life (performance prior to
learning are obtained by measuring the number of food tokens eaten by individuals during one epoch of life
without updating the weights). For reasons of space, performance are displayed only each 10 generations.
Average results over 10 replications of the experiment.

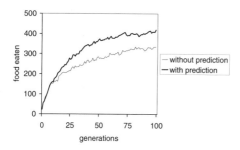

**Figure 7.5**
Average of food tokens eaten by populations of animats throughout generations for experiments with and
without learning. Each curve is the average result of 10 replications. The difference between the two curves is
statistically significant from generation 25 (see Nolfi et al., 1994a).

the evolutionary surfaces. However, since learning tries to maximize performance on the
learning task, individuals will move toward higher areas of the learning surface. Given
that the way in which individuals move in weight space affects their fitness (the total
fitness of the individual is the sum of the fitness values received during such displacements
on the weight space) evolution will tend to select individuals located in areas where, by
increasing their performance on the learning task, they also increase their performance on
the evolutionary task.

Consider for example two individuals, *a* and *b*, which are located in two distant loca-

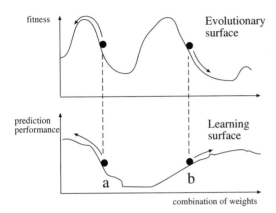

**Figure 7.6**
Fitness surface for the evolutionary task and performance surface for the learning task (sensory prediction) for all possible weight matrices. Movements due to learning are represented as arrows. Point *a* is in a region in which the two surfaces are dynamically correlated. Even if *a* and *b* have the same fitness on the evolutionary surface at birth, *a* has more probability to be selected than *b* since it is more likely to increase its fitness during life than *b*.

tions in weight space but have the same fitness at birth; i.e., the two locations correspond to the same height on the fitness surface (see figure 7.6). However, individual *a* is located in a region where the fitness surface and the learning surface are dynamically correlated; i.e., a region where movements that result in an increase in height with respect to the learning surface cause an increase with respect to the fitness surface, on the average. Individual *b*, on the other hand, is located in a region where the two surfaces are not dynamically correlated. If individual *b* moves in weight space it will go up in the learning surface but not necessarily in the fitness surface. Because of learning, the two individuals will move during their lifetime in a direction that improves their learning performance, i.e., in a direction in which their height on the learning surface tends to increase. This implies that individual *a*, which is located in a dynamically correlated region, will end up with a higher fitness than individual *b* and, therefore, will have a better chance to be selected. The final result is that evolution will have a tendency to progressively select individuals which are located in dynamically correlated regions. In other words, learning forces evolution to select individuals which improve their performance with respect to both the learning and the evolutionary task.·

Two surfaces are dynamically correlated even if some changes that produce an increase in height with respect to the learning surface produce a corresponding decrease with respect to the evolutionary surface. As shown in figure 7.4, for example, the changes due to learning which occur during the last part of lifetime, in the case of individual *a*, produce a decrease in performance with respect to the evolutionary task. Despite of that, changes due to learning tend to produce an increase in performance on the evolutionary task, on the average. Also notice that when the evolutionary surface present a small peck (as in the left part of figure 7.6) evolution will tend to select individuals located down the peck as the individual *a* (i.e., individuals that while move following the gradient of the learning surface spend as much time as possible on the peck itself).

These results show that although evolution and learning are two distinct types of change occurring in two distinct entities (populations and individual organisms), they strongly influence each other. The influence of evolution on learning is not surprising. Evolutionary change leaves its trace in the genotype. Hence, each individual inherits a genome which is the cumulative result at the level of evolutionary changes that have occurred at the level of the population. Since an individual's genome partially specifies the resulting phenotypic individual and it constrains how the individual will behave and what it will learn, the way is open for an influence of evolution on learning. However, the experiments described in this and in the previous section clearly show that the reverse is also true: learning affects evolution. The interaction between the two processes is so profound that learning tends to produce a positive effect on evolution even if the learning task and the evolutionary task are different (and, apparently, independently from what the learning task is, see Parisi et al. 1992).

It should be noted that in these experiments characters initially acquired through learning are not assimilated in the individuals' genotype in successive generations, at least completely, even if the assimilation would increase individuals' fitness (i.e., individuals which acquire fit behaviors through learning start with lower performance and therefore collect less fitness in the first part of their lifetime). This may be explained by considering that: (a) the cost of learning can be reduced by increasing the learning speed (as can be observed in figure 7.4, evolved individuals reach optimal performance in the very first epochs of their lifetime); (b) the learning space and the evolutionary space are not completely correlated (for the correlation between the learning space and the evolutionary space see Mayley 1997). In fact, although learning and evolution operate on the same entities (i.e., the connection weights), the genetic operators and the learning operators are quite different (mutations are accomplished by adding randomly selected values to a set of randomly selected connection weights while learning is accomplished by backpropagation). This implies that points which are close in the learning space may be far apart in the evolutionary space. In other words, points which can be reached with few learning cycles, may require a prohibitively long list of mutations. As we claimed in the previous section the probability to genetically assimilate characters acquired through learning is inversely proportional to the correlation between the learning and the evolutionary space.

In the next sections we will analyze other aspects of the interaction between learning and evolution.

### Is there a new factor in evolution?

In two recent articles, Harvey (1996, 1997) proposed a different explanation of the interaction between evolution and learning than the one described in this section. He claimed that improvements in average performance observed in learning individuals described in figures 7.5 and 7.6 is not due to an interaction between learning and evolution but "rather from a relearning effect on weights perturbed by mutation" (Harvey 1997, p. 328). Harvey's hypothesis is based on evidence that by perturbing the weights of a neural network previously trained with back-propagation on a set of input-output pairs and then retraining the network on a new training set, uncorrelated with the original one, performance also improves on the patterns belonging to the original training set (Harvey and Stone 1996).

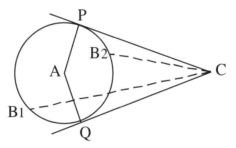

Harvey's explanation is based on a geometrical argument. Briefly stated, the trajectory of the network in the weight space during training on the second set is very likely to transit by the original point where it was before being perturbed by noise. Assume that A represents the weights of the network trained on the original training set, B1 and B2 are two possible positions of the network after perturbation, and C is the position of the network after being trained on the second training set. Finally, assume that performance on the original set is inversely proportional to the distance from point A. Therefore, whenever B lies outside the outer arc PQ (e.g., B1), its trajectory gets closer to A for some time; instead, whenever B lies inside the inner arc PQ (e.g., B2), its trajectory always goes away from A. Regardless of the position of C, the former situation happens at least 50% of the times for a two dimensional weight space and much more often in a high dimensional weight space (Harvey 1997); furthermore, it happens 100% of the times when C lies within the circle.

---

**Is there a new factor in evolution?** (continued)

On the basis of this new explanation, Harvey claims that the beneficial effects of learning a different task than the evolutionary task can be explained by considering a highly converged evolved population sitting on point A (food finding) being pulled away by mutations to point B, and then transiting to point C with prediction learning. As a consequence he hypothesized that "if one substituted for the elite member of a population evolved on the food finding task one individual trained by back-propagation using an external teacher (or any other learning mechanism) on the same task, then one should expect similar responses after weight perturbations" (Harvey 1986, p. 83).

In order to test this prediction, Nolfi (1999) measured the performance of individuals of successive generations which were allowed to learn for the first time (i.e., individuals which had the same architecture of learning individuals but which evolved without being exposed to learning during lifetime). In contrast with Harvey's expectation, learning to predict produces a significant decrease in performance of these individuals even though their weights have been perturbed by mutations (exactly like the weights of individuals which were exposed to learning in previous generations). This and other results described in Nolfi (1999) suggest that: (a) the advantages produced by lifetime learning are due to the interaction between learning and evolution; (b) in the case of learning individuals, the population does not converge on A but on some point on the left side of A which ensures that by learning (i.e., by moving toward C) individuals will spend most of their lifetime close to A. This explanation fits nicely the suggestion given above that evolution tends to select individuals that are located in dynamically correlated regions of the fitness and learning surfaces.

---

## 7.5   Evolving the adaptation mechanisms

In all the experiments described so far the weights were genetically inherited although they were also subjected to changes during the lifetime of individuals. However in most of the species the genome does not contain all the information necessary to build the corresponding phenotype. It is therefore unlikely that fine details such as initial weight values could be precisely encoded on the genotype.

In this section we will describe an experiment (Floreano and Mondada 1996a) where the synaptic weights are not precisely encoded into the genotype, but are continuously modified during lifetime through a learning process in which genetically inherited learning rules interact with information coming from the external environment. In other words,

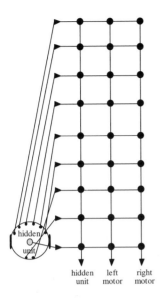

hidden          left          right
unit           motor         motor

**Figure 7.7**
The architecture of the neural network employed. Black disks are synapses; the circle in the middle of the robot body represents the hidden neuron. The activation of the three units correspond, respectively, to the hidden unit, the left motor, and the right motor.

the genotype encodes only the architecture and learning rules of the synapses, but not their precise strengths. Every time that a chromosome is decoded into the corresponding neural controller, all the synapses are intialized to small random values. As soon as the robot begins to move and sensory signals flow through the network, synaptic values can change according to the genetically encoded rules. These genes for one synapse include four possible learning rules, a learning rate, and chemical properties of the synapse, such as whether it is excitatory or inhibitory and whether it drives or modulates the postsynaptic neuron (see chapter 2). Therefore, the accurate balance between weighted signals necessary to drive the motor neurons in a coordinated fashion must be learned during lifetime according to the genetically specified instructions.

The neural network employed in this experiment was composed of three units: one hidden neuron and two motor neurons, each one receiving input/activation via synaptic connections from all eight infrared sensors and from the hidden neuron itself (figure 7.7). Therefore, there was a total of 27 connections whose meta-properties were encoded on the genotype.[4] Signals going through the synaptic connections, which could have a driving or a modulatory effect on the postsynaptic neuron, were combined in a two component activation function (Phillips et al. 1995) that generated an output between 0 and 1. For the motor neurons, the sum of the driving signals determined the direction of rotation of the wheel, whereas the sum of modulatory signals could enhance or reduce rotation speed, but could not change the direction of rotation (more details can be found in Floreano and Mondada 1996a).

The meta-properties of each synapse were individually encoded on the chromosome by six bits: driving or modulatory (1 bit), excitatory or inhibitory (1 bit), four learning rule (2 bits), and four learning rate (2 bits). Each individual synapse could change its strength according to one of four hebbian learning rules (Willshaw et al. 1990): pure hebbian, postsynaptic, presynaptic, and covariance (see chapter 2). These learning rules included a decay factor so that synaptic strengths were always bound within the interval [0.0, 1.0] and their signs were genetically specified (second bit of each gene). The final weight values were not coded back into the genotype.

As soon as a neural network was decoded and attached to the sensors and motors of the robot, synaptic weight values were initialized to small random values (i.e., the initial strengths of the synapses were not inherited) in the range [0.0, 0.1] and updated every 300 ms according to the following discrete time equation:

$$w^t = w^{t-1} + \eta \Delta w^t \tag{7.1}$$

where $\eta$ was the genetically encoded learning rate, which could assume one of four values {0.0, 0.3, 0.7, 1.0}. If the learning rate was 0.0, the corresponding synapse did not change its strength during the life of the individual. Robots were evolved in a real environment and selected for their ability to navigate as fast as possible while keeping far from obstacles. The environment, fitness function, and evolutionary algorithm employed were the same as those described in section 4.2. By maintaining everything similar to the previous experiment, we could compare these results with those obtained when synaptic weight values were genetically evolved.

Three evolutionary runs were made. In all runs the fitness values of the best individuals reached a maximum of 0.23, ±0.09 (similar to the value obtained by the best individual displayed in the experiment of chapter 4) after approximately 50 generation. All the best individuals of the last generation exhibited smooth trajectories around the looping maze (figure 7.8). In all the three runs the best individuals of the last generation displayed an emergent frontal direction corresponding to the side with more infrared sensors, just like in the experiment of chapter 4. However, in this experiment the navigation ability was not present "at birth," as in the previous experiment. Here, the neural networks learned to navigate starting from random initial values assigned to the synapses. The acquisition of this ability was very fast: in less than 10 sensory motor loops the best individuals were already capable of moving forward without getting stuck into walls.

Figure 7.8 shows the trajectory of one of the best evolved controllers in two successive

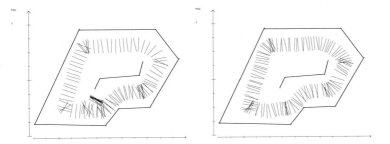

**Figure 7.8**
Trajectory of an evolved robot learning to navigate during its lifetime. Position data, visualized as bars
representing the axis connecting the two wheels, were acquired with an external laser positioning device every
100 ms. (see section 3.2) **Left:** Trajectory during the first lap (the robot starts in the lower portion of the
environment and turns counterclockwise). **Right:** Trajectory at the second lap.

laps of the looping maze. Initially, the synapses were randomly initialized and the robot was
positioned facing a corner of the inner wall (figure 7.8, left; initial position corresponds to
the set of superimposed bars in the lower portion of the environment). During the first
2 seconds (6–7 synaptic updates), the robot adjusted its position alternating back and
forth movements until it found a wall on its right side. This initial behavior was quite
stereotypical: it was displayed for any starting position. Once a wall had been found, the
robot moved forward keeping it at a distance of 2 cm from its own right side. Every second
or third action, it slightly turned toward the wall and then continued forward. This sort of
jerky behavior was gradually reduced when coasting a straight long wall (e.g., the north
and east walls). If the wall was slightly bent, the robot could still follow it without reducing
speed, but when it encountered a convex angle smaller than 90 degrees (which means that
most of the front infrared sensors were active) the robot stopped, backed rotating to the
right, and then resumed forward motion in the new direction. After one lap around the
maze, the path became smoother with less trajectory adjustments and more tuned to the
geometric outline of the environment (figure 7.8, right).

The development of such behavior can be understood by studying the internal dynamics of the evolved network. Figure 7.9 plots the strengths of all synapses in the network
during the first 100 actions (sensory-motor loops) visualized in figure 7.8 using the same
format of figure 7.7. Without going into much details (which can be found in Floreano
and Mondada 1996a), one of the most remarkable results was that synapses continuously
changed while the behavior of the robot became rather stable after a few seconds.

In the conventional view, synapses are relatively slow changing and stable components
of the nervous system (see chapter 2). Synaptic change is identified with learning of
new skills or acquisition of new knowledge, while neural activation is identified with

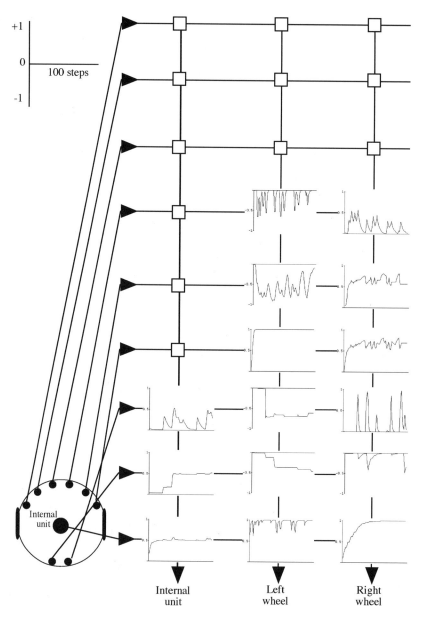

**Figure 7.9**
Synaptic strengths recorded every 300 ms during the first 100 actions of the robot. Small white boxes represent synapses that remain close to zero.

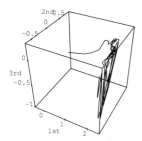

**Figure 7.10**
State-space representation of synaptic dynamics during the first 100 actions plotted as trajectory within the space of the first three principal components. Arrows indicate starting position and range of oscillation between action sequences 20–80 and 80–100. Oscillations within the subspace of the third (smallest) component correspond to fine trajectory adjustments. Method: Sanger's network (Sanger, 1989) for extracting the first three principal components of the input correlation matrix was trained to stability on the 27-component vectors corresponding to the synaptic activity recorded during the first 100 actions of the robot visualized in figure 7.9. After training, input vectors were presented again to the network and output unit activations were plotted in the resulting 3-dimensional space.

behavior (or short term memory, as we wrote at the beginning of this chapter). Typically, it is assumed that acquisition of a stable behavior in a static environment (for example, learning to distinguish faces) corresponds to reaching a stable state—no further change—of synapses in the network (e.g., see Hertz et al. 1989). This assumption is explicitly included into the objective functions from which—both supervised and unsupervised—conventional learning algorithms are analytically derived: least mean square error minimization, energy reduction, maximization of node mutual information, etc. Since synaptic stability was not included in the fitness function employed in this experiment, which was defined solely in behavioral terms, the evolved neurocontrollers were free to explore and exploit different ways of using synaptic change.

One way of looking at a dynamical system such as this evolved neural network is to analyze its state space behavior, that is the development of the synaptic vector in its 27 dimensional space over 100 updates (which correspond to two laps around the looping maze). Since it is impossible to draw a 27-dimensional space, a more convenient representation could be that of displaying how the 27 dimensional vector varies over 100 time steps. Principal Component Analysis does just that by extracting the directions of maximum variance of the distribution of data (our 100 synaptic vectors). Once we have extracted the first, say, three directions of maximum variance, we have a 3 dimensional space on which we can sequentially plot each of the 100 vectors. Figure 7.10 shows the trajectory of synaptic change in the reduced state space of the first three principal components of the recorded synaptic vectors during the first 100 actions of the individual displayed in figure 7.8 and 7.9.

During the first six actions the neural network moves toward a subregion of the space for which there is no change in the first two principal components; residual variation along the slice of space corresponding to the third principal component corresponds to fine trajectory adjustments and is further reduced as the robot gradually tunes its path to the geometry of the environment. This means that, after an initial phase of strong variation, the synapses as a whole change in a systematic and coordinated fashion. In other words, the stable behavior acquired during life is regulated by continuously changing synapses which are dynamically stable. Roughly speaking, this means that when one synapse goes up, there will be another synapse going down. Other solutions might exist that produce similar fitness values and correspond to a similar behavior. For example, the synapses might reach a static state after a few steps, as in most artificial neural networks. However, this solution was never observed in the individuals analysed.

The synapses evolved in this experiment are responsible for both learning and behavior regulation. Knowledge in the network is not expressed by a final stable state of the synaptic configuration, but rather by a *dynamic equilibrium point* in an *n* dimensional state space (where *n* is the number of synapses). Learning can be seen as a displacement of the entire system from a dynamically unstable state to a new dynamically stable state. Whether biological synapses can play a similar role or not, is an issue that remains to be investigated.

Learning of the evolved controller relies on simple genetically inherited abilities. For example, the controller analyzed above always starts by moving backward until it finds some object; then it rotates to the right until its rightmost sensors become active and synapses begin to change. These two simple motor programs result from weak sensory signals (mostly noise) filtered and amplified through the synaptic matrix of excitatory and inhibitory weights. They represent the basis from which learning can start to operate and are similar to instincts in that they are both genetically inherited and represent primitives upon which the organism can start to explore its environment. In other words, evolution not only shapes the learning modality, but also bootstrap learning by selecting basic behaviors useful for learning.

The analysis of the evolved behavior described above clearly indicates that the environment plays a great role in shaping the ontogenetically developed behavior. Behavior is an emergent property of the interaction between inherited instructions and the environment not only because evolution exploits the complexity of the environment and of the interaction between the robot and the environment, but also because inherited instructions only indirectly constrain how the robot reacts in the environment. The way in which the robot reacts to different sensory states itself is affected by the previous interactions of the robot with the environment. In this way the amount of information encoded in the genotype may be reduced given that part of the information will be filled up by the interaction between

inherited instructions and the environment. This property may also allow evolution to select individuals capable of adapting during lifetime to different environments or to rapid
changes in the same environment, as we shall see in the next section (see also Todd and
Miller 1991).

This model is also interesting from the point of view of the issues described in the
previous two sections. In the Hinton and Nowlan's model described in section 7.3, learning
is modeled as a random search process without any directionality. Instead, in the model
described in the previous section, learning has a directionality but the learning task is fixed
and predetermined by the experimenter. In the model described in this section, learning
has a directionality and the learning task itself (i.e., the learning constraints) is evolved.
Interestingly some constraints on what can be learned are determined by the interaction
between the robot and the environment. Only the weights departing from the sensors which
are activated in a given environment can be affected by learning (for example, the weights
departing from the left sensors will never learn because the robot follows walls on its
right side). Instead, other constraints (e.g., the learning rates and the learning rules) are
genetically inherited and therefore are subjected to the evolutionary process. This implies
that in this model the exploration of the phenotypic space around the point corresponding
to the individual at birth has a directionality which is determined by both environmental
and genetic constraints.

A further point that should be stressed is the fact that in this model evolution and
learning operate on two different synaptic entities (the meta-properties and the weight
strengths, respectively) while in the experiments described in the previous two sections
they operate on the same entity (i.e., the weight strengths).

Finally, since this strategy forced the evolved systems to adapt on-line to the environment, it can cope with unpredictable changes without requiring additional evolution. We
shall come back on this point in the conclusions of this chapter.

## 7.6   Adaptation to fast changing environments

As we claimed above, another limitation of the experiment by Hinton and Nowlan was
the learning mechanism employed. Even assuming that evolution and learning are working
toward the same goal (for example, the development of suitable food gathering strategies),
biological learning seems to be more directional than random switching of synapses. The
experiments conducted by Ackley and Littman (1991) in simulated environments not only
represent a step forward with respect to this issue, but also introduce a novel self-teaching
architecture that could be used right away on real autonomous robots.

A variable size population of artificial organisms lives in a simulated environment

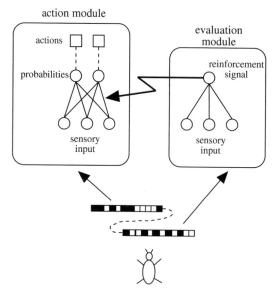

**Figure 7.11**
Evolutionary Reinforcement Learning (Ackley and Litmann 1991). The genetic string of an individual encodes
the connection strengths of the two modules composing the control system. The action module also modifies its
own connection strengths during life, but such changes are not written back into the genetic code.

containing predators, different types of food tokens, and other objects. Each organism
is controlled by a neural network composed of two modules: an *action module* and an
*evaluation module*, as in classic reinforcement learning architectures (Barto et al. 1983,
1990). The action module is a feedforward network mapping sensory information into
probabilities of executing a certain action; the evaluation module provides an evaluation of
the sensory information which is used as a reinforcement signal for the action module
(figure 7.11). The value of the reinforcement signal depends on the variation of the
output of the evaluation module over time. A genetic algorithm evolves the synaptic
weight values of both the action and the evaluation modules, but during the life of the
individual the action module also modifies the genetically inherited weights using the
reinforcement signal provided by the evaluation module. The basic principle behind the
weight change rule is that positive reinforcements cause strengthening of active synapses,
whereas negative reinforcements cause weakening of active synapses. As in darwinian
evolution, final synaptic weight values are not copied back into the genotype.

Each organism can reproduce when it has accumulated enough energy (eating food
while escaping predators) and has found another organism ready for reproduction; offspring are formed by crossing over and randomly mutating the chromosomes of the par-

ents. Organisms die if they cannot maintain a sufficient energy level or when they become too old. As compared to traditional genetic algorithms (Holland 1975), here the energy level plays the role of an intrinsic fitness function.[5]

The authors have compared three different situations: evolution without learning, learning without evolution, and the combination of both. The latter condition, also named *evolutionary reinforcement learning* (ERL), outperformed both other conditions managing to keep the population alive for over three thousand generations. A longitudinal study of the behavioral characteristics of the artificial organisms showed that during the first 600 generations the action modules were not capable of reaching food at birth, but had to learn it during life. In later generations however, food gathering strategies were already present at birth.

These experiments are similar to the situation described by Hinton and Nowlan because learning and evolution are synergetic mechanisms working toward the same goal. Consequently, here the Baldwin effect manifests itself in its most intuitive aspects: an evolutionary advantage of learning individuals and a gradual genetic assimilation of the features learned during life. The distinctive aspect of the approach employed by Ackley and Littman is that evolution effectively decides how to shape learning, that is when and how to provide positive and negative reinforcements to the action module. In the reinforcement learning literature, the decision of when and how a reinforcement signal of a certain type is provided to the learning system (by the environment) is called a *reinforcement program* (RP). In practice, choosing an appropriate RP makes the difference between a successful learning session and a serious failure. By letting evolution decide under what conditions different reinforcement signals are received by the action module, Ackley and Littman have created an autonomous self-learning that decides *when* and *what* should be learned.

A similar approach has been taken more recently by Nolfi and Parisi (1997) in experiments resorting to more realistic simulations of a mobile robot (which will be described below), and showed to be a very effective procedure in dynamic environments that are unpredictable on the evolutionary time scale.

Consider the case of a Khepera robot that should find a target in an arena where walls change color from black to white. The color of the walls significantly affects the response of the infrared sensors of the robot. Since the target is invisible, the robot should explore the environment as much as possible. In order to do so it should adapt during lifetime to the different color of the walls. The experiments described in this section have been conducted in simulation using the sensor sampling technique described in chapter 3.

The environment used for the experiments is a $60 \times 20$ cm arena surrounded by walls (figure 7.12). The target area is a circle of 2 cm of diameter and is positioned at randomly chosen locations. Although the robots cannot directly perceive the target area, the fitness function selects individuals that can reach the target area in the shortest amount of time.

**Figure 7.12**
Two environments with a target area (small black circle) and the Khepera robot (large white circle). The target area is painted on the floor and therefore it cannot be detected by the robot's sensors. The two environments differ in the color of the walls. The wall of the environment on the right reflect six times more light than those of the environment on the left. The environments measure 60x20 cm, the target area has a diameter of 2 cm.

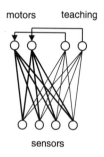

**Figure 7.13**
Self-teaching network. The output of the two teaching units is used as teaching signal for the two motor units. The delta rule is used to change the weights from the input units to the motor units. The weights from the input units to the teaching units do not change during the lifetime of an individual.

This selection criterion indirectly encourages robots to explore the arena efficiently in order to increase their chance to end up on the target area.

Robots can live in two different types of environments: (a) an environment with dark walls, and (b) an environment with bright walls, i.e. walls that reflect six times more light than dark walls. In the dark environment infrared sensors are activated within a distance of about 1 cm from the wall whereas in the light environment this distance is 6 cm. The robot should behave differently in the two environments in order to explore as much as possible the arena. If it lives in environment (a) the robot should move very carefully when sensors are activated because dark walls are detected only when they are very close. In contrast, if the robot lives in environment (b) the walls can be detected from farther away; therefore, if the robot wants to explore the portion of the arena which is close to the walls, it should begin to avoid them only when the sensors are strongly activated. Consider however that individual robots do not know in which type of environment they are going to live. Hence they should be capable of detecting the type of environment in which they are currently

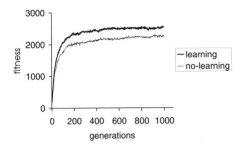

**Figure 7.14**
Fitness of the best individuals along 1000 generations for the population with learning during life (thick curve)
and for the population without learning (thin curve). Each curve represents the average of 10 replications.

placed and should adapt to it through lifetime accordingly.

Robots are controlled by a feedforward neural network consisting of just an input and
an output layer (figure 7.13). The input layer includes four units that encode the activation
level of the robot's sensors. The first input unit encodes the average activation level of
sensors 1 and 2, the second unit the average activation of sensors 3 and 4, etc. Hence,
the network has four receptors: front, back, left, and right. These four input units are
connected to four output units. The first two output units encode the speeds of the two
wheels of the Khepera robot. The remaining two output units represent two *teaching units*
that encode a teaching signal for the first two output units. (A more detailed description
of this type of architecture is given in Nolfi and Parisi 1993a, 1994). This self generated
teaching signal is used to change the weights from the input units to the two motor units
with the delta rule (Widrow and Hoff 1960). In other words, the neural architecture includes
two distinct sub-networks that share the same input units but have separate output units.
The first sub-network (*standard network*; thick connections in figure 7.13) determines
the robot's motor actions. The second sub-network (*teaching network*; thin connections
in figure 7.13) determines how the information coming from the environment is used
to change the connection weights of the standard network. All connection weights are
genetically encoded and evolved, but the connection weights of the teaching network
(teaching weights) do not change during the robot's lifetime while the connection weights
of the standard network (standard weights) do change.[6]

The way in which these robots may adapt to different environments during their life
becomes clear if one considers that the output of the teaching network, which functions
as teaching signal for the standard network, depends on two factors: the connection
weights of the teaching network and the activation value of the four sensory units. While
the connection weights of the teaching network are genetically inherited and are not
directly influenced by the current environment, the sensory input does reflect the external

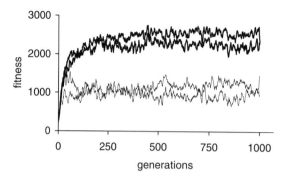

**Figure 7.15**
Performance of robots that have lived and learned in either a dark or a bright environment and are then tested in the same or different environment. The test is applied only to the best individual of each generation. Thick curves represent the performance of individuals that are tested in the same environment in which they have lived and learned (either dark or light). Thin curves represent the performance of individuals that are tested in a different environment (either dark or bright). Average results of 10 replications.

environment. As a consequence, the teaching signal generated by the teaching network may be influenced by the external environment and can teach different things in different environments. Evolution has the possibility to select robots that are able to adapt to changing environments by selecting teaching weights that produce teaching signals that are different in different environments and that produce changes that are appropriate to the current environment.

By comparing the performance of individuals which were subjected to lifetime learning with individuals which were not allowed to do so we observed that, after few generations, learning individuals outperform non learning individuals (figure 7.14).

To understand whether learning robots were actually capable of learning to adapt to the particular environment they happen to be born in, we tested "adult" robots (that is, robots at the end of their life and, therefore, of their learning) both in the environment in which they had developed and in an environment which was different from the one they experienced during their life. We made two copies of the weights of the best individual in each generation (prior to learning) and we left one copy live and learn in the bright environment and the other copy live and learn in the dark environment. At the end of life (learning) the two resulting networks were tested, with their weights frozen, in both environments. As shown in figure 7.15, individuals perform better (i.e., they obtain more fitness) if the environment in which they are tested is the same environment in which they have lived and learned. This shows that characters acquired through learning are adapted to the particular environment in which the learning takes place.

How is such adaptation to the current environment actually accomplished? How can

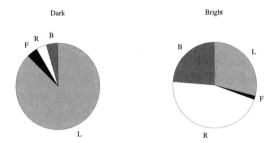

**Figure 7.16**
Percentage of time each of the four input units is the most active one during one epoch without learning (i.e., using the weight values inherited at birth) in both the dark and bright environment. The measures are carried out on an individual evolved to learn during lifetime. (F = front sensor (black); B = back sensor (dark-gray); L = left sensor (light-gray); R = right sensor (white)).

robots "recognize" the type of environment they happen to be born in and how can they modify themselves to adapt to that environment?

If we examine the type of stimuli that the two identical copies of the best individual of each generation experience in the dark and in the bright environment, we see that these stimuli differ both quantitatively and qualitatively depending on the environment where the individual lives. We measured the activation level of the sensors during the entire lifetime of the best individuals of each generation and we found that the average activation level was 0.11 for the copy living in the dark environment and 0.24 for the copy living in the bright environment. In addition, we found that the percentage of times each of the four input units (corresponding to the left, right, front, and back pairs of sensors) is the most active one significantly varies at birth, i.e., prior to learning, between the two environments (figure 7.16). This measure is obtained by allowing an individual to live for one epoch prior to learning in the two environments while measuring the percentage of times each of the four input units is the most active one.

The different types of stimuli the robots experience in the two environments affect the type of teaching signal computed by the teaching network and allow the robots to modify their standard weights (i.e., the weights that determine their motor behavior) differently in the two environments.

At this point we may ask ourselves what is the role of the inherited standard weights in the case of individuals that are allowed to learn during their life. One might think that the standard weights incorporate the same general solution adopted by non learning individuals and that learning is used to refine the inherited strategy by taking into consideration the specificity of the current environment. If we compare the performance exhibited prior to learning by evolved individuals belonging to the learning population with the performance

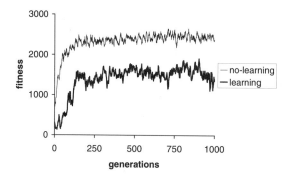

**Figure 7.17**
Performance of learning (thick curve) and non-learning (thin curve) individuals at birth across 1000 generations.
The performance of learning individuals has been assessed by letting these individuals live for 10 epochs
without any learning. Average of 10 replications.

of individuals belonging to the non learning population, we discover that this is not the case
(see figure 7.17). Individuals belonging to the learning population perform on the basis of
their inherited standard weights less well than individuals of the non learning population.[7]
This result contrasts with the comparison between the two populations when performance
is assessed after learning. In these circumstances the individuals of the learning population
outperform those of the non learning population (see figure 7.14).

This result implies that inherited standard weights of learning individuals are selected
not only for their ability to solve the task (as shown by their performance at birth prior
to learning), but also for how well they can learn. In other words, the genes (i.e., the
inherited standard weights plus the inherited teaching weights) of evolved individuals
that are allowed to learn do not incorporate a predisposition to behave efficiently, but a
*predisposition to learn* to behave efficiently.

To understand what a predisposition to learn can mean in the case of our robots we
should consider two facts (see chapter 2): a) initial conditions (e.g., initial weights) can
determine the course of learning by error minimization (Kolen and Pollack 1990), and
b) evolution can select appropriate initial weights for learning (Belew et al. 1991). The
former result, applied to our case, implies that the values of standard weights can strongly
affect the learning process. If we allow our individuals to learn starting from random
initial weights instead than from their inherited standard weights, their performance will
remain constantly low throughout their life (result not shown). Although the learning error
will progressively decrease, the weight change does not improve the efficiency of their
exploration of the environment even if the inherited teaching weights are left intact (see
Nolfi and Parisi 1997).

## The effect of the sequence of training patterns on learning

That the sequence of training patterns has a significant effect on the outcome of learning has been shown by several authors within "classical" neural networks studies. Plunkett and Marchmann (1991) have shown how a neural network can be successfully trained to classify a set of sensory states only if the network experiences sensory states which are difficult to be categorized more often than the others. They trained a neural network which received as input the stem of both regular and irregular English verbs to produce as output the correct past tense form (a well studied ability in language acquisition literature) and showed that presenting each verb token just one time for each training epoch resulted in a disastrous performance for the irregular verbs. Successful performance was only achieved by manipulating the frequency of the verbs types in the training set. In particular, they showed that the network is able to produce the correct output for all verbs only if irregular verbs are presented more often to the network than the regular verb (something which approximates what is known about the linguistic input of the real children). These results can be explained by considering that "the high token frequency of the irregular verbs afforded them some degree of protection from regular verb interference" (Elman and al. 1996, pp. 139). Elman (1993) showed that complex tasks can be learned only if the network is exposed first to simple cases and then to progressively more complex cases. The author trained a recurrent neural network to predict the next word in sentences of a pseudo natural language. To solve this task the network should take into account features with different level of complexity such as verb/subject number agreement and long distances (cross clausal) dependencies. As in the previous case, the network was unable to learn this task if sentences of any length were experienced from the beginning. Success could only be achieved either by: (a) dividing the training data into graded batches beginning with simple sentences and gradually introducing more and more complex ones; (b) by resetting the context units (which formed the memory of the network) initially after two or three words and than at increasingly long intervals. These results can be explained by considering that in both cases the role of the simple sentences is enhanced in the first part of the training (In the former case because the network experiences only simple sentences in the first part of training. In the latter, because the limitation in the memory span prevents the tractability of the long sentences but not of the short sentences which impose fewer demands). Short sentences provide the right entry point to the problem because they allow the network to develop internal representations than in turn will allow the network to deal with more complex sentences.

**The effect of the sequence of training patterns on learning** (continued)

In this type of research, where neural networks are not embodied and are studied in isolation, the input sequence is determined by the experimenter. In the case of robots that "live" and learn by interacting with an external environment, instead, the sequence of input states is determined by the environment and by the robot itself through its motor actions. As we claimed in chapter 5, this implies that sensory-motor coordination tends to assume additional functions in plastic individuals. Generally speaking we can say that evolving plastic individuals display initial behaviors that ensure the experience of input sequences suitable to be learnt, even if these behaviors do not directly contribute to increase individuals' fitness. This might be accomplished in a variety of different ways. The initial back and rotate behavior observed in evolved individuals described in section 7.5, for example, seems to have the function of channeling the learning process in the right direction (i.e., to allow the robot to experience a certain input sequence which, in turn, produces certain modifications in the weights of the controller). Moreover, the initial behavior displayed by the individuals described in this section, allows individuals to perceive quite different input sequences in the two environments which, in turn, facilitates the problem of producing different modifications depending on the type of environment. It should be noted that these are only two of the possible functions that sensory-motor coordination can assume in plastic individuals. As in the case of the experiments described above, we may expect that sensory-motor coordination will also be used to increase the frequency of important sensory states and of input sequences that allow the development of internal features necessary to master other, more complex, input sequences.

A predisposition to learn to explore the environment more efficiently, therefore, is at least in part incorporated in the inherited standard weights. However, the inherited teaching weights also incorporate a predisposition to learn (or, more precisely, to produce adaptive changes in the standard weights). If we allow our individuals to modify the genetically inherited standard weights but we randomize the teaching weights, in this case too learning will destroy whatever ability to explore is present at birth rather than increasing that ability (see Nolfi and Parisi 1997). Moreover, if we let our robots move using the output of the teaching units instead of the output of the standard units, once again we obtain a significant decrease in performance (see Nolfi and Parisi 1997) with respect to the case in which self generated teaching is used to modify the standard weights that determine how the robots behave.

Therefore both the standard weights and the teaching weights incorporate a genetically

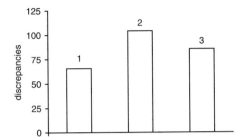

**Figure 7.18**
Difference in the percentage of time each of the four input units is the most activated one in the two environments for (1) nonlearning individuals at birth, (2) learning individuals at birth, and (3) learning individuals at the end of their life. Individuals evolved for learning behave so that input units are activated more differently in the two environments. This means that their behavior enhances perceptual differences.

inherited predisposition to learn rather than a predisposition to behave. The behavior of evolved robots emerges from the interaction between the two set of weights and cannot be traced back in part to one set and in part to the other set. More precisely, behavior is the emergent result of the interaction between standard weights, teaching weights, and the environment.

Interestingly, the predisposition to learn does not only consist in an ability to use the sensory patterns coming from the sensors to adapt to the environment, but also in an ability to modify the patterns received from the environment in order to select patterns which produce adaptive changes. In other words evolved individuals have *a predisposition to select useful learning experiences*. (See inset box on the role of the sequence of training patterns on learning). It was found, in fact, that evolved robots learning during lifetime behave at birth in a way that enhances the perceived difference between the two environment with respect to non learning robots (see figure 7.18).

To determine how the two environments differ in the inputs that they make available to the learning and nonlearning robots, we computed the percentage of cycles in which each of the four input units was the most active and we compared these percentages in the two environments for both learning and non learning individuals (details of how the measurement has been conducted can be found in Nolfi and Parisi 1997). The differences in the activation level among the four input units in the two environments reflect the different behaviors of an organism in the two environments. The first column of figure 7.18 shows the average difference between the stimuli perceived at birth in the two environments by non learning individuals. The second column shows the same average difference for the learning individuals at birth, i.e., before any learning. The third column shows the average difference for the learning individuals at the end of life, that is, after learning has had its effect. These data indicate that learning individuals perceive at birth the two environments as more different than non learning individuals (i.e., the difference between the first and second column is statistically significant, see Nolfi and Parisi 1997). In other words, learning individuals behave at birth in a way that enhances perceived differences between the two environments which in turn allow them to learn to produce two different behaviors in the two environments.

## 7.7  Conclusions

In this chapter we have investigated how learning can enhance the adaptive power of evolution. In section 7.3 we saw that learning can help and guide the evolutionary search even if characters acquired through lifetime learning are not inherited. In particular we saw that learning and evolution might solve tasks that evolution alone is unable to solve. Moreover, in section 7.4, we showed that learning can produce an increase in performance both ontogenetically and phylogenetically even if the learning task differs from the task for which individuals are selected.

We also showed that learning individuals outperform non learning individuals in non stationary environments by adapting during lifetime to their current environment (section 7.6). Evolved individuals are capable of detecting the type of environment in which they are placed and of modifying accordingly their behavior during lifetime in order to maximize their fitness. We will discuss another example of adaptation to a dynamically changing environment in chapter 8.

In section 7.5 we showed that some characters (i.e., the connection weights in this case) can be extracted from the environment instead of being specified into the genotype. In the model described in that section, the weight values emerge from the interaction between genetically specified instructions and the environment.

We saw that information extracted from the environment can channel evolutionary search into promising directions. In section 7.5, for example, we saw that only weights departing from sensors which are stimulated in a given environment (i.e., only weights which have an effect on the corresponding behavior) change during lifetime. In other words, the information coming from the environments allows learning to explore the most interesting dimensions of the search space.

Finally, we saw that evolution may channel learning into promising direction. In the case of the experiments described in section 7.5 and 7.6, the directionality of learning is not fixed but is determined by the inherited constraints (the combination of learning parameters and the teaching weights respectively) which are themselves under evolution. Therefore the directionality of learning is selected by evolution (i.e., evolution selects the learning task).

Since lifetime learning affects the fitness of the individuals and consequently affects also the choice of individuals selected for reproduction, evolution will tend to select individuals that display good learning directions. In other words evolution will tend to select inherited constraints that produce ontogenetic changes which are adaptive.

By exploring the adaptive functions of learning we discovered that the interaction between learning and evolution deeply alters both the evolutionary and the learning process themselves. Evolution in interaction with learning displays dynamics very different from those which are observed in evolution alone. While in non plastic individuals the inherited characters are directly selected for their ability to produce successful behaviors, in the case of individuals that learn, the characters are selected for their ability to incorporate a *predisposition to learn*. This genetically inherited predisposition to learn may consist of different things:

- the presence of starting conditions at birth (e.g., initial weights for learning) that canalize learning in the right direction. Evolution may select initial weight matrices or network architectures that cause a better and/or a faster learning. This happens either when the learning task and the evolutionary task are the same or are different. In the latter case, evolution does not only select individuals that have a predisposition to better learn, but also individuals that, by learning a certain task, improve their performance with respect to the evolutionary task.

- an inherited tendency to behave in such a way that the individual is exposed to the appropriate learning experiences. Evolution tends to select characters that produce initial behaviors that enhance the possibility to learn and/or that increase the probability to acquire adaptive characters through learning. In other words evolution tends to select individuals which have an initial behavior suitable for learning and not necessarily for solving the evolutionary task.

Learning within an evolutionary perspective has quite different characteristics from learning studied in isolation, as in "traditional" connectionist research (Rumelhart and Mc-Clelland 1986). While in individuals that learn but are not subjected to an evolutionary process (e.g., neural networks trained with supervised methods) learning is usually accomplished by ignoring the characters of the individual prior to learning (which are typically generated at random), in evolving plastic individuals learning exploits such starting conditions. In other words, when the learning process itself is subjected to an evolutionary process, learning does not necessarily tend to incorporate the right solution to the problem; rather it tends to pull the learning individual in a direction that maximizes the chances of acquiring adaptive characters by taking into consideration its initial state. This explains the surprising result described in section 7.6 that self generated teaching signals do not correspond to the desired motor actions although they are capable of producing changes that generate suitable motor actions (see also Nolfi and Parisi 1993a, 1994).

The strategy described in section 7.5, i.e., the evolution of learning rules, presents a distinctive feature: the genetic string does not encode any synaptic weight of the control network (only the sign). Therefore, individuals are evolved mainly for their ability to adapt on-line to the environment and develop behavioral abilities that satisfy the selection criterion. Therefore, one may expect that these individuals can cope with unpredictable changes that happen during their lifetime, that is changes that have not been experienced during the evolutionary process. In a series of very recent experiments, we have indeed shown that robots evolved with this strategy can re-adapt on-line to several types of changes without requiring further evolutionary training. We have applied the changes only after evolution and have compared evolved adaptive robots with genetically determined robots (whose genetic string encodes only the weights, but not the learning rules). We have studied three types of changes: a) sensory changes; b) environmental changes; c) morphological changes. In the first case (a), we have used the environment shown in figure 7.12 of section 7.6. Adaptive robots evolved only in white environments were capable of adapting immediately during their lifetime to both black and gray environments whereas genetically determined robots failed to do so (Urzelai and Floreano 1999). In the second case (b), we evolved robots in an environment with different areas that required different behaviors and then we randomly changed the locations of these areas. Once again, adaptive robots managed to modify their behavior during lifetime and report the same fitness, whereas genetically determined robots failed to do so (Urzelai and Floreano 2000). In the third case (c), we transferred evolved controllers from the Khepera to the Koala robot and showed that adaptive controllers managed to adapt during their lifetime to the new morphology whereas genetically determined individuals could not (Urzelai and Floreano 2000). We also showed that evolving the learning rules, instead of the synaptic weights, does not allow robots to use minimalistic strategies that rely on environmental features discovered during evolution. As a consequence, these robots can develop more complex abilities and solve tasks that genetically determined robots cannot (Floreano and Urzelai 1999). Finally, since this strategy does not require encoding of synaptic weights, one can apply the same learning rule for all the connections of a neuron in the network. This means that the length of the genetic string is now proportional to the number of neurons, not to the number of connections in the network. We could show that evolved adaptive robots report the same performance even when we added twenty fully recurrent internal neurons (that is, 400 new connections) to the control network, whereas genetically determined individuals failed to evolve any meaningful behavior (Floreano and Urzelai 1999). Therefore, not only this strategy generates more efficient and robust controllers, but it may well be used to evolve architectures of controllers where one cannot specify in advance all the weights of the network.

Finally, another interesting issue on which we shall return in chapter 8 is to imagine that learning allows evolving individuals to solve complex tasks by using a collection of simple strategies instead of a single strategy that might be too difficult (or maybe impossible) to evolve. In these cases, learning allows individuals to detect current needs and to modify their strategy accordingly.

# 8 Competitive co-evolution

## 8.1 Introduction

Competitive co-evolution (i.e., the evolution of two or more competing populations with coupled fitness) has several features that may potentially enhance the adaptation power of artificial evolution.

Co-evolution of competing populations may produce increasingly complex evolving challenges. As discussed by Dawkins and Krebs (1979), competing populations may reciprocally drive one another to increasing levels of behavioral complexity by producing an evolutionary "arms race." Consider for example the well studied case of two co-evolving populations of predators and prey (Miller and Cliff 1994): the success of predators implies a failure of prey and viceversa. Evolution of a new behavior in one species represents a new challenge for the other species which is required, on its turn, to evolve a new strategy. The continuation of this process may produce increasingly higher levels of complexity in the behavioral strategies of the two competing species (although this does not necessarily happen, as we will see below). As Rosin and Belew (1997) point out, from the point of view of one of the two species this corresponds to a *pedagogical* series of challenges that gradually require more complex solutions.

We have already mentioned the benefits of incremental training for neural networks that must learn a complex task which cannot be learned at once (see inset box in chapter 7 on the effect of sequence of training patterns on learning). Similarly, artificial evolution might fail to find a solution to a complex task if starting from scratch, but it is very likely to succeed if it is asked first to find a solution to a simple task and later to progressively more complex tasks. As we have seen in earlier chapters, one might implement incremental evolution by gradually modifying the fitness function and/or the characteristics of the environment (Floreano 1992; Harvey et al. 1994; Floreano and Mondada 1996a), but this requires careful attention and planning by the experimenter. Consider instead the case of predators and prey. At the beginning of the evolutionary process, both predators and prey display, on average, very poor behaviors. Therefore, for some predators it might be relatively easy to catch several prey and produce offspring for the next generation; a similar situation holds for the prey. Gradually, both populations and their evolving challenges will become progressively more and more complex. Therefore, even if the selection criterion and the layout of the physical environment remain the same, the task effectively faced by each species may become progressively more complex.

Another potentially beneficial factor regards the variety of tasks faced by every single individual. During its lifetime an organism might encounter a certain number of opponents both from the same generation or from earlier generations (if we consider some type of generational overlap). In both cases, the opponents faced by the organism are likely to be different and to change over generations. Therefore, the ability for which individuals are selected is more general[1] (i.e., it has to cope with a variety of different cases) than in the case of evolution of a single population where the task and the environment are always the same. Consider also that if we evolve predators to catch always one single prey, we may easily fail. In fact, if the prey is very efficient, the probability that a predator from the first generation with a randomly generated genotype can catch it is very low. As a consequence, all individuals would be scored with the same null value and selective reproduction could not operate. On the contrary, if we ask the evolutionary process to find a predator able to catch a variety of different prey, it is much more likely that at least one individual of the initial generations will catch at least one prey, thus providing the necessary conditions for selective reproduction and possibly setting the stage for progressive development of more complex strategies.

Finally, competing co-evolutionary systems are computationally appealing because the ever changing fitness landscape caused by changes in the co-evolving species is potentially useful in preventing stagnation in local minima. Before moving on to the experimental investigations, in the next section we will review some possible situations that may limit the power of competitive co-evolution.

## 8.2   Co-evolutionary complications

As already pointed out, co-evolution could spontaneously produce a form of incremental evolution which might allow it to select individuals with progressively more complex competencies. Indeed, as hypothesized by some biologists, "arm races" could be one of the main sources of evolutionary innovation and adaptation in natural evolution (Van Valen 1973; Dawkins 1986; Ridley 1993)

However, a continuous increase in complexity is not guaranteed. Co-evolving populations might in fact drive one another along twisting pathways where each new solution is just good enough to counter balance the current strategies implemented by the co-evolving population, but is not necessarily more complex than solutions discovered some generations earlier. Furthermore, the new solution may be ineffective against strategies which previous solutions were able to defeat.

For instance, co-evolving populations may cycle between alternative classes of strategies that, although do not represent progress in the long run, may be temporarily effective against the co-evolving population.

## Theoretical models of competitive co-evolution

The first formal studies of predator prey dynamics date back to the mid 1920's when Lotka (1925) and Volterra (1926) independently developed a simple model composed of two differential equations. The Lotka and Volterra model describes how population densities $N_1$ and $N_2$ of two co-evolving competing species vary during evolutionary time $t$

$$\frac{\partial N_1}{\partial t} = N_1\left(r_1 - b_1 N_2\right), \quad \frac{\partial N_2}{\partial t} = N_2\left(-r_2 + b_2 N_1\right)$$

where $r_1$ is the increment rate of the prey population in the absence of predators, $r_2$ is the death rate of predators in the absence of prey, $b_1$ is the death rate of prey due to be eaten by predators, and $b_2$ is the ability of predators in catching prey.

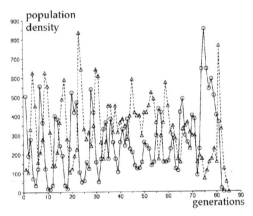

Probabilistic versions of this simple model have been used to explain several biological observations, such as the oscillatory dynamics of co-evolving host-parasite populations, and predict oscillation periods and stability conditions (Renshaw 1991; Murray 1993). For example, the figure above shows variations in population size of co-evolving biological parasites (triangles) and hosts (circles) (redrawn from Utida 1957) whose oscillatory dynamics can be easily predicted by Lotka-Volterra models (extinction of both populations at generation 85 was caused by external factors).

It is important to notice that Lotka-Volterra models focus on variations of population size and assume a given performance (fitness) for both predators and prey which remains fixed across generations. Therefore, they cannot be used to assess whether competitive co-evolution can generate incremental progress in performance of the two species.

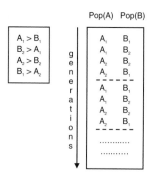

**Figure 8.1**
The same strategies (A1 and A2 in population A) and (B1 and B2 in population B) may be selected over and over again throughout generations, as shown on the right-hand side of the figure, if (1) the interaction between them obeys to the relationships outlined on the left-hand side of the figure, and (2) different strategies are close on the genotype space. In this case the cycle corresponds to four different combinations of strategies.

Imagine, for example, that at a particular moment population A adopts strategy $A_1$ giving it an advantage over population B which has strategy $B_1$. Imagine now that there is a strategy $B_2$ (genotypically close to $B_1$, i.e., which can be easily reached from $B_1$ on the genotype space) that gives population B an advantage over strategy $A_1$. Population B is very likely to find and adopt strategy $B_2$. Imagine now that there is a strategy $A_2$ (genotypically close to $A_1$) that provides an adaptive advantage over strategy $B_2$. Population A will easily find and adopt strategy $A_2$. Finally, imagine that previously discovered strategy $B_1$ provides an advantage over strategy $A_2$. Population B will go back to strategy $B_1$. At this point also population A will go back to strategy $A_1$ (because, as explained above, it is effective against strategy $B_1$) and this cycling of the same strategies will be repeated over and over again (figure 8.1). Notice that the cycling may involve not only two or more different strategies for each population, but also two or more different groups of strategies.

If this phenomenon occurs early on during co-evolution, it may cancel out several of the previously described advantages because the solutions evolved might be few and trivial. Instead of discovering progressively more complex strategies, evolution might rediscover previously selected strategies that could be adopted with only a few genetic changes (i.e., very quickly or in a few generations).

Another difficulty in competitive co-evolution is related to changes in the fitness landscape and to the external assessment of progress (figure 8.2). In co-evolving populations, in fact, changes in one species affect the reproductive value of specific trait combinations in the other species. In other words, a particular combination of genetic traits evolved over some generations might quickly become ineffective in later generations if the opponent

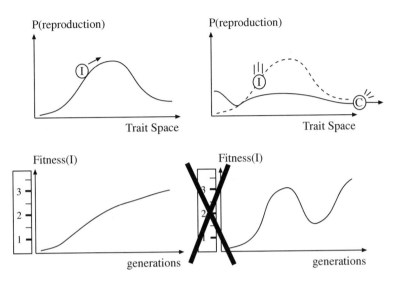

**Figure 8.2**
**Top, left:** Fitness landscape of a single species I under evolution in a static environment. Selective reproduction and mutations tend to drive the individual towards zone of the genotype that correspond to higher reproduction probability (fitness). **Bottom, left:** In the single-agent static-environment case, evolutionary progress can be measured using average and best fitness scores reported by species I across generations. **Top, right:** Reproduction probability of species I under competitive co-evolution with species C. Adaptive changes in species C cause a modification of the fitness landscape of I by making ineffective genetic traits that were beneficial some generations earlier. **Bottom, right:** In competitive co-evolution, fitness scores reported by species I depend on the strategies used by the competitive species C and do not provide an absolute measure of performance. In other words, a decrement in fitness scores might be caused by an improvement in the strategies of C and not necessarily by an absolute deterioration of I's strategies.

species changes its behaviors. This effectively corresponds to a modification of the fitness landscape. It might thus happen that progress achieved by one lineage is reduced or eliminated by the competing species. This phenomenon, which is referred to as the *Red Queen effect*[2] (van Valen 1973; Ridley 1993), makes it hard to monitor progress by using conventional indicators, such as average population fitness or fitness of the best individual. In fact, since immediate fitness scores are relative to a co-evolving set of traits in the opponent, they are no longer a valid indicator of absolute performance. Apparent oscillations might hide true progress and periods of stasis might correspond to tightly coupled co-evolutionary changes in both species.

In the context of artificial co-evolution, where all the data are available to the researcher, this problem can be easily solved by developing appropriate measuring techniques. Cliff and Miller (1995) have suggested to monitor progress by testing the performance of the best individual at each generation against all the best competing ancestors.

The measurements obtained in this way have been called *CIAO* data (*current individual vs. ancestral opponents*). We have proposed proposed another simple measure called *master tournament* (Floreano and Nolfi 1997a). It consists in testing the performance of the best individual at each generation against the best competitors of all generations. Both techniques, by reporting the average performance of one strategy against other discovered strategies, can be used to measure co-evolutionary progress (i.e., the discovery of more general and effective solutions). The latter technique, which takes into account all opponent strategies (not only those discovered up to the current generation as in the CIAO technique), may be used to select the best solutions from an optimization point of view (see Floreano and Nolfi 1997a).

Despite these complications, one can find in the computational literature some examples where co-evolution generates powerful solutions to difficult problems. Hillis (1990) reported a significant improvement in the evolution of sorting programs when parasite programs (deciding the test conditions for the sorting programs) were co-evolved, and similar results were found by Angeline and Pollack (1993) on co-evolution of players for the Tic Tac Toe game.

*But does sustained competition really lead to smooth directional evolutionary progress, or to noisy, unreliable, fits and starts, or to endless cycling through different evolutionary unstable strategies? How important is tight co-evolution among two or a few competing lineages, versus diffuse co-evolution among many? These issues are critical to the debate between those who view evolution as a smoothly running engine of adaptation (e.g. Dawkins 1986), and other theorists who view it as a more contingent history of genetic drift, ad hoc modification, and developmental limitation (e.g. Gould 1989). The Red Queen question is a microcosm of the ancient debate over the links between evolution, life, teleology, and progress.*

From Cliff and Miller 1995, pp. 200–201

In this chapter we will investigate the role of co-evolution in the context of evolutionary robotics. Moreover, we will try to understand under which conditions, if any, co-evolution can lead to "arms races" where two populations reciprocally drive one another to increasing levels of complexity.

After introducing our experimental framework in section 8.3, we will describe the result of an initial simple experiment in section 8.4. As we will see, by co-evolving two populations of predator and prey robots we can easily obtain a large variety of interesting behavioral strategies. However, the innovations produced in this first experiment may easily be lost because the evolutionary process quickly falls into a cycling phase where the same type of solutions are adopted over and over again by the two co-evolving populations. In section 8.5 we will show that the tendency to cycle between the same types of strategies may be reduced by preserving all previously discovered strategies and by using all of them to test each individual of the current population (this technique is referred to as "hall of fame" co-evolution, Rosin and Belew 1997). We will also point out that this technique, which is biologically implausible, has its own drawbacks. As we will show in section 8.6 in fact, "hall of fame" co-evolution does not necessarily produce better performance than simple co-evolution. On the contrary, in the case of the experiment described in this section, simple co-evolution tends to outperform "hall of fame" co-evolution. In section 8.6 we will also see that "arms races" can emerge and indeed produce increasingly better solutions. In section 8.7 we will see that co-evolution can solve problems that evolution alone cannot. In other words, we will show that under some circumstances competitive co-evolution has a higher adaptive power than evolution of a single population. Finally, in section 8.8 we will discuss the role of ontogenetic plasticity in the case of co-evolving populations. As we will see, predators allowed to change ontogenetically exploit the possibility to quickly adapt to the strategy of their current competitors during their own lifetime. This allows them to develop general strategies and reduces the risk that the co-evolutionary process ends up in a cycling behavior.

## 8.3   Co-evolving predator and prey robots

Several researchers have investigated predator-prey co-evolution in simulation (Koza 1991, 1992; Cliff and Miller 1995, 1996). Our investigations are based on a combination of experiments with Khepera robots (Floreano et al. 1998) and realistic simulations based on those robots (Floreano and Nolfi 1997a, 1997b; Nolfi and Floreano 1999). In this section, we will describe our experimental framework and in the next sections we will give an overview of the results obtained.

We used two Khepera robots (figures 8.3 and 8.9), one of which (the *Predator*) was equipped with a vision module while the other (the *Prey*) had a maximum available speed set to twice that of the predator. Both species were also provided with eight infrared proximity sensors (six on the front side and two on the back). In the environment used for these experiments, the infrared sensors could detect a wall at a distance of approximately 3 cm, but could detected the other robot at only half that distance (because the reflecting surface is much smaller).

The two robots evolved within a square arena of 47x47 cm delimited by high white walls so that the predator could always see the prey (if within the visual angle) as a black spot on a white background.

The two robots were connected to a desktop workstation equipped with two serial ports through a twin aerial cable providing the robots with electric power and data communication to/from the workstation. The two cables ended up in two separate rotating contacts

**Figure 8.3**
**Right:**The Predator is equipped with the vision module (1D-array of photoreceptors, visual angle of 36 degrees). **Left:** The Prey has a black protuberance which can be clearly detected by the predator at a distance up to 70 cm, but its maximum speed is twice that of the predator. Both Predator and Prey are equipped with eight infrared proximity sensors (max detection range was 3 cm in our environment).

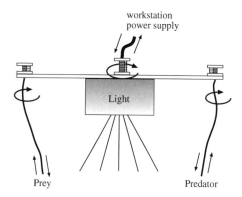

**Figure 8.4**
The suspended bar with the three rotating contacts and a white box casting light over the arena.

firmly attached to the far ends of a suspended thin bar. Both wires then converged into a single rotating contact at the center of the bar and ended up in the serial ports of the workstation (figure 8.4). The thick rotating contact allowed the bar to freely rotate around its center while the remaining two contacts allowed free rotations of the two robots. A halogen lamp (20 W output) attached under the bar provided illumination over the arena.

Both robots were also fitted with a conductive metallic ring around their base so that they could detect when they hit each other (instead of a wall). The vision module of the predator consisted of a one dimensional array of 64 photoreceptors that provided a linear

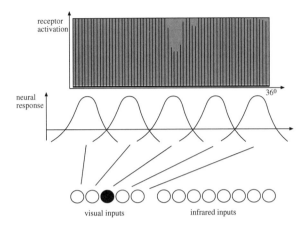

**Figure 8.5**
**Top:** A snapshot of the visual field of the predator looking at the prey. The heights of vertical bars represent the activations of corresponding photoreceptors. The black protuberance of the prey looks like a large valley in the center of the image. The small dip on the right corresponds to the cable. In standard illumination conditions, the image was refreshed at a rate of approximately 15 Hz. **Bottom:** Visual filtering with five *center/off-surround/on* neurons. A neuron is maximally activated when the projection of the prey falls in its receptive field. The most active neuron is set to 1, all the remaining neurons are set to 0 in a winner-take-all fashion.

image composed of 64 pixels of 256 gray levels each subtending a total view angle of $36^o$. In the simple environment employed for these experiments, the prey looks like a blackspot against the white walls (figure 8.5, top).

The controllers of the two robots were two simple neural networks with recurrent connections at the output layer. The neural controller of the prey had eight input units clamped to eight infrared sensors and two motor units controlling the speed of each wheel, as in the experiments described in early chapters. The neural controller of the predator was very similar, but its input layer had an additional set of five units that received information from the vision module. Each of these visual units, which covered approximately $13^o$ and was inspired upon the complex cells found in the early parts of the nervous systems of most animals with a vision system, responded whenever the retinal projection of the prey fell within their receptive field. However, the maximum speed of the predator was set to half that of the prey. Thus, we had a good sighted—but slow—predator and an almost blind—but fast—prey.

Two genetic algorithms were run in parallel, one for the predator and the other for the prey. The genetic algorithms were running on the workstation CPU, but each newly decoded neurocontroller was downloaded through the serial line into the microcontroller Motorola MC68331 of the Khepera robots which was sufficiently capable of storing the set

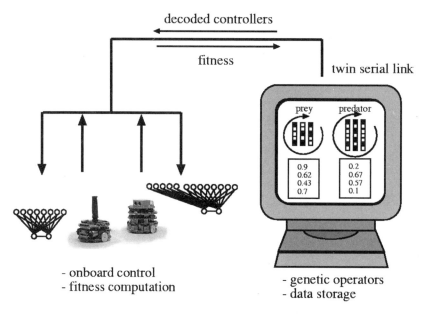

**Figure 8.6**
The genetic operators run on the main workstation, which also manages data storage and analysis; the neural controllers are automatically downloaded on the microcontrollers of the robots through the serial link. In the predator, a microprocessor on the vision module performs visual preprocessing and sends data at 15 Hz frequency to the main microcontroller.

of instructions and variables necessary to handle all input/output routines and neural states (figure 8.6). The speed of the input/output cycles was set to approximately 15 Hz for both prey and predator. In the predator image acquisition and low level visual preprocessing was handled by a private 68HC11 processor installed on the vision turret. Upon receipt of a new neurocontroller from the workstation, each robot set its internal clock (a cycle counter) to zero and began to move. A tournament ended either when the predator hit the prey or when 500 sensory motor cycles (corresponding to approximately 50 seconds) were performed by the prey without being hit by the predator. Upon termination, the prey sent back to the workstation CPU the value of the internal clock (ranging between 0 and 499) which was used as fitness value for both prey and predator. High values corresponded to high fitness for the prey and to low fitness for the predator.

Along with the physical robots, we built a realistic simulator based on the sampling technique described in chapter 3. This simulator allowed us to explore very quickly several variations of the experiments carried out on the physical robots and also perform some computationally expensive analysis of the fitness landscape (see Floreano et al. 1998).

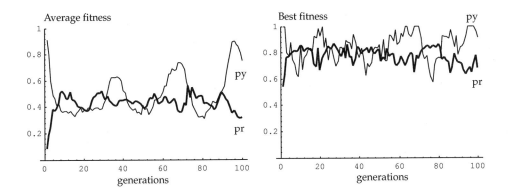

**Figure 8.7**
Co-evolutionary fitness measured in simulation. **Left:** Average population fitness. **Right:** Fitness of the best individuals at each generation. Pr = predator; py = prey. At each generation, the fitness values of the two species do not sum to one because each individual is tested against the best opponents recorded from the previous 10 generations.

## 8.4    Evolution of predator and prey robots: a basic experiment

An initial set of exploratory experiments was investigated in simulations (see Floreano and Nolfi 1997a).[3] The same co-evolutionary procedure was later applied to the physical robots without human intervention. Figure 8.7 shows the average population fitness (left graph) and the fitness of the best individual at each generation (right graph).

As expected, initially the prey score very high, whatever they might do, because the predators are not good at catching them; for the same reason, initially the predators score very low. Very quickly a set of counter phase oscillations emerge in the two populations, as also reported by other authors (Sims 1994, p. 36), but we never observed dominance of one population on the other in any of our evolutionary runs (even when continued for 500 generations). However, the fitness for the prey always tended to generate higher peaks due to position advantage (even in the case of the worst prey and best predator, the latter will always need some time to reach the prey). A similar pattern is observed for the fitness of the best individuals (right graph).

As we mentioned in the previous section, these data cannot be taken as a measure of progress. The only information that they provide is the relative performance of the two species within a window of ten generations. They indicate that progress in one species is quickly counter balanced by progress in the competing species, but do not tell us whether evolutionary time corresponds to true progress, or how to choose the best prey and the best predator from the point of view of optimization. A simple way to learn more about

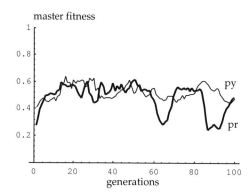

**Figure 8.8**
Master fitness for species evolved in simulation. Each data point is the average fitness of all tournaments of the corresponding individual against all the best 100 opponents recorded during co-evolution.

absolute performance of the two species is to organize a master tournament where the best individuals for each generation are tested against the best competitors from all generations. For example, the best prey of generation 1 is tested against the 100 best predators and the scores of these tournaments are averaged. The master fitness values reported in figure 8.8 indicate that—in absolute terms—individuals of later generations are not necessarily better than those from previous ones.

The results of the experiments carried out on the physical robots (figure 8.9) displayed a trend similar to that observed in simulations.[4] Figure 8.10 shows the average fitness of the population (left graph) and the fitness of the best individual (right graph) along generations for both species. Very quickly the two scores become closer and closer until after generation 15 they diverge again. A similar trend is observed for the fitness of the best individuals at each generation.

25 generations are sufficient to display one oscillatory cycle. Once the relative fitness values of the two species reach the same value, one party improves over the other for some generations until the other counter adapts (the best predators of the last three generations already show a fitness gain). Figure 8.11 shows the master fitness values for the two robot species. The best prey and predators can be found at generation 20. It can also be noticed that fitness oscillations of the best individuals between generation 9 and 16 (figure 8.10, right) do not show up in the master fitness, indicating that they are due to tight interactions between the two competing species which can amplify the effects of small behavioral differences.

A remarkable aspect of these co-evolutionary experiments is the variety and complexity of behavioral strategies displayed by the two species. Figure 8.12 shows some typical

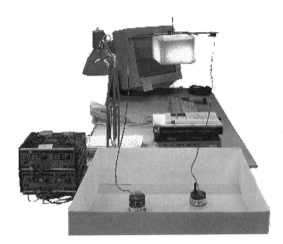

**Figure 8.9**
Experimental setup used for co-evolving physical robots without human intervention.

tournaments recorded from individuals at generation 13, 20, and 22. At generation 13 the prey moves quickly around the environment and the predator attacks only when the prey is at a certain distance. Later on, at generation 20, the prey spins in place and, when the predator gets closer, it rapidly avoids it. Prey that move too fast around the environment sometimes cannot avoid an approaching predator because they detect it too late (remember that the other robot is more difficult to detect by infrared sensors than a large white wall). Therefore, it pays off for the prey to wait for the slower predator and accurately avoid it. However, the predator is smart enough to perform a small circle after having missed the target and reattack until, by chance, the prey is caught on one of the two sides (where wheels and motors do not leave space for sensors). The drop in performance of the predator in the following generations is due to a temporary loss of the ability to avoid walls (which was not required in the few previous generations because the predator very quickly localized and approached the prey). At the same time the prey resumes a rapid wall following and obstacle avoidance which forces the predator to get closer to walls and collide if the prey is missed (right of figure 8.12).

By analyzing the behavior obtained in simulations throughout a longer evolutionary time, however, it can be shown that the same type of strategies are rediscovered over and over again (Nolfi and Floreano 1999). This does not imply that the co-evolutionary process is unable to find interesting solutions, as we just saw. It only means that effective strategies may be lost instead of being retained and refined. Such good strategies, in fact, are often replaced by other strategies that, although providing an advantage over the current

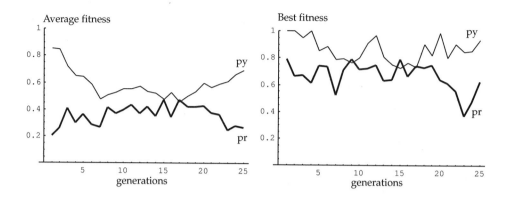

**Figure 8.10**
Co-evolutionary fitness measured on the real robots. **Left:** Average population fitness. **Right:** Fitness of the best individuals at each generation. pr = predator; py = prey.

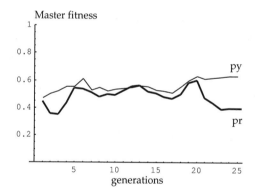

**Figure 8.11**
Master fitness for species evolved on the real robots. Each data point is the average fitness of all tournaments of the corresponding individual against all the best 25 opponents recorded during co-evolution.

opponents, are much less general and effective in the long run. In particular, this type of process may lead to the cycling process described in section 8.2 in which the same strategies are lost and rediscovered over and over again.

If we take a look at the qualitative aspects of the behavior of the best individuals of successive generations we see that in all replications, evolving predators discover and rediscover two main classes of strategies: ($A_1$) track the prey and try to catch it by approaching it; ($A_2$) track the prey while remaining more or less in the same area and

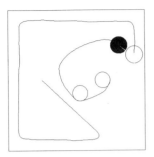 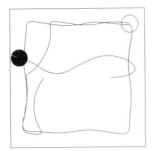 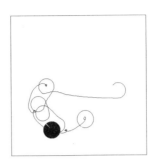

**Figure 8.12**
Typical strategies of the best predator and prey in the experiments with real robots. Full circle is the predator, empty circle is the prey. Trajectories have been plotted running a tournament with simulated individuals who display the same behavioral strategies observed with the real robots. From left to right: generation 13, 20, and 22.

attacking the prey only on very special occasions (when the prey is in a particular position relative to the predator). Similarly the prey cycles between two classes of strategies: ($B_1$) stay still, or "hidden" near a wall (predators usually stay away from walls in order to avoid crashes), waiting for the predator and eventually trying to escape when the IR sensors detect the predator; ($B_2$) move fast in the environment, avoiding both the predator and the walls.

Now, as in figure 8.1, strategy $A_1$ is generally effective against $B_1$; in fact the predator will reach the prey if the prey does not move too fast and has a good chance of succeeding given that the prey can only detect predators approaching from certain directions because of the uneven distributions of the infrared sensors around the body. Strategy $B_2$ is effective against strategy $A_1$ because the prey is faster than the predator and so, if the predator tries to approach a fast moving prey, it has little chance of catching it. Strategy $A_2$ is effective against strategy $B_2$ because, if the prey moves fast in the environment, the predator may be able to catch it easily by waiting for the prey itself to come close. Finally, strategy $B_1$ is very effective against strategy $A_2$. In fact, if the predator does not approach the prey and the prey stays still, the prey will never risk being caught. This type of relation between different strategies produces a cycling process similar to that described in figure 8.1. The cycling process is driven in general by prey that, after adopting one of the two classes of strategies for several generations, suddenly shift to the other strategy. This switch forces predators to shift their strategy accordingly.

What actually happens in the experiments (both in simulations and with the physical robots) is not as simple as in the description we have just given because of several factors: (1) the strategies observed are not single strategies but classes of similar strategies. So, for example, there are plenty of different ways for the predator to approach the prey and different ways may have different probabilities of being successful against the same opposing strategies; (2) the advantage or disadvantage of each strategy against another strategy varies quantitatively and is probabilistic (each strategy has a given probability of beating a competing strategy); (3) populations at a particular generation do not include only one strategy but a certain number of different strategies, although they do tend to converge toward a single one; (4) different strategies may be easier to discover or rediscover than others. However the cycling process between the different classes of strategies described above can be clearly identified.

## 8.5   Testing individuals against all discovered solutions

In a recent article, Rosin and Belew (1997), in order to encourage the emergence of "arms races" and avoid cycling, suggested saving and using as competitors all the best individuals of previous generations ("hall of fame" co-evolution):

*So, in competitive co-evolution, we have two distinct reasons to save individuals. One reason is to contribute genetic material to future generations; this is important in any evolutionary algorithm. Selection serves this purpose. Elitism serves this purpose directly by making complete copies of top individuals.*

*The second reason to save individuals is for purposes of testing. To ensure progress, we may want to save individuals for an arbitrarily long time and continue testing against them. To this end, we introduce the "Hall of Fame", which extends elitism in time for purposes of testing. The best individual from every generation, is retained for future testing.*

From Rosin and Belew (1997), pp. 8.

This type of solution is implausible from a biological point of view (although some-thing similar may occur in one population if the lifecycle of the competing population is much shorter). Moreover, we may expect that, by adopting this technique, the adaptive power of the co-evolutionary dynamics will be progressively reduced throughout genera-tions with the increase in number of previous opponents. In fact, as the process goes on, there is less and less pressure to discover strategies that are effective against the opponent of the current generation and greater and greater pressure to develop solutions capable of improving performance against opponents of previous generations.

However, as the authors show, in some cases this method may be more effective than "standard" co-evolution where individuals compete only with opponents of the same or of the previous generation. More specifically, it may be a way to overcome the problem of cycling through the same strategies. In this framework, in fact, behaviors that compete successfully against the opponent of the current generation, but do not generalize to opponents of previous generations, are unlikely to be selected for reproduction. To test

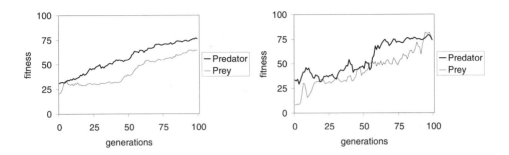

**Figure 8.13**
Experiments with "hall of fame". Performance of the best individuals of each generation tested against all the best opponents of each generation (master tournament). **Left:** Average result of 10 different replications. **Right:** Best replication (i.e., the simulation in which predators and prey attain the best performance). Data were smoothed using a rolling average over three data points.

this hypothesis we ran a new set of experiments in simulation by using the "hall of fame" selection regime: each individual is tested against 10 opponents randomly selected from *all* previous generations (whereas in the previous experiments we selected 10 opponents from the immediately preceding generations).[5]

Figure 8.13 shows that in this case the master fitness of the best individuals tested against all best competitors progressively increases throughout generations. True progress is clearly displayed also by the CIAO analysis (Cliff and Miller 1995) described in section 8.2 above. The plot on the left side of figure 8.14 shows an ideal situation where predators are capable of catching all prey of previous generations, and prey are capable of escaping all predators of previous generations (see figure legend). The plot at the center shows the results from a control experiment where competitors are taken only from the previous 10 generations (as in the experiments described in the previous section). The plot on the right instead shows the data for the experiments carried out under the "hall of fame" selection regime. Although the results only approximate the ideal situation, evolutionary progress is clearly visible.

If we look at the individual strategies selected throughout generations in these experiments, we see that they are of the same class of those described in the previous section. However, in this case, the strategies are evolutionarily more stable (i.e., in general they are not suddenly replaced by another strategy of a different class). This enables the co-evolutionary process to progressively refine current strategies instead of cycling between different classes of strategies, restarting each time from scratch.

The fact that individuals are tested against quite different strategies (i.e., competitors randomly selected from all previous generations) should enable the evolutionary process

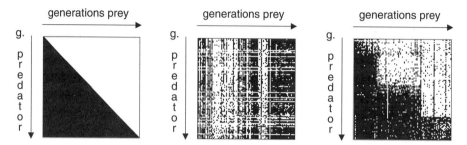

**Figure 8.14**
Performance of the best individuals of each generation tested against all the best opponents of each generation.
Black dots represent individual tournaments in which the predators win while white dots represent tournaments
in which the prey wins. **Left:** An ideal situation in which predators are able to catch all prey of previous
generations and the prey are able to escape all predators of previous generations. **Center:** Typical result of a
control simulation in which each individual is tested against opponents selected from the 10 immediately
preceding generations. **Right:** Typical result of the "hall of fame" simulation in which each individual is tested
against 10 opponents randomly selected from all previous generations. **Center, right:** Result in the best
replication, i.e., the simulation in which predators and prey attain the best performance.

to find strategies that are more general (i.e., that are effective against a larger number
of counter strategies) than those obtained in the experiments described in the previous
section. In order to investigate this hypothesis we tested the best 10 predators and prey
obtained with "standard" co-evolution against the best 10 predators and prey obtained
with "hall of fame" co-evolution (i.e., the best predator and prey of each replication were
selected) all other parameters being the same. From the summary data reported on the
left side of figure 8.15, one can see that "standard" individuals have a higher probability
of defeating "standard" individuals than "hall of fame" individuals. Moreover, "hall of
fame" individuals have a higher probability of defeating "standard" individuals than "hall
of fame" individuals (right side of figure 8.15). One could conclude that "hall of fame" co-
evolution tends to produce more general solutions than "standard" co-evolution. However,
variability across replications is quite high (see error bars in the graphs) and differences in
performance are not as great as one could expect from the trends of the master tournaments
in the two conditions, which are quite different (we will return to this point later on).

## 8.6 How the length of "arms races" may vary in different conditions

One of the simplification we adopted in our experiments is that the sensory-motor system
of the two species was fixed. As we shall show below, the structure of the sensory system
can indeed affect the course of the co-evolutionary process and the length of "arms races."

In all the experiments described above the prey has a limited sensory system that

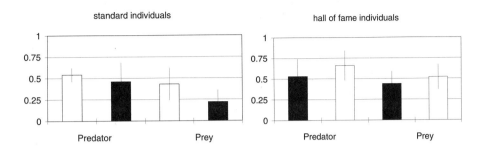

**Figure 8.15**
**Left:** Graphs showing the average performance obtained by testing "standard" individuals against "standard" or "hall of fame" competitors (white and black histograms, respectively). **Right:** Graphs showing the average performance obtained by testing "hall of fame" individuals against "standard" or "hall of fame" competitors (white and gray histograms, respectively). Vertical bars indicate standard deviation. Individuals are selected by picking the predator and the prey with the best score in the master tournament of each replication. Y-axis indicates the percentage of defeated competitors. Each column is the results of a separate test (individuals start with different randomly assigned orientations).

enables it to perceive predators only at a very limited distance and not from all directions (there are no infrared sensors pointing to the rear-left and rear-right side where wheels and motors are positioned). One might speculate that the prey cannot improve its strategy above a certain level because of this limitation. Therefore, the only way it might compete with co-evolving predators is that of suddenly changing behavior when predators adopt an effective strategy. Consequently, if the prey's sensory system is improved, one might expect that it will be able to defend itself from predators by gradually refining its behavior instead of radically changing it every now and then.

We ran a new set of simulations in which the prey was also provided with a vision system capable of detecting the predators' relative position. Although these new experiments were carried out only in simulations, the vision system accurately modeled an existing vision turret consisting of a one dimensional array of 150 photoreceptors of 256 gray levels subtending a total view field of 240° (Landolt 1996). We chose this wider camera because escape behaviors might need visual systems covering more than only the frontal direction. As for predators, the visual field was divided into five sectors of 48° corresponding to five simulated photoreceptors. As a consequence, in this experiment, both predator and prey were controlled by a neural network with 13 sensory neurons. Moreover, in this case, both predator and prey could see their competitors as a black spot against a white background. Standard co-evolution was used, i.e., individuals were tested against the best competitors of the 10 previous generations (not against competitors selected from all previous generations as in the "hall of fame" case). All the other parameters were the same of those described in section 8.5.

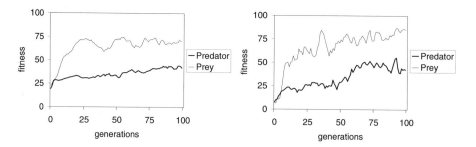

Figure 8.16
Experiments with "standard" co-evolution (i.e., not "hall of fame") where the prey is equipped with a wide-angle camera. Performance of the best individuals of each generation tested against all best opponents of each generation (master tournament). Data were smoothed using a rolling average over three data points. **Left:** Average result of 10 different replications. **Right:** Best replication (i.e., the experiment in which predators and prey attain the best performance).

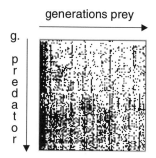

Figure 8.17
Performance of the best individuals of each generation tested against all the best opponents of each generation. Black dots represent individual tournaments in which the predators win while white dots represent tournaments in which the prey wins. Results from the best replication (the same shown in figure 8.16, right).

Under these new sensory conditions, a significant and progressive performance increment is observed in both populations through out generations (figures 8.16 and 8.17), although the prey in general is more successful than predators.[6]

These results show that by changing the initial conditions (in this case by changing the sensory system of one population) "arms races" can continue to produce better and better solutions in both populations for several generations without falling into cycles.

Interestingly, in simulations where the sensory system of two co-evolving populations was under evolution, Cliff and Miller observed that "... pursuers usually evolved eyes on the front of their bodies (like cheetahs), while evaders usually evolved eyes pointing sideways or even backwards (like gazelles)." (Cliff and Miller 1996, pp. 506).[7]

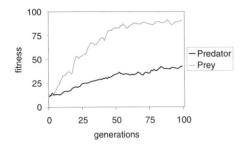

**Figure 8.18**
Experiments with "hall of fame"; the prey is equipped with vision too. Performance of the best individuals of each generation tested against all the best opponents of each generation (master tournament). Average result of 10 different replications. Data were smoothed using a rolling average over three data points.

To investigate whether also in this case "hall of fame" co-evolution outperforms "standard" co-evolution we ran another set of experiments identical to those described in this section but using the "hall of fame" selection regime. Figure 8.18 shows master tournament measures obtained for this second set of experiments.

Although performances increase very dramatically across generations (especially for the prey), if we test individuals obtained with "standard" co-evolution against individuals obtained with "hall of fame" co-evolution we find that the latter do not outperform the "standard" individuals (see figure 8.19). On the contrary, individuals obtained with "standard" co-evolution tend to outperform individuals obtained with "hall of fame" co-evolution (figure 8.19, left). Moreover, "hall of fame" prey has a higher probability of defeating "hall of fame" than "standard" predators, but "hall of fame" predators are more likely to defeat "standard" than "hall of fame" prey (figure 8.19, right). Notice however that also in this case, there is a high variability between different replications.

From these results it may be concluded that although the "hall of fame" selection regime always tends to reduce the probability of falling into limit cycles (see figure 8.18 which shows how progressively more general solutions are selected), it does not necessarily produce more general solutions that "standard" co-evolution (see figure 8.19). When, as in the case described in this section, "standard" co-evolution can produce arms races of significant length, it may outperform "hall of fame" co-evolution. Furthermore, by continuing the evolutionary process, the "hall of fame" selection regime might be even less effective than "standard" co-evolution given that, as mentioned earlier, co-evolutionary dynamics tend to become progressively less effective throughout the generations with an increasing probability of opponents from previous generations being selected.

The fact that the structure of the sensory-motor system of the two species can significantly affect the course of the evolutionary process demonstrates the importance of using

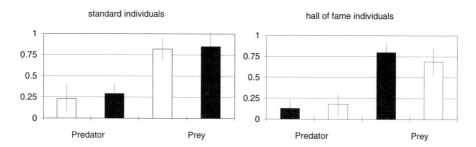

**Figure 8.19**
**Left:** Graphs showing the average performance obtained by testing "standard" individuals against "standard" or "hall of fame" competitors (white and black histograms, respectively). **Right:** Graphs showing the average performance obtained by testing "hall of fame" individuals against "standard" or "hall of fame" competitors (white and gray histograms, respectively). Vertical bars indicate standard deviation. Individuals are selected by picking the predator and the prey with the best score in the master tournament for each replication. Y-axis indicates the percentage of defeated competitors. Each column is the results of a separate test (individuals start with different randomly assigned orientations).

real robots instead of idealized agents. Real robots and living organisms, in fact, have sensory-motor systems that rely on measures of physical entities (light, speed, etc.), have limited precision, are affected by non uniform noise, etc. Idealized agents instead, often adopt sensors and motors which have simple and often irrealistic characteristics (e.g., sensors which have infinite precision or which measure abstract entities such as distances between objects). These properties may introduce constraints which channel the experiment in a certain direction producing artifactual results.

## 8.7    How co-evolution can enhance the adaptive power of artificial evolution

In the previous sections we showed that "arms races" between co-evolving populations can indeed arise in some circumstances. At this point we should try to understand whether co-evolution can really enhance the adaptive power of artificial evolution. In other words, can artificial co-evolution solve tasks that cannot be solved using a simple evolutionary process?

There are two reasons for hypothesizing that co-evolution can have a higher adaptive power than evolution. The first reason is that individuals evolving in a co-evolutionary framework experience a larger number of different environmental events. The second and more important reason is that, as we claimed in section 8.1, co-evolution may produce an evolutionary "arms race."

In order to see whether co-evolution can produce solutions to problems that evolution alone is unable to solve, we evolved predators against the best prey obtained using co-

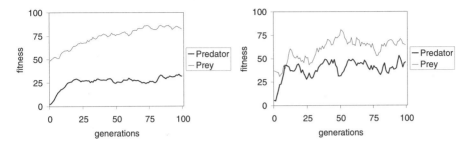

**Figure 8.20**
Experiments with the complex environment and predators and prey equipped with ambient light sensors ("standard" co-evolution). Performance of the best individuals of each generation tested against all the best opponents of each generation (master tournament). Data were smoothed using a rolling average over three data points. **Left:** Average result of 10 different replications. **Right:** Result of the best replication (i.e., the experiment in which predators and prey attain the best performance).

evolution. Likewise, we evolved prey against the best predator obtained by co-evolution. If evolution of a single population fails, at least in some cases, to produce individuals capable of defeating opponents obtained by co-evolution, we may conclude that co-evolution can select better individuals than simple evolution can. In other words, we may conclude that co-evolution is capable of producing solutions to problems that evolution is unable to solve.

The parameters used in this set of experiments were the same as those described in section 8.5, but here only one population was subjected to the evolutionary process: evolving individuals were tested 10 times throughout 100 generations always against the same opponent. In all cases simple evolution was capable of producing increasingly better individuals until optimal or close to optimal performance was obtained. In other words, in these conditions evolution was capable of selecting a very effective strategy against the best single strategy developed by co-evolution. In order to produce a serious challenge for simple evolution it was necessary to change the sensory system of the predator and prey and use a more complex environment than the simple arena involved in the experiments described above.

We ran a new set of co-evolutionary experiments in which predators and prey were not equipped with cameras but were allowed to use the 8 ambient light sensors already present on each Khepera robot. We added a 1 watt lamp on the top of both predator and prey so that each individual could obtain an indirect measure of the relative position of the other robot. Both predator and prey had 16 sensory units (8 for the infrared sensors and 8 for the ambient light sensors) and two motor units. The genotype was 8 x 34 bits long in both cases (the total number of synapses was 16 x 2 + 2 thresholds). We used an $60 \times 60$ cm arena with 13 cylindrical obstacles distributed inside it. The "standard" selection regime was used. For all other parameters the same values described in section 8.5 were used.

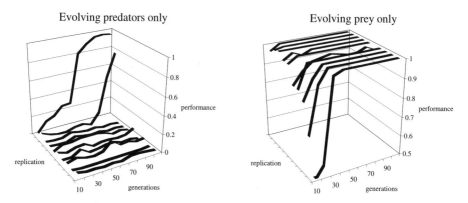

**Figure 8.21**
**Left:** Results obtained by evolving a single population of predators for the ability to catch one of the best
co-evolved prey. **Right:** Results obtained by evolving a single population of prey for the ability to escape one of
the best co-evolved predator. Each graph shows the results of 10 experiments in which the best prey and predator
obtained in the 10 co-evolutionary experiments described above were used as fixed opponents. Average results
of 10 succeeding generations are shown. Results have been sorted on the replication axis to enhance readability.

Also in this condition, a significant performance increment can be observed from all
master fitness indicators (figure 8.20). Unlike the experiments described in the previous
section, in this case predators of the very first generations have close to null performance.
This implies that most of them are unable to catch most of the prey of succeeding generations.

We then ran a new set of experiments in which simple evolution (i.e., evolution of a
single population against a fixed opponent) was used to select predators against the best
co-evolved prey obtained in the experiments just described. Similarly, we ran another set
of experiments where prey were selected against the best co-evolved predators.

As one can see in figure 8.21, that shows the performance of the best evolving predators
and prey, in 8 cases out of 10 simple evolution failed to select predators capable of catching
the co-evolved prey. Conversely, in the co-evolutionary experiments described in figure
8.20, the best co-evolved predators were able to catch the best co-evolved prey at least 25%
of the time in 9 out of 10 simulations (result not shown). The reason why simple evolution
is not always successful is that predators of the first generations are almost always unable
to catch the prey and therefore the selection mechanism could not operate properly.

In this case co-evolution could produce more complex challenges than in the other
experiments because the prey could exploit the information coming from ambient light
sensors. Most of the co-evolved prey waited for the predator until it reached a distance
of about 10 cm and only then did they start to escape. This strategy forced the predator to
follow them with little chance of catching them given the difference in speed. Furthermore,

this behavior eliminated the risk of encountering the predator head on, something that instead could happen if the prey moved very fast also when the predator was far away.

The fact that "standard" evolution can generate very effective prey against the best co-evolved predators (see figure 8.21, right side) implies that in this case it is always possible to find a simple strategy for defeating the predator. As we mentioned above, this is what happens for both predators and prey in all experiments described in the previous sections.

## 8.8   The role of ontogenetic plasticity in co-evolution

In the previous section we could show that, at least in one case, co-evolution can produce a strategy that is too complex for simple evolution to cope with. However, in the other 3 cases examined in sections 8.4, 8.5, and 8.6 simple evolution was capable of generating individuals that proved very effective against co-evolved strategies. This happened also with the strategies obtained in the experiments described in section 8.5 and 8.6 in which master tournament measures clearly indicated a progress throughout generations. This means that, although increasingly more powerful (general) strategies were selected in these co-evolutionary experiments, it was always possible to select individuals capable of defeating these strategies by using "standard" evolution (i.e., by evolving a single population of individuals starting from scratch). Further proof of this is that if we look at the performance of the best individuals of the last generations we see that, even though they score increasingly better against individuals of previous generations on average, they may sometimes be defeated by individuals of many generations earlier (see, for example, figures 8.14 and 8.17).

These results point to the conclusion that in certain tasks it is always possible to find a simple strategy capable of defeating another single, albeit complex and general, strategy (although such simple strategy is a specialized strategy, i.e. it is able to defeat only that particular complex and general strategy and, of course, other similar strategies). If this is really true, in other words, if completely general solutions do not exist in some cases, we should reconsider the "cycling problem." From this point of view, the fact that co-evolutionary dynamics lead to a limit cycle in which the same type of solutions are adopted over and over again should not be considered as a failure but as an optimal solution. We cannot complain that co-evolution does not find a more general strategy capable of coping with all the strategies adopted by the co-evolving population during a cycle if such general strategies do not exist, given the existing conditions (environment, sensory motor system, architecture of the neurocontroller, etc.). The best that can be done is to select the appropriate strategy for the current counterstrategy, which is what actually happens when co-evolutionary dynamics end in a limit cycle.

More generally we can predict that co-evolution will lead to a progressive increase in complexity when complete general solutions (i.e., solutions which are successful against all strategies adopted by previous opponents) exist and can be reached by progressively moving on the genotype space. Conversely, if complete general solutions do not exist or the probability of finding them is too low, co-evolution may lead to cycling dynamics in which selected solutions will be such that: 1) they are appropriate to the current strategy of the co-evolving opponents and 2) they can be easily modified so to defeat new strategies adopted by the opponents in later generations. In other words, when general solutions cannot be found, it becomes important for each evolving population to be able to dynamically change its own strategy into one of a set of appropriate strategies. From the individuals' point of view, we may say that individuals with a predisposition to quickly change in certain directions will be selected.

Interestingly, a cycling dynamics is an ideal situation for the emergence of ontogenetic adaptation (lifetime learning). The ability to adapt during one's lifetime to the opponent's strategy would in fact produce a significant increment in the adaptation power of a single individual because ontogenetic adaptations are much faster than phylogenetic ones. Therefore, we may hypothesize that when a co-evolving dynamics lead to a limiting cycle, there will be a high selective pressure in the direction of ontogenetic adaptation. At the same time, the cycling dynamics will create the conditions in which ontogenetic adaptation may more easily arise because, as we have seen, individuals with a predisposition to change in certain directions will be selected. It is plausible to argue that, for such individuals, a limited number of changes during ontogeny will be able to produce the required behavioral shift. In other words, we can argue that it will be easier for co-evolving individuals to change their behavior during their lifetime in order to adopt strategies already selected by their close ancestors thanks to the cycles occurring in previous generations.

Let us distinguish between two types of individuals: *full general* and *plastic general* (see also inset box on intelligence and generality). Full general individuals have a single strategy capable of defeating a certain set of opponent strategies. Plastic general individuals instead possess a set of different strategies, each one capable of defeating a different single opponent strategy of the same set. Although these two types of individuals seem equivalent, there are some subtle differences. Plastic general individuals should be able to select the appropriate strategy for their current competitor. In other words, they should be able to adapt through ontogenetic adaptation. From this point of view full general individuals will be more effective because they do not require such adaptation process and may provide immediately the correct answer to the current competitor. On the other hand, as we said above, it may be that in certain conditions a full general individual cannot be selected because a full general strategy does not exist or because it is too difficult to find for the evolutionary process. In this case, the only option left is that of plastic general solutions.

## Intelligence and generality

A key feature of intelligent systems is generality, i.e., the ability to carry out a certain task in different environmental conditions or the ability to carry out different tasks. In the context of predators and prey, for example, predators should be able to catch different types of prey.

Most of the systems which we have described in this book (including the predator and prey which we described in the previous sections) are interesting but lack generality. These systems are interesting because can solve non trivial tasks in simple ways. However, they are strongly dependent on the current state of the environment. If the environment changes (e.g., the strategy of the competitor changes) they may become unable to solve their task. These two aspects (i.e., simplicity and lack of generality) are the two side of the same coin. As we showed in chapter 5, these systems are able to solve non trivial task with simple strategies because they exploit the regularities available in the environment (including the physical characteristics of their own sensory-motor system). One might conclude that, in order to be general, systems should be more autonomous from the environment. In other words, intelligent systems should rely less on the regularities available in the environment and more on their internal "nervous mechanisms." Such systems will probably require more internal complexity than the simple non general systems which we described. The attempt of (Good Old Fashioned) Artificial Intelligence to build general purpose systems (e.g., universal planners) mostly ignoring the characteristics of the external and of the internal environment is a natural consequence of this line of thought.

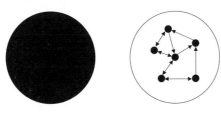

full-general            plastic-general

Fortunately, this is not the only available option. Generality may also be achieved by systems that, instead of incorporating a single general strategy, posses a collection of simple strategies that are appropriate in different environmental circumstances and a mechanism which is able to select the strategy which is appropriate to the current environment.

---

**Intelligence and generality** (continued)

Although both type of systems may be described as general and might produce similar types of behaviors they will significantly differ in their internal organization. Full general systems will posses a single general strategy (see the large black circle, left figure) which will require a quite complex control system. This type of systems, by not relying on the regularities present in the internal and external environment, will be quite different from the type of systems which we described in the previous sections. Plastic general systems, instead, will include a set of simple strategies (see the small black circles, right figure) of the same type of those which we described in the previous sections and a mechanism for selecting the strategy which is appropriate to the current environment (see the arrows, right figure).

---

As a final remark, it should be noticed that also plastic general solutions might be difficult to obtain because they require the following conditions: 1) that the individual is capable of displaying a variety of different strategies; 2) that it is also capable of selecting the right strategy at the right moment (depending on the behavior of the current competitor). The interesting point is that, when a full general strategy cannot be found, co-evolution will fall into cycling dynamics where a set of "specialistic" strategy will be discover over and over again across generations. Now, since during this phase the best thing individuals can do to improve the chances of survival of their offspring is to produce offspring which can evolutionary change their strategy as fast as possible (in other words individuals which have a predisposition to change in certain directions), we may expect that the length of the cycles will be progressively shortened throughout successive generations. At this point, we might speculate that co-evolution could favor the emergence of individuals with the ability to modify their behavior during lifetime in the most appropriate directions (the same directions for which a predisposition to change have been genetically acquired), if the genotype could allow for some type of phenotypic modification.

We have conducted a set of exploratory experiments to investigate whether competitive co-evolution can exploit ontogenetic adaptation (Floreano and Nolfi 1997b). As for the experiments described in section 7.5, the genotype encodes a set of parameters describing synaptic properties and learning rules, but not the weights of the connections which are always initialized to small random values. The genotype encoded the sign of the corresponding connection (1 bit), the learning rule (2 bits), and the learning rate (2 bits). All other parameters are the same of those described in section 8.4. Therefore, the individuals of these experiments are allowed to change during lifetime according to evolved genetic

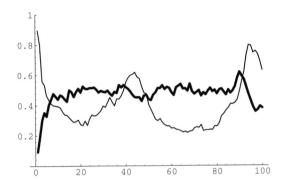

**Figure 8.22**
Average fitness across generations. Thick line = predator; thin line = prey.

instructions and, in principle, might be able to adapt ontogenetically to the strategy of their
current competitor.

Under these conditions the predators reported higher average and best fitness values
than prey in all six runs, except for short temporary oscillations (figure 8.22). Furthermore,
in all runs, the average fitness of the predator population was more stable than that of the
prey. Relative performance of the two species (i.e., how many times one species wins over
the other) in this condition significantly differed from the experiments described in section
8.4 (figure 8.7, left) in which individuals were not allowed to change during lifetime.
Although also in this case behavioral strategies specifically tuned to the behavior of the
competitor can be found, this pattern was less marked than in the experiments with non
plastic controllers.

More information can be gained by observing behavioral patterns of the two competitors during individual tournaments (figure 8.23). There is not much variation in the
behavior of the predator. It always displays a very good tracking ability across generations:
once the prey has been locked in its visual field, it quickly accelerates to maximum speed
until contact. As compared to the experiments described in section 8.4, where the predator
tended to efficiently track in only one direction, here it can turn in both directions at equal
speed. For non learning controllers proper tracking in both directions would have required
accurate settings of all synaptic strengths from visual inputs (a rare solution that might
be difficult to find on the genotype space). Here, instead, since synapses are temporarily increased depending on active visual units (Floreano and Mondada 1996a), individual
adjustments of synapses take place when and where required depending on current sensory input. The trajectory in the center image of figure 8.23 shows an evident example
of synaptic adjustment. Here, while the prey rotates always around the same circle, the
predator performs three turns on itself during which synaptic values from the visual units

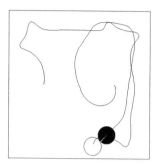 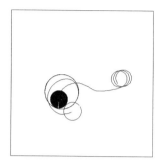 

**Figure 8.23**
Behaviors of co-evolved individuals with ontogenetic learning. Full circle is predator, empty circle is prey. **Left:** Generation 20. **Center:** Generation 70. **Right:** Generation 95.

are gradually increased; at the fourth turn, the synaptic values will be sufficiently high to cause a straight pursuit (eventually, the prey will try to avoid the predator without success). Finally, the temporary drop in performance of the predator after generation 90 is due a more precise tracking combined with a slower motion (right image of figure 8.23). Such behavior was probably developed because the prey were also slower and more careful in avoiding obstacles (including the predator).

Although activity dependent synaptic change is exploited by the far sighted predator, not the same happens for the prey. Prey are faster with respect to the experiment described in section 8.4, especially when turning near walls (where IR sensors become active and synapses temporarily strengthen), but plasticity does not allow an increment of their behavioral repertoire because their sensory system is quite limited. Not even can they improve it because volatile changes of the synaptic values imply that most of the time they must redevelop on the fly appropriate strengths. Although this can be well suited for avoidance of static obstacles, it does not represent an advantage when facing another fast moving object such as the predator.

These results indicate that plastic predators are capable of adapting their strategies to the strategy adopted by the current competitor during lifetime. Almost all predators are able to adapt to the two different classes of strategies adopted by the prey which we described in section 8.4 (i.e., $B_1$: stay still or hidden close to a wall waiting for the predator and eventually trying to escape when the IR sensors detect the predator; $B_2$: move fast in the environment, avoiding both the predator and the walls) by selecting the appropriate counter strategy during lifetime. This explain why in these experiments predators are not compelled to abandon their strategy when prey suddenly change their counter strategy. Predators, by having the possibility to develop plastic general strategies, can keep and refine their strategy. This is also reflected by the fact that their fitness is more stable than that of the prey across generations. Instead, since the prey cannot develop more effective strategies because of their limited sensory ability, they display cyclic behaviors (as revealed by both fitness values and behavioral analysis). The limitation of the prey prevents the emergence of real "arm races" in these experiments. However, the results indicate that plastic general solutions can be developed in some cases and that this might be another factor against limit cycles.

## 8.9    Conclusions

To sum up, competitive co-evolution is interesting from several points of view. First, it is interesting because it allows the study of adaptation in an ever changing environment. As we have shown in section 8.4, this allows the evolutionary process to produce a much larger variety of behaviors with respect to the experiments conducted in static environments. Second, competitive co-evolution is interesting because it might produce incremental evolution without requiring additional supervision from the designer. Our experimental results, however, indicate that this happens only in some circumstances (i.e., when general solution exists). In the other cases, as we have seen in section 8.4, the co-evolutionary process tends to fall into a limit cycle in which the same solutions are adopted by both populations over and over again (we will refer to this problem as the *cycling problem*). What happens is that at a certain point one population, in order to overcome the other population, finds it more useful to suddenly change its strategy instead of continuing to refine it. This is usually followed by a similar rapid change of strategy in the other population. The overall result of this process is that most of the characters previously acquired are not appropriate in the new context and therefore are lost. However, later on, a similar sudden change may bring the two populations back to the original type of strategy so that previous characters are likely to be rediscovered again.

The effect of the cycling problem may be reduced by preserving all the solutions previously discovered for testing the individuals of the current generations (Rosin and Belew 1997). However, this method has drawbacks that may affect some of the advantages of co-evolution (beside being biological implausible). In fact, as the process goes on, there is less and less pressure to discover strategies that are effective against the opponent of the current generation and increasing pressure to develop solutions able to improve performance against opponents of previous generations which are no longer under co-evolution. While in some cases testing individuals against a sample of all previously selected competitors may produce better performance (as shown in section 8.5), in other cases this might not be true. Indeed it may even result in less effective individuals (see section 8.6).

We believe that the cycling problem, like the local minima problem in gradient descent methods (i.e., the risk of getting trapped in a sub optimal solution when all neighboring solutions produce a deterioration of performance), is an intrinsic problem of co-evolution that cannot be eliminated completely. However, as we have shown in sections 8.6 and 8.7 the cycling problem does not always affect co-evolutionary dynamics so strongly as to prevent the emergence of "arms races." When both co-evolving populations can produce better and better strategies, "arms races" may last several generations and produce progressively more complex and general solutions. On the other hand, if one or both populations cannot improve their current strategy sufficiently, the co-evolutionary dynamics will probably quickly lead to a limit cycle in which similar strategies are rediscovered over and over again. As we saw in section 8.7, in fact, co-evolution succeeds in producing individuals able to cope with very effective competitors (by selecting the competitors at the same time) whereas simple evolution is unable to do so.

Finally, competitive co-evolution pushes the evolutionary process to find general strategies (i.e., strategies that are effective in different environmental circumstances). As we discussed in section 8.8 this is a fundamental issue in the study of natural and artificial intelligence. Our results suggest that, at least in the case of our experimental framework, generality might be obtained by evolving plastic individuals (i.e., individuals which incorporate a set of simple non general strategies and a mechanisms for adapting their current strategy to the environment). Indeed, ontogenetic plasticity may limit the effect of the cycling problem. Plastic individuals, in fact, may be able to cope with different classes of strategies adopted by the other population by adapting to the opponent's strategy during lifetime. This in turn reduces the necessity to produce generational shifts of behavior which cause the cycling problem.

In an additional set of experiments (Floreano and Nolfi 1997b), we left the choice of whether to use ontogenetic plasticity to the evolutionary process. This was achieved by adding an extra gene for each synapse. If the gene was 0, then the remaining bits for that synapse were interpreted by the decoding process as the strength of the synapse, otherwise they were interpreted as the learning rule and learning rate and the synapse was initialized to a small random value. These results showed that while predators quickly (in few generations) and consistently exploited ontogenetic plasticity, prey did not do so (results for the prey varied both across generations and across different replications). As one might expect, predators also reported higher performance than prey across all co-evolutionary runs. These experiments suggest that whether an individual can benefit from the ability to adapt during life depends not only on the challenges that it faces, but also on its sensory-motor characteristics. In other words, the sensory system of the prey is not rich enough to afford the potential advantages and costs of ontogenetic adaptation. The experiments also suggest that if the physical properties of the individual are suitable such as in the case of the predator, dynamic environments favor the emergence of ontogenetic plasticity in evolving populations.

# 9  Encoding, mapping, and development

## 9.1  Introduction

A cornerstone of biology is the distinction between inherited genetic code (genotype) and the corresponding organism (phenotype). What is inherited from the parents is the genotype. The phenotype is the complete individual that is formed, in interaction with the environment, driven by the instructions specified in the genotype.

Evolution is critically dependent on the distinction between genotype and phenotype, and on their relation, i.e. the *genotype-to-phenotype mapping*. The fitness of an individual, on which selective reproduction is based, is given by the phenotype, but what is inherited is the genotype, not the phenotype. Furthermore, while the genotype of an individual is one single entity, the organism can be considered as a succession of different phenotypes taking form during the genotype-to-phenotype mapping process, each derived from the previous one under genetic and environmental influences.

When the genotype-to-phenotype mapping process takes place during individuals' lifetime we can talk of *development*. In this case, each successive phenotype, corresponding to a given stage of development, has a distinct fitness. The total fitness of a developing individual is a complex function of these separate successive fitness. Evolution must ensure that these distinct successive forms are all viable and, at the same time, that they make a well formed sequence where each form leads to the next one until a mostly stable (adult) form is reached. This puts various constraints on evolution but it also offers new means for exploring novelty. Small changes in the developmental rates of different components of the phenotype, for example, can have huge effects on the resulting phenotype. Indeed it has been hypothesized that in natural evolution changes affecting regulatory genes that control the rates of development play a more important role than other forms of change (Gould 1977).

Although the role of the genotype-to-phenotype mapping and of development has been ignored in most of the experiments involving artificial evolution, there is now an increasing awareness of its importance. Wagner and Altenberg (1996) write: "In evolutionary computer science it was found that the darwinian process of mutation, recombination and selection is not universally effective in improving complex systems like computer programs or chip designs. For adaptation to occur, these systems must possess *evolvability*, i.e. the ability of random variations to sometimes produce improvement. It was found that evolvability critically depends on the way genetic variation maps onto phenotypic variation, an issue known as the representation problem." (p. 967).

In nature, the genotype-to-phenotype mapping is the result of the evolutionary process and, presumably, has been organized so to ensure evolvability (we will come back to this point in the next section). In artificial evolution, instead, the rules that determine the relations between genotype and phenotype are decided quite arbitrarily by the experimenter and, in most cases, are not under genetic control. Moreover, the relation between genetic information—whatever is encoded in the genotype—and phenotype is usually so simple that it is even questionable whether there is a distinction between genotype and phenotype. All these considerations suggest that progress in this area would significantly improve the adaptive power of artificial evolution. Also, considering that the relation between development and evolution is far from being well understood in biology (Gottlieb 1992), investigations in artificial evolution may help understand the role of development in natural evolution.

In section 9.2 we will discuss this problem in more detail. In section 9.3 and 9.4 we will present some of the most representative studies in the area. It should be noted that the experiments described in this chapter are only inspired on biological data and do not intend to be a detailed model of biological processes. The main goal of these models is to identify a set of general mechanisms that might capture some key aspects of development in natural organisms and, consequently, might enhance the adaptive power of artificial evolution.

## 9.2   Genetic encodings

Before running an evolutionary experiment we should decide how to encode the robot control system in the genotype in a manner suitable for the application of genetic operators. In most cases, all phenotypical characteristics are directly or indirectly coded (see chapter 2) in an uniform manner so that the description of an individual at the level of the genotype assumes the form of a string of identical elements (such as binary or floating point numbers). The transformation of the genotype in a full fledged organism is called genotype-to-phenotype mapping.

In direct encoding schemes there is a one-to-one correspondence between genes and the phenotypical characters subjected to the evolutionary process. Aside from being biological implausible, simple one-to-one mappings has several drawbacks. One problem, for example, is scalability. Since the length of the genotype is proportional to the complexity of the corresponding phenotype, the space to be searched by the evolutionary process increases exponentially with the increment of the number of phenotypical characters. A larger space does not necessarily mean that evolutionary search is more difficult. In fact, *if a suitable encoding is used*, the number of solutions could increase proportionally with the size of the space. The problem is that it is difficult to find a suitable encoding schema. Consequently, it can happen that longer genotypes make evolution harder. For example, our experience shows that direct encoding of synaptic strengths requires more generations for larger neural networks. A more desirable strategy is an encoding schema where the length of the genotype only weakly reflects the complexity of the corresponding phenotype.

Another related problem with direct encoding is the impossibility to encode repeated structures (think of the vertebrae of a snake or of the neural modules in visual cortex) in a compact way. If we assume a one-to-one mapping in fact, elements that are repeated at the level of the phenotype must be repeated at the level of the genotype as well. This does not only affect the length of the genotype and the corresponding search space, but also the evolvability of individuals. A full genetic specification of a phenotype with repeated structures, in fact, implies that adaptive changes affecting repeated structures should be independently rediscovered by all genetic areas that encode the same characteristics. A better solution would be a genotype where the common features of repeated phenotypical structure are encoded only once in the genotype. For example this seems to be the case for the development of the snake body, which is composed of several similar segments (Dawkins, 1986).

A good genetic encoding should exhibit several properties. A first requirement is *expressive power*, i.e. the possibility to encode many different phenotypical characteristics such as the architecture of the controller, the morphology of the robot, the rules that control the plasticity of the individual, and eventually the rules that determine the genotype-to-phenotype process itself. Only the features that are encoded in the genotype, in fact, can be developed through the self-organization process instead of being predesigned and fixed. Moreover, only by encoding different features in the genotype, the evolutionary process can exploit the interaction between them and select individuals with co-adapted sub-components (e.g. individuals with co-adapted bodies and brains—we will come back to this issue in chapter 11).

A second requirement is *compactness*, i.e. genotype-to-phenotype mappings where the length of the genotype only weakly reflects the complexity of the corresponding phenotype. The length of the genotype in fact, can affect the dimensionality of the space to be searched by the genetic algorithm that, along with the characteristics of the fitness surface, may affect the result of the evolutionary process. Compactness could be achieved by means of different mechanisms. A mechanism is that of having genotypes that vary in length (Harvey 1992, 1993). The complexity of an individual's phenotype may vary during the evolutionary process. If we assume that the length of the genotype is proportional to the complexity of the phenotype, the genotype length could vary with the complexity of the phenotype. A second mechanism is plasticity. Genotype length could be reduced by letting some characteristics of the phenotype to be defined by an adaptive mechanism during lifetime. Finally, another interesting mechanism is the possibility of encoding repeated structures, such as similar subcomponents of the controller, using a single set of genetic

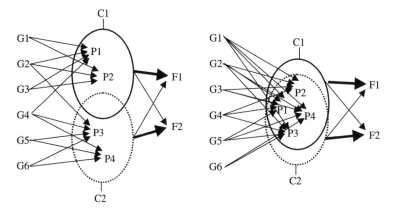

**Figure 9.1**
**Left:** Example of a modular genotype-to-phenotype organization. **Right:** Example of a non modular genotype-to-phenotype organization. Complexes of phenotypical characters C1 = [P1, P2] and C2 = [P3, P4] serve both functions F1 and F2. However C1 is mainly involved in F1 while C2 is mainly involved in F2 (thickness of the corresponding lines). The genotype-to-phenotype mapping is modular in the left case because a first group of genes [G1, G2, G3] have primarily pleiotropic effects on the characters in complex C1 and a second group of genes [G4, G5, G6] have primarily pleiotropic on the characters in complex C2. In the right case, on the contrary, most of the genes have pleiotropic effects on both complexes. Therefore C1 and C2 are quite separated in the left case while they strongly overlap in the right case. (Redrawn with modifications from Wagner and Altenberg 1996.)

instructions.[1]

A third requirement is *evolvability*, i.e. the ability to produce improvements through the application of genetic operators (Wagner and Altenberg 1996). The probability that an offspring will be fitter than its parent(s) is a function of three different entities: the shape of the fitness surface in the area around the parent (i.e., better offspring can be selected only if better genotypes are located in the neighborhood of the current parent), the genetic operators that determine which type of variations occur in the genotype of the offspring, and the genotype-to-phenotype mapping that determines how genotypic variations affect the phenotype.

An aspect that negatively affects evolvability is *pleiotropy* (Wagner and Altenberg 1996), that is the fact that a single gene can affect several different phenotypical characters. Once the population has converged to a local maximum, genetic operators tend to have negative effects, on the average. This means that changes in genes which affect different characters will produce negative effects on most of these characters. To produce an improvement, a variation of a single gene should positively affect at least a single phenotypical character, but not affect negatively all the other characters related to that gene. As a consequence, the probability that a change affecting a gene will produce a positive effect is inversely proportional to the pleiotropy of that gene (i.e., to the number of phenotypical characters affected by that gene). A good mapping therefore, should reduce pleiotropic effects among characters serving different adaptive functions. Independent functions, in other words, should be coded as independently as possible so that improvements of each function can be realized with minimal interference to other structures serving other functions.

To better illustrate this point let us consider figure 9.1 that schematically represents two individuals with different types of genotype-to-phenotype mappings. G1 to G6 are the genes, P1 to P4 are phenotypical characters (e.g. different control substructures), and F1 and F2 are two adaptive functions (e.g. different behavioral abilities necessary to gain fitness). Arrows represent the relation between genes and phenotypical characters, and between phenotypical characters and adaptive functions. The schema on the left represents an individual with a modular genotype-to-phenotype organization. In this individual the first three genes mainly influence the complex of phenotypical feature C1 which in turn mainly influences the adaptive function F1. Similarly the other three genes primarily influence C2 which in turn influence F2. On the contrary, the individual represented on the right presents a larger level of pleiotropy and does not display a modular organization. In the case of this individual, in fact, the two sets (complexes) of phenotypical characters serving the two functions are affected by almost all genes and therefore strongly overlap in genotype space.

A good genotype-to-phenotype mapping should allow the emergence of modular genotype-to-phenotype organization like that shown in the left part of figure 9.1. Individuals adopting such a form of organization would display a higher level of evolvability. A modular genotype-to-phenotype organization is also a prerequisite for the possibility of re-using the same genetic information to encode repeated phenotypical structures. If a phenotypical structure is coded in a relatively short portion of the genotype, in fact, it is possible to imagine that additional phenotypical structures can be obtained by using the same portion of the genotype. This can be obtained in two ways: (1) by using a genetic operator which might duplicate a portion of the genotype during the reproductive process, thus producing offspring that have more copies of the same portion of the genotype in their genome; (2) by including a distinction between germinal cells and somatic cells and by allowing the latter ones to replicate and differentiate during the genotype-to-phenotype mapping (see section 9.4). In this case the genotype contains a single copy of the instructions for building a given phenotypical structure.

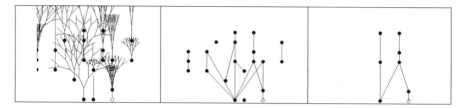

**Figure 9.2**
Development of the neural network of an evolved organism. **Left:** The growing and branching process of axons. **Center:** The resulting neural network after removal of nonconnecting branches. **Right:** The functional network after elimination of isolated and nonfunctional neurons and groups of interconnected neurons. The lower layer represents sensory neurons, the upper layer represents motor neurons, the remaining layers represents internal neurons which can be arranged up to a maximum of seven layers.

## 9.3   Growing methods

The genotype-to-phenotype process is not only an abstract mapping of information from genotype-to-phenotype. It is also a process of physical growth, growth in size and in physical structure. Instead of encoding the entire phenotypical structure in the genotype, one may encode only growing instructions. The phenotype is progressively built by executing the growing instructions specified in the genotype.

Nolfi et al. (1994b) used a growing encoding scheme to evolve the architecture and the connection weights of neural networks controlling a Khepera robot (see also Nolfi and Parisi 1992). These controllers were composed by a collection of artificial neurons distributed over a two dimensional space with growing and branching axons (see figure 9.2, left). Inherited genetic material specifies instructions that control the axonal growth and branching process of a set of neurons. The growing process occurs during individuals' lifetime. During the growth process, when a growing axonal branch of a particular neuron reaches another neuron a connection between the two neurons is established (figure 9.2, center). The axons grow and brunch only if the activation variability of the corresponding neurons is larger than a genetically specified threshold. This simple mechanism is based upon the idea that the sensory information coming from the environment has a critical role in the maturation of the connectivity of the biological nervous system and, more specifically, that the maturation process is sensitive to the activity of single neurons (see Purves 1994; Quartz and Sejnowski 1997). The developmental process of these individuals therefore is determined both by genetic and environmental factors. On the right side of figure 9.2, the resulting network controller after the elimination of isolated and non functional neurons is shown.

The genotype of evolving robots is divided in blocks each coding for the characteristics

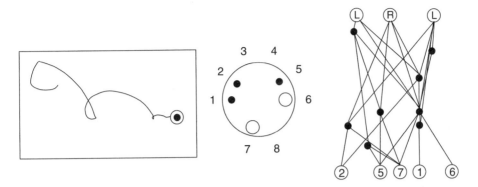

**Figure 9.3**
A typical evolved individual developing in a "light" environment. **Left:** Behavior of the robot. The rectangular box represents the arena, the empty circle represents the target area, the small full circle represent the light source, the remaining line represents the trajectory of the robot. **Center:** The sensors on which the individual relies. Large empty circles represent ambient light sensors and small full circles represent infrared sensors. **Right:** The evolved neural architecture. The bottom layer contains sensory neurons (numbers indicate the position of the corresponding neuron), the upper layer contains motor neurons ("L" and "R" indicate whether the neuron control the left or the right wheel).

of a corresponding neuron. Sensory, internal, and motor neurons were encoded by 10, 17, and 5 blocks, respectively. Each block of the genotype contains instructions that determine the properties of the corresponding neuron and the growing instruction of the axon. For sensory neurons, the corresponding sensors of the robot is indicated (within the 8 infrared and 8 ambient light sensors). Similarly, for motor neurons, the corresponding motor of the robot is indicated (within the two available motors controlling the left and the right wheels).

The environment was a $60 \times 35$ cm arena surrounded by walls. Individuals should find as quickly as possible a target area of circular shape with a diameter of 2 cm randomly positioned in the arena. The target area may or may not be illuminated by a 1 watt lightbulb positioned *right above the area*. Since the area is illuminated only in odd generations, evolving individuals have 50% of probability to be exposed to one of the two illumination conditions. Experiments have been carried out in simulation using the sampling technique described in chapter 3.[2]

Evolved individuals were able to reach the target area most of the times both in dark and in light environments although performances were clearly better in light environments (Nolfi et al. 1994b). Figures 9.3 and 9.4 show examples of behaviors displayed by the same evolved individual developing in the two different environments. In the case of the "light" environment, the individual explores the arena until it happens to perceive the light source and then approaches the target area following the light gradient (figure 9.3, left). In

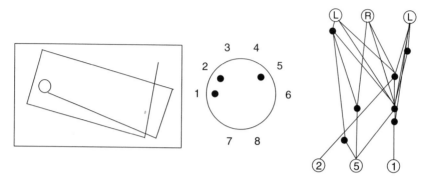

**Figure 9.4**
The same individual (i.e., with the same genotype) of figure 9.3 developing in a "dark" environment. See legend of figure 9.3.

the "dark" environment instead, the individual explores the arena trying to minimize the possibility to end up in portions of the environment that have already been visited (figure 9.4, left).

In this experiments both the synaptic weights and the neural architecture are evolved. Moreover, some aspects of the sensory-motor system of evolving individuals are under genetic control, such as the number and type of sensory and motor neurons.[3] This has two advantages: (1) it releases the designer from the burden of designing architecture and sensory-motor system, and (2) it allows the evolutionary process to shape and select architectures that are adapted to the current task and to the current environmental situation (see also box on self-adapting neural architectures). Some of these aspects (namely the architecture and the selected sensors and motors) are also under the control of the developmental process because neurons only grow and establish connections if the variation in their activation level is larger than a genetically specified threshold. This developmental process, being influenced by the external environment, displays a form of phenotypic plasticity. As in the case of some of the experiments described in chapter 7, in fact, these individuals are able to adapt to the particular environment in which they happen to "live" and develop. However, in this case the ontogenetic adaptation process involves also the architecture and the sensory-motor system of the robot and not only the synaptic weights. The individual described in figures 9.3 and 9.4 indeed, are the results of two identical copies of the same genotype (clones). Individuals developing in different environments therefore tend to develop different neural architectures, to rely on different sensors, and to exhibit different behaviors.

Husbands (1994) proposed a similar method where the free ends of dendrites grow according to a set of differential equations (see also Husbands et al. 1994). The genotype encodes the properties of each neuron (the type of neuron, the relative position with respect to the neuron created previously, the initial direction of growth of the dendrites and the parameters of the equations governing the growth process). In this case, the whole genotype-to-phenotype mapping takes place before that the robot is put in the environment and therefore it cannot display phenotypical plasticity as in the example described above. During the genotype-to-phenotype process the genetic string is scanned from left to right until a particular marker is found. When a special marker that indicates the beginning of the description of a neuron is encountered, the next bits are read and interpreted as parameters for a new neuron. The presence of an additional marker, however, might indicate that the parameters of the current neuron are specified in a previous portion of the string. This mechanism may potentially allow the emergence of phenotypes with repeated structures formed by re-expression of the same genetic instructions.

---

### Self adapting neural architectures

Although uniformly connected neural networks are universal approximators (i.e., for any given function there is a feedforward neural network able to approximate that function; see Hornik et al. 1989) the type of functions that can be learned by a given neural network are significantly affected by the topology of its architecture.

The ability to generalize (i.e., the ability to produce correct responses for sensory patterns never experienced before) is affected by the number of free parameters (connection weights) determined by the network architecture. While too small networks cannot accurately learn the desired input-output mapping, too large networks may not generalize well (Denker et al. 1987; Weigend et al. 1991). Highly connected networks are more affected by conflicting learning demands. By training neural networks with different topologies to perform visual object recognition (what) and spatial localization (where) task, Rueckl et al. (1989) showed that a fully connected feedforward neural network learns more slowly than a network where the "what" and "where" output units receive connections only from two different subsets of the hidden units. According to the authors, the difference between the two network topologies resulted from the fact that hidden units of the fully connected network received inconsistent training information because they were connected to the output units encoding both the "what" and "where" tasks. These experiments were conducted using back-propagation, but this type of problem it is not limited to networks trained using this algorithm.

Within connectionist research, three classes of approaches have been developed to automatically shape the topology of the neural architecture: growing, pruning, and decomposition methods.

**Self adapting neural architectures** (continued)

Growing methods start with networks that are too small to solve a problem and add neurons and connections during the training process. For example, in the *cascade correlation learning algorithm* proposed by Fahlman and Lebiere (1990) the initial architecture includes only direct connections from input to the output units. During the learning process, however, if the error does not decrease below a user specified threshold after a certain number of training cycles, a new internal neuron connected to all the input and output units and to all previously created internal neurons is added. Among other related approaches are the *dynamic node creation* developed by Ash (1989) and the *local growing method* proposed by Hanson (1990).

Pruning methods start which a large network and progressively reduce the network size by eliminating connections until the error becomes unacceptable. In the case of the *weight decay method* proposed by Weigend, Rumelhart and Huberman (1991), for example, the learning algorithm tries to minimize the size of the connection weights in addition to the learning error. Weights getting close to 0 can then be eliminated. For a related approach, see LeCun, Denker and Solla (1990).

Decomposition methods, such as the *adaptive mixture of local experts* proposed by Jacobs and Jordan (1991), does not operate at the level of single connections or single neurons, but at the level of larger entities (i.e., sub-networks). The process starts with a neural network composed of a certain number of hand designed sub-networks that have the same input and output units, but that might differ in their internal organization. These sub-networks may compete to learn the training patterns or to control different subsets of the output units (Jacobs, Jordan and Barto 1991). As a consequence, at the end of the learning process, different sub-networks may be responsible for different sets of patterns or for producing different parts of the output, and therefore compute different functions. In other words, the network learns to partition the task into two or more functionally independent tasks by allocating different networks to each task. Moreover, sub-networks with different topology tend to be allocated to the tasks for which their topology is best suited.

These methods and the methods based on artificial evolution reviewed in this chapter share the goal of developing an appropriate neural architecture through a self-organizing process. There are several differences however that should be noted.

The methods described in this box, are based on the back-propagation algorithm and, as a consequence, can be applied only when a detailed description of the desired output of the network is available at each time step (an exception to this is ART, a self-organizing network where new output units are dynamically added to encode new input classes [Grossberg 1987]).

> **Self adapting neural architectures** (continued)
>
> The methods based on artificial evolution, instead, can rely on a much more limited feedback such as how well the neural network is performing for a certain number of trials (during individuals' lifetime). The methods described in this box rely on an abstract view of neural networks in which the input and the output patterns are provided and interpreted by the experimenter. On the contrary, the methods described in the remaining of the chapter are based on an embodied and situated view of neural networks. This, as we will see below, offers the possibility to co-adapt the neural architecture and the structure of the sensory and motor system. In the case of the methods relying on artificial evolution, any characteristic of a system (e.g. the connection weights, the topology of the neural architecture, the sensory-motor system, the body structure) may be encoded in the genotype and subjected to the same adaptive process. Finally, in the methods described in this box changes occur only at one time scale (the learning process) while in the methods relying on artificial evolution changes might occur at two different time scales: phylogenesis and ontogenesis. This might represent an advantage when changes should affect smaller or larger entities, such as the connection weights and the architecture of the network.

## 9.4   Cellular encodings

In natural organisms the development of the nervous system begins with a folding in of the ectodermic tissue which forms the neural crest. This structure gives origin to the mature nervous system through three phases: the genesis and proliferation of different classes of neurons by cellular duplication and differentiation, the migration of the neurons toward their final destination, and the growth of neurites (axons, dendrites). The growing process described in the previous section therefore characterizes very roughly only the last of these three phases. A number of attempts have been made to include other aspects of this process in artificial evolutionary experiments.

Cangelosi et al. (1994), for example, extended the model described in the previous section by adding a cell division and migration stage to the already existing stage of axonal growth shown in figure 9.2. The genotype, in this case, is a collection of rules governing the process of cell division (a single cell is replaced by two "daughter" cells) and migration (the new cells can move in the 2D space). The genotype-to-phenotype process therefore starts with a single cell which, by undergoing a number of duplication and migration processes, produces a collection of neurons arranged in a 2D space. These neurons grow their axons and establish connections until a neural controller is formed. The number of duplications is genetically specified and cannot exceed a maximum number. The genotype-to-phenotype mapping process occurs before the lifetime of the individuals begin (for other related approaches see Vaario 1993; Dellaert and Beer 1994).

Gruau (1994) proposed a genetic encoding scheme for neural networks based on a cellular duplication and differentiation process. The genotype-to-phenotype mapping starts with a single cell that undergoes a number of duplication and transformation processes ending up in a complete neural network. In this scheme the genotype is a collection of rules governing the process of cell divisions (a single cell is replaced by two "daughter" cells) and transformations (new connections can be added and the weights of the connections departing from a cell can be modified).

In Gruau's model connection links are established during the cellular duplication process. For this reason there are different forms of duplication, each determining the way in which the connections of the mother cells are inherited by the daughter cells. For example, one of two daughter cells may inherit from the mother the input links while the other may inherit the output links and be connected with newly established synapses; alternatively, both daughters may inherit input and output connections from the mother cell; or, a part of the links may be inherited by the first cell and the remaining links by the other cell; and so forth. Additional operations include the possibility to add or remove connections and to modify the connections weights.

The instructions contained in the genotype are represented as a binary tree structure and evolved as in genetic programming. During the genotype-to-phenotype mapping process, the genotype tree is scanned starting from the top node of the tree and then following each ramification. The top node represents the initial cell that, by undergoing a set of duplication processes, produces the final neural network. Each node of the genotype tree encodes the operations that should be applied to the corresponding cell. The two subtrees of a node specify the operations that should be applied to the two daughter cells. The neural network is progressively built by following the tree and applying the corresponding duplication instructions. Terminal nodes of the tree (i.e., nodes that do not have sub trees) represent terminal cells that will not undergo further duplications. Inspired by Koza's work on automatic discovery of reusable programs (Koza 1994), Gruau also considered the case of genotypes formed by many trees where the terminal nodes of a tree may point to other trees. This mechanism allows the genotype-to-phenotype process to produce repeated phenotypical structures (e.g. repeated neural sub-networks) by re-using the same genetic informations. Trees that are pointed to more than once, in fact, will be executed more times. This encoding method has two advantages: (a) compact genotypes can produce complex phenotypical networks, and (b) evolution may exploit phenotypes where repeated substructures are encoded in a single part of the genotype. Since the identification of substructures that are read more than once is an emergent result of the evolutionary process,

| single-tree: | tree 1: |
|---|---|
| A(A(U_3)(S(L3(M3(M9))))(P(T(L4(M1))(D_6(G(D2(P(L_8( F6(F1)))(S(L8(D_1(M3)))(I_5(M1(F1))))))(L4(M3(M9))))))( A(U7(M2))(A(H((L_8(M1(L2(M3))))(S(2(M1))(U_5))))(C_ 3(T(L_1(M1))(U_5)))))))))(R(T(S(L_2(M1(L4(L))))(T(D_8( W(F2)))(T(T(S(R(A(A(S(A(L_1)(L8))(R(L3(M3))))(S(G(L_ 9(M1))(D7(M3(F1))))(L6))(W(S(A(S(D_5(T(T9(U_1))(L_7( L(F1)))))(S(L_6(M2))(U2())))(R(L2(M1))))(T(L3(L_5))(L_7 (M1)))))))(F1))(L_3(M2)))(L_3))))(H(I8(P(S(H(P(L_2(M2( M1)))(R(U9(M1))))(S(U4)(U5(U_2(M1)))))(A(M1)(T(L5)(I _5(U_1)))))(A(T(T(C(A(P(G(C(T(C_4(A(P(G(C6(L4(U_5( M1)))))(W(U_8))(I3(L_2)))(U_7)))(F1)))(M1(L_6(L(M3))))) (U6))(U9)))(G(T(P(D1(L2))(M1))(T(D_2(L6(M1)))(S(L8)(U _4(M1)))))(R(T(M1)(C_3(L8))))))(E(W(T(A(A(S(A(L_3)(L _7))(R(L1(M3)))(S(G(L(M1))(D7(M3(F1))))(L6))))(W(S(A( S(D(T(I_9(U_1))(I_7(L_3(F1)))))(S(L_6(M1))(U2(S(G(L(M 1))(D7(M3(f1))))(L6))))(R(L2(M1))))(T(L3(L5))(L7(M1)))) ))(L_9(M1(M3)))))))(G(H(G(L2(M1(C9(F1)))(D_2(L_1)))( D_1(D7(S(T(I(L6))(H(L8(L_2(M1(L_4(L_5))))(L_5))))(U_9 )))))(U2)))))(G(U6)(M2))))) | (A(A(n2)(n2))(n2)) |
|  |  |
|  | tree 2: not used |
|  |  |
|  | tree 3: |
|  | P(T(C_7(C_7(D5(M3(C_7(C_7(D5(M3(M2(C_9(I2(U_5(C2 (I8(U1(M2(F2(M2(L_1(F2(M4(U))))))))))))))))))))))(D5(D5( M3(M2(I2(M2(I4(F4(F3))))))))(T(C_7(C_7(C_7(D5(M3( M2(I7(W(F2(M3(M2(I4(F2(F4)))))))))))))))(R(U6(M2))) |

**Figure 9.5**
**Left:** Genotype of an individual evolved without ADNS. In this experiment the genotype is composed by a single tree that develops 260 nodes. **Right:** Genotype of an individual evolved with ADNS. In this case the genotype is composed of three trees. In the case of this individual, however, the second tree is not functional. The first tree, in fact, includes three terminal nodes "n2" that point to the third tree and no pointer to the second tree. The total number of nodes in the case of this individual is 65. For reasons of space, trees are represented as a nested list of instructions. (Redrawn from Gruau 1994. Reprinted with permission)

Gruau defined this method *Automatic Definition of Neural Subnetworks* (ADNS) (Gruau 1994).

Gruau (1994) applied this method to evolve neural controllers for a simulated hexapod robot. The model of the robot was a simplified version of the insect model developed by Beer and Gallagher (1992) reported later in chapter 10. Gruau compared two experimental settings with and without ADNS. In ADNS experiments the genotypes consisted of three trees and terminal nodes could potentially point to another threes (the terminal nodes of the first tree could point to the two other trees, the terminal nodes of the second tree could point only to the third tree, the terminal nodes of the last tree could not point to any tree). In this case the crossover operator could exchange both subparts or complete trees. In experiments without ADNS the genotype consisted of a single tree and crossover could only exchange subtrees.[4]

For time reasons, Gruau ran only two replications of the experiments for each condition. The evolutionary process evolved a walking pattern (see also chapter 10) for both replications with ADNS, but only in one replication without ADNS. The genotype of evolved individuals were significantly more compact in the case of experiments with ADNS (see figure 9.5). Moreover, the resulting phenotypical networks were much more structured in the case of experiments with ADNS (see figure 9.6). In the example dis-

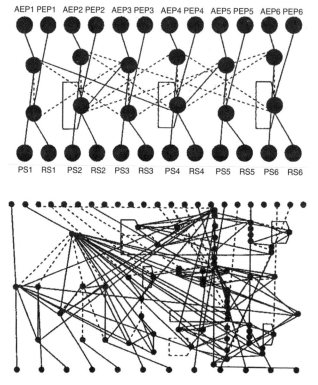

**Figure 9.6**
**Top:** Phenotypical networks of an individual evolved with ADNS. PEP = Posterior extreme position, PS = power stroke; RS = return stroke, AEP = Anterior extreme position. **Bottom:** Phenotypical networks of an individual evolved without ADNS. For space reasons the label of the sensor and motor neurons are not shown in this case. (Reprinted with permission from Gruau 1994.)

played in figure 9.6 the network included three repeated sub-networks controlling two legs each.

By running additional experiments with a more detailed model of the robot (Beer and Gallagher 1992), Gruau (1994) showed that a walking pattern could be solved without hand coding the architecture of the controller and without providing any information about how to decompose the problem into subcomponents. He showed that this harder problem could only be solved by using ADNS, that is by using a modular genotype-to-phenotype mapping where the same genetic information can be re-used to produce repeated phenotypical structures.[5] The evolutionary process, however, required about one million of evaluations to evolve successful controllers for this simulated walking robot. When it came to apply this method to the real octopod robot, Gruau attempted to reduce the number of evaluations by using syntacting constraints to shrink the search space, by including handmade problem decomposition, and by giving subjective fitness values upon visual inspection of the behavior (Gruau 1997, see also section 10.3).

Kodjabachian and Meyer (1998a) proposed a related approach that was applied to the same problem, that is the evolution of neural controllers for a simulated hexapod robot based on the model developed by Beer and Gallagher (1992). In this encoding scheme, called *simple geometry oriented cellular encoding* (SGOCE), neurons grow their connections in a two dimensional matrix substrate where their actual positions affect the types of connections that are established. As in the case of Gruau's model, the genotype was formed by a tree of instructions and crossover was accomplished by exchanging subtrees (genetic programming). Genotypes included only 6 different instructions: a) a cellular division instruction (DIVIDE) that takes as parameters the distance and the relative angle of the daughter cell; b) two instructions (GRAW and DRAW) that create efferent or afferent connections, respectively, and take as parameters the angle and distance of the neuron with which the connection should be made and its connection weight; c) two instructions (SETTAU and SETBIAS) that specify the values of the time constant and bias threshold of the cell; d) an instruction (DIE) that causes a cell to die.[6]

When compared to the encoding scheme proposed by Gruau, Kodjabachian and Meyer handcrafted a set of important phenotypical properties: the size of the substrate over which the network develops, the positions of the sensory cells and of the motor neurons, and the number and position of precursor cells. Six precursor cells were used and were located in the center of the six corresponding sectors of the substrate. These six cells developed according to a unique set of genetic instructions.[7] The substrate, the sensory and motor neurons, and the precursor cells are shown in figure 1.3 (left) and correspond to the rectangular area, the empty circles, and the black circles respectively. The handcrafting of these features is probably one of the reasons why the authors observed the emergence of walking behaviors in significantly shorter time (after about 100,000 evaluations) than in Gruau's experiments. A stable walking behavior was obtained in one out of five replications of the experiment. On the top-right of the same figure, the genotype of an evolved individual is displayed (parameter value are not shown). Finally, on the bottom of the figure we can see the resulting phenotypical network after that useless interneurons and connections have been removed. Solid and dotted lines represent excitatory and inhibitory connections respectively.

The authors were able to evolve behaviors of increasing complexities in an incremental fashion. The experiment described above, in fact, was saved and used as a building block for evolving more complex controllers. In a second evolutionary stage an additional module was evolved. This module received sensory information through additional sensory cells and influenced the walking behavior by establishing connection with the cells of the first module. In one experiment described in Kodjabachian and Meyer (1998b), for instance, a gradient following module was evolved in an additional substrate placed just on the left of the first substrate which was provided with two precursor cells and two photoreceptor sensors. In this second phase, individuals were selected for their ability to approach the light source as quickly as possible. Individuals capable of approaching the light in five different conditions were obtained after about 20,000 evaluations in five out of five replications of the experiment. Capitalizing on the development of these two modules, the authors were able to evolve a third obstacle avoidance module that received information from two additional contact sensors. After another 20,000 evaluations, the authors obtained simulated robots able to approach the light source while avoiding obstacles. However, it should be noted that the fitness functions employed for the various stages explicitly used metric distances between the simulated robot, the obstacles, and the goal. This type of information is not readily available when a physical robot is employed or requires careful manipulations of the evolutionary environment (as it will be shown later on). The SGOCE approach has also been used for incremental evolution of navigation behaviors in robots with wheels (Chavas et al. 1998).

## 9.5   Conclusions

The encoding scheme and the mapping from genotype-to-phenotype have strong effects on the evolvability of a system. In this chapter we have discussed various ways of encoding the characters of an evolving control systems into genetic representations that are suitable for artificial evolution. We have described some methods to design genetic encodings and genotype-to-phenotype mappings that have desirable properties such as expressive power, compactness, and evolvability. Despite these preliminary results, this is an open field of research for the future. In particular, in all the methods described in this chapter there are several arbitrary assumptions whose consequences are not yet fully tested and understood.

An important point to notice is that in most computational methods the genotype-to-phenotype mapping is conceived as an instantaneous process that takes place before testing an individual in the world. In other words, it is as if these individuals were born as full blown adult organisms. The only case where the genotype-to-phenotype process takes place while the individual interacts with the environment is the growing scheme proposed in section 9.3. In those experiments the control system develops while the robot interacts with the environment and is affected by early experiences during growth. The results indicate that this form of developmental plasticity increases the adaptability of the individual to the specific characteristics of the environment where it happens to be born. Among other things, it would be interesting to study the implications of variable developmental rates in different types of environments.

Finally, most encoding schemes described in this chapter use rather complex rules and building blocks pre-specified by the designer in order to solve a specific problem. The experimental evidence is not yet strong enough to show that such methods generate results that are competitive with more direct encoding schemes applied to a pre-specified architecture. In most cases, the complexity of the genetic encoding comes from the fact that different neuron types and connectivity patterns must be included in the genotype. Recently, we have explored a way to overcome this problem by combining compact encodings (where the genetic string encodes only few properties of a generic neuron) with ontogenetic adaptation described in section 7.5 (see also Floreano and Urzelai 2000). In other words, the genotype specifies only the sign and learning properties of each neuron in the network (therefore genotype length is proportional to the number of neurons, not to the number of connections); consequently, all incoming connections to a neuron will adapt during lifetime using the same learning rule associated to that neuron, but will develop different strengths depending on the activations of presynaptic neurons. The results show that: a) such encoding strategy is more effective than one where adaptive rules are specified independently for each synapse; b) the performance of the evolutionary system is not degraded by adding a large number of additional neurons to the network; c) when evolution can choose whether to use an encoding scheme based on neurons or on synapses by adding an extra gene that tells the decoding scheme how to read the genetic material, it consistently selects the former (Urzelai 2000). These explorations make us believe that developmental schemes may benefit by the addition of ontogenetic plasticity to reduce the complexity and length of genotypes.

# 10 Complex hardware morphologies: Walking machines

## 10.1 Introduction

Walking robots require a greater effort of low level sensory-motor coordination than wheeled robots do. Even in a mechanically simple walking robot, each leg has at least 2 degrees of freedom (the same as a two wheeled robot); a six leg (hexapod) robot has at least 12 degrees of freedom (figure 10.1). The traditional geometric approach to control, based on modeling of the robot and derivation of leg trajectories, is computationally expensive and requires fine tuning of several parameters in the equations describing direct/inverse kinematics. Some authors have recently employed genetic algorithms for optimizing these parameters (for example, see Arakawa and Fukuda 1997). In the behavior-based approach trajectories emerge from the coordination of several control modules with local computation often inspired upon biological mechanisms of walking. In this chapter we shall describe mainly evolutionary experiments within a behavior-based and bioinspired framework.

The complexity of controlling a legged robot can be considerably reduced if one takes into account the symmetries of the body. For example, if a six leg robot is symmetric along its displacement axis, one may assume that the two corresponding legs across this axis use the same type of low level control architecture. Furthermore, if the three legs on each side of the robot have the same morphology, one might further assume that they use the same

**Figure 10.1**
Hexapod robot and its major axes (white lines). The complexity of leg control can be decomposed by considering symmetries across and (possibly) along the displacement axis (thick white line). A common solution consists of developing only one low-level controller, replicate it over all legs, and coordinate the timing of leg movements. (Adapted from Brooks 1989. Reprinted with permission.)

control architecture too. At this point, it is sufficient to develop only a single leg controller, replicate it over the six legs, and coordinate the timing of the movement of each leg both across and along the main axis.

---

### Static and dynamic gaits

The robots described in this chapter are quadrupeds (4 legs), hexapods (6 legs), and octopods (8 legs). There are other types of walking robots, ranging from single leg to wheel leg hybrids, but they will not be covered here.

Independently of the robot considered, we can distinguish between two types of gait: static and dynamic. *Static gait* is called so because the robot remains upright also when the legs stop moving. This gait requires that the projection of the center of mass of the robot on the ground lies within the support polygon formed by feet on the ground. This type of motion is common to many insects and it is easier for control of robots. Examples of static gaits are tripod, tetrapod, and wave gait. Tripod gait applies to hexapod robots. It consists of keeping three legs (frontmost and backmost legs on one side, middle leg on the other side) on the ground at any one time and shift the remaining three in the air. Similarly, tetrapod gait applies to octopod robots: four alternating legs (two on each side) stay on the ground while the remaining four swing in the air. Instead, in wave gait corresponding legs move forward together two at a time while all remaining legs keep contact with the ground.

*Dynamic walk* is called so because the projection of the center of mass of the robot is continuously displaced inside and outside of the support polygon when the legs move. If the legs stop moving the robot may fall down. This type of gait requires faster motion of the limbs and is computationally more complex because it is necessary to take into account the mass and inertia of the robot. The advantages of dynamic walk are better flexibility on irregular terrains, high speed motion (running, jumping, etc), and several types of gaits. It works better for robots with large bodies (longer time in the air) and greater mass (larger inertia). Two examples of quadruped dynamic gaits are pacing and trotting. In both cases only two legs are in contact with the ground at any one time. During pacing the legs along the body diagonal move at the same time whereas during trotting the legs on the same side move together.

---

There is some evidence that walking in biological organism relies on coordination of decentralized control systems replicated for each leg (Pearson 1976). In the bioinspired architecture described by Brooks (1989) for a hexapod robot (figure 10.1), the controller of each leg was implemented as a hand designed finite state machine replicated over all legs. Each finite state machine modified its own state on the basis of its local program and of the state returned by other machines within a loosely coupled architecture. It was later shown

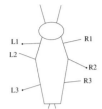

**Figure 10.2**
The model of insect used in the work by Beer and Gallagher (1992). Thick endpoints indicate that the foot are on the floor. (Adapted from Beer and Gallagher 1992. Reprinted with permission.)

that coordination among these finite state machines could be learned by trial and error (Maes and Brooks 1990). A trailing wheel attached to the robot provided positive feedback when it rolled forward and touch sensors under the robot provided negative feedback when the robot fell down. A reinforcement learning algorithm used this feedback to update the table of state-conditions under which each leg initiated a swinging movement.

## 10.2   Evolving simulated insects

Artificial evolution of walking robots has often resorted to the type of functional and architectural decomposition described above. Beer and Gallagher (1992) conducted some pioneering work on evolution of walking for simulated hexapod insects. Their methodology is often used as source of inspiration in more recent work with physical robots. Starting from their model (Beer 1990) of a simple insect with six legs (figure 10.2), the authors showed that artificial evolution can find robust locomotion controllers without much a priori knowledge (as compared to, for example, the works by Brooks 1989, and Brooks and Maes 1990 mentioned above).

In Beer's simulated insect each leg has a foot that can be either up or down. When the foot is down, the leg provides support and can generate forces moving the body forward (*stance phase*). When the foot is up, the forces generated by the controller can swing the leg in the air (*swing phase*). The insect can move only if it is statically stable (see inset box). In conditions of static stability, the displacement of the body is computed under Newtonian dynamics by summing the forces exerted by all stancing legs. If the insect is not statically stable, it falls down and its velocity drops to zero. Each leg contains three effectors: one controls the state of the foot (up or down), while the other two control—respectively—the forward swing and the backward swing of the leg in a manner similar to antagonist muscles found in biological organisms for limb control. Each leg also has a sensor that measures the angle between the leg and the body of the robot.

**A**

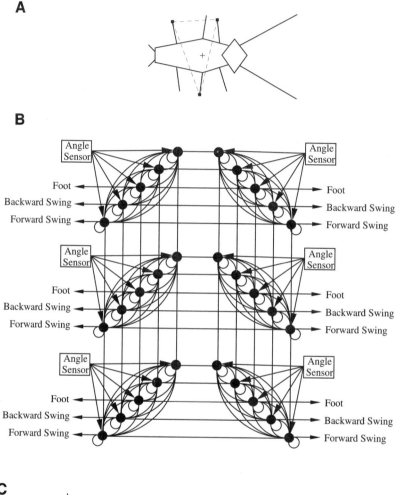

**B**

**C**

**Figure 10.3**
The walking task. **A**: Body Model. **B**: Controller network architecture. **C**: The performance of a walking agent is evaluated by measuring the forward distance that the body moves in a fixed amount of time. (Reprinted with permission from Beer 1997.)

A leg is controlled by a five neuron, fully interconnected, continuous, dynamical neural network (figure 10.3, B). Three neurons correspond to the three effectors described above while two remaining neurons function as hidden units. Each neuron receives an additional weighted input from the angle sensor. A leg controller is thus defined by 40 parameters: 25 interconnections, 5 connections from the angle sensor, 5 thresholds, and 5 time constants. In order to limit the number of interconnections, the authors assumed that each neuron is connected only to its corresponding neighboring neurons (figure 10.3, B), that the cross body (5) and intersegmental (5) connections are identical, and that each controller has the same connection weights. This architecture, inspired upon the neural circuitry used by cockroaches for locomotion (Pearson et al. 1973; Pearson 1976), has only 50 free parameters that must be found by the genetic algorithm.

A population of 500 individuals, each encoding the 50 parameters of the architecture on 200 bit binary string, was evolved from scratch using the simple genetic algorithm described in chapter 2. An individual was evaluated by randomizing the insect's initial leg positions and neuron states and allowing it to run for a fixed amount of time. The fitness function was the forward distance travelled by the insect within the allocated time normalized by the total distance it could have travelled if it had moved forward at maximum speed (behavioral fitness). This fitness function encouraged stable support, forward motion, and speed. Each individual was tested in two different trial and its fitness averaged: in one trial the neurons received information from the angle sensor, in the other they did not. This solution was devised to evolve robust controllers capable of generating the appropriate amplitude, phase, and duration of movements even in absence of external input.

In all evolutionary runs, artificial evolution discovered a pattern of leg movement known as tripod gait (figure 10.4), a type of gait used by all fast moving insects (Graham 1985). The evolved controllers displayed a higher stepping frequency and more regular phasing in the presence of sensory input (figure 10.4, top), but were capable of moving forward even in its absence (figure 10.4, bottom). In all evolutionary runs, the authors detected four different evolutionary phases. In the first phase, insects moved forward by putting down all six feet and pushing forward until they fell down. In the second phase, they learned to swing their legs in an uncoordinated fashion making some progress forward, but falling down often. In the third phase, the best insects began to display stable static gait which was further refined in the fourth final phase.

In a related earlier work, de Garis (1990) evolved a fully recurrent, discrete time, neural network (12 nodes) to control walking of a simulated biped with two joint stick legs. The control architecture was incrementally evolved in two steps. In the first step, the fitness function was designed to evolve a single coordinated step of the two legs. In the second step, the last population of controller was evolved to cover as much forward distance as possible within a limited amount of time. In this experiment, the fitness function used

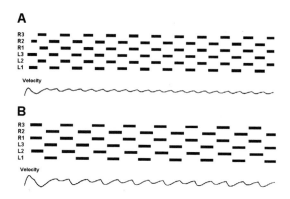

**Figure 10.4**
Behavior of a mixed locomotion controller. (A) with and (B) without its sensors. The legs are labeled L for left and R for right and numbered from 1 to 3 starting from the front of the insect (see also figure 10.2) Black bars denote the swing phase of a leg, and the space between bars represents a stance phase. (Reprinted with permission from Beer and Gallagher 1992.)

an error measure that explicitly computed the difference between the actual and desired trajectories, and the simulation was rather simple and purely kinematic. In other words, this work was mainly aimed at demonstrating evolvability of walk.

When Beer and Gallagher attempted to use the incremental approach advocated by de Garis, i.e. evolving first a single controller for one leg and later the coordination among copies of this controller, they found that the performance of evolved insects was not as good as that of insects that were evolved from scratch on the full locomotion problem. Similarly, a leg controller evolved together with the coordination parameters for the locomotion task, did not function well as a standalone leg controller.

The apparently contradicting results from the two research groups can be explained by considering that Beer and Gallagher controller has relatively few free parameters as compared to de Garis model. In the latter case, evolutionary search can be helped by an incremental approach that explores one region of the search space at a time, whereas in the former case the search space is small enough to allow the development of a fully coordinated solution. However, both authors did not provide enough data to understand whether de Garis model could have taken advantage from full evolution of a more constrained architecture, or whether the reduced search space of Beer and Gallagher presented only spatially separated local minima, one for a single leg controller and the other for the full locomotion controller, and thus could not benefit from an incremental approach.

From a methodological perspective, it would be advisable to use an approach that resorts to behavioral and simple fitness functions, such as in Beer and Gallagher work. On the one hand, simple fitness functions computed using information available through the sensors of the robot are more easily implemented on autonomous physical robots. On the other hand, the more constrained the fitness function and the assumptions involved in the design of the evolutionary experiment, the less appealing artificial evolution becomes with respect to other adaptive techniques (see also the discussion on fitness space in chapter 2). Finally, a functional a priori decomposition of the problem at hand, although reasonable from an engineering perspective, might impose a heavy burden on the biological or ethological significance of the results obtained.

## 10.3   Evolution of walking machines

The first attempt to evolve a physical walking machine has been carried out at the University of Southern California (Lewis et al. 1992).[1] The goal was to evolve a neural network to generate a sequence of signals that can drive the legs of an hexapod robot with two degrees of freedom for each leg (lift and swing). Inspired upon the work of Beer and Gallagher and of de Garis described above, the authors resorted to incremental evolution (they called it *staged evolution*) and functional decomposition between evolution of single leg controller and of coordination of evolved controllers. Motivated by developmental observations in biology (Coghill 1964), the authors decided to approach the problem of locomotion in two phases: a) evolution of a single oscillator to be replicated over each leg; b) evolution of the coordination links between already evolved controllers.

The experiments were carried out on a six leg robot similar to that shown in figure 10.1. The robot was approximately 35 cm long and 12 cm large. Each leg was actuated by two servomotors providing leg elevation and swing. The motors were controlled by an onboard Motorola 68332 processor. The robot *did not* use sensors for locomotion. A population of 10 individuals, each encoding the synaptic weights of neurocontrollers using grey coding, was evolved using the simple genetic algorithm described in chapter 2. The two best individuals were preserved for the next generation (elitism). The genetic code of each individual was used as input to a neural network descriptor that simulated and displayed the activations of the neurons on a computer. The sequence of neural activations was then downloaded into the robot controller where the program was executed. The resulting behavior was scored by the experimenter using a combination of objective measures and visual inspection, and the score was fed back to the genetic algorithm as fitness.

The positions of the two joints were driven by the states of two corresponding neurons (figure 10.5, left). The activation dynamics of each neuron were analogous to those used by Beer and Gallagher without the contribution of external sensory input. For certain

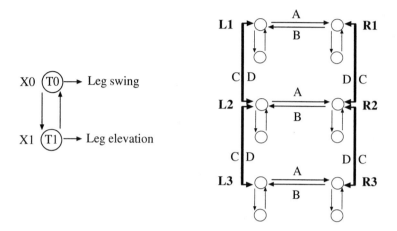

**Figure 10.5**
**Left:** Simple oscillator circuit for controlling two joints of a single leg. T0 and T1 are the time constants of the two neurons X0 and X1 respectively. **Right:** Coupled oscillator circuit composed of six replicas of simple oscillators, linked by additional weights. Weights with the same letter (A, B, C, or D) are forced to take the same value. Thick connections represent two weights (C and D). Legs are labeled as in Beer and Gallagher's insect model depicted in figure 10.2. (Adapted from Lewis et al. 1992. Reprinted with permission.)

combinations of weight and threshold parameters, the two neurons began to oscillate at a particular frequency and phase. By connecting one neuron to the motor controlling leg elevation and the other to the motor controlling leg swing, when the two neurons oscillated with a phase difference of 90 degrees, this coupled oscillator produced a stepping motion.

The first phase of evolution concentrated on finding the parameters for a suitable oscillator circuit. The genetic string encoded two weights and two thresholds. Each parameter was encoded on 8 bits using grey coding and randomly initialized in the range $[-8, 8]$. Total string length was 32 bits. Evaluation was performed by visual inspection of the temporal behavior of the oscillating neurons on the computer screen and scored according to the following criteria. If both neurons are in the same state, the fitness score is 0. If one neuron is $>0$ and the other $<0$, the fitness score is 5. If at least a neuron moves from one state to the other, then the score is 10. In case of oscillations damping to 0 the fitness is 25. If these oscillations do not damp to zero, but their magnitude is not yet 1, the fitness is 40. For sustained oscillations over the entire range $[0, 1]$, the fitness score is 60. When at least half of the population reached maximal scores of 60 (about 17 generations), the experiment moved on to the second phase.

In the second phase, the genetic string encoded both the parameters of the oscillators and four additional parameters for the links between the oscillators, for a total of 65 bits. The interconnection links, encoded on 8 bits each, were constrained to take the same

value across the axis of the robot and along each side (figure 10.5, right), similarly to
Beer and Gallagher's methodology, and were all initialized to 0. Instead, the parameters
of the oscillators were those evolved in the first phase. The 65th bit determined whether
the leg swing neuron caused a forward or a backward motion. In this way, it was easy to
transition between forward and backward motion without a full recoding of all weights. It
took between 10 and 35 additional generations to obtain efficient walking patterns. In all
replications of the experiment, the robot evolved tripod gait, as for the simulated insect of
Beer and Ghallagher. Before stabilizing into this type of gait, during some early generations
the robot displayed wave gait, another type of gait frequently observed in insects. However,
due to the particular construction of the robot, the tripod gait produced faster motion than
the wave gait and dominated in the populations of later generations.

## Online evolution

Gomi and Ide (1998) evolved walking patterns for an octopod robot designed to mimick
the body of a lobster (figure 10.6, left). As in the work of Lewis et al. described above,
the authors did not take in consideration sensory information, but here the evolutionary
process was carried out entirely on the physical robot using an automated evaluation
process similar to that described in section 10.2. To this end, the robot was designed so
that it could operate both on batteries and on an external DC power source to enable
sustained periods of evolution. The weight of the robot was approximately 3800 grams,
including batteries. Each leg has two degrees of freedom, lift and swing. The genetic string
encoded the parameters of all eight legs (figure 10.6, right). Each leg was characterized by
8 parameters describing its motion. These were: the amount of delay (up to 5 seconds) after
which the leg begins to move, the current status of the leg (two bits indicating the direction
of the leg's vertical and horizontal motions), end positions of both vertical and horizontal
swings of the leg ($-64$ to 64, zero being center for both down/up and back/front maxima),
and vertical and horizontal angular speeds of the leg ($-10$ to 10, negative being upward
and forward speed).

The motor current sensors and two belly contact sensors were used for the evaluation
of the fitness function. This function was designed to favor evolution of a robot that could
stand up, coordinate its leg motions, and advance forward. The electric current required to
drive a leg was monitored at the corresponding servo motor and the current values for the
horizontal and vertical axis of the leg (swing and lift, respectively) were used to identify the
"proper loading" condition for each leg. Summarizing, positive feedback was given when
a front to back stroke of a leg occurred while there was sufficient but not excessive vertical
load. Positive feedback was given also when a leg swinged back to a starting position with
no load. All other movements, as well as the activation of the touch sensors located on the
belly of the robot, caused negative feedback.

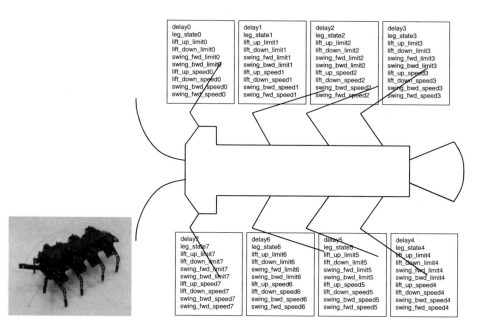

**Figure 10.6**
**Left:** OCT-1b, an octopod robot designed to mimic a lobster. Each leg is composed of a single rod of bent metal. It has two degrees of freedom: lift and swing. The robot is 30 cm long, has four infrared sensors that point forward and to the sides, 10 ambient light sensors positioned around the body, and front bumpers and wiskers. **Right:** The genotype encodes the parameters of the eight legs. Each leg is characterized by 10 parameters that define its motion. (Both figures courtesy of Applied AI Systems Inc.)

Each of the 50 individuals of the population was tested for 40 seconds. Forward movements were evolved after a few dozen generations, but continuous improvements could be detected for over 100 generations. It took about 10 generations to evolve robots that could stand up and another dozen for the appearance of forward movements. In most cases the robots developed a tetrapod gait, although some time a wave gate was also observed. The relatively longer evolution time of this experiment with respect to that of Lewis et al. was probably due to the longer genetic string that individually encoded the parameters of all eight leg controllers.

**From simulations to physical robots**

In the attempt to reduce the number of evaluations required on the physical robot, Jakobi (1998) evolved neural control architectures for the octopod robot described above in "minimal simulations" (see chapter 3). As compared to Gomi and Ide's work, the author provided to the control system the sensory information coming from infrared and bumper sensors available on the robot. The aim of the experiment was to evolve neural networks that would allow the robot to wander around its environment avoiding objects with its infrared sensors and backing away from objects that hit with its bumpers. The simulator was extremely simple and computed the speeds of the left side and of the right side of the robot using position and displacement information from the eight legs (see Jakobi 1998 for details). The fitness evaluation was based on four tests, one for each of four sensory scenarios lasting five simulated seconds. At the end of every test, the fitness of the individual was incremented by the resulting value $\delta$. The four test cases were: 1) If there were no objects within sensor range, $\delta$ was the sum of the left and right side speeds; 2) If there was an object within infrared sensor range on the right side, $\delta$ was the right side speed minus the left side speed; 3) If there was an object within infrared sensor range on the left side, $\delta$ was the left side speed minus the right side speed; 4) If the robot hit an obstacle with the bumpers, $\delta$ was set to minus the sum of the left side and right side speeds.

The control architecture and genetic encoding used in Jakobi's experiment was similar to that used in Beer and Gallagher experiment described in section 10.2. Each leg controller consisted of six fully connected neurons, one of which controlled the horizontal angle and another the vertical angle of the leg. In addition, each synapse of a leg controller received a gating signal from three weighted sensor neurons (infrared, bumper, bias unit set to 1). If the sum of the weighted sensors was negative, the synapse was temporarily set to 0. Instead, if the sum was positive, the synapse value was unaffected.[2]

Reliably fit controllers evolved within around 3500 generations. When downloaded on the physical robot, the best evolved controllers made the octopod walk around its environment using tetrapod gait. The robot turned away from objects that fell within infrared range and backed away from objects hit with the bumpers. However, Gomi and Ide, who had the opportunity to compare Jakobi's evolved controller with their own, remarked that Jakobi's evolved behaviors were too demanding for the mechanics and motors of the robot. They claimed that this was due to the fact that simulations are not sufficient to take into account mechanical stress and other electromechanical characteristics of the robot. Instead, by evolving the controllers on the physical robot, Gomi and Ide found that current profiles generated by their evolved controllers matched better the constraints of robot hardware (Gomi and Ide 1998).

**Evolving architectures**

In all the work described so far, the architecture of the controller has been predesigned and fixed during evolution. Gruau has applied his cellular encoding method (see chapter 9) to the evolution of gait for the octopod robot Oct-1b described above (figure 10.6, left). As we reported in chapter 9, in the case of a simulated hexapod robot (Gruau 1994) shown that the 6 leg locomotion task could be automatically decomposed into the problem of generating a neural network controlling two legs and coordinating the three resulting sub-networks. It took a parallel machine and one million evaluations to evolve successful controllers for that simulated robot. When it came to apply this method to the real octopod robot, Gruau attempted to reduce the number of evaluations by using syntacting constraints to shrink the search space, by including handmade problem decomposition, and by giving subjective fitness values upon visual inspection of the behavior (Gruau 1997). With regard to this latter aspect and to the fact that the controllers do not have access to sensory information, Gruau's approach is similar to the method of visual inspection initially adopted by Lewis et al. (1992). However, as compared to Lewis et al., Gruau selected the controllers in a more subjective way while attempting to maintain diversity in a first phase and to encourage convergence and fine tuning in a second phase. The syntactic constraints were such that specific types of cell duplications were enforced (for example, cloning) and that the number of certain recursive operations were bound to limits that matched the number of legs of the robot.

As in Lewis et al., Gruau approached the problem by decomposing it into two sequential subproblems: first evolve a leg controller and later evolve the coordination among eight copies of this controller. During the first phase 20 individuals were evolved for 20 generations. The fitness was manually given depending on the ability of the controller to start the swing sequence at the right time, to exploit the full range of lift space, and to keep the leg on the floor during the power stroke. Two types of neurons evolved, one using temporal delay to control the duration of the movement and another using spatial summation to control the intensity of the motor power. During the second phase, 32 individuals were created, each having 8 copies of the controller evolved during the first phase. After 5 generations the population size was halved while the mutation rate of the parameters specifying connection weights was increased in order to obtain fine tuning of a converged population. Although the author reported only one successful controller out of five repetitions of the experiment, in the successful case a fast quadripod gait was evolved in only seven generations.

As we reported in chapter 9, a related approach has been pursued by Kodjabachian and Meyer (1998a, 1998b), but so far it has been tested only on a simulated hexapod robot inspired upon the insect model by Beer and Gallagher described above in section 10.2. Behaviors of increasing complexity have been evolved in an incremental fashion. In the first evolutionary stage, simple locomotion controllers are evolved for the insect model. At the end of this stage, the developmental program corresponding to the best evolved controller is selected to be the locomotion module for more complex, sensory driven controllers. At a later stage, a gradient following module is evolved that receives information from two sensors, each measuring the intensity of an odour signal perceived at the tip of an antenna. By affecting the locomotion module, this added module can generate efficient goal seeking behaviors. Using a similar procedure, the authors showed evolution

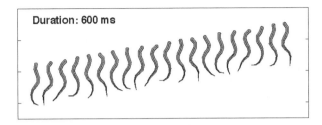

**Figure 10.7**
Swimming sequence of a simulated lamprey produced by an evolved central pattern generator. The horizontal axis represents time, the vertical axis represents space. (Figure courtesy of Auke Jan Ijspeert.)

of obstacle avoidance locomotion and combination of goal seeking and obstacle avoidance.

## 10.4   From swimming to walking

Capitalizing on the observation that locomotion controllers are relatively similar across several vertebrate species, Ijspeert (Ijspeert et al. 1998) has incrementally evolved walking controllers out of previously evolved swimming controller. Although the experiments have been carried out only in simulation, the approach seems sufficiently realistic to be applicable to physical robots. As a matter of fact, Lewis (1996) previously reported in his PhD thesis experiments where he evolved swimming controllers for a simulated lamprey and then incrementally evolved walking controllers for a quadruped robot with a flexible spine. Unfortunately, these results were not described in sufficient detail to be reliably reproduced and sensory input was not taken into consideration.

Considering this previous work, in a first phase Ijspeert has evolved bioinspired swimming controllers for a simulated lamprey. The controller consisted of a *central pattern generator* (CPG) that, provided with suitable parameter values, was capable of producing oscillatory patterns even in the absence of external inputs. These oscillations were used for rythmic muscle contraction in both swimming and locomotion. The control architecture for the simulated lamprey was composed of interconnected segmental oscillators. During swimming each segment oscillated with a small phase lag that generated a wave of neural activity. Each of these oscillators was connected to two muscles on the sides of the body segment causing rythmic bending of the segment. The resulting wave of neural activity generated a complete undulation of the body.

The swimming controllers were evolved in three stages (Ijspeert et al. 1999) using a procedure similar to that of Lewis et al. (1992) described in section 10.3 for the first two stages. In the first stage an individual segmental oscillator was evolved using a fitness

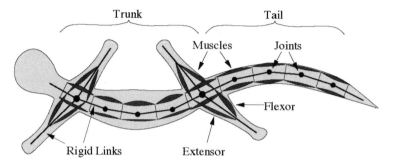

**Figure 10.8**
Mechanical configuration of the evolutionary salamander. The main body, reproduced from the body of the lamprey, is composed of 10 rigid links connected by one degree of freedom joints. Four additional rigid links corresponding to the legs are added. A total of 26 muscles, modeled as a combination of springs and dampers, are connected in parallel to each joint. Muscles are contracted by corresponding motorneurons producing a bending of the joint between two adjacent segments. (Adapted from Ijspeert et al. 1998. Reprinted with permission.)

function that rewarded the production of regular oscillations, increments in oscillation frequency induced by external excitation, and a minimal number of connections. In the second stage, the author evolved the coordination of several copies of previously evolved segmental oscillators. Finally, in the third stage sensory connections from cells sensitive to body stretch were incrementally evolved in order to allow the controller to compensate for varying water currents. The evolved controllers produced swimming patterns similar to those observed for biological animals (figure 10.7). In addition, evolution was repeated by constraining the space of possible controllers to those that preserved the connectivity and neuron sign observed in real lampreys. The evolved connections corresponded very closely to those observed in the real animal, including the sensory feedback from stretch sensitive cells, suggesting that natural evolution might have exploited sensory feedback in order to cross speed barriers due to water currents. Finally, by employing the SGOCE methodology described in section 9.4, it was shown that swimming patterns could be evolved in a single evolutionary stage (Ijspeert and Kodjabachian 1999).

In a second stage, Ijspeert evolved walking controllers for a simulated salamander based on two interconnected oscillatory networks which were copies of the evolved segmental oscillators of the swimming controller (1998). The mechanical model of the salamander (figure 10.8) was derived from the model of the lamprey by adding 4 rigid links corresponding to the limbs and 2 interconnected segmental oscillators for control of these limbs. When put into the water, all segments of the body (including the limbs) were subject to water inertial forces. Instead, when put on land, each segment (including the limbs) was subject to friction forces by assuming that the trunk of the salamander slides on the ground

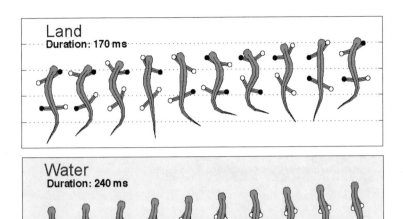

**Figure 10.9**
**Top:** Walking sequence of salamander produced by an oscillating neural architecture incrementally evolved from a previously evolved lamprey controller (see figure 10.7). A filled circle indicate that the limb is on the ground. **Bottom:** The same salamander is capable of swimming when put into the water. Horizontal axis represents time, vertical axis represents space. (Adapted from Ijspeert et al. 1998. Reprinted with permission.)

when it is walking. In addition, the contact of a limb with the ground was considered as an extra mechanical constraint in the movement of the body. The goal was to evolve controllers that can switch between walking and swimming depending on which part of the controller architecture is excited: the walking oscillators or the swimming oscillators. The author manually switched between the two modes during evolution, but one could easily imagine an extra set of touch sensors to detect whether the simulated salamander is in the water or on the ground (Ijspeert, personal communication).

The chromosome consisted of 39 real valued numbers encoding the synaptic weights of the connections from the two walking oscillators to the motoneurons of the limbs, and the weights of the connections from the brain stem. The latter were used to send excitation to the walking architecture. A left/right simmetry was assumed. A simple genetic algorithm (see chapter 2) was employed to evolve a population of 40 individuals. Individuals were evaluated by an objective fitness function that rewarded fast walking on a straight line, a large range of speeds depending on the amount of excitation sent to the oscillator from the brainstem, and usage of all four limbs. The mathematical definition of the fitness function was a product of these three components. Ten evolutionary runs were carried out, one set

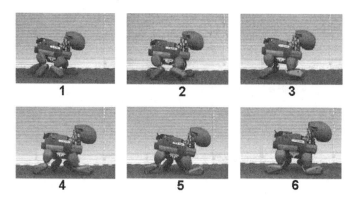

**Figure 10.10**
Sequence of evolved trot gait for quadruped robot (Hornby et al., 1999). (Figure courtesy of Sony Corporation.)

of five being incremental evolution of walking from artificial controllers of the lamprey, the other set being evolution from biologically plausible controllers of the lamprey. After 40 generations, all runs converged to controllers capable of producing a gait with speed proportional to the level of excitation sent from the brainstem (figure 10.9, top). When the swimming circuit was excited and the flexor muscles of the limbs were excited as well (in order to bring them close to the body), the salamander was still capable of swimming, but its speed was approximately 35% lower than that of the lamprey due to extra inertial forces produced by the limbs (figure 10.9, bottom).

## 10.5   Dynamic gait for a quadruped robot

All the experiments described so far aimed at evolving static gait. Recently, a group of researchers at Sony Corporation attempted to evolve locomotion controllers for dynamic gait of their quadruped robot (Hornby et al. 1999). The Sony quadruped is an autonomous robot with the shape of a dog (Fujta and Kitano 1998). The head and the four legs have three degrees of freedom and the tail has an additional degree of freedom. The body is 18 cm long (without head and tail) and the legs are 12 cm tall (measured from the joint of the shoulder). The head is equipped with a micro camera and fast color detection processing, stereo microphones, infrared sensors pointing forward from the nose, and a touch sensor. Each foot is provided with a touch sensor and the body houses a gyroscope and accelerometers.

The authors (Hornby et al. 1999) aimed at evolving two types of dynamic gaits: pace and trot (see inset box above). Both these gaits cannot be easily programmed by hand and

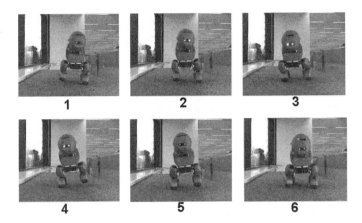

**Figure 10.11**
Sequence of evolved pace gait for quadruped robot (Hornby et al., 1999). The evolved gait is twice as fast as the best hand-designed pace gait. (Figure courtesy of Sony Corporation.)

would require extremely complex computations to be simulated. Therefore the researchers decided to employ artificial evolution on the physical robot. The whole evolutionary process was completely autonomous according to the methodology outlined in chapter 3. The robot was tethered to a workstation through a serial cable providing energy supply. The fitness function was computed using only information available through onboard sensors. After each evaluation the robot was automatically repositioned by simple onboard behaviors without human intervention.

The locomotion controller were preprogrammed modules characterized by 20 real valued parameters. These parameters specify the position and orientation of the body, the swing trajectory and speed, the oscillation of the body location and orientation, and three additional gain parameters to smooth the overall behavior. Artificial evolution was used to find suitable values of these parameters. The authors evolved two types of locomotion modules: a module for pace gait and a module for trot gait (see inset box).

The goal was to evolve controllers capable of moving in a straight line as fast as possible without using sensory information. A steady state genetic algorithm with tournament selection was run on the CPU available on the robot. The chromosome encoded the locomotion parameters as real values. In order to narrow the search space, the parameters could assume a value within a predefined range that corresponded to locomotion behaviors. The initial population was randomly generated testing each individual. If the individual was not capable of standing, it was replaced by a newly generated chromosome until a predefined number of chromosomes was found.

The robot was placed in a rectangular arena with two colored vertical stripes painted on each end. The robot started on one end, centered itself by using visual information about the position of the stripe on the opposite end and measured its distance from the opposite wall using the infrared sensors available on the head. The current chromosome was tested for 7 seconds. At the end the robot searched again for the stripe moving its head until it centered it in its visual field and then measured again the distance from the wall. The fitness function was based on the difference between the final distance and the initial distance, and on the final orientation of the robot with respect to the opposite wall (measured as rotation angle of the head). If the robot fell down or could not find the stripe after 7 seconds of test, the individual was rated with zero fitness. This fitness function encouraged speed and straightness of locomotion. Preprogrammed behaviors were used to rotate the robot at the end of each test and to stand up from the floor after falling.

Starting from a population of 30 individuals, it took about twenty generations to evolve a trot gait (figure 10.10) moving at 6.5 meters per minute and about 10 generations to evolve a pace gait (figure 10.11) at a speed of 10.2 meters per minute. The evolved trot gait was not truly dynamic because the evolved individuals dragged their forward moving legs on the floor and, consequently it was slower than the pace gait. On the other hand, the pace gait was very effective and almost twice as fast as the best hand programmed locomotion controller.

## 10.6  Conclusions

Despite the variety of simulated and physical robots described in this chapter, almost all approaches are remarkably similar in the following four aspects.

- *Staged evolution.* In the first stage the controller for a single leg is evolved in isolation. In the second stage, the evolved controller is replicated for each leg and evolution is used to set the connections among the controllers for coordinated movement. In those experiments where there is not a distinction of evolutionary phases (for example, Beer and Gallagher of section 10.2), the architecture of the controller preserves a structural distinction between single leg control and leg coordination control. This distinction shows up both in the structure of the controller itself (neural module, behavior module) and in the genetic encoding (the space allocated for leg control is clearly separated from that for leg coordination, or coordination is explicitly predefined as in the case of Sony quadruped).

- *Sensor-less walk.* The control system has no access to sensory information and artificial evolution is mainly used to develop a straight navigation without taking into account the external environment. Two exceptions are the experiments by Jakobi and by Kodjabachian and Meyer (section 10.3), but they both have been carried out in simulation. In the case of Sony quadruped, Hornby et al. use vision information from the robot onboard camera only to evaluate the fitness of the individual, but this information is not passed to the evolutionary control system.

• *Coupled oscillators.* When neural networks are used, they often consist of coupled oscillators (with the exception of experiments using cellular encoding strategies). These oscillators can rapidly synchronize and are well suited for generating regular rhythmic patterns required by walk, but one may wonder how well can they integrate external modulation for different patterns of control. For example, in Jakobi's work (section 10.3) sensory informations temporarily shut down synaptic transmission within the oscillator, effectively disrupting oscillatory patterns.

• *Static walk.* With the notable exception of Sony quadruped, all other experiments have concentrated on static walk. This is mainly due to the fact that robots with six or more legs are intrinsically static (see inset box). It should be noticed, however, that in the case of the quadruped the basic behaviors and coordination mechanisms were already largely predefined in the program modules whose parameters were evolved.

These results indicate that artificial evolution can develop robust low level walking patterns for physical robots without using modeling, but much work remains to be done in order to extend the flexibility and control of walk. For example, one further step would be runtime shifting between different walking patterns depending on the robot's speed, terrain, and hardware behavior. All this could still be achieved by monitoring angles and speeds at leg level. The next step would be integration of high level control for online gait modulation, steering, speed adaptation, and alternative gait styles (from walking to hopping, for example) depending on incoming sensory information. Legged robot will require powerful sensory processing abilities because the oscillation of the robot chassis and of onboard sensors will cause rapid variations in sensor readings.

Considering the current complexity and fragility of walking hardware, simulations can be a useful aid if the experiment is planned in an incremental fashion with partial test on the physical robot (see chapters 3 and 4) and, possibly, transfers from mechanically simple robots to more complex ones (see section 10.3 above and chapter 4). Current mechanical solutions use the same hardware conception of wheeled robots (step motors, gears, etc.) and thus are not well suited to capture the flexibility, durability, and power displayed by biological muscles and required by walk. Improvement of this technology and development of alternative hardware solution (for example artificial muscles) will provide increased flexibility, dynamics, and ultimately benefit from a model free evolutionary approach.

# 11 Evolvable hardware

## 11.1 Introduction

*Evolvable hardware* (usually abbreviated as EHW) are systems that can change their hardware structure by means of artificial evolution. We can identify two types of hardware evolution: evolution of electronic circuits and evolution of robot bodies. These will be the topics of the next two sections of this chapter.

There are several good reasons for evolving the hardware of a robot. In this book we have shown several times that an evolving behavioral system is intimately related to its environment. The physics of the interaction between the robot and the environment, often difficult to anticipate and to include in software models, play a major role in the evolutionary development of the observed behavior and of the control mechanisms that support it. Nevertheless, in all cases described so far, evolutionary robots could only adapt the software running within their processors, but could not change the physical properties of their circuits, sensors, motors, or even the shape of their body. This situation puts strong limits to the ability of an evolving robot to adapt and exploit the physics of the interaction with an environment. The adaptive power of artificial evolution is limited by the constraints of traditional circuit design, programming languages, choice of sensory-motor system, and design of body shape. It may thus happen that a robot must evolve complex control systems because its hardware configuration (processor, sensors, or shape) cannot exploit simpler solutions. Eventually, the choice of the hardware configuration constrains the evolvability of a robot and ultimately affects the type of behaviors and control mechanisms that it will display.

One may argue that "good engineering practice" can help to choose the best circuits, processors, and actuators for a given problem. Although even this dogma is being challenged by evolvable hardware, a major problem is that the structure of conventional hardware is not adaptive. This has two major consequences for an evolving system. The first consequence is that a given hardware configuration may fit well a family of control systems, but not another. For example, a robot with many degrees of freedom, several types of sensors, and a complex shape may be suitable for a fully formed complex control system, but may be extremely hard to manage for an initial population of random controllers. Co-evolution of hardware structure and control system thus is an important issue for evolvability. The second consequence is that the system is less robust to environmental variations and becomes quickly obsolete over time. We believe that an important aspect of artificial evolution is open ended adaptation to an ever changing environment, not only automatic discovery of a solution for a predefined problem. In this perspective, all components of

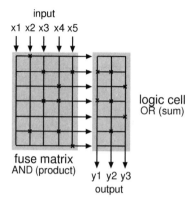

input
x1 x2 x3 x4 x5

logic cell
OR (sum)

fuse matrix
AND (product)

y1 y2 y3
output

**Figure 11.1**
Schematic structure of a programmable logic device. Fused interconnections (crossed nodes) enable input
signals and combine them with the logic operator AND (equivalent to a product). The logic cell provides the
output signal by combining the products with OR functions (equivalent to a sum) or other programmable logic
functions. A configuration bit string describes the set of all gates in the circuit.

an evolving system—not only its software—should be capable to continuously mutate,
co-evolve, and adapt to characteristics of the environment where they happen to be.

## 11.2   Electronic circuits

Pioneering work in evolvable hardware has been done by Tetsuya Higuchi on evolution
of electronic circuits (Higuchi et al. 1993). Instead of evolving a software program that is
later compiled into a set of instructions for configuring the circuit hardware, the main idea
is that of evolving directly the set of instructions. Bypassing the programming language
allows to achieve functionalities that require less hardware resources, run faster, and
can exploit physical characteristics of the circuit that would normally be ignored by
traditional compilers. It also offers a schema for online autonomous adaptation of the
circuit configuration (and thus of its functionality) without passing through a compilation
phase.

### Programmable circuits

Evolution of electronic circuits is based on recent availability of reconfigurable devices (for
a clear and short introduction to reconfigurable devices, see Sanchez 1995). *Programmable
logic devices* (PLD) are simple forms of reconfigurable circuits.

A PLD can be visualized as a matrix of fuses and a logic cell (figure 11.1). A fuse
acts like a gate. An input signal can flow through only if the fuse is burnt. If multiple

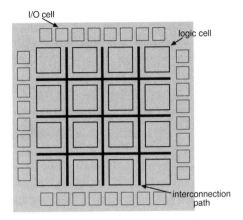

**Figure 11.2**
Schematic representation of a field programmable gate array. The circuit is composed of several interconnected cells. Each logic cells can be programmed to execute a specific logic function. The configuration bit string, that in some models resides in a piece of static RAM, defines the functions of the cells and their interconnection pattern. FPGA can be reconfigured in few milliseconds and implement complex multilevel logic functions.

fuses are burnt on a row, the corresponding input signals are combined by an AND function (product). Each row can implement a different combination of inputs. A logic cell combines the signals coming from the rows, for example with OR functions (summation). In some cases the logic cell is fixed, in other cases it is a set of programmable gates. Such a PLD circuit is capable of implementing any logical combination function as a sum of products. The configuration of the circuit is a string of bits that specifies the set of fused gates. Evolvable hardware uses modern PLD where the configuration of gates is reversible. Whereas in traditional engineering practice the configuration bit string is created by a compiler from a high level program, in evolvable hardware this string represents the genotype of the individual. This string can be very long because it specifies the states of all gates in the circuit and in some cases it can require long evolutionary time. In order to overcome this problem, Higuchi et al. (1993) used a variable length genotype including only the bits of "fused" gates. In more recent work this method has been applied to evolution of field programmable gate arrays for pattern recognition and robotic welding problems (Higuchi et al. 1995).

A *field programmable gate array* (FPGA) is a reconfigurable circuit composed of several interconnected logic cells (figure 11.2). The configuration bit string defines the logic function of each cell and also the pattern of connectivity among cells. This functionality makes FPGA more powerful than traditional PLD in that it allows implementation of multilevel logic functions.

The flexibility of FPGA has made them the preferred tool for evolutionary electronics over the last few years. For example, De Garis (1995) has been working at a machine built out of several FPGA capable of growing large modular neural networks. These modules, their architectures and patterns of connectivity are expected to grow in real time according to the instructions specified in the genotype, but it remains to be seen how such a network will be used and what for.

A different approach has been taken by Adrian Thompson who argues that evolvable hardware circuits need not be constrained by the logic abstractions of digital design. Thompson considers physical electronic circuits as continuous time dynamical systems that:

*"[...] can display a broad range of dynamical behavior, of which discrete-time systems, digital systems and even computational systems are but subsets. These subsets are much more amenable to design techniques than dynamical electronic systems in general, because the restrictions to the dynamics that each subset brings support design abstractions, as described above. Intrinsic [online] EHW does not require abstract models, so there is no need to constrain artificially the dynamics of the reconfigurable hardware being used."*

(Thompson, Harvey, and Husbands 1995, p. 150).

As an example, he mentions that engineers consider transistors as on/off devices and are not concerned with the analogue behavior given by transient states during switching. In order to maintain consistency between abstract digital design and hardware implementation, various parts of the circuit are constrained to wait until all transient have disappeared, usually by means of a global clock that synchronizes signal transmission. By lifting this temporal constraint and other constraints related to the spatial configuration of the circuit, Thompson could evolve extremely compact circuits with rich dynamics and complex time dependent behaviors (Thompson et al. 1995). It was later shown that some of these circuits exploited physical properties of the environment to perform their computation, such as magnetic fields generated by neighboring cells and environmental temperature (Thompson 1997).

Yet another approach to evolvable hardware is the "Embryonic Project" by Mange et al. (1995) whose goal is the development of very large scale integrated circuits capable of self-repair and self-reproduction. An embryonic system is a multicellular organization where each cell contains the full genome of the organism, but performs only its own unique function. The genome is composed of several genes, each gene corresponding to a function and a position. Since a cell of an embryonic system occupies a position in space, it implements the function described by the gene at the corresponding position. An embryonic system develops from a mother cell that occupies position 1 through a process of successive replications. Daughter cells assume the function corresponding to their own position coordinates. Since each cell contains the whole genome and is implemented as an FPGA based module capable of implementing any function in the genome, an embryonic is capable of self-repair. Provided that the system contains a number of spare cells, whenever a cell dies, a neighboring cell will assume its function and all other cells will be shifted by one position and reconfigured accordingly.

**Evolutionary circuits in robotics**

The first example of an evolved hardware circuit for robot control has been described by Thompson (1995). According to the dynamical approach advocated above, Thompson evolved the configuration of a standard electronic architecture without the dynamical limitations imposed by digital design. Since at the time of the experiment, existing FPGAs did not yet allow *any* type of reconfiguration, it was necessary to implement it with standard electronics. When the appropriate new family of FPGA (Xilinx XC6200) became available, Thompson replicated the evolutionary experiment online with a Khepera robot equipped with an evolvable hardware module (Thompson 1997b). The original experiment consisted of evolving a *dynamic state machine* (analogous to a reconfigurable circuit with programmable temporal dynamics) that could perform a wall avoidance behavior. The robot was equipped with two lateral sonars and two lateral wheels. The sonars fired simultaneously every 200 ms and set their state from 0 to 1; as soon as they detected the echo, they set their state back to 0. In conventional digital design, the length of time a sonar remains in state 1 would be transformed into a measure of the distance of an object (time flight of sound); this information would then be passed on to a controller whose output would set the speeds of the wheels. Thompson instead fed directly the sonar pulses into the dynamic state machine whose output controlled directly the speeds of the wheels. The configuration bit string included a look up table (32 bits) used to describe the logic function of 4 signals (2 from the sonars and 2 recurrent signals), the period of the clock from 2Hz to several kHz (16 bits), and whether each signal was clocked or unclocked. The robot was evolved in a rectangular arena.[1]

The circuit was evolved in real time and controlled the wheels of the robot. However, the robot was suspended in the air. A real time simulation computed the displacement of the robot from the wheel rotation and the pulses of the sonars (with addition of noise) that were fed into the circuit. However, the evolving circuit could not be simulated because the effects of asynchronous evolved signals depended on the characteristics of the hardware. The evolved controllers were capable of moving away from walls and maintain the robot close to the center of the arena (figure 11.3). Evolved circuits, that could be described by a few bits of RAM, used internal asynchronous dynamics to transform raw sonar pulses into appropriate motor actions. The dynamics of these compact circuits were coupled with the waveforms of the sonars and the characteristics of the robot environment interaction.

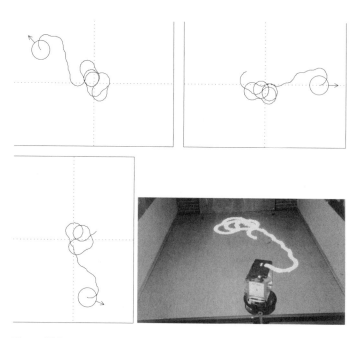

**Figure 11.3**
Evolved wall-avoidance behavior in simulation and on the real robot. The evolved circuit employs genetically determined clocks and asynchronous dynamics to transform raw sonar pulses into appropriate motor commands. (Reprinted with permission from Thompson 1995.)

Similar results were obtained later with an FPGA module mounted on a Khepera robot (Thompson 1997b).

Keymeulen et al. (1996, 1998) evolved an FPGA controller for a vision based robot expected to develop a tracking behavior while avoiding obstacles on its way (figure 11.4). The robot was equipped with two mobile cameras. The two cameras, each pointing on one side of the robot, were equipped with a color discrimination mechanism capable of detecting a yellow ball within a 360° visual field. The output of the cameras was reduced to 2 bits, i.e. in which of the four visual sectors (90° each) the ball was positioned. 10 infrared sensors around the body of the robot returned the presence of an object within a distance of 30 cm and their output was mapped into 6 bits. The motor output consisted of 8 possible actions coded into 3 bits: 2 translations, 2 rotations, and 4 combinations of translations and rotations. The evolvable hardware circuit was composed of two transputers and two FPGA. One transputer preprocessed infrared and vision inputs, while the other transputer controlled the two FPGAs. One FPGA was used to execute the robot behavior while the other was used to simulate the evolutionary process, as it will be explained below. The

**Figure 11.4**
A vision-based robot is evolved to approach a colored ball and avoid obstacles on its way. The evolvable
hardware circuit consists of two FPGA, one used to implement the controller of the robot and the other to evolve
a population of simulated controllers in a model of the environment. (Reprinted with permission from
Keymeulen et al. 1998.)

architecture of the evolvable control circuit was similar to that depicted in figure 11.1. The
8 input signals were fed into a fuse matrix whose rows ended into three OR gates providing
the motor outputs. In order to represent all possible combinations of inputs, the fuse matrix
should have $2^8 = 256$ rows. In order to reduce the length of the genetic string, the authors
reduced the matrix size to 50 rows assuming that 5 input states are mapped to the same
output. A population of such controllers was evolved in an approximate simulation of the
environment running on one FPGA. Every 10 generations, the best circuit was transferred
to the other FPGA and used to control the robot in the real world. While the robot was
moving, the simulation FPGA gathered data to improve the model and continue evolution.
This *model based on line evolution*, as defined by the authors, could evolve in 5 minutes
circuits capable of satisfactory tracking behaviors with obstacle avoidance.

Nordin and Banzhaf (1996) evolved machine code for the 68331 Motorola controller
of the Khepera robot. This is not a case of evolvable hardware strictly speaking because the
physical structure of the circuit is not changed. However the methodology is similar in that
the genotype encodes the binary sequence read by the machine to map input states into
output states. The authors employed a variant of genetic programming and developed a
special crossover operator to manipulate variable length linear chromosomes and make
meaningful combinations of instructions. An obstacle avoidance behavior was evolved
using a combination of model based evolution and real world testing, similarly to the
method described in the previous paragraph.

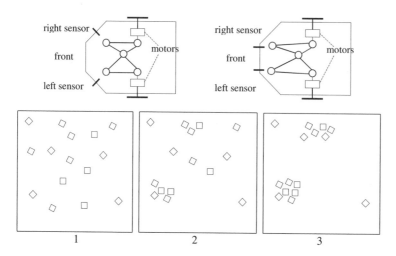

**Figure 11.5**
**Top, left:** The robot with two wheels and two infrared sensors on its frontal side oriented 45 degrees left and right. **Top, right:** The same robot with the two sensors oriented toward the front. **Bottom:** The environment consisting of an arena with randomly distributed cubes in three successive phases. The picture on the left displays the initial state of the environment in which the cubes are randomly distributed. The other two pictures display how the cubes tend to cluster as a result of the behavior of the robot shown in the top-left of the figure. Clustering cannot be achieved by the robot shown in the top-right which has the same control system but sensors oriented in a different way. (Adapted from Scheier et al. 1998.)

## 11.3  Body structures

The control system of a robot is only one of the aspects that determine the resulting behavior. More precisely, behavior results from the interaction between the control system, the robot body, and the external environment. Just like a control system, the body of a robot should also be evolved to best support the behavior of the individual. This suggests that both the control system and the body of a robot should be coadapted. Lund et al. (1997a) write: "A human brain would not be of much help to a parrot, and an elephant brain would not be appropriate to control a human body."

The characteristics of the body strongly affect the complexity of the control system required to solve a certain task in a given environment (Chiel and Beer 1997). This point can be illustrated with a simple example described by Maris and Boekhorst (1996; also reported in Scheier et al. 1998). Consider the case of the robot illustrated in figure 11.5 (top-left) that is capable of clustering the cubes randomly distributed in the arena shown on the bottom of the figure.

The robot has a rectangular shape and two infrared sensors pointing $45^o$ left and $45^o$ right on its frontal side (figure 11.5, top-left) and is controlled by a very simple neural network that turns right when the left sensor is activated, turns left when the right sensor is activated, and goes forward otherwise. This robot just performs obstacle avoidance. On the other hand, when the robot happens to encounter a cube head on, it pushes the cube until it encounters another cube on its own front-left or front-right side. The robot is "unaware" of pushing cubes because it has no sensors on its own front side. However, once the robot starts to form a cluster with two cubes (by pushing one cube close to another), the probability that additional cubes will be deposited close to the existing cluster will progressively increase with the size of the cluster itself.[2] The final result is that the robot will progressively produce clusters of cubes as shown in the bottom-center and bottom-right of figure 11.5. Clearly in this example the shape of the body, the position of the sensors, and the environment play a key role in the resulting behavior. If the position of the two sensors is slightly changed as shown in the top-right of figure 11.5, the simple obstacle avoidance program described above will be no longer capable to produce clusters. In other words, by changing the layout of the sensors, not only the resulting behavior changes, but also the task itself becomes significantly harder.

A biological example of how the structure of the body can significantly simplify the task faced by the control system is the case of the cricket described by Webb (1995) and by Lund et al. (1997b). Female crickets can discriminate the song of a male belonging to their own species from sounds emitted by other species and can approach the male on the basis of its song even if other males of the same species are producing almost identical songs. This discrimination task is rather hard given that there is little difference in the strength and amplitude of the sound received through the ears for songs of different species. The only difference is the arrival time of sound at the two ears. However, since the auditory neurons cannot detect this difference which is in the order of microseconds, the cricket has evolved a solution that relies on its own body structure. The cricket has four auditory openings: two ears located on each upper foreleg where tympani are located and two additional openings called spiracles on each side of the frontal section of the body. These four openings are connected by tracheal tubes. As a consequence each tympanum receives both the signal directly through the ear and a delayed version of the same signal through the tracheal tube from the other ear. These two stimuli reinforce or cancel one another according to their relative phase. Given that the length of the tracheal tubes (which affects the amount of the delay) is tuned to the wavelength of the desired calling song, ears are stimulated only by the sound corresponding to the right calling song. Moreover, given that the amplitude of the sound is proportional to the traveled distance, the amplitude of the stimulation is larger in the tympanum closer to the sound. This difference provides an indication of the direction of the selected sound. For more details see Webb (1995) and Lund et al. (1997b).

Lund et al. (1997b) showed that a Khepera robot equipped with an auditory circuit based on these principles is capable of discriminating and approaching a singing male

**Figure 11.6**
The Khepera robot with the auditory sensory system developed at the Department of Artificial Intelligence of the University of Edinburgh. The two microphones are position on the top pointing forward. (Reprinted with permission from Lund et al. 1997b.)

of a certain species (see figure 11.6). This circuit collects sounds through two or four microphones and generates delayed copies of the sounds which are then added together to construct the response at the level of the tympani. If the response is larger than a given threshold in one of the two tympani, the robot turns in the corresponding direction, otherwise it produces a forward movement. The robot was able to discriminate the right song among other songs corresponding to different species and approach the sound source effectively. The songs used in the experiments were recorded from real crickets.

These two examples show that the control system and body structure (type, number, and position of sensors and actuators; size and shape of the body) fit well each other in ways that take into account the characteristics of the environment and of the task faced by the robot. In an evolutionary perspective, this implies that control systems and body structures should be co-evolved (Cliff et al. 1993). The reason is that, aside from very simple cases such as the two examples described above, it is extremely difficult to handcraft the body structure of a robot in a way that matches the environment, the control system, and the expected behavior. In chapter 4 we have shown a case where the control system evolutionarily adapts to a different body structure (from Khepera to Koala), but it would be desirable to co-evolve both the control system and the structure of the robot body. Some preliminary attempts have been made in this direction. In the next sections we will review some experiments where the number and type of sensors were allowed to vary and where

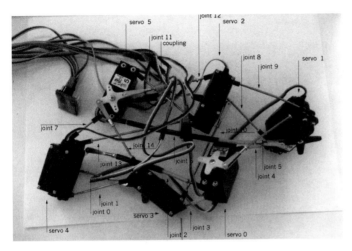

**Figure 11.7**
Random-Morphology robot inspired upon Sims' creatures. The robot is composed of six servo motors arbitrarily coupled by thin metal joints. Each servo motor has two degrees of freedom and the connecting joints can be reconfigured (manually) at run time. (Photo by A. Burgel. Reprinted with permission from Dittrich et al. 1998.)

the positions of sensors and motors and the size of the robot were co-evolved together with the control system.

Jordan Pollack and his group have exlored the possibility of evolving the structure of physical robots (Pollack et al. 1999). In preliminary work they used an offline method for evolving structures of bridges and moving cranes using simulated Lego bricks and later built the evolved structures out of real bricks (Funes and Pollack 1998). More recently, they evolved the control system (sigmoid neurons) and the body description of robots composed of linear actuators, bars, and joints (Lipson and Pollack 2000). The entire configuration was evolved for a given task and some individuals were automatically built out of thermoplastic material with a 3D printer. The printer takes as input the genetic description of the robot morphology and its temperature-controlled head lays down thermoplastic material layer by layer with holes for motors and joints, which are snapped in later on. The authors demonstrated this technology in the case of robots evolved for straight navigation where the fitness function was the distance covered by the robot. These robots displayed various forms of locomotion, including crawling and pedalism, both in simulation and in reality.

## Co-evolution of robot bodies and control systems

There have been attempts to co-evolve robot bodies along with the control systems of artificial organisms. Although co-evolution of robot bodies and control systems would greatly benefit from evolvable materials, the methodology currently used consists of using simu-

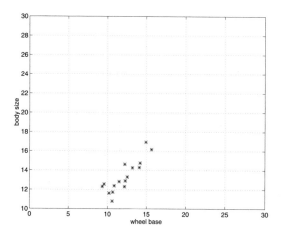

**Figure 11.8**
Body size plotted against wheel base for the best evolved robots of 16 replications of the experiment. (Figure courtesy of Henrik Hautop Lund.)

lations and, in some cases, build the robot according to the resulting evolved morphology.

One of the earliest examples is the experiment on visually guided robots described in section 4.3, where the chromosomes are organized into two parts, one specifying the network architecture and the other the morphology of the visual system. The authors (Cliff et al. 1993) used virtual receptors obtained by averaging the values of 25 pixels uniformly scattered around target points whose locations were genetically evolved. In this way, different individuals could rely on different visual receptors without the need to reconfigure the hardware of the vision system.

Sims (1994) used a uniform graph representation for both the body and the brain of simulated three dimensional creatures whose body was formed of three dimensional segments. The morphologies of the body and of the controller were encoded in the genotype using a graph made up of nodes that included information about the dimension of the segment, the joints connecting it to the parent node, the connection to other nodes, and the local set of neurons. Sensors were located in the segments of the body. Joint angle sensors measured the relative position between two segments, contact sensors could detect a physical contact of a segment with another object, photosensors could detect ambient light. The motor effectors were also located in the segments of the body and could control the motion of joints with two degrees of freedom. Sims was able to evolve a great variety of creature morphologies and behaviors. The goal of these experiments, however, was not to build real robots. The segments of the creatures overlapped at the joints and sensors and motors were considered to have infinite precision.

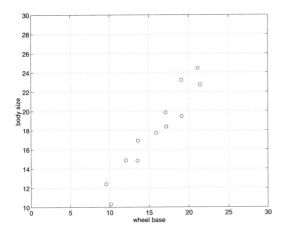

**Figure 11.9**
Body size plotted against wheel base for the best evolved robots of 12 replications of an experiment where sensor detection range is twice as much that of the experiments shown in figure 11.8. (Figure courtesy of Henrik Hautop Lund.)

Inspired by the work of Karl Sims, Dittrich et al. (1998) have built a random morphology robot (figure 11.7) whose geometry can be manually reconfigured at run time. The robot is composed of a set of servomotors arbitrarily connected by thin metal bars. Each motor has two degrees of freedom and is attached with wires to a microcontroller via a serial line. The authors used genetic programming to evolve a controller capable of advancing this robot. The fitness function was the distance covered by the robot within a given amount of time. The distance was measured by a mouse attached to the robot that returned its displacement on the plane.

In their experiments on co-evolved simulated predator and prey, Cliff and Miller (1996) used simulated photoreceptors whose position within the perimeter of the body, orientation, and angle of acceptance were genetically specified. Cliff and Miller (1996) reported that "... pursuers usually evolved eyes on the front of their bodies (like cheetahs), while evaders usually evolved eyes pointing sideways or even backwards (like gazelles)." (p. 506).

Lund et al. (1997a) co-evolved in simulation the control system and some characteristics of the body of wheeled robots that were selected for their ability to navigate while avoiding obstacles. The genotype consisted of a tree structure encoding the neural controller (including the number of sensors and their position) and of a list of real numbers encoding aspects of the robot body, such as the diameter of the body, the width of the wheel base, the wheels radius, and a motor time constant.[3]

The authors analyzed the distribution in morphological space of evolved robots. Figure

11.8 shows the body size plotted against wheel base of the best evolved robots in a number of replications of the experiment. These results showed two main aspects: a) relatively small body sizes turned out to be best suited for obstacle avoidance; and b) there was an almost linear relationship between body size and wheel base (the correlation coefficient was 0.8694).

When the experiments were repeated with a double detection range for the sensors, the relationship between body size and wheel base of evolved individuals remained constant, but their absolute dimension increased significantly (see figure 11.9). This could be explained by considering that robots were capable of detecting obstacles from further away and therefore had more time to avoid them. Consequently, they could afford larger body sizes. Lund et al. (1997a) inferred that "the upper limit of the size and base of a robot is constrained by the sensor range."

## 11.4   Conclusions

Evolvable hardware is a new approach to electronic and mechanical engineering, but the technology necessary for online implementation of all the ideas and experiments described in this chapter is not yet available. This is the reason why several researchers still use an offline method where the system is first evolved in simulation and later implemented in hardware according to the evolved instructions.

The most advanced area of EHW is evolutionary electronics, thanks to the availability of new reconfigurable circuits that allow arbitrary settings of their configuration parameters. Getting closer to the substrate where the computation is performed requires a more stringent consideration of its physical characteristics. An important question in circuit evolution is whether the biological metaphors used in software approaches are applicable or can take advantage from direct hardware implementation. For example, Thompson et al. (1995) argue that it may be unwise to limit circuit evolution to implementation of neural architectures because biological neurons have slower dynamics than electronics do, and exploit a rich three dimensional connectivity whereas VLSI is restricted mainly to two dimensional wiring. We share their view that:

*"For engineering purposes, 'VLSI-plausible' architectures are required, not 'biologically-plausible' ones. [...] The aim is to arrive at an implementation of artificial evolution that is inspired by nature, but suited to the facilities available"*

(Thompson et al. 1995, p. 155).

The situation is technologically less advanced in the realization of evolvable body structures. Despite the initial interesting attempts described in the previous section to co-evolve control and morphology of robots, it is not yet clear to what extent the whole process can be wholly automated. Major advancement in evolvable body hardware is likely to come from material science with the synthesis of new materials capable of predefined growth according to evolved specifications. This may imply abandoning traditional engineering tools like servo motors, printed boards, gears, etc.

# Conclusions

In this book we have provided an evolutionary perspective to the autonomous self-organization of machines viewed as artificial organisms with sensors and actuators. An organism is an embodied system that lives and acts in an environment. In artificial intelligence this obvious statement is often overlooked even by biologically inspired approaches, such as connectionism, where cognition is considered as a structure that develops in an abstract environment. In that context, it is implicitly assumed that we will know the intrinsic nature of cognition when the laws that govern the dynamics of our brain have been discovered. However, an organism is not only a collections of neurons; it is also immersed in a physical environment and, using the sensory-motor apparatus, actively extracts information from the environment. Therefore, if we want to understand intelligent life and cognition we must investigate also how organisms autonomously interact with their environment, that is how they behave.

Underestimation of behavior can be partially explained by considering that behavior is an emergent result of the interaction between the organisms and the environment that is hard to describe analytically by trying to identify key components that have rather independent functions. Emergent functionality of behaviors results from the interaction of a large number of primitive components among themselves and with the external environment. A promising method is to use a synthetic approach such as evolutionary robotics where sensory-motor systems can develop their own skills in close interaction with the environment and where human intervention and design is reduced as much as possible. Throughout this book we have emphasized artificial evolution of robots as a way to study and develop intelligent systems that self-organize at several levels while they autonomously interact with the environment.

Self-organization does not mean that an evolutionary system is entirely free of human design. On the contrary, humans often play a role in one or more of the following aspects: (a) the choice of a fitness function; (b) choice of a fixed genotype-to-phenotype mapping; (c) evolutionary conditions, such as the number of individuals in the population and genetic operators, the testing conditions, etc.; (d) the choice of a control architecture; (e) the choice of electronics, hardware components, and morphology of the robot. Although in the book we have shown that all these aspects could be evolved, often one makes a set of minimal assumptions and concentrates on other aspects of the evolving system. For example, in most of the experiments described in the book, we have not been concerned with the mechanics of the genetic algorithm and thus did not attempt to vary the population size, the genetic operators, etc. Nonetheless and even when other aspects, such as body morphology and neuron model, were kept unchanged, we showed that a large variety of different mechanisms and abilities emerged by simply varying the fitness function. These include (a) obstacle avoidance (section 4.2); (b) exploration (section 7.6); (c) discrimination among different objects (sections 5.3 and 5.4); (d) oriented navigation (section 5.5); (e) escaping predators (chapter 8), to mention only a few.

The point is that artificial evolution can be employed so to leave more room to self-organization than other approaches, even when several aspects of the evolving individuals have been fixed (see also the discussion of fitness space in section 3.4). Evolutionary robotics also fits nicely and provides a further adaptive dimension to other approaches for the study of behavioral systems.

For example, one interesting approach described by Pfeifer and Scheier (1998, 1999) is based on the identification of a set of design principles which may guide a researcher in designing behavioral systems and, by doing so, in understanding natural systems. The authors point out that models and experimental tools often rely on the implicit intuition of the designer and on her view of intelligence. The purpose of design principles is to make this knowledge explicit and to take inspiration from systematic studies of biological systems instead of from implicit assumptions. Notice that in Pfeifer and Scheier's view, design principles are heuristics for the construction and study of autonomous agents and not detailed models. This level of description leaves room for emergence. As the authors point out, "Emergence is required because behavior cannot be reduced to an internal mechanism only.... For example, if we want to achieve wall following behavior we should not design a module for wall following within the agent, but we should define basic processes which together, in the interaction with the environment, lead to this desired behavior. This is called design for emergence" (Pfeifer and Scheier 1998, p. 15). Evolutionary robotics fully shares this view of intelligence. Indeed design principles may provide a theoretical background for evolutionary robotics and help the researcher to understand the results of the evolutionary process. Understanding how evolved agents solve their task is difficult because: (1) behavior is an emergent property of the interaction between the agent and the environment; and (2) the way in which evolved agents solve their tasks is usually very different from the way in which we would design systems for solving the same tasks. Design principles, by providing new ways of describing behavioral systems, may solve the second of these two problems in that they can serve hypotheses which might help us to understand evolved systems. On the other hand, our understanding of emergent behavior in evolving agents (natural and artificial) may help us to discover new design principles and/or discard existing ones. Finally, design principles may help us to design the characteristics which are not subjected to the evolutionary process (e.g., an hypothetical design principle may be that although both the connection weights and the architecture of evolving agents should be subjected to an evolutionary process, the genotype-to- phenotype mapping should ensure that the latter changes less frequently than the former).

Another approach to the study of behavioral systems consists of collecting neurophysiological and ethological data on natural organisms and building biologically-plausible embodied systems. When this is possible at a sufficient level of detail, it can have very strong explanatory power for understanding mechanisms of behavior in biological systems. A clear example is the work of Franceschini where he carefully studied the vision system of the fly and came up with a model so detailed that not only it was possible to implement it in a mobile robot capable of navigating in an environment by visuo-motor coordination, but also provided further insights on the role of specific neurophysiological circuits through the observation of the robot behavior (Franceschini 1997). In this context, evolutionary robotics can play at least two roles. On the one hand, it can use those models and mechanisms as building blocks to evolve further abilities. On the other hand, it can add an evolutionary dimension that may provide hypotheses of how and why those circuits came into existence. This brings us to the next question.

To what extent does evolutionary robotics help us to understand biological systems? The processes and models employed in evolutionary robotics are extremely simplified with respect to the biological processes they are supposed to capture. Furthermore, since artificially evolved systems are the result of an adaptation to their own environment, they may share very few characteristics with natural systems evolved in natural environments. Therefore, we think that evolutionary robotics may be useful to understand general principles of natural evolution and adaptive behavior or to test theoretical hypothesis (if all relevant aspects of the phenomena are included in the experiment). However, when we move from general issues (e.g., the role of co-evolution between competing species in the emergence of complex behavior, or the effects of the interaction between learning and evolution) to more specific issues (e.g., how rats navigate in a certain environment), it becomes more and more questionable whether the results obtained are of any relevance for explaining the object of study. In the latter case (for example, in the study of an individual species) the solutions found by artificial evolution can be used as counter examples. In modeling a given form of behavior biologists or ethologists often make implicit assumptions. For example, they may assume that an observed behavior performed by an organism necessarily implies a certain type of strategy. By evolving an artificial organism—a robot—for the ability to perform the same behavior one may show that other solutions can exist (for example, see section 5.6). Although this is not a proof that the strategy selected through artificial evolution is that actually adopted by the natural organism, it is useful to discover that other hypotheses are viable and that previous assumptions may be questionable.

A related question is whether evolutionary robotics should resort to, or be constrained by, biologically plausible mechanisms. We think that this should not always be the case for at least the following three reasons: (1) biological mechanisms are not necessarily optimal for a given task and/or do not always represent the only way of achieving a given functionality (think, for example, of flight by birds and airplanes); (2) available or convenient hardware may not always match or exploit the characteristics of biological mechanisms (see, for example, the discussion on evolvable electronics in section 11.4); (3)

there is no reason why one should restrict the range of possibilities offered by current and future technologies for developing autonomous self-organizing machines.

Our philosophy throughout this book and our daily work has been to be guided by bio-inspired principles and mechanisms to the extent to which they provide some advantage with respect to other technologies or trigger interesting scientific questions where artificial evolution could provide some insight. In this book, we have attempted to show that, whatever one's perspective is, evolutionary robotics represents a powerful methodology to generate autonomous machines that, although not always biologically plausible, display the biology, technology, and intelligence allowing them to self-organize and survive in the environment.

# Notes

## Chapter One

1   Unsupervised learning algorithms, such as hebbian learning or Kohonen self-organized maps, do not need any supervision at all. However, although these algorithms can be used to train subparts of the control systems, they seem unable to produce mapping between sensory inputs into motor states by themselves unless the architecture is constrained in such a way that the system converges toward certain solutions (Verschure et al. 1992). We will discuss an example in which they can be successfully used to learn goal-directed behavior in conjunction with evolution in section 7.5

2   This does not imply that connectionism is the only possible way for studying behavior and cognition within a uniform conceptual framework.

3   This does not imply that evolutionary robotics is the only possible methodology for studying adaptive behavior. Pfeifer and Scheier (1997), for example, proposed a list of design principles which should help researchers both to design artificial agents and to understand natural organisms. Another possibility, of course, is to use evidence from neurophysiology when it is available at a sufficient level of detail (see, for example, Franceschini 1997). We will return to this issue at the end of this chapter.

## Chapter Two

1   Genetic drift refers to the fact that genetic traits can reach fixation in a population even if they do not provide any adaptive advantage (Kimura 1983).

2   For sake of simplicity, let us assume that each location on a chromosome corresponds to a different genetic trait.

3   In this book we shall use both conventions making sure that it is clear what we refer to.

4   Consider a network with three neurons: 1 input, 1 hidden, and 1 output. If both the hidden unit and the output unit use a linear output function, the output of a network is a linear transformation of a linear transformation of the input, which is equivalent to a single linear transformation with a weight equal to the product of the two weights in the multilayer network. In other words, multilayer networks with linear output functions can always be reduced to a network without hidden units and therefore can learn only linearly separable mappings.

5   We can consider the learning process as a parameter estimation problem. The weights are the parameters that must be estimated and the training patterns are the sample data. It

is known in statistics that such a problem is ill-defined if the size of the sample is smaller or equal to the number of the parameters to estimate. In other words, a rule of thumb is that the number of training pairs should be larger than the number of weights in the network.

6   CRBP does not tell the network what actions should be encouraged when a negative feedback is reiceved.

7   However, GP is not bound to Lisp. Several authors use C or C++.

## Chapter Three

1   Khepera and Koala were designed and built at the Laboratory of Microprocessors and Interfaces, Swiss Federal Institute of Technology in Lausanne (Mondada et al. 1993). They are currently distributed and supported by K-Team S.A. (www.k-team.com).

2   This section is based on technical data from the Khepera user manual and on personal communications by Francesco Mondada.

3   This belongs to the same family of processors once used on the second generation of Macintosh computers. It combines floating point operation with low power consumption.

4   For example, transmission of the eight values from the infrared sensors can take less than 3 ms.

5   This is only a partial indication. Several other factors can affect the autonomy of an evolving system, such as constraints in the control architecture, limitations in the actions that it can perform, the choice of mapping from genotype-to-phenotype, the constraints imposed by hardware, etc.

## Chapter Four

1   By manipulating the combination of sensory motor wirings, Braitenberg showed that one can create different types of vehicles displaying increasing behavioral complexity. He even suggested the possibility of evolving vehicles. The prewired solution mentioned here is inspired upon vehicle type 3c described in his book (1984).

2   Synaptic connections (16 for sensors, 4 recurrent, and 2 for bias unit) were coded as floating point numbers on the chromosome. The network architecture was maintained fixed. Each individual was left free to move for 80 sensory motor loops (sensor reading, network activation, and wheel speed setting) while its performance $\Phi$ was automatically computed and accumulated. Each sensory motor loop lasted 300 ms while the wheel speed

was kept constant. After testing an individual, a pair of random speeds was applied to the wheels of the robot for 5 seconds in order to put it to a new position. A population of 80 individuals was evolved using a genetic algorithm with fitness scaling and roulette wheel selection, biased mutations with probability 0.2 for each location, and one-point crossover with probability 0.1. The weight values of the initial population were randomly initialized in the range $[-0.5, 0.5]$. The values added to weights selected for mutation were randomly extracted in the range $[-0.5, 0.5]$. The same experiment was later repeated using binary encoding of the weights with 4 bit precision. The same results described below were obtained, but in 30% less generations.

3    The term *emergent* is used to indicate an adaptive solution (mechanism or behavior) that is not designed or expected.

4    CMOS is a technology that requires a single type of alimentation at low voltage and can be easily integrated with processing units, whereas the standard CCD technology requires several types of alimentation and an external framegrabber unit.

5    A population of 30 individuals was evolved by a genetic algorithm using linear rank selection and elitism, ensuring that the best individual was twice as likely to be reproduced as the median. The crossover operator allowed small changes in the length of the network chromosome only; the mutation rate was set to 1 bit for each visual chromosome and 1.8 bits for each network chromosome.

6    The term *affordance* has been coined by J. J. Gibson (1979) to indicate that an object in the world is more than its retinal projection for an organism. Objects and features "afford" actions and have meanings associated to the ecological niche of the animal.

7    Each individual was positioned at a new random location in the arena and evaluated over 500 sensory motor loops. The neural network used to control the robot had the same architecture of that described in section 4.2 above, but without the recurrent connections on the output units. The synaptic (16) and bias (2) connections of the network were encoded on the genotype as floating point numbers. The genetic algorithm was based on fixed ranked selection. The best 20 individuals were allowed to reproduce by making 5 copies each. The crossover operator was not used, but 25% of the weights of each network were randomly mutated by adding a small value randomly extracted from a distribution centered around zero (i.e., the weights could become stronger or weaker).

**Chapter Five**

1    The term *regularities* refers to features of the sensory patterns which can be used to

discriminate between classes of sensory patterns requiring different answers. The exact meaning of the term will become clear later on.

2   The training set was presented 5000 times during learning with learning rate 0.02 and no momentum. For each architecture we ran 10 training trials starting from different randomly-assigned initial weights.

3   Evolving individuals were allowed to "live" for 5 epochs with each epoch consisting of 5000 actions. Individuals' fitness was increased at each time they were close to a large object and decreased when they were close to a small object or a wall. Connections were represented in the genotype by a 6-bit string where 1 bit determined whether the connection was to be used or not and 5 bits coded for the strength of the corresponding weight. Population size was 50. Ten best individuals of each generation were allowed to reproduce by generating 5 copies of their genotype which were mutated by replacing 5% of randomly selected bits with a new randomly chosen value. The experiment was replicated 30 times using 4 different network architectures (with and without recurrent connections and with and without hidden units). Similar results were obtained for all types of architecture.

4   Evolving individuals were allowed to "live" for 5 epochs, each epoch consisting of 500 actions (the speed of the two wheels was updated each 100ms). Individuals' fitness was increased at each time step when they were close to the cylindrical object. Connection weights were represented in the genotype by 8-bits strings and normalized between −10 and +10. Population size was 100. The best 20 individuals of each generation were allowed to reproduce by generating 5 copies of their genotype with 3% of their bits replaced with a new randomly selected value. The experiment was replicated 10 times.

5   The position of the attractor area varies in different replications of the experiment. Often it overlaps the border between areas where the sensory patterns can and cannot be discriminated by a passive agent. Only in a minority of cases the attractor area is located within the discriminative area.

6   Evolving individuals were allowed to "live" for 100 epochs with each epoch consisting of 200 actions. Each epoch individual were initially placed in a randomly selected cell of the environment. Individuals' fitness was increased each time individuals ended up in the left part of the environment after 200 cycles. Connection weights were binarily represented in the genotype that was 20 bits long. Population size was 100. The best 20 individuals of each generation were allowed to reproduce by generating 5 copies of their genotype with 2% of their bits replaced with a new randomly selected value. The experiment was replicated 10 times.

7   In the case of the individual shown in the right part of figure 5.13, one of the three attractors is located at border between the two sides of the environment. When the agent falls within this attractor it starts to oscillate between the left and the right side of the environment. However this does not happen often because the basin of attraction is quite small. In other words, there are few starting positions from which the agent arrives here.

8   The term map or cognitive map is often used with different meanings. In this particular case it is used to indicate a two-dimensional map of the environment in which information is represented in Euclidean terms.

9   The architecture of the network was fixed and consisted of a fully connected perceptron with 8 sensory and 2 motor neurons. Individuals' fitness was increased each time individuals ended up in the target area (i.e., each time their distance from the intersection corresponding to the position of the food was less than 7.5 cm after 80 cycles). Each connection weight was represented in the genotype by an 8-bit string and normalized between $-10$ and $+10$. Population size was 100. The best 20 individuals of each generation were allowed to reproduce by generating 5 copies of their genotype with 4% of their bits replaced with a new randomly selected value.

## Chapter Six

1   Evolving individuals were allowed to "live" for 15 epochs. At the beginning of each epoch the robot and the target objects were randomly positioned in the arena as far as possible from each other. Epochs terminated after 200 actions or after an object had been correctly released outside the arena. Connection weights were represented in the genotype with 8-bit precision and normalized between $-10$ and $+10$. Population size was 100. The best 20 individuals of each generation were allowed to reproduce by generating 5 copies of their genotype with 2% of their bits replaced with a new randomly-selected value. For each architecture the experiment was replicated 10 times. Genotypes had a total length of: (A) 256, (B) 416, (C) 480, (D) 480, and (E) 1024 bits, respectively, for the 5 different architectures described. Individuals were evolved in simulation by using the sampling technique described in chapter 3 and then tested on the real robot.

2   These sub-behaviors have been pre-designed to simplify the experiment and take into account the fact that the robot must be very close to an object to recognize it with the infrared sensors, but a little more distant to grip it correctly.

3   In principle, different strategies can be developed by robots with architecture (c) that, having recurrent connections, may discriminate cylindrical objects from another position

and pick-up the object later on from the frontal side. However, the analysis of evolved individuals with this architecture did not show differences from this point of view.

4   Individuals with architecture (c) which have recurrent connections cannot be subjected to this test because their motor output is not only function of the current sensory state but also of the previous sensory states.

5   The real battery charger would grab the Khepera when it perceives it by means of a simple sensor placed on the black platform; the neural network is automatically discon-nected, and the robot built-in battery is charged; then, the neural network is attached again to the sensors and motors, and the robot is left free to move.

6   Indeed most of the time 0.0: due to the small size of the area and to the vicinity of the walls, both components are very close to zero.

7   Evolving individuals were allowed to "live" for a single epoch consisting of a minium of 50 and a maximum of 150 actions (lasting 380ms each). Between each individual and the next, a random velocity was applied to each wheel of the robot for 5 seconds in order to avoid artifactual influences between successive individuals in the same population. Selective reproduction consisted of a linear scaling of the fitness values followed by a probabilistic allocation of a number of offspring proportional to the fitness value of each individual (roulette wheel selection). Population size was 80. Connection weights and neuron thresholds were individually coded as floating point numbers on the chromosome (value for the first generations were randomly generated between −0.5 and +0.5). All offspring, simple copies of their parents, were then randomly paired and a random single-point crossover was performed with a 0.1 probability. Each value of the newly obtained strings was then mutated with 0.2 probability by adding a small random value within a negative and positive mutation range.

8   The facing direction corresponded to the direction of motion of the evolved robot.

9   We tried to combine the two measuring procedures by disconnecting the motor neurons from the wheels and recording the node activations for a few seconds at all location in the environment. In this situation all the neurons started to display an asynchronous and cyclic pattern of activity that was completely uncorrelated with any external and internal parameter (position, orientation, battery status).

## Chapter Seven

1   Similar views were expressed in the same period by Morgan (Morgan, 1896) and Osborn (Osborn, 1896).

2   One might wonder whether Lamarckian evolution (i.e., an evolutionary process where characters acquired through learning are directly coded back into the genotype and transmitted to offspring) could be more effective that darwinian evolution (i.e., an evolutionary process in which characters acquired through learning are not coded back into the genotype). Ackley and Littman (1994) for instance claimed that in artificial evolution, where inherited characters can be easily coded into the genotype given that the mapping between genotype and phenotype is generally quite simple, there is no reason for not using Lamarckian evolution. Indeed the authors showed that Lamarckian evolution is far more effective than darwinian evolution in a stationary environment. On the other hand, as shown by Sasaki and Tokoro (1997), darwinian evolution largely outperforms lamarkian evolution when the environment is not stationary or when different individuals are exposed to different learning experiences.

3   Each sensorimotor cycle is repeated for 20 epochs (life span) during which the animat is allowed to spend 50 actions in 5 environments with randomly different food distributions (for a total of 5000 cycles). The initial population is composed of 100 individuals, each with the architecture described in figure 3 and randomly assigned connection weights in the $\pm 1.0$ interval. At the end of life the 100 individuals are ranked in terms of their fitness (total number of food elements eaten during life) and the best 20 individuals are allowed to reproduce by generating 5 copies each of their connection weights. The inherited original weight matrices (changes due to learning during life are discarded) are mutated by selecting 5 weights at random and perturbing the weight's value by adding a quantity randomly selected in the $\pm 1.0$ interval. The process is repeated for 100 generations.

4   It should be noticed that such encoding is rather irrealistic from a biological point of view and one might correctly argue that biological genotypes do not encode characteristics of individual synapses. However, here the point is that of studying the interaction between learning and evolution by preventing evolution alone to find a precise behavioral solution and giving it the possibility to exploit lifetime learning.

5   These types of environments, which are more biologically plausible, are also known as Latent Energy Environments (Menczer and Belew 1996). One way of comparing the effect of different manipulations of the parameters of these artificial world consists in observing how long a population survives.

6   When a network is placed in the environments described above the following sequence of events will occur. Sensory input is received on the input units. Activation flows up reaching the two motor units and the two teaching units. The activation value of the two motor units is used to move Khepera, thereby changing the sensory input for the next cycle. The activation value of the two teaching units (teaching signal) is used to change the weights that connect the input units to the motor units. Then the next cycle begins. The total fitness of an individual is the sum of its fitnesses in the 10 epochs of its life. An epoch ends when the robot finds the target or after 500 cycles. Individuals of even generations lived in an arena with dark walls while individuals of odd generations lived in an arena with bright walls. At every new epoch the position of the target area is randomly determined. Weights are encoded as floating point values in the genotype and are randomly initialized between $-1.0$ and $1.0$ in the initial generations. During the copying process 10% of the weights are mutated by adding a quantity randomly selected in the interval $\pm$ 1.0 to the weight's current value. In each epoch the fitness of an individual is increased by $500 - N$ units, where N is the number of cycles needed to reach the target area in that epoch. In other words, individuals with high fitness are individuals that are able to reach the target area quickly.

7   This result is also obtained with evolved self-teaching networks living in a stationary environment (see Nolfi and Parisi 1993, 1994).

**Chapter Eight**

1   We will use the term 'general strategy' or 'general solution' to indicate selected individuals able to cope with different tasks. In the context of predator and prey we will indicate with the term 'general' the strategy adopted by a predator which is able to catch a large number of prey adopting different, not necessarily complex, strategies.

2   The Red Queen is an imaginary chess character described in Lewis Carroll's *Through the Looking Glass* who was always running without making any advancement because the landscape was moving with her.

3   In order to keep things as simple as possible and given the small size of the parameter set, we used direct genetic encoding: each parameter (including recurrent connections and threshold values of output units) was encoded on five bits, the first bit determining the sign of the synapse and the remaining four its strength. Therefore, the genotype of the predator was 5 x (30 synapses + 2 thresholds) bits long while that of the prey was 5 x (20 synapses + 2 thresholds) bits long. Two populations of 100 individuals each were co-evolved for 100 generations. Each individual was tested against the best competitors of

the previous ten generations (a similar procedure was used in [Sims 1994; Reynolds 1994; Cliff and Miller 1995, 1996] in order to improve co-evolutionary stability). At generation 0, competitors were randomly chosen within the same generation, whereas in the other 9 initial generations they were randomly chosen from the pool of available best individuals (2 at generation 3, 3 at generation 4, etc.). For each competition, the prey and predator were always positioned on a horizontal line in the middle of the environment at a distance corresponding to half the environment width, but always at a new random orientation. The competition ended either when the predator touched the prey or after 500 motor updates (corresponding to 50 seconds at maximum on the physical robot). The fitness function for each competition did not require any sensor or motor measurement, nor any global position measure; it was simply TimetoContact normalized by the maximum number of motor updates for the predator and 1-TimetoContact for the prey further averaged over the number of competitions. Therefore the fitness values were always between 0 and 1, where 0 means worst. Individuals were ranked after fitness performance in descending order and the best 20 were allowed to reproduce. One-point crossover was applied on all randomly paired strings with a probability pc, and random mutation (bit switching) was applied to each bit with constant probability pm=0.05.

4   Two populations (one for the prey, the other for the predator) of 20 individuals each were co-evolved for 25 generations (P(crossover)=0.6; P(mutation)=0.05 per bit) in approximately 40 hours of continuous operation (time might vary in different replications, depending on the relative performances of the two species). Each individual was tested against the best competitors from the most recent 5 generations. After each tournament, the two robots were allowed to move in the environment for 5 seconds in obstacle avoidance mode.

5   The parameters used in these simulations are mostly the same as those described in the previous section. However, in these experiments we used a simpler fitness function. The fitness function for each competition was simply 1 for the predator and 0 for the prey if the predator was able to catch the prey and, conversely, 0 for the predator and 1 for the prey if the latter was able to escape the predator. Moreover, to keep the number of parameters as small as possible, we did not use crossover. In the previous experiments, in fact, we did not notice any significant difference in experiments conducted with different crossover rates. Finally, each weight (including recurrent connections and threshold values of output units) was encoded using 8 bits.

6   This may be due to the fact that in this and in the experiments that will be presented in the next section the sensory systems of the prey have been enriched with respect to the experiments described in sections 8.4 and 8.5.

7   The authors did not provide enough data in their paper to understand whether their simulations fell into cycles. However, even though both the nervous system and the sensory system were under co-evolution in their case, it seems that Cliff and Miller did not observe any co-evolutionary progress toward increasingly general solutions. In fact, they report that "co-evolution works to produce good pursuers and good evaders through a pure bootstrapping process, but both types are rather specially adapted to their opponents' current counter-strategies." [2, pp. 506]. It should be noted that there are several differences between Cliff and Miller experiments and ours. The fitness function used in their experiments, in fact, is more complex and includes additional constraints that attempt to force evolution in a certain direction (e.g., predators are scored for their ability to approach the prey and not only for their ability to catch it). Moreover, the genotype-to-phenotype mapping is much more complex in their cases and includes several additional parameters that may affect the results obtained.

**Chapter Nine**

1   Grau (1992), in addition to compactness and scalability, mentioned other properties such as "completeness" (any neural architecture may be potentially encoded in the geno-type) and closure (any genoma should code for a valid architecture).

2   Evolving individuals were allowed to "live" for 10 epochs consisting of 500 cycles each. At the beginning of each epoch the robot and the target area were randomly posi-tioned in the arena. The genotype was a bit string divided up into 32 blocks where each block coded for the characteristics of a corresponding neuron. Sensory, internal, and motor neurons were encoded by 10, 17, and 5 blocks, respectively. Each block of the genotype contains instructions that determine the properties of the corresponding neuron. A *thresh-old expression gene* determines the threshold in the activation variability over which is triggered a growth process of the corresponding neuron. Two *physical position genes* spec-ify the Cartesian coordinates of the neuron in two-dimensional space (the 'y' coordinate however was predetermined and fixed for sensory and motor neurons). A *branching angle gene* and a *segment length gene* determine the angle and the length of the branching seg-ments. A *synaptic weight gene* determines the synaptic coefficients of all the connections that will be established by the neuron (i.e., all connections departing from the same neuron have the same weight). A *bias gene* represents the activation bias of the neuron. Finally, a *neuron type gene* indicates the type of the corresponding sensory neuron (within the 8 infrared and 8 ambient light sensors) or of the corresponding motor neuron (the motor controlling the left or the right wheel). If more than a single output neuron codifying the same motor information exists, the actual motor output is taken to be the average of the activation levels of the different neurons. Population size was 100. The best 20 individuals

of each generation were allowed to reproduce by generating 5 copies of their genotype. Random mutations were introduced in the copying process. Individuals were scored with $(500 - N)$ units each time they were able to reach the target area, where N represents the number of actions spent to reach the target area. For other details see Nolfi, Miglino and Parisi (1994).

3   In this case, evolution can only select a subset of the 16 available sensors (8 infrared sensors and 8 ambient light sensors). More complex cases will be described in section 9.3.

4   Evolving individuals were evaluated starting with up to 7 different configurations of the legs in different epochs (to save time, however, an individual entered in the successive epoch only if performance in the previous epochs was close to optimal). Although all individuals were evaluated on the basis of the walking distance, the initial configurations of the legs varied in different sub-populations. Genotypes are formed by tree structures composed of 14 different symbols (alleles) encoding the corresponding operations. Some of these symbols have an argument. For example the symbol 'C', which cuts connection links, takes as argument the number of links to be deleted. The genetic operators were applied until a genetic code was found that developed into a well formed neural network or until the allocated time of 2 hours elapsed. The initial population had randomly generated trees with 60 nodes (the number of nodes could increase in evolving individuals up to a maximum of 600 nodes). To maintain genetic diversity, the population was divided in 32 islands arranged on a 2D torus with each island consisting of 64 individuals organized into a 2D grid. The total population therefore was composed by 2048 individuals. The mating probability was proportional to the distance of the individuals in this 2D space. Offspring were created either through the recombination of two other individuals or by exchanging subtrees of a single reproducing individual. Every time an offspring is created all alleles are mutated with a 0.005 probability. Neurons were updated in a continuum fashion as in Beer and Gallagher (1992). For all other parameters see Gruau (1994).

5   In the case of the complete model, the experiments without ADNS failed to produce a correct walking behavior in five out of five replications.

6   The fitness function was the distance covered during the evaluation period increased by a term encouraging any leg motion. A steady-state evolutionary algorithm was used. Population size was 200. The genotypes can be imagined as distributed over a circle. To create a new individual the following sequence of operations occurs: (1) a point P is randomly selected within the circle; (2) two individuals close to P are selected (the probability to select an individual is inversely proportional to the distance from P); (3) selected individuals are allowed to reproduce; (4) the new individual is evaluated; (5)

an individual in the neighborhood of P is replaced by the newly created individual. The individual to be replaced is selected by using a 2-tournament anti-selection scheme. During reproduction a crossover operator and two forms of mutations are applied. Crossover is realized by exchanging subtrees between the two reproducing individuals. Mutations can affect both a subtrees (which is replaced by another compatible randomly selected subtree) or the parameters of the instructions. No more than three successive divisions can occur and the number of connections created by any cell is limited to four. To reduce the size of the search space the structure of the genotype was constrained by requiring that all subprograms were well-formed trees according to a given grammar. For all other parameters, see Kodjabachian and Meyer (1998a, 1998b).

7   Given that the same program was called six times, the corresponding sub-networks differed only because of spatial interactions.

**Chapter Ten**

1   This could also be considered the first experiment in Evolutionary Robotics, although the methodology employed does not fully exploit the interaction between the controller and the environment.

2   The genetic string encoded as real numbers 36 connection weights of the leg controller, 12 cross-body and along-body connection weights, 36 gating weights from the infrared sensor, 36 gating weights from the bumper sensor, 36 gating weights from the bias unit, 9 thresholds (6 for the controller neurons, 1 for the infrared sensor, 1 for the bumper sensor, and 1 for the bias unit), 9 time constants, and 3 connection weights for the infrared sensor, for the bumper sensor, and for the bias unit (a total of 177 numbers in the range from 0 to 99). A genetic algorithm with tournament selection, elitism, single-point crossover (probability 1.0), and mutation (probability 0.02) were used.

**Chapter Eleven**

1   The robot has a circular body with a diameter of 46 cm and a height of 63 cm. The evolutionary arena has a rectangular shape measuring 2.9m by 4.2m. The fitness function encouraged motion of the wheels, but distance from the walls. Each individual was tested four times for 30 seconds starting from different positions and orientations. The value of the worst test was taken as the fitness of the individual. A population of 30 individuals was evolved for 35 generations with crossover probability 0.7 and 1 bit mutated per each individual.

2   Therefore, the resulting behavior changes because the world changes, not because something changes inside the robot (Scheier et al. 1999).

3   The simulated robot had a circular body, two lateral wheels controlled by two motors, and a number of sensors positioned around it pointing radially outward (its shape was similar to that of a Khepera robot). Sensors detected the distance of objects up to a distance of 30 cm and within an angle of 20 degrees. The motor system was modeled by first-order differential equations taking into account the wheel radius and the distance between the two wheels. 5% of random noise was added both to the sensors and to the motors. The control system consisted of a neural network encoded in a tree structure. The tree structure included the specification of the number and relative positions of sensors; these were encoded as terminal nodes of the tree. The time constant was restricted between 0.5 and 2.5 second, wheel radius between 1.0 cm and 3.5 cm, the diameter of the body between 10 cm and 25 cm, and the wheel base was constrained to be not larger than the body size. To increase diversity, the population was divided into two groups of 40 individuals. The evolutionary process consisted of 50 generations and a tournament selection method. Given their different representation, the tree structures (controllers) and the string of real numbers encoding the structure of the body were manipulated by different crossover and mutation operators. As in the case of the experiment described in section 4.2, the fitness function included three components that encouraged speed, straight movement, and obstacle avoidance (8 sensors evenly spaced around the robot body were used to detect the distance of the nearest object at each time step). Individuals were evaluated for 15 epochs of 500 sensory-motor cycles each. For other details see Lee et al. 1996.

# References

Abeles M. (1991). *Corticonics*. Cambridge:Cambridge University Press.

Ackley D.H. and Littman M. L. (1990). Generalization and scaling in reinforcement learning. In D. S. Touretzky (Ed.), *Advances in Neural Information Processing Systems 2*. San Mateo, CA: Morgan Kaufmann.

Ackley D.H. and Littman M.L. (1991). Interaction between learning and evolution. In C.G. Langton et. al (Eds.), *Proceedings of the Second Conference on Artificial Life*. Reading, MA: Addison-Wesley.

Angeline P.J. and Pollack J.B. (1993). Competitive environments evolve better solutions for complex tasks. In S. Forrest (Ed.), *Proceedings of the Fifth International Conference on Genetic Algorithms*. San Mateo, CA: Morgan Kaufmann.

Arakawa T. and Fukuda T. (1997). Natural motion generation of biped locomotion robot using hierarchical trajectory generation method consisting of GA, EP layers. In *Proceedings of the IEEE Conference on Robotics and Automation*. New York: IEEE Press.

Arbib M.A. (1989). *The Methaphorical Brain 2*. New York: Wiley.

Arkin R.C. (1989). Motor schema-based mobile robot navigation. *International Journal of Robotics Research*, 8:92–112.

Arkin R.C. (1990). The impact of cybernetics on the design of a mobile robot system: A case study. *IEEE Transaction on Systems, Man, and Cybernetics*, 20:1245–1257.

Arkin R.C. (1998). *Behavior-Based Robotics*. Cambridge, MA: MIT Press.

Ashby W.R. (1956). *An Introduction to Cybernetics*. London: Chapman and Hall.

Bajcsy R. (1988). Active perception. *Proceedings of the IEEE*, (76)8:996–1005.

Baldwin J.M. (1896). A new factor in evolution. *American Naturalist*, 30:441–451.

Barnett L. (1998). Ruggedness and neutrality: The NKp family of fitness landscapes. In C. Adami, R. Belew, H. Kitano and C. Taylor (Eds.), *Artificial Life IV: Proceedings of the Sixth International Conference on Artificial Life*. Cambridge, MA: MIT Press.

Barto A.G., Sutton R.S. and Anderson C.W. (1983). Neuronlike elements that can solve difficult learning control problems. *IEEE Transactions on Systems, Man, and Cybernetics*, 13(5):835–846.

Barto A.G., Sutton R.S. and Watkins C.J. (1990). Learning and sequential decision making. In M. Gabriel and J.W. Moore (Eds.), *Learning and Computational Neuroscience*. Cambridge, MA: MIT Press/Bradford Books.

Barto A.G., Bradtke S.J. and Singh S.P. (1995). Learning to act using real-time dynamic programming. *Artificial Intelligence*, 6:105–122.

Baxter J. (1994). The evolution of learning algorithms for artificial neural networks. *Technical Report*, School of Information Science and Technology, The Flinders University of South Australia.

Beer R.D. (1990). *Intelligence as Adaptive Behavior: An Experiment in Computational Neuroethology*. New York: Academic Press.

Beer R.D. (1997). The dynamics of adaptive behavior: A research program. *Robotics and Autonomous Systems*, 20:257–289.

Beer R.D. and Gallagher J.C. (1992). Evolving dynamical neural networks for adaptive behavior. *Adaptive Behavior*, 1:91–122.

Belew R.K., McInerney J. and Schraudolph N.N. (1992). Evolving networks: using the genetic algorithm with connectionistic learning. In C.G. Langton et. al (Eds.), *Proceedings of the Second Conference on Artificial Life*. Reading, MA: Addison-Wesley.

Belew R.K. and Mitchell M., Eds. (1996). *Adaptive Individuals in Evolving Populations*. Reading, MA: Addison-Wesley.

Biro Z. and Ziemke T. (1998). Evolution of visually-guided approach behavior in recurrent artificial neural network robot controllers. In R. Pfeifer, B. Blumberg, J-A. Meyer and S.W. Wilson (Eds.), *From Animals to Animats V, Proceedings of the Fifth International Conference on Simulation of Adaptive Behavior*. Cambridge, MA: MIT Press.

Booker L., Godberg D.E. and Holland J.H. (1989). Classifier systems and genetic algorithms. *Artificial Intelligence*, 40:235–282.

Braitenberg V. (1984). *Vehicles*. Cambridge, MA: MIT Press.

Brooks R.A. (1986). A robust layered control system for a mobile robot. *IEEE Journal of Robotics and Autonomation*, 2:14–23.

Brooks R.A. (1989). A robot that walks: Emergent behaviors from a carefully evolved network. *Neural Computation*, 1:253–262.

Brooks R.A. (1991a). Intelligence without reason, In J. Mylopoulos and R. Reiter (Eds.), *Proceedings of 12th International Joint Conference on Artificial Intelligence*. San Mateo, CA: Morgan Kaufmann.

Brooks R.A. (1991b). New approaches to Robotics. *Science*, 253:1227–1232.

Brooks R.A. (1992). Artificial life and real robots. In F. J. Varela and P. Bourgine (Eds.), *Toward a Practice of Autonomous Systems: Proceedings of the First European Conference on Artificial Life*. Cambridge, MA: MIT Press/Bradford Books.

Brooks R.A. (1999). *Cambrian Intelligence*. Cambridge, MA: MIT Press.

Calabretta R., Nolfi S., Parisi D. and Wagner G. P. (1998). A case study of the evolution of modularity: towards a bridge between evolutionary biology, artificial life, neuro- and cognitive science. In C. Adami, R. Belew, H. Kitano and C. Taylor (Eds.), *Proceedings of Artificial Life VI*. Cambridge, MA: MIT Press.

Cangelosi A., Nolfi S. and Parisi D. (1994). Cell division and migration in a "genotype" for neural networks. *Network*, 5.497–515.

Cecconi F., Menczer F. and Belew R.K. (1996). Maturation and the evolution of imitative learning in artificial organisms. *Adaptive Behavior*, 4: 29–50.

Chalmers D.J. (1990). The evolution of learning: An experiment in genetic connectionism. In D.S. Touretzky, J.L. Elman, T.J. Sejnowski and G.E. Hinton (Eds.), *Proceedings of the 1990 Connectionist Models Summer School*. San Mateo, CA: Morgan Kaufmann.

Chavas J., Corne C., Horvai P., Kodjabachian J. and Meyer, J-A. (1998). Incremental evolution of neural controllers for robust obstacle-avoidance in Khepera. In P. Husbands and J-A. Meyer (Eds.), *Evolutionary Robotics. First European Workshop*, pp. 227–247. Berlin: Springer-Verlag.

Cheng K. (1986). A purely geometric module in the rat's spatial representation. *Cognition*, 23:149–178.

Chiel H.J. and Beer R.D. (1997). The brain has a body: Adaptive behavior emerges from interactions of nervous system, body and environment. *Trends in Neurosciences*, 20: 553–557.

Churchland P. M. and Sejnowski T. J. (1992). *The Computational Brain*. Cambridge, MA: MIT Press.

Clark A. and Thornton C. (1997). Trading spaces: Computation, representation, and the limits of uniformed learning. *Behavioral and Brain Sciences*, 20:57–90.

Cliff D. (1991). Computational neuroethology: A provisional manifesto. In J-A. Meyer and S.W. Wilson (Eds.), *From Animals to Animats: Proceedings of the First International Conference on Simulation of Adaptive Behavior*. Cambridge MA: MIT Press/Bradford Books.

Cliff D., Harvey I. and Husbands P. (1993). Explorations in evolutionary robotics. *Adaptive Behavior*, 2:73–110.

Cliff D. and Miller G.F. (1995). Tracking the Red Queen: Measurements of adaptive progress in co-evolutionary simulations. In F. Moran, A. Moreno, J.J. Merelo and P. Chacon (Eds.), *Advances in Artificial Life: Proceedings of the Third European Conference on Artificial Life*. Berlin: Springer Verlag.

Cliff D. and Miller G.F. (1996). Co-evolution of pursuit and evasion II: Simulation methods and results. In P. Maes, M. Mataric, J-A Meyer, J. Pollack, H. Roitblat and S. Wilson (Eds.), *From Animals to Animats IV: Proceedings of the Fourth International Conference on Simulation of Adaptive Behavior*. Cambridge, MA: MIT Press-Bradford Books.

Coghill G.E. (1964). *Anatomy and the Problem of Behavior*. London: MacMillan.

Collins R. and Jefferson D. (1991). Selection in massively parallel genetic algorithms. In R. K. Belew and L.B. Booker (Eds.), *Proceedings of the Fourth International Conference on Genetic Algorithm (ICGA-91)*. San Francisco, CA: Morgan Kaufmann.

Colombetti M., Dorigo M. and Borghi G. (1996). Behavior analysis and training: A methodology for behavior engineering. *IEEE Transactions on Systems, Man, and Cybernetics—Part B*, 3, 365–380.

Cramer N.L. (1985). A representation for the adaptive generation of simple sequential programs. In J. J. Grefenstette (Ed.), *Proceedings of the First International Conference on Genetic Algorithms and Their Applications*. Hillsdale, NJ: Erlbaum.

Dasdan A. and Oflazer K. (1994). Genetic synthesis of unsupervised learning algorithms, *Technical Report*. Department of Computer Engineering and Information Science, Bilkent University of Ankara, Turkey.

Dawkins R. and Krebs J.R. (1979). Arms races between and within species. *Proceedings of the Royal Society of London B*, 205:489–511.

Dawkins R. (1986). *The Blind Watchmaker*. New York: Norton Cooper.

Dellaert F. and Beer R. D. (1994). Toward an evolvable model of development for autonomous agent synthesis. In R. Brooks and P. Maes (Eds.), *Proceedings of the Fourth Conference on Artificial Life*. Cambridge: MIT Press.

Denker J., Schwartz D., Wittner B., Solla S., Hopfield J., Howard R. and Jackel L. (1987). Automatic learning, rule extraction, and generalization. *Computer Systems*, 1:877–922.

Dill M., Wolf R. and Heisenberg M. (1993). Visual pattern recognition in Drosophila involves retinotopic matching. *Nature*, 355:751–753.

Dittrich P., Bürgel, A. and Banzhaf W. (1998). Learning to Move a Robot with random Morphology. In P. Husbands and J-A. Meyer (Eds.), *Evolutionary Robotics. First European Workshop*. Heidelberg: Springer Verlag.

Dorigo M. and Schnepf U. (1993). Genetic-based machine learning and behavior based robotics: A new synthesis. *IEEE Transaction on Systems, Man, and Cybernetics*, 1:141–154.

Dorigo M. and Colombetti M. (1994). Robot shaping: Developing autonomous agents through learning. *Artificial Intelligence*, 71:321–370.

Dorigo M. and Colombetti M. (1997). *Robot Shaping: An Experiment in Behavior Engineering*. Cambridge, MA: MIT Press/Bradford Books.

Elman J.L. (1990). Finding structure in time. *Cognitive Science*, 14:179–211.

Elman J.L. (1993). Learning and development in neural networks: The importance of starting small. *Cognition*, 48:71–99.

Elman J.L., Bates E.A., Johnson M.H., Karmiloff-Smith A., Parisi D. and Plunket K. (1996). *Rethinking Innateness. A Connectionist Perspective on Development*. Cambridge, MA: MIT Press.

Enquist M. and Arak A. (1994). Symmetry, beauty, and evolution. *Nature*, 372:169–172.

Fahlman S.E. and Lebiere C. (1990). The cascade-correlation learning architecture. In D.S. Touretzky (Ed.), *Advances in Neural Information Processing Systems 2*. San Mateo, CA: Morgan Kaufmann.

Floreano D. (1992). Emergence of home-based foraging strategies in ecosystems of neural networks. In J. Meyer, H.L. Roitblat and S.W. Wilson (Eds.), *From Animals to Animats 2, Proceeding of the International Conference on Simulation of Adaptive Behavior*. Cambridge, MA: MIT Press.

Floreano D. (1997a). Reducing human design and increasing adaptability in evolutionary robotics. In T. Gomi (Ed.), *Evolutionary Robotics: From Intelligent Robots to Artificial Life*. Ontario, Canada: AAI Books.

Floreano D. (1997b). Engineering Adaptive Behavior. *Adaptive Behavior*, 5(3/4):407–416.

Floreano D. (1998). Evolutionary robotics in behavior engineering and artificial life. In T. Gomi (Ed.), *Evolutionary Robotics. From Intelligent Robots to Artificial Life (ER98)*. Ontario, Canada: AAI Books.

Floreano D. and Mondada F. (1994). Automatic creation of an autonomous agent: genetic evolution of a neural-network driven robot. In D. Cliff, P. Husbands, J. Meyer and S.W. Wilson (Eds.), *From Animals to Animats 3: Proceedings of Third Conference on Simulation of Adaptive Behavior*. Cambridge, MA: MIT Press/Bradford Books.

Floreano D. and Mondada F. (1996a). Evolution of plastic neurocontrollers for situated agents. In P. Maes, M. Mataric, J-A. Meyer, J. Pollack and S. Wilson. (Eds.), *From Animals to Animats 4, Proceedings of the International Conference on Simulation of Adaptive Behavior*. Cambridge, MA: MIT Press.

Floreano D. and Mondada F. (1996b). Evolution of homing navigation in a real mobile robot. *IEEE Transactions on Systems, Man, and Cybernetics—Part B: Cybernetics*, 26(3):396–407.

Floreano D. and Mondada F. (1998). Evolutionary neurocontrollers for autonomous mobile robots. *Neural Networks*, 11:1461–1478.

Floreano D. and Nolfi S. (1997a). God save the Red Queen! Competition in co-evolutionary robotics. In J.R. Koza, D. Kalyanmoy, M. Dorigo, D.B. Fogel, H. Garzon, H. Iba and R.L. Riolo (Eds.), *Genetic Programming 1997: Proceedings of the Second Annual Conference*. San Francisco, CA: Morgan Kaufmann.

Floreano D. and Nolfi S. (1997b). Adaptive behavior in competing co-evolving species. In P. Husbands and I. Harvey (Eds.), *Proceedings of the Fourth European Conference on Artificial Life*. Cambridge, MA: MIT Press.

Floreano D. and Urzelai J. (2000). Evolutionary robots with on-line self- organization and behavioral fitness. *Neural Networks*, in press.

Floreano D., Nolfi S. and Mondada F. (1998). Competitive co-evolutionary robotics: From theory to practice. In R. Pfeifer, B. Blumberg and H. Kobayashi (Eds.), *Proceedings of the Fifth International Conference of the Society for Adaptive Behavior (SAB98)*. Cambridge, MA: MIT Press.

Fontanari J. F. and Meir R. (1991). Evolving a learning algorithm for the binary perceptron. *Network*, 2:353–359.

Franceschini N. (1997). Combined optical, neuroanatomical, electrophysiological and behavioral studies on signal processing in the fly compound eye. In C. Taddei-Ferretti (Ed.), *Biocybernetics of Vision: Integrative Mechanisms and Cognitive Processes*. London: World Scientific.

Fujita M. and Kitano H. (1998). Development of an autonomous quadruped robot for robot entertainment. *Autonomous Robotics*, 5:1–14.

Funes P. and Pollack J. (1998). Evolutionary Body Building: Adaptive physical designs for robots. *Artificial Life* 4: 337–357.

Gallistel C.R. (1990). *The Organization of Learning*. Cambridge, MA: MIT Press.

de Garis H. (1990). Genetic programming: Building artificial nervous systems using genetically programmed neural network modules. In B.W. Porter and R.J. Mooney (Eds.), *Proceedings of the Seventh International Conference on Machine Learning*, pp. 132–139. San Mateo, CA: Morgan Kaufmann.

de Garis H. (1995). CAM-BRAIN: The Evolutionary Engineering of a Billion Neuron Artificial Brain by 2001 Which Grows/Evolves at Electronic Speeds Inside a Cellular Automata Machine. In E. Sanchez and M. Tomassini (Eds), *Towards Evolvable Hardware. The Evolutionary Engineering Approach*, pp. 76–98. Berlin: Springer Verlag.

Gibson J.J. (1979). *The Ecological Approach to Visual Perception*. Boston: Houghton Mifflin.

Glasner A.S. (1989). *An Introduction to Ray Tracing*. London: Academic Press.

Goldberg D.E. (1989). *Genetic Algorithms in Search. Optimization, and Machine Learning*. Redwood City, CA: Addison-Wesley.

Gomi T. and Ide K. (1998). Emergence of gait of a legged robot by collaboration through evolution. In P. K. Simpson (Ed.), *IEEE World Congress on Computational Intelligence (WCCI'98)*. New York: IEEE Press.

Gottlieb G. (1992). *Individual Development and Evolution: The Genesis of Novel Behavior*. New York: Oxford University Press.

Gould S.J. (1977). *Ontogeny and Phylogeny*. Cambridge, MA: Harward University Press.

Gould S.J. (1989). *Wonderful Life: The Burgess Shale and the Nature of History*. New York: W.W. Norton.

Graham D. (1985). Pattern and control of walking in insects. *Advances in Insect Physiology*, 18:31–140.

Grossberg S. (1987). Competitive learning: From interactive activation to adaptive resonance. *Cognitive Science*, 11:23–63.

Gruau F. (1992a). Genetic systems of boolean neural networks with a cell rewriting developmental process. In D. Whitley and J. D. Schaffer (Eds.), *Combination of Genetic Algorithms and Neural Networks*. Los Alamitos, CA: IEE Computer Society Press.

Gruau F. (1992b). Cellular encoding of genetic neural networks. *Technical Report* 92–21, Laboratoire de l'Informatique du Parallelisme, Ecole Normale Superieure de Lyon.

Gruau F. (1994). Automatic definition of modular neural networks. *Adaptive Behavior*, 3:151–183.

Gruau F. (1997). Cellular encoding for interactive evolutionary robotics. In P. Husbands and I. Harvey (Eds.), *Proceedings of the Fourth European Conference on Artificial Life*, pp. 368–377. Cambridge, MA: MIT Press.

Hancock P.J.B. (1992). Genetic algorithms and permutation problems: A comparison of recombination operators for neural structure specification. In D. Whitley (Ed.) *Proceedings of the International Workshop on the Combination of Genetic Algorithms and Neural Networks*. Baltimore: IEEE Press.

Harnad S. (1990). Symbol grounding problem. *Physica D*, 42:335–464.

Harp S.A., Samad T. and Guha A. (1989). Toward the genetic synthesis of neural networks. In J.D. Schaffer (Ed.), *Proceedings of the Third International Conference on Genetic Algorithms*. San Mateo, CA: Morgan Kaufmann.

Harvey I. (1992a). The SAGA cross: The mechanics of recombination for species with variable length genotypes. In R. Manner and B. Manderick (Eds.), *Parallel Problem Solving from Nature 2*. Amsterdam: North-Holland.

Harvey I. (1992b). Species adaptation genetic algorithms: A basis for a continuing SAGA. In F. Varela and P. Bourgine (Eds.), *Toward a Practice of Autonomous Systems: Proceedings of the First European Conference on Artificial Life*. Cambridge, MA: MIT Press.

Harvey I. (1993). Evolutionary robotics and SAGA: The case for hill crawling and tournament selection. In C. Langton (Ed.), *Artificial Life 3: Proceedings of the Santa Fe Conference*. Reading, MA: Addison-Wesley.

Harvey I. (1995). The artificial evolution of adaptive behavior. *Ph.D. Thesis*. School of Cognitive and Computing Science, University of Sussex, UK.

Harvey I. (1996). Relearning and evolution in neural networks. *Adaptive Behavior*, 4(1):81–84.

Harvey I. (1997). Is there another new factor in evolution?. *Evolutionary Computation*, 4(3): 313–329.

Harvey I. (1997b). Artificial evolution for real problems. In T. Gomi (Ed.) *Evolutionary Robotics: From Intelligent Robots to Artificial Life (ER'97)*. Ontario, Canada: AAI Books

Harvey I. and Stone J.V. (1996). Unicycling helps your French: spontaneous recovery of associations by learning unrelated tasks. *Neural Computation*, 8: 697–704.

Harvey I. and Thompson A. (1996). Through the labyrinth, evolution finds a way: A silicon ridge. In T. Higuchi, M. Iwata and W. Liu (Eds.), *Proceedings of the First*

*International Conference on Evolvable Systems: From Biology to Hardware.* Tokyo: Springer-Verlag.

Harvey I., Husbands I. and Cliff D. (1994). Seeing the light: artificial evolution, real vision. In D. Cliff, P. Husbands, J-A Meyer and S. Wilson (Eds.), *From Animals to Animats 3, Proceedings of the Third International Conference on Simulation of Adaptive Behavior.* Cambridge, MA: MIT Press/Bradford Books.

Harvey I., Husbands P., Cliff D., Thompson A. and Jakobi N. (1997). Evolutionary robotics: The Sussex approach. *Robotics and Autonomous Systems*, 20:205–224.

Haykin S. (1994). *Neural Networks. A Comprehensive Foundation.* Englewood Cliffs, NJ: Macmillan.

Hebb D.O. (1949). *The Organization of Behavior.* New York: Wiley and Sons.

Hertz J., Krogh A. and Palmer R.G. (1991). *Introduction to the Theory of Neural Computation.* Redwood City, CA: Addison-Wesley.

Higuchi T., Iwata M., Kajitani I., Iba H., Hirao H., Furuya, T. and Manderick B. (1995). Evolvable hardware and its applications to pattern recognition and fault-tolerant systems. In E. Sanchez and M. Tomassini (Eds), *Towards Evolvable Hardware. The Evolutionary Engineering Approach*, pp. 118–135. Berlin: Springer Verlag.

Higuchi T., Niwa T., Tanaka T., Iba H., de Garis H., and Furuya, T. (1993). Evolving hardware with genetic learning: A first step towards building a darwin machine. In J-A. Meyer, H.L. Roitblat and S.W. Wilson (Eds.), *From Animals to Animats 2, Proceeding of the International Conference on Simulation of Adaptive Behavior.* Cambridge, MA: MIT Press.

Hillis W. (1990). Co-evolving parasites improve simulated evolution as an optimization procedure. *Physica D*, 42:228–234.

Hinton G.E. and Nowlan S.J. (1987). How learning guides evolution. *Complex Systems*, 1:495–502.

Hinton G. and Plaut D. (1987). Using fast weights to deblur old memories. In *Proceedings of the 9th Annual Conference of the Cognitive Science Society.* Hillsdale, NJ: Lawrence Erlbaum Associates.

Holland J.H. (1975). *Adaptation in Natural and Artificial Systems.* Ann Arbor, MI: University of Michigan Press.

Hornby G.S., Fujita M., Takamura S, Yamamoto T. and Hanagata O. (1999). Autonomous evolution of gaits with the Sony quadruped robot. In W. Banzhaf, J. Daida, A. E. Eiben, M. H. Garzon, V. Honavar, M. Jakiela, and R. E. Smith (Eds.), *GECCO-99: Proceedings of the Genetic and Evolutionary Computation Conference.* San Francisco, CA: Morgan Kaufmann.

Hornik K., Stinchcombe M. and White H. (1989). Multilayer feedforward networks are universal approximators. *Neural Networks*, 2:359–366.

Horswill I. (1993). A simple, cheap, and robust visual navigation system. In J-A. Meyer, H.L. Roitblat and S.W. Wilson (Eds.), *From Animals to Animats 2, Proceedings of the Second International Conference on Simulation of Adaptive Behavior*, pp. 129–136. Cambridge, MA: MIT Press.

Husbands P. (1994). A force field development scheme for use with genetic encodings of network-based sensorymotor control systems. *Technical Report* CSRP-326, School of Cognitive and Computing Sciences, University of Sussex.

Husbands P. and Harvey I. (1992). Evolution versus design. Controlling autonomous robots. In *Integrating perception, planning and action: Proceedings of the Third Annual Conferences on Artificial Intelligence*. Los Alamitos, CA:IEEE Press.

Husbands P., Harvey I. and Cliff D. (1993). An evolutionary approach to situated AI. In A. Sloman, D. Hogg, G. Humphreys, and A. Ramsay (Eds.), *Proceedings of AISB93 Ninth Biennial Conference of the Society for the Study of Artificial Intelligence and the Simulation of Behavior.* Birmingham, UK: IOS Press.

Husbands P., Harvey I., Cliff D. and Miller G. (1994). The use of genetic algorithms for the development of sensorimotor control systems. In P. Gaussier and J-D. Nicoud (Eds.) *From Perception to Action.* Los Alamitos CA: IEEE Press.

Husbands P., Smith T., Jakobi N. and O'Schea M. (1998). Better living through chemistry: Evolving GasNets for robot control. *Connection Science*, (10)3–4:185–210.

Indiveri G. and Verschure P. (1997). Autonomous vehicle guidance using analog VLSI neuromorphic sensors. In W. Gerstner, A. Germond, M. Hasler and J-D. Nicoud (Eds.), *Artificial Neural Networks—ICANN'97*, pp. 811–816. Berlin: Springer Verlag.

Ijspeert A.J., Hallam J. and Willshaw D. (1998). From lampreys to salamanders: Evolving neural controllers for swimming and walking. In R. Pfeifer, B. Blumberg, J-A. Meyer, and S.W. Wilson (Eds.), *From Animals to Animats 5, Proceedings of the Fifth International Conference on the Simulation of Adaptive Behavior*, pp. 390–399. Cambridge, MA: MIT Press.

Ijspeert A.J., Hallam J. and Willshaw D. (1999). Evolving swimming controllers for a simulated lamprey with inspiration from neurobiology. *Adaptive Behavior*, 7:247–269

Ijspeert A.J. and Kodjabachian J. (1999). Evolution and development of a central pattern generator for the swimming of a lamprey. *Artificial Life*, 5: 247–269

Jacobs R. and Jordan M. (1991). Adaptive mixtures of local experts. *Neural Computation*, 3(1): 79–87.

Jacobs R., Jordan M. and Barto A.G. (1991). Task decomposition through competition in a modular connectionist architecture: the what and where vision tasks. *Cognitive Science*, 15:219–250.

Jakobi N. (1997a). Half-baked, ad-hoc and noisy: Minimal simulations for evolutionary robotics. In P. Husbands and I. Harvey (Eds.), *Fourth European Conference on Artificial Life*, pp. 348–357. Cambridge, MA: MIT Press.

Jakobi N. (1997b). Evolutionary robotics and the radical envelop of noise hypothesis.*Adaptive Behavior*, 6(1):131–174.

Jakobi N. (1998). Running across the reality gap: Octopod locomotion evolved in a minimal simulation. In P. Husbands and J-A. Meyer (Eds.), *Evolutionary Robotics. First European Workshop*, pp. 39–58. Berlin: Springer-Verlag.

Jakobi N., Husbands P. and Harvey I. (1995). Noise and the reality gap: The use of simulation in evolutionary robotics. In F. Moran, A. Moreno, J. Merelo and P. Chancon (Eds.), *Advances in Artificial Life: Proceedings of the Third European Conference on Artificial Life*. Berlin: Springer Verlag.

Jordan M.I. (1989). Serial Order: A parallel, distributed processing approach. In J. L. Elman and D. E. Rumelhart (Eds.), *Advances in Connectionist Theory*. Hillsdale, NJ: Erlbaum.

Kaelbling L.P., Littman M.L. and Moore A.W. (1996). Reinforcement Learning: A Survey. *Journal of Artificial Intelligence Research*, 4, 237–285.

Keymeulen D., Durantez M., Konaka K., Kuniyoshi, Y. and Higuchi T. (1996). An evolutionary robot navigation system using a gate-level evolvable hardware. In T. Higuchi, M. Iwata and W. Liu (Eds.), *Proceedings of the First International Conference on Evolvable Systems: from Biology to Hardware*. Heidelberg: Springer Verlag.

Keymeulen D., Iwata M., Konaka K., Suzuki R., Kuniyoshi, Y. and Higuchi T. (1998). Off-line model-free and on-line model-based evolution for tracking navigation using evolvable hardware. In P. Husbands and J-A. Meyer (Eds.), *Evolutionary Robotics. First European Workshop*. Heidelberg: Springer Verlag.

Kimura M. (1983). *The Neutral Theory of Molecular Evolution*. Cambridge, UK: Cambridge University Press.

Kitano H. (1990). Designing neural networks using genetic algorithms with graph generation system. *Complex Systems*, 4:461–476.

Kodjabachian J. and Meyer J.A. (1998a). Evolution and development of modular control architectures for a 1-D locomotion is six-legged animats. *Connection Science,* (10)3–4: 211–254.

Kodjabachian J. and Meyer J.A. (1998b). Evolution and development of neural controllers for locomotion, gradient-following, and obstacle-avoidance in artificial insects. *IEEE Transactions on Neural Networks*, 9:796–812.

Kohonen T. (1982). Self-organized formation of topologically correct feature maps. *Biological Cybernetics*, 43:59–69.

Kolen J.F. and Pollack J.B. (1990). Back-propagation is sensitive to the initial conditions. *Complex Systems*, 4:269–280.

Koza J.R. (1991). Evolution and co-evolution of computer programs to control independently-acting agents. In J.A. Meyer and S. Wilson (Eds.), *From Animals to Animats: Proceeding of the First International Conference on Simulation of Adaptive Behavior.* Cambridge, MA: MIT Press.

Koza J.R. (1992). *Genetic Programming: On the Programming of Computers by Means of Natural Selection.* Cambridge, MA: MIT Press.

Koza J.R. (1994). *Genetic Programming II: Automatic Discovery of Reusable Programs.* Cambridge, MA: MIT Press.

de Lamarck J.B.P.A. (1990). *Zoological Philosophy.* London: MacMillan, 1914. Relevant excerpts reprinted in Belew and Mitchell, 1996.

Landolt O. (1996). Description et mise en oeuvre du chip ED084V2A, *Technical Report 16-11-95,* Centre Suisse d'Electronique et Microtechnique, Switzerland.

Langton C. (1992). Artificial Life. In C. Langton (Ed.), *Artificial Life.* Reading, MA: Addison-Wesley.

LeCun Y, Denker J.S. and Solla S.A. (1990). Optimal brain damage In D.S. Touretzky (Ed.), *Advances in Neural Information Processing Systems 2.* San Mateo, CA: Morgan Kaufmann.

Lee W.P., Hallam J. and Lund H.H. (1996). A hybrid GP/GA approach for co-evolving controllers and robot bodies to achieve fitness-specified tasks. In *Proceedings of IEEE Third International Conference on Evolutionary Computation.* New York: IEEE Press.

Lewis M.A. (1996). Self-organization of locomotory controllers in robots and animals, *Ph.D. Thesis,* Faculty of the Graduate School, University of Southern California.

Lewis M.A., Fagg A.H. and Solidum A. (1992). Genetic programming approach to the construction of a neural network for control of a walking robot. In *Proceedings of the IEEE International Conference on Robotics and Automation.* New York: IEEE Press.

Lipson H. and Pollack J.B. (2000). Towards continuously reconfigurable robotics. In *Proceedings of the 6th International Conference on Robotics and Automation.* San Francisco, CA: IEEE Press.

Lotka A.J. (1925). *Elements of Physical Biology.* Baltimore: Williams and Wilkins.

Lund H.H. and Hallam J. (1996) Sufficient neurocontrollers can be surprisingly simple. *Technical Report n. 824.* Department of Artificial Intelligence, University of Edinburgh.

Lund H.H. and Miglino O. (1997). Evolving and breading robots. In P. Husbands and J-A Meyer (Eds.), *Proceedings of the First European Workshop on Evolutionary Robotics.* Berlin: Springer Verlag.

Lund H.H., Hallam J. and Lee W.P. (1997a). Evolving robot morphology. In *Proceedings of the Fourth International Conference on Evolutionary Computation*. New York: IEEE Press.

Lund H.H., Web B. and Hallam J. (1997b). A robot attracted to the cricket species gryllus bimaculatus. In P. Husbands and I. Harvey (Eds.), *Proceedings of Fourth European Conference on Artificial Life*. Cambridge MA: MIT Press/Bradford Books.

Lund H.H., Miglino O., Pagliarini L., Billard A. and Ijspeert A. (1998). Evolutionary Robotics—A children's game. In *Proceedings of IEEE 5th International Conference on Evolutionary Computation*. New York: IEEE Press.

Maes P. (1992). Learning behavior networks from experience. In F. J. Varela, P. Bourgine (Eds.), *Toward a Practice of Autonomous Systems: Proceedings of the First European Conference on Artificial Life*. Cambridge, MA: MIT Press/Bradford Books.

Maes P. and Brooks R. A. (1990). Learning to coordinate behaviors. In *Proceedings of the Eight National Conference on Artificial Intelligence—AAAI-90*, pp. 796–802. San Mateo, CA: Morgan Kaufmann.

Mahadevan S. and Connell J. (1992). Automatic programming of behavior-based robots using reinforcement learning. *Artificial Intelligence*, 55:311–365.

Mange D., Goeke M., Madon D., Stauffer A., Tempesti G. and Durand S. (1995). Embryonics: A new family of coarse-grained field-programmable gate array with self-repair and self-reproducing properties. In E. Sanchez and M. Tomassini (Eds), *Towards Evolvable Hardware. The Evolutionary Engineering Approach*. Berlin: Springer Verlag.

Margules J. and Gallistel C.R. (1988). Heading in the rat: determination by environmental shape. *Animal Learning and Behavior,* 16:404–410.

Marjanovic M., Scassellati B. and Williamson M. (1996). Self-taught visually-guided pointing for a humanoid robot. In P. Maes, M.J. Mataric, J-A. Meyer, J. Pollack and S.W. Wilson (Eds.), *From Animals to Animats 4*, *Proceedings of the Fourth Conference on Simulation of Adaptive Behavior*, pp. 35–44. Cambridge, MA: MIT Press.

Marr D. (1982). *Vision*. New York: Freeman.

Maris M. and Boekhort R. (1996). Exploiting physical constraints: heap formation through behavioral error in a group of robots. In *Proceedings of the IEEE/RSJ International Conference on Intelligent Robots and Systems (IROS'96)*. New York: IEEE Press.

Mataric M.J. and Cliff D. (1996). Challenges in evolving controllers for physical robots. *Robotics and Autonomous Systems*, 1:67–83.

Mayley G. (1997). Landscapes, learning costs, and genetic assimilation. *Evolutionary Computation*, 4(3):213–234.

Mayley G. (1999). Explorations into the interactions between learning and evolution using genetic algorithms, *Ph.D. Thesis*. School of Cognitive and Computing Science, University of Sussex, UK.

McCulloch W. and Pitts W. (1943). A logical calculus of the ideas immanent in nervous activity. *Bulletin of Mathematical Biophysics*, 5:115–133.

McFarland D.J. and Houston A. (1981). *Quantitative Ethology: the State-Space Approach*. London: Pitman Books.

Medeen L.A. (1996). An incremental approach to developing intelligent neural network controllers for robots. *IEEE Transactions on Systems, Man, and Cybernetics—Part B*, 26 (3):474–485.

Meyer J-A. and Guillot A. (1991). Simulation of adaptive behavior in animats: Review and prospects. In J-A. Meyer and S.W. Wilson (Eds.), *From Animals to Animats: Proceedings of the First International Conference on Simulation of Adaptive Behavior*. Cambridge MA: MIT Press/Bradford Books.

Menczer F. and Belew R.K. (1996a). From complex environments to complex behaviors. *Adaptive Behavior*, 3–4:317–364.

Menczer F., Belew R.K. (1996b). Latent Energy Environments. In R.K. Belew and M. Mitchell (Eds.), *Adaptive Individuals in Evolving Populations: Models and Algorithms*. SFI Studies in the Sciences of Complexity Vol. XXIII, Reading, MA: Addison Wesley.

Miglino O. (1996). Orientamento spaziale in a open field box. Organismi biologici ed artificiali a confronto, *Ph.D. Thesis*, University of Palermo, Italy.

Miglino O., Nafasi K. and Taylor C.E. (1994). Selection for wandering behavior in a small robot. *Artificial Life*, 2:101–116.

Miglino O., Lund H. and Nolfi, S. (1995). Evolving mobile robots in simulated and real environments. *Artificial Life*, 2:417–434.

Miglino O., Nolfi S. and Parisi D. (1996). Discontinuity in evolution: how different levels of organization imply pre-adaptation. In Belew, R.K, Mitchell, M. (Eds.), *Adaptive Individuals in Evolving Populations*. SFI Studies in the Science of Complexity, Vol. XXVI, Reading, MA:Addison-Wesley.

Miller G.F. and Cliff D. (1994). Co-evolution of pursuit and evasion I: Biological and game-theoretic foundations, *Technical Report* CSRP311, School of Cognitive and Computing Sciences, University of Sussex.

Miller G.F. and Todd P.M. (1990). Exploring adaptive agency I: Theory and methods for simulating the evolution of learning. In D.S. Touretzky, J.L. Elman, T.J. Sejnowski and G.E. Hinton (Eds.), *Proceedings of the 1990 Connectionist Models Summer School*. San Matteo, CA: Morgan Kaufmann.

Miller G.F., Todd P.M. and Hedge S.U. (1989). Designing neural networks using genetic algorithms. In L. Nadel and D. Stein (Eds.), *Proceedings Third International Conference on Genetic Algorithms*, pp. 379–384. San Mateo, CA: Morgan Kaufmann.

Miller G.F. and Todd P.M. (1990). Exploring adaptive agency I: theory and methods for simulating the evolution of learning. In D.S. Touretzky, J.L. Elman, T.J. Sejnowski and G.E. Hinton (Eds.), *Proceedings of the 1990 Connectionist Models Summer School*. San Matteo, CA: Morgan Kaufmann.

Mitchell M. (1996). *An Introduction to Genetic Algorithms*. Cambridge, MA: MIT Press.

Mondada R., Franzi E. and Ienne P. (1993). Mobile robot miniaturization: A tool for investigation in control algorithms. In T.Y. Yoshikawa and F. Miyazaki (Eds.), *Proceedings of the Third International Symposium on Experimental Robots*. Berlin, Springer-Verlag.

Mondada F. and Floreano D. (1995). Evolution of neural control structures: Some experiments on mobile robots. *Robotics and Autonomous Systems*, 16:183–195.

Montana D. and Davis L. (1989). Training feed forward neural networks using genetic algorithms. In *Proceedings of the Eleventh International Joint Conference on Artificial Intelligence*. San Mateo, CA: Morgan Kaufmann.

Morgan C.L. (1896). *Habit and Instinct*. London: Arnold.

Murray J.D. (1993). *Mathematical Biology*. Berlin: Springer Verlag, Second, Corrected Edition.

Neisser U. (1976). *Cognitive Psychology*. New York: Appleton-Century-Crofts.

Nolfi S. (1996). Adaptation as a more powerful tool than decomposition and integration. In T. Fogarty and G. Venturini (Eds), *Proceedings of the Workshop on Evolutionary Computing and Machine Learning*, 13th International Conference on Machine Learning, Bari.

Nolfi S. (1997a). Using emergent modularity to develop control system for mobile robots. *Adaptive Behavior*, 3–4:343–364.

Nolfi S. (1997b). Evolving non-trivial behaviors on real robots: A garbage collecting robot. *Robotics and Autonomous System*, 22:187–198.

Nolfi S. (1997c). Evolving non-trivial behavior on autonomous robots: Adaptation is more powerful than decomposition and integration. In T. Gomi (Ed.), *Evolutionary Robotics: From Intelligent Robots to Artificial Life*. Ontario, Canada: AAI Books.

Nolfi S. (1999). The power and the limits of reactive agents. *Technical Report*. Rome, Institute of Psychology, National Research Council.

Nolfi S. (1999). How learning and evolution interact: The case of a learning task which differs from the evolutionary task. *Adaptive Behavior*, 7 (2):231-236.

Nolfi S. and Floreano D. (1999). Co-evolving predator and prey robots: Do "arm races" arise in artificial evolution?. *Artificial Life*, 4 (4):311–335.

Nolfi S. and Marocco D. (in press). Evolving visually-guided robots able to discriminate between different landmarks. In J-A. Meyer, A. Berthoz, D. Floreano, H.L. Roitblat and Wilson S. (Eds.), *From Animals to Animats 6. Proceedings of The Sixth International Conference on the Simulation of Adaptive Behavior*. Cambridge, MA: MIT Press/Bradford Book.

Nolfi S. and Parisi D. (1992). Growing neural networks, *Technical Report*, Institute of Psychology, Rome

Nolfi S. and Parisi D. (1993a). Auto-teaching: networks that develop their own teaching input. In J.L. Deneubourg, H. Bersini, S. Goss, G. Nicolis and R. Dagonnier (Eds), *Proceedings of the Second European Conference on Artificial Life*, pp. 845–862. Brussels: Université Libre de Bruxelles.

Nolfi S. and Parisi D. (1993b). Self-selection of input stimuli for improving performance. In G. A. Bekey (Ed.), *Neural Networks and Robotics,* Kluwer Academic Publisher.

Nolfi S. and Parisi D. (1994). Desired responses do not correspond to good teaching input in ecological neural networks. *Neural Processing Letters*, (1)2:1–4

Nolfi S. and Parisi D. (1995). "Genotypes" for Neural Networks. In M. A. Arbib (Ed.), *The Handbook of Brain Theory and Neural Networks*. Cambridge, MA: MIT Press/ Bradford Books.

Nolfi S. and Parisi D. (1997). Learning to adapt to changing environments in evolving neural networks. *Adaptive Behavior*, 5: 99–105

Nolfi S. and Tani J. (1999). Extracting regularities in space and time through a cascade of prediction networks: The case of a mobile robot navigating in a structured environment, *Connection Science,* (11)2:129–152.

Nolfi S., Elman J.L. and Parisi D. (1990). Learning and Evolution in Neural Networks. CRL *Technical Report* 9019, University of Southern California, San Diego, United States.

Nolfi S., Elman J.L. and Parisi D. (1994a). Learning and evolution in neural networks. *Adaptive Behavior*, (3)1:5–28

Nolfi S., Miglino O. and Parisi D. (1994b). Phenotypic plasticity in evolving neural networks. In J-D. Nicoud and P. Gaussier (Eds.), *Proceedings of the Conference From Perception to Action*. Los Alamitos, CA: IEE Computer Society Press.

Nolfi S., Floreano D., Miglino O. and Mondada F. (1994c). How to evolve autonomous robots: different approaches in evolutionary robotics. In R.A. Brooks and P. Maes (Eds.), *Proceedings of the Fourth International Conference on Artificial Life.* Cambridge, MA: MIT Press.

Nordin P. and Banzhaf W. (1997). An on-line method to evolve behavior and to control a miniature robot in real time with genetic programming. *Adaptive Behavior*, 5:107–140

O'Keefe J. and Nadel L. (1978). *The Hippocampus as a Cognitive Map.* Oxford: Clarendon Press.

O'Reilly U-M. and Oppacher F. (1992). An experimental perspective on genetic programming. In R. Männer and B. Manderick (Eds.), *Parallel Problem Solving from Nature 2*, Amsterdam: North-Holland.

Osborn H.F. (1896). Ontogenetic and phylogenetic variation. *Science*, 4:786–789.

Parisi D. (1997). Artificial life and higher level cognition. *Brain and Cognition,* 34:160–184.

Parisi D. and Nolfi S. (1996). How learning can influence evolution within a non-Lamarckian framework. In Belew, R.K, Mitchell, M. (Eds.) *Adaptive Individuals in Evolving Populations.* SFI Studies in the Science of Complexity, Vol. XXVI, Reading, MA: Addison-Wesley

Parisi D., Nolfi S. and Cecconi F. (1992). Learning, Behavior and Evolution. In F. Varela and P. Bourgine (Eds.), *Toward a Practice of Autonomous Systems*, pp. 207–216. Cambridge, MA: MIT Press.

Pearson K.G. (1976). The control of walking. *Scientific American*, 235:72–86.

Pearson K.G., Fourtner C. R. and Wong R. K. (1973). Nervous control of walking in the cockroach. In R. B. Stein, K. G. Pearson, R. S. Smith and J. B. Redford (Eds.), *Control of posture and locomotion.* New York: Plenum Press.

Pfeifer R. and Scheier C. (1997). Sensory-motor coordination: The metaphor and beyond. In R. Pfeifer and R. Brooks (Eds.), *Robotics and Autonomous Systems*, 20: 157–178.

Pfeifer R. and Scheier C. (1998). Embodied cognitive science: A novel approach to the study of intelligence in natural and artificial systems. In T. Gomi (Ed.), *Evolutionary Robotics: From Intelligent Robots to Artificial Life.* Ontario, Canada: Applied AI Books.

Pfeifer R. and Scheier C. (1999). *Understanding Intelligence.* Cambridge, MA:MIT Press

Phillips W.A., Kay J. and Smyth D. (1995). The discovery of structure by multi-stream networks of local processors with contextual guidance. *Network*, 6:225–246.

Plunkett K. and Marchman V. (1991). U-shaped learning and frequency effects in a multi-layered perceptron: implications for child language acquisition. *Cognition*, 38:43–102.

Pollack J.B., Lipson H., Ficici S., Funes P., Hornby G. and Watson R.A. (1999). Evolutionary Techniques in Physical Robotics. In J. Miller, A. Thompson, P. Thomson and T.C. Fogarty (Eds.), *Evolvable Systems: From Biology to Hardware: Proceedings of the Third International Conference.* Berlin: Springer Verlag.

Purves D. (1994). *Neural Activity and the Growth of the Brain.* Cambridge: Cambridge University Press.

Quartz S. and Sejnowski T.J. (1997). The neural basis of cognitive development: A constructivist manifesto, *Behavioral and Brain Science*, 4:537–555.

Radcliffe N.J. (1991). Formal analysis and random respectful recombination. In R. K. Belew and L. B. Booker (Eds.), *Proceedings of the Fourth International Conference on Genetic Algorithms*. San Mateo, CA: Morgan Kaufmann.

Ram A., Arkin R.C., Boone G. and Pearce M. (1994). Using genetic algorithms to learn reactive control parameters for autonomous robotic navigation. *Adaptive Behavior,* 3:277–305.

Reynolds C.W. (1994). Competition, coevolution and the game of tag. In R. Brooks and P. Maes (Eds.), *Proceeding of the Fourth Workshop of Artificial Life*. Boston MA: MIT Press.

Renshaw E. (1991). *Modeling Biological Populations in Space and Time*. Cambridge: Cambridge University Press.

Ridley M. (1993). *The Red Queen: Sex and the Evolution of Human Nature*. London: Viking Press.

Rosin C.D. and Belew R.D. (1997). New methods for competitive coevolution. *Evolutionary Computation*, 5(1):1–29.

Rueckl J.G., Cave K.R. and Kosslyn S.M. (1989). Why are "what" and "where" processed by separate cortical visual systems? A computational investigation. *Journal of Cognitive Neuroscience*, 1:171–186.

Rumelhart D.E. and McClelland J.L. (1986). *Parallel Distributed Processing*. Cambridge, MA: MIT Press.

Rumelhart D.E., Hinton G.E. and Williams R.J. (1986). Learning representation by back-propagation of errors. *Nature*, 323:533–536.

Sanger T.D. (1989). Optimal unsupervised learning in a single-layer feedforward neural network. *Neural Network*, 2:459–473.

Sanchez E. (1995). Field Programmable Gate Array (FPGA) Circuits. In E. Sanchez and M. Tomassini (Eds), *Towards Evolvable Hardware. The Evolutionary Engineering Approach*, pp. 1–18.Berlin: Springer Verlag.

Sasaki T. and Tokoro M. (1997). Adaptation toward changing environments: Why darwinian in nature?. In P. Husbands and I. Harvey (Eds), *Proceedings of the Fourth European Conference on Artificial Life*. Cambridge, MA: MIT Press.

Schaffer J.D., Whitley L.D. and Eshelman L.J. (1992). Combinations of genetic algorithms and neural networks: A survey of the state of the art. In L.D. Whitley and J.D. Schaffer (Eds.), *Proceedings of an International Workshop on the Combination of Genetic Algorithms and Neural Networks*. Los Alamitos: CA, IEEE Press.

Scheier C. and Pfeifer R. (1995). Classification as sensorimotor coordination: A case study on autonomous agents. In F. Moran, A. Moreno, J.J. Merelo and P. Chacon

(Eds.), *Advances in Artificial Life: Proceedings of the Third European Conference on Artificial Life*. Berlin: Springer Verlag.

Scheier C., Pfeifer R. and Kuniyoshi Y. (1998). Embedded neural networks: exploiting constraints. *Neural Networks*, 11:1551–1596.

Schraudolph N.N. and Belew R.K. (1992). Dynamic parameter encoding for genetic algorithms. *Machine Learning*, 9:9–21.

Sharkey N.E. (1997). The new wave in robot learning. *Robotics and Autonomous Systems,*. 22:179–186.

Sharkey N.E. and Heemskerk J. (1997). The neural mind and the robot. In A.J. Browne (Ed.), *Neural Network Perspectives on Cognition and Adaptive Robotics*. Bristol U.K.: IOP Press.

Shrager J. and Johnson M H. (in press). Modelling the development of cortical function. In B. Julesz and I Kowacs (Eds.), *Maturational Windows and Cortical Plasticity in Human Development: Is There a Reason for an Optimistic View?*. Reading, MA: Addison Wesley.

Sibly R.M. and McFarland D.J. (1974). A state-space approach to motivation. In D.J. McFarland (Ed.), *Motivational Control Systems Analysis*. London: Academic Press.

Sims K. (1994). Evolving 3D morphology and behavior by competition. In R. Brooks and P. Maes (Eds.), *Proceedings of Fourth Conference on Artificial Life*. Cambridge, MA: MIT Press.

Sims K. (1995). Evolving 3D morphology and behavior by competition. *Artificial Life*, 1:353–372.

Singer W. (1987). Activity-dependant self-organisation of synaptic connections as a substrate of learning. In J. P. Changeaux and M. Konishi (Eds.), *The Neural and Molecular Bases of Learning*. London, UK: Wiley and Sons.

Skinner B.F. (1938). *The Behavior of Organisms: An Experimental Analysis*. New York: Appleton Century.

Smith T.M.C. (1998). Blurred vision: Simulation-reality transfer of a visually guided robot. In P. Husbands and J-A. Meyer (Eds.), *Evolutionary Robotics: First European Workshop*, pp. 152–164. Berlin: Springer-Verlag.

Stanton P.K. and Sejnowski T.J. (1989). Associative long-term depression in the hyppocampus induced by Hebbian covariance. *Nature*, 339:215–218.

Steels L. (1993). Building agents out of autonomous behavior systems. In L. Steels and R. Brooks (Eds.), *The Artificial Life Route to Artificial Intelligence. Building Situated Embodied Agents*. New Haven: Lawrence Erlbaum.

Steels L. (1994). The Artificial Life roots of Artificial Intelligence. *Artificial Life*, 1:75–110.

Steels L., Ed. (1995). *The Biology and Technology of Intelligent Autonomous Agents.* Berlin: Springer Verlag, NATO ASI Series.

Stent G. S. (1973). A physiological mechanism for Hebb's postulate of learning, *Proceedings of the National Academy of Sciences USA*, 70, 997–1001.

Sutton R.S. and Barto A.G. (1998). *Introduction to Reinforcement Learning.* Cambridge, MA: MIT Press.

Taube J.S., Muller R.U. and Ranck J.B. Jr. (1990). Head-direction cells recorded from the postsubiculum in freely moving rats. I: Description and quantitative analysis, *Journal of Neuroscience*, 10:420–435.

Thompson A. (1995). Evolving Electronic Robot Controllers that Exploit Hardware Resources. In F. Moran, A. Moreno, J.J. Merelo and P. Chacon (Eds.), *Advances in Artificial Life: Proceedings of the Third European Conference on Artificial Life.* Berlin: Springer Verlag.

Thompson A. (1997a). Temperature in Natural and Artificial Systems. In P. Husbands and I. Harvey (Eds.), *Proceedings of the Fourth European Conference on Artificial Life.* Cambridge, MA: MIT Press.

Thompson A. (1997b). Artificial Evolution in the Physical World. In T. Gomi (Ed.), *Evolutionary Robotics. From Intelligent Robots to Artificial Life.* Ontario, Canada: AAI Books.

Thompson A., Harvey I. and Husbands P. (1995). Unconstrained Evolution and Hard Consequences. In E. Sanchez and M. Tomassini (Eds), *Towards Evolvable Hardware. The Evolutionary Engineering Approach*, pp. 136–165. Berlin: Springer Verlag.

Thornton C. (1997). Separability is a learner's best friend. In J.A. Bullinaria, D.W. Glasspool, and G. Houghton (Eds.), *Proceedings of the Neural Computation and Psychology Workshop: Connectionist Representations.* London: Springer Verlag.

Todd P.M. and Miller G.F. (1991). Exploring adaptive agency II: simulating the evolution of associative learning. In J. A. Meyer and S.W. Wilson (Eds), *From Animals to Animats. Proceedings of the First International Conference on Simulation of Adaptive Behavior.* Cambridge, MA: MIT Press.

Tolman E.C. (1948). Cognitive maps in rats and men. *Psychological Review*, 55:189–208.

Urzelai J. and Floreano D. (1999). Incremental Evolution with Minimal Resources. In U. Rueckert and F. Mondada (Eds.), *Proceedings of the First International Khepera Workshop.* Padeborn: Heinz-Nixdorf Institute Press.

Urzelai J., Floreano D., Dorigo M. and Colombetti M. (1998). Incremental robot shaping. *Connection Science*, 10(3–4):341–360. '

Utida S. (1957). Population fluctuations. In *Proceedings of the XXII CSHL Symposium on Population Studies: Animal Ecology and Demography*, Cold Spring Harbor Laboratory, NY.

van Valen L. (1973). A new evolutionary law. *Evolution Theory*, 1:1–30.

Varela F.J., Thompson E. and Rosch E. (1991). *The Embodied Mind: Cognitive Science and Human Experience*. Cambridge, MA: MIT Press.

Vaario J. (1993). An Emergent Modeling Method for Artificial Neural Networks, *Doctor Dissertation*, The University of Tokyo.

Verschure P.F.M. J., Kröse B.J.A. and Pfeifer R. (1992). Distributed adaptive control: The self-organization of structured behavior. *Robotics and Autonomous Agents*, 9:181–196.

Volterra V. (1926). Variazioni e fluttuazioni del numero di individui in specie animali e conviventi. *Memorie dell'Accademia dei Lincei*, 2, 31–113. Variations and fluctuations of the number of individuals in animal species living together. Translation in: R. N. Chapman, *Animal Ecology*. New York: McGraw Hill, 1931, pp. 409–448.

Waddington C.H. (1942). Canalization of development and the inheritance of acquired characters. *Nature*, 150:563–565.

Wagner G.P. and Altenberg L. (1996). Complex adaptations and the evolution of evolvability. *Evolution* 50:967–976.

Watson R.A., Ficici S.G. and Pollack J.B. (1999). Embodied evolution: A response to challenges in evolutionary robotics. In J.L. Wyatt and J. Demiris (Eds.), Eighth European Workshop on Learning Robots.

Webb B. (1995). Using robots to model animals: A cricket test. *Robotics and Autonomous Systems*, (16)2–4:117–132.

Weigend A.S., Rumelhart D.E. and Huberman B.A. (1991). Back-propagation, weight-elimination and time series prediction. In D.S. Touretzky (Ed.), *Connectionist Models: Proceedings of the 1990 Summer School*. San Mateo, CA: Morgan Kaufmann.

Whitehead S.D. and Ballard D.H. (1991). Learning to perceive and act by trial and error. *Machine Learning*, 7:45–83.

Whitley D., Starkweather T. and Bogart C. (1990). Genetic algorithms and neural networks: Optimizing connections and connectivity. *Parallel Computing*, 14:347–361.

Widrow B. and Hoff M.E. (1960). Adaptive switching circuits. In *IRE WESCON Convention Record*, vol IV, 96–104. Reprinted in Anderson J.A. and Rosenfield E. Eds. (1988). *Neurocomputing: Foundations of Research*. Cambridge, MA: MIT Press/Bradford Books.

Willshaw D. and Dayan P. (1990). Optimal plasticity from matrix memories: What goes up must come down. *Neural Computation*, 2:85–93.

Wilson S.W. (1987). Classifier systems and the animat problem. *Machine Learning*, 2:199–228.

Wilson S.W. (1991). The animat path to AI. In J-A. Meyer and S.W. Wilson (Eds), *From Animals to Animats: Proceedings of the First International Conference on Simulation of Adaptive Behavior*. Cambridge MA: MIT Press/Bradford Books.

Withley D., Gordon S. and Mathias, K. (1994). Lamarkian evolution, the Baldwin effect and function optimization. In Y. Davidor, H.P. Schwefel and R. Manner (Eds.), *Parallel Problem Solving from Nature (PPSNIII)*, Berlin: Springer-Verlag.

Yao X. (1993). A review of evolutionary artificial neural networks. *International Journal of Intelligent Systems*, 4:203–222.

Yamauchi B. and Beer R. (1994). Integrating reactive, sequential, and learning behavior using dynamical neural networks. In D. Cliff, P. Husbands, J-A Meyer and S. Wilson (Eds.), *From Animals to Animats 3. Proceedings of the Third International Conference on Simulation of Adaptive Behavior*. Cambridge, MA: MIT Press/Bradford Books

Yamauchi B. and Beer R.D. (1995). Sequential behavior and learning in evolved dynamical neural networks. *Adaptive Behavior*, 2(3):219–246.

# Index

## Date Due

| MAY 0 5 2003 | | | |
|---|---|---|---|
| | | | |
| | | | |
| | | | |
| | | | |
| | | | |
| | | | |
| | | | |
| | | | |
| | | | |
| | | | |
| | | | |
| | | | |
| | | | |
| | | | |
| | | | |